PRAISE FOR *INVENT YOUR OWN COMPUTER GAMES WITH PYTHON, 4TH EDITION*

"It's a great introduction to Python and a great introduction to building fairly simple but interesting games. The author's not just a talented coder, but a Python maestro. And his programming techniques provide good lessons on how to approach programming tasks."

—Sandra Henry-Stocker, Computerworld

"Games are a great way to engage kids, and Python is a perfect language for them to see immediate results on the screen as they code. *Invent Your Own Computer Games with Python* should be a hit."

—James Floyd Kelly, GeekDad

"This is an excellent way to learn Python, if you are a kid or not. Little kids can learn with their adult guide, and older kids will eat this book up in an afternoon or two."

—Greg Laden, National Geographic's *ScienceBlogs*

"This book is a great entry point for beginning programmers that 'gamifies' coding, allowing readers to immediately apply the concepts covered, rather than teaching basics with little application."

—School Library Connection

"Excellent . . . a great place to start [learning Python], as it is modeled on the 1980s style of programming books."

—Alex Handy, *Software Development Times Blog*

INVENT YOUR OWN COMPUTER GAMES WITH PYTHON

4TH EDITION

by Al Sweigart

San Francisco

INVENT YOUR OWN COMPUTER GAMES WITH PYTHON, 4TH EDITION.

Printed in USA

Seventh printing

25 24 23 22 21 7 8 9 10 11

ISBN-10: 1-59327-795-4
ISBN-13: 978-1-59327-795-6

Publisher: William Pollock
Production Editor: Laurel Chun
Cover Illustration: Josh Ellingson
Interior Design: Octopod Studios
Developmental Editor: Jan Cash
Technical Reviewer: Ari Lacenski
Copyeditor: Rachel Monaghan
Compositor: Susan Glinert Stevens
Proofreader: Paula L. Fleming
Indexer: Nancy Guenther

The sprite images in Figure 20-1 on page 302, from left to right, were created by fsvieira, przemek.sz, LordNeo, and Suppercut. The grass sprite image in Figure 20-2 on page 302 was created by txturs. These images have been dedicated to the public domain with a CC0 1.0 Public Domain Dedication.

For information on distribution, translations, or bulk sales, please contact No Starch Press, Inc. directly:
No Starch Press, Inc.
245 8th Street, San Francisco, CA 94103
phone: 1.415.863.9900; info@nostarch.com
www.nostarch.com

Library of Congress Cataloging-in-Publication Data

Names: Sweigart, Al, author.
Title: Invent your own computer games with Python / by Al Sweigart.
Description: San Francisco : No Starch Press, Inc., [2017]
Identifiers: LCCN 2016037817 (print) | LCCN 2016044807 (ebook) | ISBN 9781593277956 | ISBN 1593277954 | ISBN 9781593278113 (epub) | ISBN 159327811X (epub) | ISBN 9781593278120 (mobi) | ISBN 1593278128 (mobi)
Subjects: LCSH: Computer games--Programming. | Python (Computer program language)
Classification: LCC QA76.76.C672 S785 2017 (print) | LCC QA76.76.C672 (ebook) | DDC 794.8/1526--dc23
LC record available at https://lccn.loc.gov/2016037817

To Caro

About the Author

Al Sweigart is a software developer, tech book author, and hoopy frood who really knows where his towel is. He has written several programming books for beginners, including *Automate the Boring Stuff with Python* and *Scratch Programming Playground*, also from No Starch Press. His books are freely available under a Creative Commons license at his website *https://inventwithpython.com/*.

About the Technical Reviewer

Ari Lacenski is a developer of Android applications and Python software. She lives in the Bay Area, where she writes about Android programming at *http://gradlewhy.ghost.io/* and mentors with Women Who Code.

BRIEF CONTENTS

Acknowledgments xix
Introduction xxi
Chapter 1: The Interactive Shell 1
Chapter 2: Writing Programs 11
Chapter 3: Guess the Number 21
Chapter 4: A Joke-Telling Program 39
Chapter 5: Dragon Realm 45
Chapter 6: Using the Debugger 63
Chapter 7: Designing Hangman with Flowcharts 77
Chapter 8: Writing the Hangman Code 87
Chapter 9: Extending Hangman 111
Chapter 10: Tic-Tac-Toe 121
Chapter 11: The Bagels Deduction Game 149
Chapter 12: The Cartesian Coordinate System 163
Chapter 13: Sonar Treasure Hunt 171
Chapter 14: Caesar Cipher 197
Chapter 15: The Reversegam Game 209
Chapter 16: Reversegam AI Simulation 239
Chapter 17: Creating Graphics 255
Chapter 18: Animating Graphics 273
Chapter 19: Collision Detection 285

Chapter 20: Using Sounds and Images. 301
Chapter 21: A Dodger Game with Sounds and Images 311
Index 335

CONTENTS IN DETAIL

ACKNOWLEDGMENTS **xix**

INTRODUCTION **xxi**

Who Is This Book For? xxii
About This Book. xxiii
How to Use This Book. xxiv
    Line Numbers and Indentation xxiv
    Long Code Lines xxv
Downloading and Installing Python xxv
Starting IDLE xxvi
Finding Help Online. xxvii

1
THE INTERACTIVE SHELL **1**

Some Simple Math. 2
    Integers and Floating-Point Numbers 2
    Expressions 3
Evaluating Expressions 3
Syntax Errors. 4
Storing Values in Variables 5
Summary 8

2
WRITING PROGRAMS **11**

String Values. 12
String Concatenation 13
Writing Programs in IDLE's File Editor. 13
    Creating the Hello World Program 14
    Saving Your Program. 15
    Running Your Program. 16
How the Hello World Program Works 17
    Comments for the Programmer 17
    Functions: Mini-Programs Inside Programs 18
    The End of the Program 19
Naming Variables 20
Summary 20

3
GUESS THE NUMBER **21**

Sample Run of Guess the Number 22
Source Code for Guess the Number. 22
Importing the random Module 23
Generating Random Numbers with the random.randint() Function 24
Welcoming the Player 26

Flow Control Statements 26
    Using Loops to Repeat Code. 26
    Grouping with Blocks 27
    Looping with for Statements 28
Getting the Player's Guess. 29
Converting Values with the int(), float(), and str() Functions 29
The Boolean Data Type. 31
    Comparison Operators 32
    Checking for True or False with Conditions. 32
    Experimenting with Booleans, Comparison Operators, and Conditions 33
    The Difference Between = and == 34
if Statements 34
Leaving Loops Early with the break Statement 35
Checking Whether the Player Won 35
Checking Whether the Player Lost 35
Summary 36

4
A JOKE-TELLING PROGRAM 39

Sample Run of Jokes. 40
Source Code for Jokes 40
How the Code Works. 41
Escape Characters 41
Single and Double Quotes 42
The print() Function's end Keyword Parameter 43
Summary 44

5
DRAGON REALM 45

How to Play Dragon Realm 45
Sample Run of Dragon Realm 46
Flowchart for Dragon Realm 46
Source Code for Dragon Realm 47
Importing the random and time Modules. 48
Functions in Dragon Realm 49
    def Statements 49
    Calling a Function. 49
    Where to Put Function Definitions 50
Multiline Strings 50
How to Loop with while Statements 51
Boolean Operators. 52
    The and Operator 52
    The or Operator 53
    The not Operator 53
    Evaluating Boolean Operators 54
Return Values. 55
Global Scope and Local Scope 56
Function Parameters 57

Displaying the Game Results 58
Deciding Which Cave Has the Friendly Dragon. 59
The Game Loop 60
    Calling the Functions in the Program 60
    Asking the Player to Play Again 61
Summary 61

6
USING THE DEBUGGER **63**

Types of Bugs 64
The Debugger 65
    Starting the Debugger 65
    Stepping Through the Program with the Debugger. 67
Finding the Bug 70
Setting Breakpoints. 73
Using Breakpoints 73
Summary 75

7
DESIGNING HANGMAN WITH FLOWCHARTS **77**

How to Play Hangman 78
Sample Run of Hangman 78
ASCII Art 79
Designing a Program with a Flowchart 80
    Creating the Flowchart. 81
    Branching from a Flowchart Box 81
    Ending or Restarting the Game 83
    Guessing Again 83
    Offering Feedback to the Player 85
Summary 86

8
WRITING THE HANGMAN CODE **87**

Source Code for Hangman 88
Importing the random Module 91
Constant Variables. 91
The Lists Data Type. 92
    Accessing Items with Indexes 92
    List Concatenation. 94
    The in Operator 94
Calling Methods 94
    The reverse() and append() List Methods 95
    The split() String Method 95
Getting a Secret Word from the Word List 96
Displaying the Board to the Player 97
    The list() and range() Functions 98
    List and String Slicing 98
    Displaying the Secret Word with Blanks. 99

Getting the Player's Guess. 101
The lower() and upper() String Methods 101
Leaving the while Loop 103
elif Statements 103
Making Sure the Player Entered a Valid Guess 104
Asking the Player to Play Again 104
Review of the Hangman Functions 105
The Game Loop 105
Calling the displayBoard() Function 106
Letting the Player Enter Their Guess 106
Checking Whether the Letter Is in the Secret Word 106
Checking Whether the Player Won 107
Handling an Incorrect Guess 107
Checking Whether the Player Lost 108
Ending or Resetting the Game. 108
Summary 109

9
EXTENDING HANGMAN **111**

Adding More Guesses 112
The Dictionary Data Type 112
Getting the Size of Dictionaries with len() 113
The Difference Between Dictionaries and Lists 113
The keys() and values() Dictionary Methods 114
Using Dictionaries of Words in Hangman 115
Randomly Choosing from a List 115
Deleting Items from Lists 117
Multiple Assignment 118
Printing the Word Category for the Player 119
Summary 120

10
TIC-TAC-TOE **121**

Sample Run of Tic-Tac-Toe 122
Source Code for Tic-Tac-Toe 123
Designing the Program 127
Representing the Board as Data 127
Strategizing with the Game AI 128
Importing the random Module 129
Printing the Board on the Screen 129
Letting the Player Choose X or O 130
Deciding Who Goes First 131
Placing a Mark on the Board 131
List References 132
Using List References in makeMove() 135
Checking Whether the Player Won 135
Duplicating the Board Data 137
Checking Whether a Space on the Board Is Free 138
Letting the Player Enter a Move 138

Short-Circuit Evaluation . . . 139
Choosing a Move from a List of Moves . . . 141
The None Value . . . 142
Creating the Computer's AI . . . 142
    Checking Whether the Computer Can Win in One Move . . . 143
    Checking Whether the Player Can Win in One Move . . . 144
    Checking the Corner, Center, and Side Spaces (in That Order) . . . 144
    Checking Whether the Board Is Full . . . 145
The Game Loop . . . 145
    Choosing the Player's Mark and Who Goes First . . . 146
    Running the Player's Turn . . . 146
    Running the Computer's Turn . . . 147
    Asking the Player to Play Again . . . 148
Summary . . . 148

11
THE BAGELS DEDUCTION GAME 149

Sample Run of Bagels . . . 150
Source Code for Bagels . . . 151
Flowchart for Bagels . . . 152
Importing random and Defining getSecretNum() . . . 153
Shuffling a Unique Set of Digits . . . 154
    Changing List Item Order with the random.shuffle() Function . . . 154
    Getting the Secret Number from the Shuffled Digits . . . 154
Augmented Assignment Operators . . . 155
Calculating the Clues to Give . . . 156
The sort() List Method . . . 157
The join() String Method . . . 158
Checking Whether a String Has Only Numbers . . . 158
Starting the Game . . . 159
String Interpolation . . . 159
The Game Loop . . . 160
    Getting the Player's Guess . . . 161
    Getting the Clues for the Player's Guess . . . 161
    Checking Whether the Player Won or Lost . . . 161
    Asking the Player to Play Again . . . 162
Summary . . . 162

12
THE CARTESIAN COORDINATE SYSTEM 163

Grids and Cartesian Coordinates . . . 164
Negative Numbers . . . 166
The Coordinate System of a Computer Screen . . . 167
Math Tricks . . . 168
    Trick 1: A Minus Eats the Plus Sign on Its Left . . . 168
    Trick 2: Two Minuses Combine into a Plus . . . 169
    Trick 3: Two Numbers Being Added Can Swap Places . . . 169
Absolute Values and the abs() Function . . . 170
Summary . . . 170

13
SONAR TREASURE HUNT 171

Sample Run of Sonar Treasure Hunt . . . 173
Source Code for Sonar Treasure Hunt . . . 175
Designing the Program . . . 180
Importing the random, sys, and math Modules . . . 180
Creating a New Game Board . . . 180
Drawing the Game Board . . . 181
    Drawing the X-Coordinates Along the Top of the Board . . . 182
    Drawing the Ocean . . . 183
    Printing a Row in the Ocean . . . 184
    Drawing the X-Coordinates Along the Bottom of the Board . . . 184
Creating the Random Treasure Chests . . . 184
Determining Whether a Move Is Valid . . . 185
Placing a Move on the Board . . . 185
    Finding the Closest Treasure Chest . . . 186
    Removing Values with the remove() List Method . . . 189
    Getting the Player's Move . . . 190
Printing the Game Instructions for the Player . . . 191
The Game Loop . . . 192
    Displaying the Game Status for the Player . . . 193
    Handling the Player's Move . . . 193
    Finding a Sunken Treasure Chest . . . 194
    Checking Whether the Player Won . . . 194
    Checking Whether the Player Lost . . . 195
    Terminating the Program with the sys.exit() Function . . . 195
Summary . . . 196

14
CAESAR CIPHER 197

Cryptography and Encryption . . . 198
How the Caesar Cipher Works . . . 199
Sample Run of Caesar Cipher . . . 200
Source Code for Caesar Cipher . . . 201
Setting the Maximum Key Length . . . 202
Deciding to Encrypt or Decrypt the Message . . . 202
Getting the Message from the Player . . . 203
Getting the Key from the Player . . . 203
Encrypting or Decrypting the Message . . . 203
    Finding Passed Strings with the find() String Method . . . 204
    Encrypting or Decrypting Each Letter . . . 205
Starting the Program . . . 206
The Brute-Force Technique . . . 206
Adding the Brute-Force Mode . . . 207
Summary . . . 208

15
THE REVERSEGAM GAME 209

How to Play Reversegam . . . 210
Sample Run of Reversegam . . . 213

Source Code for Reversegam 215
Importing Modules and Setting Up Constants 220
The Game Board Data Structure 220
Drawing the Board Data Structure on the Screen 221
Creating a Fresh Board Data Structure 222
Checking Whether a Move Is Valid 222
Checking Each of the Eight Directions 223
Finding Out Whether There Are Tiles to Flip Over 224
Checking for Valid Coordinates 225
Getting a List with All Valid Moves 226
Calling the bool() Function 227
Getting the Score of the Game Board 227
Getting the Player's Tile Choice 228
Determining Who Goes First 228
Placing a Tile on the Board 229
Copying the Board Data Structure 229
Determining Whether a Space Is on a Corner 230
Getting the Player's Move 230
Getting the Computer's Move 232
Strategizing with Corner Moves 232
Getting a List of the Highest-Scoring Moves 233
Printing the Scores to the Screen 234
Starting the Game 234
Checking for a Stalemate 234
Running the Player's Turn 235
Running the Computer's Turn 236
The Game Loop 237
Asking the Player to Play Again 238
Summary 238

16
REVERSEGAM AI SIMULATION 239

Making the Computer Play Against Itself 240
Sample Run of Simulation 1 240
Source Code for Simulation 1 241
Removing the Player Prompts and Adding a Computer Player 242
Making the Computer Play Itself Several Times 243
Sample Run of Simulation 2 243
Source Code for Simulation 2 244
Keeping Track of Multiple Games 245
Commenting Out print() Function Calls 245
Using Percentages to Grade the AIs 246
Comparing Different AI Algorithms 247
Source Code for Simulation 3 248
How the AIs Work in Simulation 3 249
Comparing the AIs 252
Summary 254

17
CREATING GRAPHICS 255

Installing pygame . . . 256
Hello World in pygame . . . 256
Sample Run of pygame Hello World . . . 257
Source Code for pygame Hello World . . . 257
Importing the pygame Module . . . 259
Initializing pygame . . . 259
Setting Up the pygame Window . . . 260
    Tuples . . . 260
    Surface Objects . . . 261
Setting Up Color Variables . . . 261
Writing Text on the pygame Window . . . 262
    Using Fonts to Style Text . . . 262
    Rendering a Font Object . . . 263
    Setting the Text Location with Rect Attributes . . . 264
Filling a Surface Object with a Color . . . 266
pygame's Drawing Functions . . . 266
    Drawing a Polygon . . . 266
    Drawing a Line . . . 267
    Drawing a Circle . . . 268
    Drawing an Ellipse . . . 268
    Drawing a Rectangle . . . 268
    Coloring Pixels . . . 269
The blit() Method for Surface Objects . . . 270
Drawing the Surface Object to the Screen . . . 270
Events and the Game Loop . . . 270
    Getting Event Objects . . . 271
    Exiting the Program . . . 271
Summary . . . 272

18
ANIMATING GRAPHICS 273

Sample Run of the Animation Program . . . 274
Source Code for the Animation Program . . . 274
Moving and Bouncing the Boxes . . . 276
Setting Up the Constant Variables . . . 277
    Constant Variables for Direction . . . 277
    Constant Variables for Color . . . 278
Setting Up the Box Data Structures . . . 278
The Game Loop . . . 279
    Handling When the Player Quits . . . 279
    Moving Each Box . . . 280
    Bouncing a Box . . . 281
    Drawing the Boxes on the Window in Their New Positions . . . 282
    Drawing the Window on the Screen . . . 282
Summary . . . 283

19
COLLISION DETECTION 285

Sample Run of the Collision Detection Program . . . 286
Source Code for the Collision Detection Program . . . 287
Importing the Modules . . . 289
Using a Clock to Pace the Program . . . 289
Setting Up the Window and Data Structures . . . 290
Setting Up Variables to Track Movement . . . 291
Handling Events . . . 292
    Handling the KEYDOWN Event . . . 293
    Handling the KEYUP Event . . . 294
Teleporting the Player . . . 295
Adding New Food Squares . . . 295
Moving the Player Around the Window . . . 296
    Drawing the Player on the Window . . . 297
    Checking for Collisions . . . 297
Drawing the Food Squares on the Window . . . 298
Summary . . . 299

20
USING SOUNDS AND IMAGES 301

Adding Images with Sprites . . . 302
Sound and Image Files . . . 302
Sample Run of the Sprites and Sounds Program . . . 303
Source Code for the Sprites and Sounds Program . . . 304
Setting Up the Window and the Data Structure . . . 306
    Adding a Sprite . . . 307
    Changing the Size of a Sprite . . . 307
Setting Up the Music and Sounds . . . 307
    Adding Sound Files . . . 308
    Toggling the Sound On and Off . . . 308
Drawing the Player on the Window . . . 309
Checking for Collisions . . . 309
Drawing the Cherries on the Window . . . 310
Summary . . . 310

21
A DODGER GAME WITH SOUNDS AND IMAGES 311

Review of the Basic pygame Data Types . . . 312
Sample Run of Dodger . . . 313
Source Code for Dodger . . . 313
Importing the Modules . . . 317
Setting Up the Constant Variables . . . 318
Defining Functions . . . 319
    Ending and Pausing the Game . . . 319
    Keeping Track of Baddie Collisions . . . 320
    Drawing Text to the Window . . . 320

Initializing pygame and Setting Up the Window 321
Setting Up Font, Sound, and Image Objects 322
Displaying the Start Screen 323
Starting the Game 324
The Game Loop 325
Handling Keyboard Events 325
Handling Mouse Movement 327
Adding New Baddies 327
Moving the Player's Character and the Baddies 328
Implementing the Cheat Codes 329
Removing the Baddies 330
Drawing the Window 330
Drawing the Player's Score 331
Drawing the Player's Character and Baddies 331
Checking for Collisions 332
The Game Over Screen 332
Modifying the Dodger Game 333
Summary 334

INDEX **335**

ACKNOWLEDGMENTS

This book would not have been possible without the exceptional work of the No Starch Press team. Thanks to my publisher, Bill Pollock; thanks to my editors, Laurel Chun, Jan Cash, and Tyler Ortman, for their incredible help throughout the process; thanks to my technical editor Ari Lacenski for her thorough review; and thanks to Josh Ellingson for yet another great cover.

INTRODUCTION

When I first played video games as a kid, I was hooked. But I didn't just want to play video games, I wanted to make them. I found a book like this one that taught me how to write my first programs and games. It was fun and easy. The first games I made were like the ones in this book. They weren't as fancy as the Nintendo games my parents bought for me, but they were games I had made myself.

Now, as an adult, I still have fun programming and I get paid for it. But even if you don't want to become a computer programmer, programming is a useful and fun skill to have. It trains your brain to think logically, make plans, and reconsider your ideas whenever you find mistakes in your code.

Many programming books for beginners fall into two categories. The first category includes books that don't teach programming so much as "game creation software" or languages that simplify so much that what is taught is no longer programming. The other category consists of books that teach programming like a mathematics textbook—all principles and concepts, with few real-life applications for the reader. This book takes a different approach and teaches you how to program by making video games. I show the source code for the games right up front and explain programming principles from the examples. This approach was the key for me when I was learning to program. The more I learned how other people's programs worked, the more ideas I had for my own programs.

All you'll need is a computer, some free software called the Python interpreter, and this book. Once you learn how to create the games in this book, you'll be able to develop games on your own.

Computers are incredible machines, and learning to program them isn't as hard as people think. A computer *program* is a bunch of instructions that the computer can understand, just like a storybook is a bunch of sentences that the reader can understand. To instruct a computer, you write a program in a language the computer understands. This book will teach you a programming language called Python. There are many other programming languages you can learn, like BASIC, Java, JavaScript, PHP, and C++.

When I was a kid, I learned BASIC, but newer programming languages like Python are even easier to learn. Python is also used by professional programmers in their work *and* when programming for fun. Plus it's totally free to install and use—you'll just need an internet connection to download it.

Because video games are nothing but computer programs, they are also made up of instructions. The games you'll create from this book seem simple compared to the games for Xbox, PlayStation, or Nintendo. These games don't have fancy graphics because they're meant to teach you coding basics. They're purposely simple so you can focus on learning to program. Games don't have to be complicated to be fun!

Who Is This Book For?

Programming isn't hard, but it *is* hard to find materials that teach you to do interesting things with programming. Other computer books go over many topics most new coders don't need. This book will teach you how to program your own games; you'll learn a useful skill and have fun games to show for it! This book is for:

- Complete beginners who want to teach themselves programming, even if they have no previous experience.
- Kids and teenagers who want to learn programming by creating games.
- Adults and teachers who wish to teach others programming.
- Anyone, young or old, who wants to learn how to program by learning a professional programming language.

About This Book

In most of the chapters in this book, a single new game project is introduced and explained. A few of the chapters cover additional useful topics, like debugging. New programming concepts are explained as games make use of them, and the chapters are meant to be read in order. Here's a brief rundown of what you'll find in each chapter:

- **Chapter 1: The Interactive Shell** explains how Python's interactive shell can be used to experiment with code one line at a time.
- **Chapter 2: Writing Programs** covers how to write complete programs in Python's file editor.
- In **Chapter 3: Guess the Number**, you'll program the first game in the book, Guess the Number, which asks the player to guess a secret number and then provides hints as to whether the guess is too high or too low.
- In **Chapter 4: A Joke-Telling Program**, you'll write a simple program that tells the user several jokes.
- In **Chapter 5: Dragon Realm**, you'll program a guessing game in which the player must choose between two caves: one has a friendly dragon, and the other has a hungry dragon.
- **Chapter 6: Using the Debugger** covers how to use the debugger to fix problems in your code.
- **Chapter 7: Designing Hangman with Flowcharts** explains how flowcharts can be used to plan longer programs, such as the Hangman game.
- In **Chapter 8: Writing the Hangman Code**, you'll write the Hangman game, following the flowchart from Chapter 7.
- **Chapter 9: Extending Hangman** extends the Hangman game with new features by making use of Python's dictionary data type.
- In **Chapter 10: Tic-Tac-Toe**, you'll learn how to write a human-versus-computer Tic-Tac-Toe game that uses artificial intelligence.
- In **Chapter 11: The Bagels Deduction Game**, you'll learn how to make a deduction game called Bagels in which the player must guess secret numbers based on clues.
- **Chapter 12: The Cartesian Coordinate System** explains the Cartesian coordinate system, which you'll use in later games.
- In **Chapter 13: Sonar Treasure Hunt**, you'll learn how to write a treasure hunting game in which the player searches the ocean for lost treasure chests.
- In **Chapter 14: Caesar Cipher**, you'll create a simple encryption program that lets you write and decode secret messages.
- In **Chapter 15: The Reversegam Game**, you'll program an advanced human-versus-computer Reversi-type game that has a nearly unbeatable artificial intelligence opponent.

- **Chapter 16: Reversegam AI Simulation** expands on the Reversegam game in Chapter 15 to make multiple AIs that compete in computer-versus-computer games.
- **Chapter 17: Creating Graphics** introduces Python's `pygame` module and shows you how to use it to draw 2D graphics.
- **Chapter 18: Animating Graphics** shows you how to animate graphics with `pygame`.
- In **Chapter 19: Collision Detection**, you'll learn how to detect when objects collide with each other in 2D games.
- In **Chapter 20: Using Sounds and Images**, you'll improve your simple `pygame` games by adding sounds and images.
- **Chapter 21: A Dodger Game with Sounds and Images** combines the concepts in Chapters 17 to 20 to make an animated game called Dodger.

How to Use This Book

Most chapters in this book will begin with a sample run of the chapter's featured program. This sample run shows you what the program looks like when you run it. The parts the user types are shown in bold.

I recommend that you enter the code for each program into IDLE's file editor yourself rather than downloading or copying and pasting it. You'll remember more if you take the time to type the code.

Line Numbers and Indentation

When typing the source code from this book, do *not* type the line numbers at the start of each line. For example, if you saw the following line of code, you would not need to type the `9.` on the left side, or the one space immediately following it:

```
9. number = random.randint(1, 20)
```

You'd enter only this:

```
number = random.randint(1, 20)
```

Those numbers are there just so this book can refer to specific lines in the program. They are not part of the actual program's source code.

Aside from the line numbers, enter the code exactly as it appears in this book. Notice that some of the lines of code are indented by four or eight (or more) spaces. The spaces at the beginning of the line change how Python interprets instructions, so they are very important to include.

Let's look at an example. The indented spaces here are marked with black circles (•) so you can see them.

```
while guesses < 10:
••••if number == 42:
••••••••print('Hello')
```

The first line is not indented, the second line is indented four spaces, and the third line is indented eight spaces. Although the examples in this book don't have black circles to mark the spaces, each character in IDLE is the same width, so you can count the number of spaces by counting the number of characters on the line above or below.

Long Code Lines

Some code instructions are too long to fit on one line in the book and will wrap around to the next line. But the line will fit on your computer screen, so type it all on one line without pressing ENTER. You can tell when a new instruction starts by looking at the line numbers on the left. This example has only two instructions:

```
1. print('This is the first instruction!xxxxxxxxxxxxxxxxxxxxxxxxxxxxxxxxxxxxxxx
   xxxxxxxxxxxx')
2. print('This is the second instruction, not the third instruction.')
```

The first instruction wraps around to a second line on the page, but the second line does not have a line number, so you can see that it's still line 1 of the code.

Downloading and Installing Python

You'll need to install software called the Python interpreter. The *interpreter* program understands the instructions you write in Python. I'll refer to the Python interpreter software as just *Python* from now on.

In this section, I'll show you how to download and install Python 3—specifically, Python 3.4—for Windows, OS X, or Ubuntu. There are newer versions of Python than 3.4, but the pygame module, which is used in Chapters 17 to 21, currently only supports up to 3.4.

It's important to know that there are some significant differences between Python 2 and Python 3. The programs in this book use Python 3, and you'll get errors if you try to run them with Python 2. This is so important, in fact, that I've added a cartoon penguin to remind you about it.

MAKE SURE YOU'RE USING PYTHON 3, NOT PYTHON 2!

On Windows, download the Windows x86-64 MSI installer from *https://www.python.org/downloads/release/python-344/* and then double-click it. You may have to enter the administrator password for your computer.

Follow the instructions the installer displays on the screen to install Python, as listed here:

1. Select **Install for All Users** and then click **Next**.
2. Install to the *C:\Python34* folder by clicking **Next**.
3. Click **Next** to skip the Customize Python section.

On OS X, download the Mac OS X 64-bit/32-bit installer from *https://www.python.org/downloads/release/python-344/* and then double-click it. Follow the instructions the installer displays on the screen to install Python, as listed here:

1. If you get the warning "'Python.mpkg' can't be opened because it is from an unidentified developer," hold down CONTROL while right-clicking the *Python.mpkg* file and then select **Open** from the menu that appears. You may have to enter the administrator password for your computer.
2. Click **Continue** through the Welcome section and click **Agree** to accept the license.
3. Select *Macintosh HD* (or whatever your hard drive is named) and click **Install**.

If you're running Ubuntu, you can install Python from the Ubuntu Software Center by following these steps:

1. Open the Ubuntu Software Center.
2. Enter `Python` in the search box in the top-right corner of the window.
3. Select **IDLE (Python 3.4 GUI 64 bit)**.
4. Click **Install**. You may have to enter the administrator password to complete the installation.

If the above steps do not work, you can find alternative Python 3.4 install instructions at *https://www.nostarch.com/inventwithpython/*.

Starting IDLE

IDLE stands for **I**nteractive **D**eve**L**opment **E**nvironment. IDLE is like a word processor for writing Python programs. Starting IDLE is different on each operating system:

- On Windows, click the **Start** menu in the lower-left corner of the screen, type `IDLE`, and select **IDLE (Python GUI)**.
- On OS X, open Finder and click **Applications**. Double-click **Python 3.*x*** and then double-click the IDLE icon.
- On Ubuntu or other Linux distros, open a terminal window and enter `idle3`. You may also be able to click **Applications** at the top of the screen. Then click **Programming** and **IDLE 3**.

The window that appears when you first run IDLE is the *interactive shell*, as shown in Figure 1. You can enter Python instructions into the interactive shell at the >>> prompt and Python will perform them. After the computer performs the instructions, a new >>> prompt will wait for your next instruction.

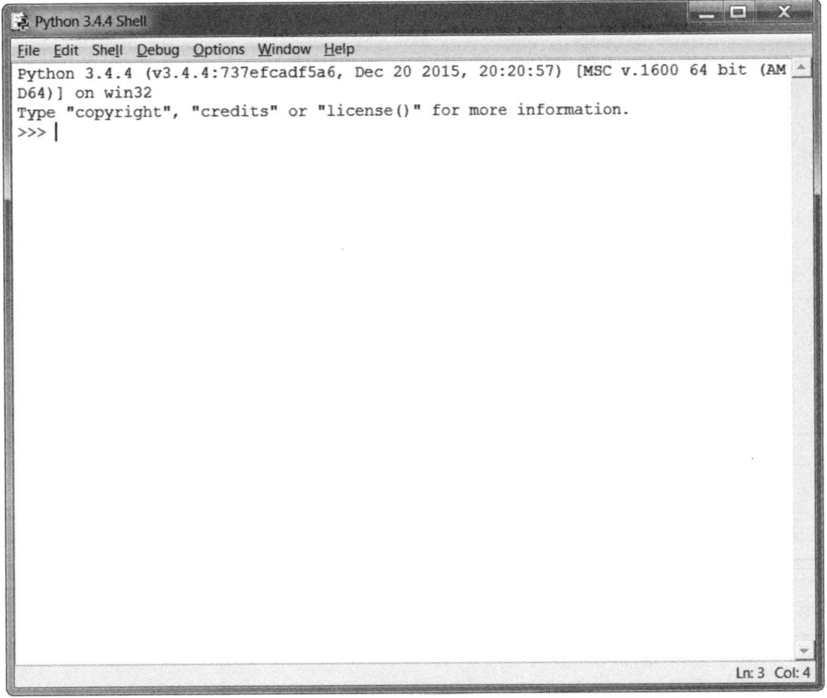

Figure 1: The IDLE program's interactive shell

Finding Help Online

You can find the source code files and other resources for this book at *https://www.nostarch.com/inventwithpython/*. If you want to ask programming questions related to this book, visit *https://reddit.com/r/inventwithpython/*, or you can email your programming questions to me at *al@inventwithpython.com*.

Before you ask any questions, make sure you do the following:

- If you are typing out a program in this book but are getting an error, check for typos with the online diff tool at *https://www.nostarch.com/inventwithpython#diff* before asking your question. Copy and paste your code into the diff tool to find any differences between the book's code and yours.
- Search the web to see whether someone else has already asked (and answered) your question.

Keep in mind that the better you phrase your programming questions, the better others will be able to help you. When asking programming questions, do the following:

- Explain what you are trying to do when you get the error. This will let your helper know if you are on the wrong path entirely.
- Copy and paste the entire error message and your code.
- Provide your operating system and version.
- Explain what you've already tried to do to solve your problem. This tells people you've already put in some work to try to figure things out on your own.
- Be polite. Don't demand help or pressure your helpers to respond quickly.

Now that you know how to ask for help, you'll be learning to program your own computer games in no time!

1

THE INTERACTIVE SHELL

Before you can make games, you need to learn a few basic programming concepts. You'll start in this chapter by learning how to use Python's interactive shell and perform basic arithmetic.

TOPICS COVERED IN THIS CHAPTER

- Operators
- Integers and floating-point numbers
- Values
- Expressions
- Syntax errors
- Storing values in variables

Some Simple Math

Start IDLE by following the steps in "Starting IDLE" on page xxvi. First you'll use Python to solve some simple math problems. The interactive shell can work just like a calculator. Type **2 + 2** into the interactive shell at the >>> prompt and press ENTER. (On some keyboards, this key is RETURN.) Figure 1-1 shows how this math problem looks in the interactive shell—notice that it responds with the number 4.

```
Python 3.4.4 Shell
File Edit Shell Debug Options Window Help
Python 3.4.4 (v3.4.4:737efcadf5a6, Dec 20 2015, 20:20:57) [MSC v.1600 64 bit (AM
D64)] on win32
Type "copyright", "credits" or "license()" for more information.
>>> 2 + 2
4
>>> |
                                                                    Ln: 5 Col: 4
```

Figure 1-1: Entering `2 + 2` into the interactive shell

This math problem is a simple programming instruction. The plus sign (+) tells the computer to add the numbers 2 and 2. The computer does this and responds with the number 4 on the next line. Table 1-1 lists the other math symbols available in Python.

Table 1-1: Math Operators

Operator	Operation
+	Addition
-	Subtraction
*	Multiplication
/	Division

The minus sign (-) subtracts numbers, the asterisk (*) multiplies numbers, and the slash (/) divides numbers. When used in this way, +, -, *, and / are called *operators*. Operators tell Python what to do with the numbers surrounding them.

Integers and Floating-Point Numbers

Integers (or *ints* for short) are whole numbers such as 4, 99, and 0. *Floating-point numbers* (or *floats* for short) are fractions or numbers with decimal points like 3.5, 42.1, and 5.0. In Python, 5 is an integer, but 5.0 is a float.

These numbers are called *values*. (Later we will learn about other kinds of values besides numbers.) In the math problem you entered in the shell, `2` and `2` are integer values.

Expressions

The math problem `2 + 2` is an example of an *expression*. As Figure 1-2 shows, expressions are made up of values (the numbers) connected by operators (the math signs) that produce a new value the code can use. Computers can solve millions of expressions in seconds.

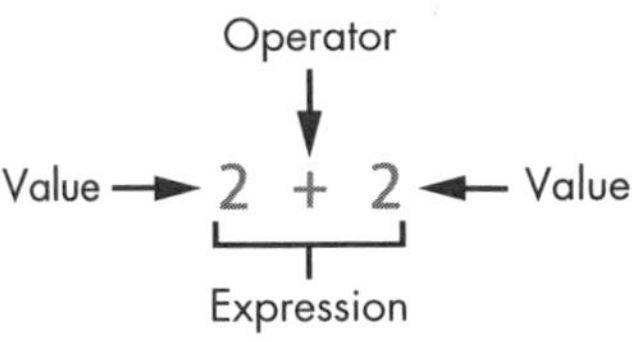

Figure 1-2: An expression is made up of values and operators.

Try entering some of these expressions into the interactive shell, pressing ENTER after each one:

```
>>> 2+2+2+2+2
10
>>> 8*6
48
>>> 10-5+6
11
>>> 2  +        2
4
```

These expressions all look like regular math equations, but notice all the spaces in the `2  +        2` example. In Python, you can add any number of spaces between values and operators. However, you must always start instructions at the beginning of the line (with no spaces) when entering them into the interactive shell.

Evaluating Expressions

When a computer solves the expression `10 + 5` and returns the value `15`, it has *evaluated* the expression. Evaluating an expression reduces the expression to a single value, just like solving a math problem reduces the problem to a single number: the answer. For example, the expressions `10 + 5` and `10 + 3 + 2` both evaluate to `15`.

When Python evaluates an expression, it follows an order of operations just like you do when you do math. There are just a few rules:

- Parts of the expression inside parentheses are evaluated first.
- Multiplication and division are done before addition and subtraction.
- The evaluation is performed left to right.

The expression `1 + 2 * 3 + 4` evaluates to `11`, not `13`, because `2 * 3` is evaluated first. If the expression were `(1 + 2) * (3 + 4)` it would evaluate to `21`, because the `(1 + 2)` and `(3 + 4)` inside parentheses are evaluated before multiplication.

Expressions can be of any size, but they will always evaluate to a single value. Even single values are expressions. For example, the expression `15` evaluates to the value `15`. The expression `8 * 3 / 2 + 2 + 7 - 9` will evaluate to the value `12.0` through the following steps:

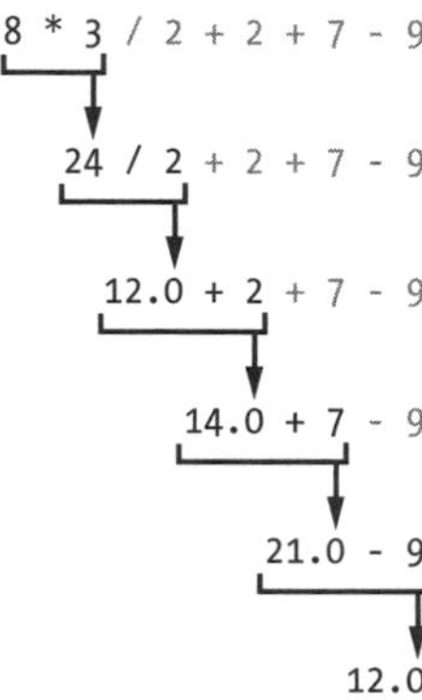

Even though the computer is performing all of these steps, you don't see them in the interactive shell. The interactive shell shows you just the result:

```
>>> 8 * 3 / 2 + 2 + 7 - 9
12.0
```

Notice that expressions with the `/` division operator always evaluate to a float; for example, `24 / 2` evaluates to `12.0`. Math operations with even one float value also evaluate to float values, so `12.0 + 2` evaluates to `14.0`.

Syntax Errors

If you enter `5 +` into the interactive shell, you'll get the following error message:

```
>>> 5 +
SyntaxError: invalid syntax
```

This error happened because `5 +` isn't an expression. Expressions have values connected by operators, and the `+` operator expects a value before *and* after it. An error message appears when an expected value is missing.

`SyntaxError` means Python doesn't understand the instruction because you typed it incorrectly. Computer programming isn't just about giving the computer instructions to follow but also knowing how to give it those instructions correctly.

Don't worry about making mistakes, though. Errors won't damage your computer. Just retype the instruction correctly into the interactive shell at the next >>> prompt.

Storing Values in Variables

When an expression evaluates to a value, you can use that value later by storing it in a *variable*. Think of a variable as a box that can hold a value.

An *assignment statement* will store a value inside a variable. Type a name for the variable, followed by the equal sign (=), which is called the *assignment operator*, and then the value to store in the variable. For example, enter the following into the interactive shell:

```
>>> spam = 15
>>>
```

The spam variable's box now stores the value 15, as shown in Figure 1-3.

Figure 1-3: Variables are like boxes that can hold values.

When you press ENTER, you won't see anything in response. In Python, you know the instruction was successful if no error message appears. The >>> prompt will appear so you can enter the next instruction.

Unlike expressions, *statements* are instructions that do not evaluate to any value. This is why there's no value displayed on the next line in the interactive shell after `spam = 15`. If you're confused about which instructions are expressions and which are statements, remember that expressions evaluate to a single value. Any other kind of instruction is a statement.

Variables store values, not expressions. For example, consider the expressions in the statements `spam = 10 + 5` and `spam = 10 + 7 - 2`. They both evaluate to `15`. The end result is the same: both assignment statements store the value `15` in the variable `spam`.

A good variable name describes the data it contains. Imagine that you moved to a new house and labeled all of your moving boxes *Stuff*. You'd never find anything! The variable names `spam`, `eggs`, and `bacon` are example names used for variables in this book.

The first time a variable is used in an assignment statement, Python will create that variable. To check what value is in a variable, enter the variable name into the interactive shell:

```
>>> spam = 15
>>> spam
15
```

The expression `spam` evaluates to the value inside the `spam` variable: `15`.

You can also use variables in expressions. Try entering the following in the interactive shell:

```
>>> spam = 15
>>> spam + 5
20
```

You set the value of the variable `spam` to `15`, so typing `spam + 5` is like typing the expression `15 + 5`. Here are the steps of `spam + 5` being evaluated:

```
spam + 5
  ↓
 15 + 5
    ↓
   20
```

You cannot use a variable before an assignment statement creates it. If you try to do so, Python will give you a `NameError` because no such variable by that name exists yet. Mistyping the variable name also causes this error:

```
>>> spam = 15
>>> spma
Traceback (most recent call last):
  File "<pyshell#8>", line 1, in <module>
    spma
NameError: name 'spma' is not defined
```

The error appeared because there's a `spam` variable but no `spma` variable.

You can change the value stored in a variable by entering another assignment statement. For example, enter the following into the interactive shell:

```
>>> spam = 15
>>> spam + 5
20
>>> spam = 3
>>> spam + 5
8
```

When you first enter `spam + 5`, the expression evaluates to `20` because you stored `15` inside `spam`. However, when you enter `spam = 3`, the value `15` in the variable's box is replaced, or *overwritten*, with the value 3 since the variable can hold only one value at a time. Because the value of spam is now 3, when you enter spam + 5, the expression evaluates to 8. Overwriting is like taking a value out of the variable's box to put a new value in, as shown in Figure 1-4.

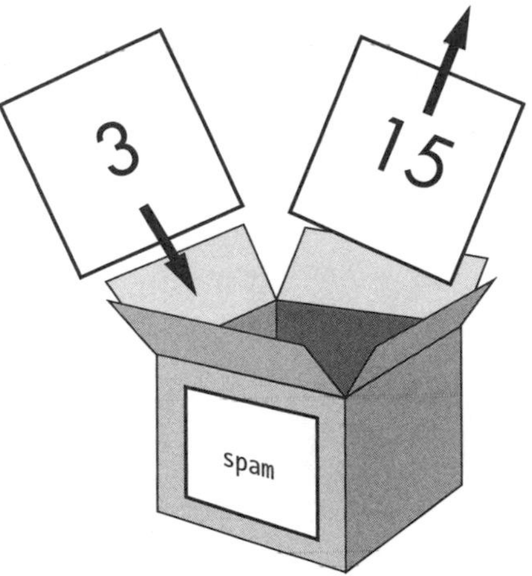

Figure 1-4: The value 15 in spam is overwritten by the value 3.

You can even use the value in the spam variable to assign a new value to spam:

```
>>> spam = 15
>>> spam = spam + 5
>>> spam
20
```

The assignment statement spam = spam + 5 says, "The new value of the spam variable will be the current value of spam plus five." To keep increasing the value in spam by 5 several times, enter the following into the interactive shell:

```
>>> spam = 15
>>> spam = spam + 5
>>> spam = spam + 5
>>> spam = spam + 5
>>> spam
30
```

In this example, you assign spam a value of 15 in the first statement. In the next statement, you add 5 to the value of spam and assign spam the new value spam + 5, which evaluates to 20. When you do this three times, spam evaluates to 30.

So far we've looked at just one variable, but you can create as many variables as you need in your programs. For example, let's assign different values to two variables named eggs and bacon, like so:

```
>>> bacon = 10
>>> eggs = 15
```

Now the bacon variable has 10 inside it, and the eggs variable has 15 inside it. Each variable is its own box with its own value, as shown in Figure 1-5.

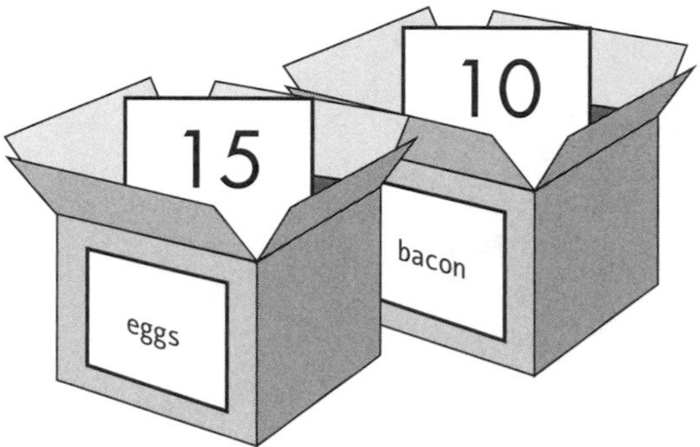

Figure 1-5: The bacon and eggs variables each store values.

Enter spam = bacon + eggs into the interactive shell, then check the new value of spam:

```
>>> bacon = 10
>>> eggs = 15
>>> spam = bacon + eggs
>>> spam
25
```

The value in spam is now 25. When you add bacon and eggs, you are adding their values, which are 10 and 15, respectively. Variables contain values, not expressions, so the spam variable was assigned the value 25, not the expression bacon + eggs. After the spam = bacon + eggs statement assigns the value 25 to spam, changing bacon or eggs will not affect spam.

Summary

In this chapter, you learned the basics of writing Python instructions. Because computers don't have common sense and only understand specific instructions, Python needs you to tell it exactly what to do.

Expressions are values (such as 2 or 5) combined with operators (such as + or -). Python can evaluate expressions—that is, reduce the expression to a single value. You can store values inside of variables so that your program can remember those values and use them later.

There are a few other types of operators and values in Python. In the next chapter, you'll go over some more basic concepts and write your first program. You'll learn about working with text in expressions. Python isn't limited to just numbers; it's more than a calculator!

2

WRITING PROGRAMS

Now let's see what Python can do with text. Almost all programs display text to the user, and the user enters text into programs through the keyboard. In this chapter, you'll make your first program, which does both of these things. You'll learn how to store text in variables, combine text, and display text on the screen. The program you'll create displays the greeting `Hello world!` and asks for the user's name.

TOPICS COVERED IN THIS CHAPTER

- Strings
- String concatenation
- Data types (such as strings or integers)
- Using the file editor to write programs
- Saving and running programs in IDLE
- Flow of execution
- Comments
- The print() function
- The input() function
- Case sensitivity

String Values

In Python, text values are called *strings*. String values can be used just like integer or float values. You can store strings in variables. In code, string values start and end with a single quote, '. Enter this code into the interactive shell:

```
>>> spam = 'hello'
```

The single quotes tell Python where the string begins and ends. They are not part of the string value's text. Now if you enter spam into the interactive shell, you'll see the contents of the spam variable. Remember, Python evaluates variables as the value stored inside the variable. In this case, this is the string 'hello'.

```
>>> spam = 'hello'
>>> spam
'hello'
```

Strings can have any keyboard character in them and can be as long as you want. These are all examples of strings:

```
'hello'
'Hi there!'
'KITTENS'
'7 apples, 14 oranges, 3 lemons'
'Anything not pertaining to elephants is irrelephant.'
'A long time ago, in a galaxy far, far away...'
'O*&#wY%*&OCfsdYO*&gfC%YO*&%3yc8r2'
```

String Concatenation

You can combine string values with operators to make expressions, just as you did with integer and float values. When you combine two strings with the + operator, it's called *string concatenation*. Enter `'Hello' + 'World!'` into the interactive shell:

```
>>> 'Hello' + 'World!'
'HelloWorld!'
```

The expression evaluates to a single string value, `'HelloWorld!'`. There is no space between the words because there was no space in either of the two concatenated strings, unlike in this example:

```
>>> 'Hello ' + 'World!'
'Hello World!'
```

The + operator works differently on string and integer values because they are different *data types*. All values have a data type. The data type of the value `'Hello'` is a string. The data type of the value `5` is an integer. The data type tells Python what operators should do when evaluating expressions. The + operator concatenates string values, but adds integer and float values.

Writing Programs in IDLE's File Editor

Until now, you've been typing instructions into IDLE's interactive shell one at a time. When you write programs, though, you enter several instructions and have them run all at once, and this is what you'll do next. It's time to write your first program!

In addition to the interpreter, IDLE has another part called the *file editor*. To open it, click the **File** menu at the top of the interactive shell. Then select **New Window** if you are using Windows or **New File** if you are using OS X. A blank window will appear for you to type your program's code into, as shown in Figure 2-1.

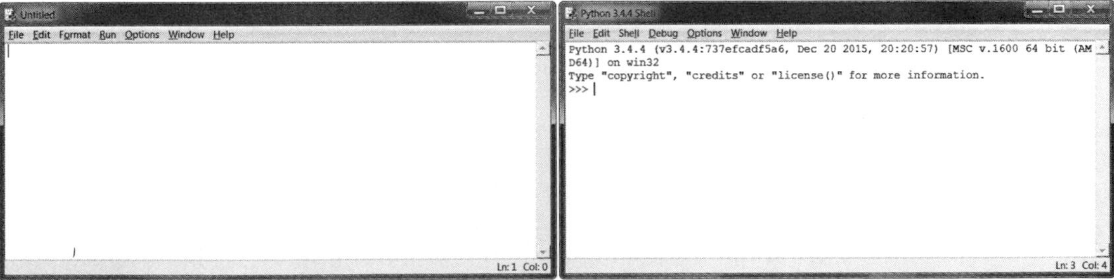

Figure 2-1: The file editor (left) and the interactive shell (right)

The two windows look similar, but just remember this: the interactive shell will have the >>> prompt, while the file editor will not.

Creating the Hello World Program

It's traditional for programmers to make their first program display `Hello world!` on the screen. You'll create your own Hello World program now.

MAKE SURE YOU'RE USING PYTHON 3, NOT PYTHON 2!

When you enter your program, remember not to enter the numbers at the beginning of each code line. They're there so this book can refer to the code by line number. The bottom-right corner of the file editor will tell you where the blinking cursor is so you can check which line of code you are on. Figure 2-2 shows that the cursor is on line 1 (going up and down the editor) and column 0 (going left and right).

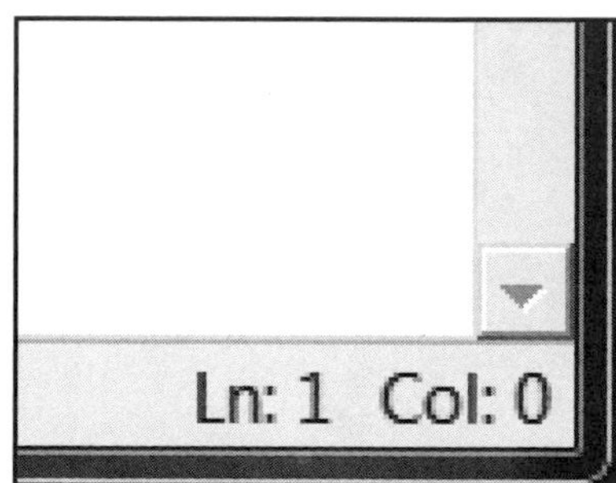
Ln: 1 Col: 0

Figure 2-2: The bottom-right of the file editor tells you what line the cursor is on.

Enter the following text into the new file editor window. This is the program's *source code*. It contains the instructions Python will follow when the program is run.

hello.py

```
1. # This program says hello and asks for my name.
2. print('Hello world!')
3. print('What is your name?')
4. myName = input()
5. print('It is good to meet you, ' + myName)
```

IDLE will write different types of instructions with different colors. After you're done typing the code, the window should look like Figure 2-3.

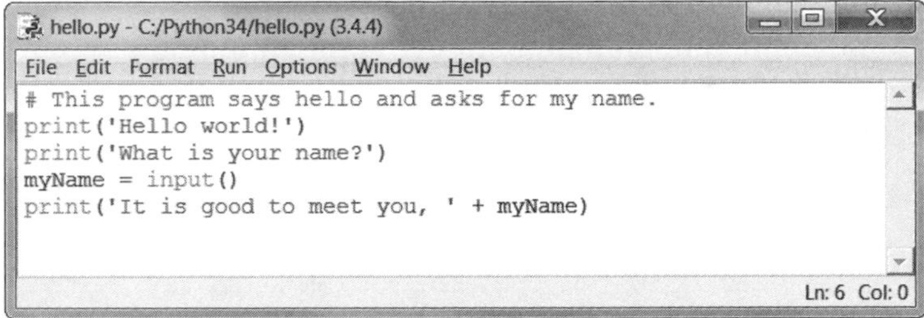

Figure 2-3: The file editor will look like this after you enter your code.

Check to make sure your IDLE window looks the same.

Saving Your Program

Once you've entered your source code, save it by clicking **File ▸ Save As**. Or press CTRL-S to save with a keyboard shortcut. Figure 2-4 shows the Save As window that will open. Enter *hello.py* in the File name text field and then click **Save**.

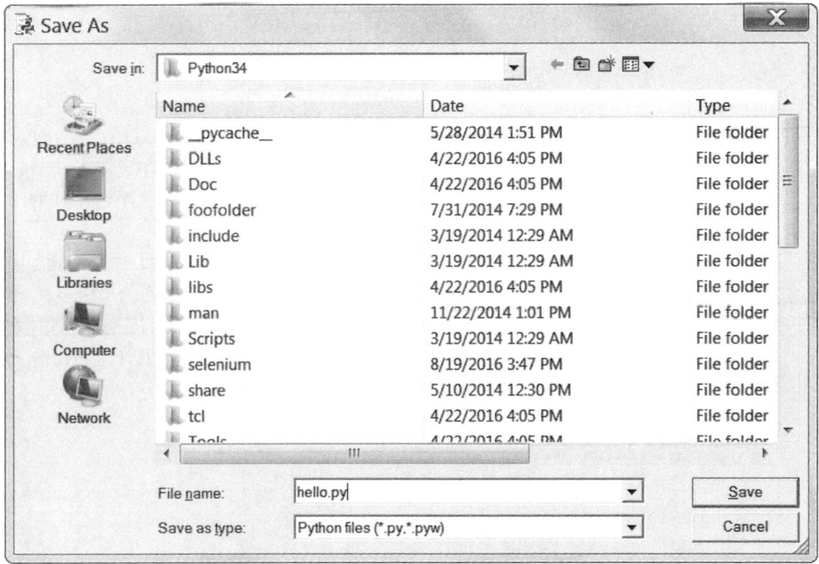

Figure 2-4: Saving the program

You should save your programs often while you write them. That way, if the computer crashes or you accidentally exit from IDLE, you won't lose much work.

To load your previously saved program, click **File ▸ Open**. Select the *hello.py* file in the window that appears and click the **Open** button. Your saved *hello.py* program will open in the file editor.

Running Your Program

Now it's time to run the program. Click **File ▸ Run Module**. Or just press F5 from the file editor (FN-5 on OS X). Your program will run in the interactive shell.

Enter your name when the program asks for it. This will look like Figure 2-5.

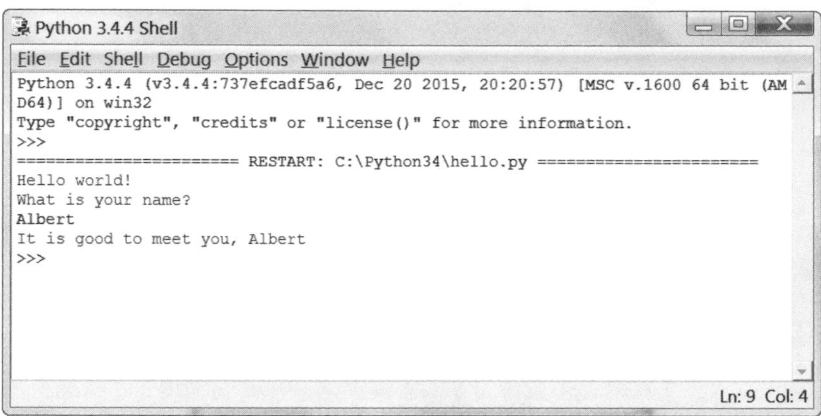

Figure 2-5: The interactive shell after you run hello.py

When you type your name and press ENTER, the program will greet you by name. Congratulations! You have written your first program and are now a computer programmer. Press F5 again to run the program a second time and enter another name.

If you got an error, compare your code to this book's code with the online diff tool at *https://www.nostarch.com/inventwithpython#diff*. Copy and paste your code from the file editor into the web page and click the **Compare** button. This tool will highlight any differences between your code and the code in this book, as shown in Figure 2-6.

While coding, if you get a `NameError` that looks like the following, that means you are using Python 2 instead of Python 3.

```
Hello world!
What is your name?
Albert
Traceback (most recent call last):
  File "C:/Python26/test1.py", line 4, in <module>
    myName = input()
  File "<string>", line 1, in <module>
NameError: name 'Albert' is not defined
```

To fix the problem, install Python 3.4 and rerun the program. (See "Downloading and Installing Python" on page xxv.)

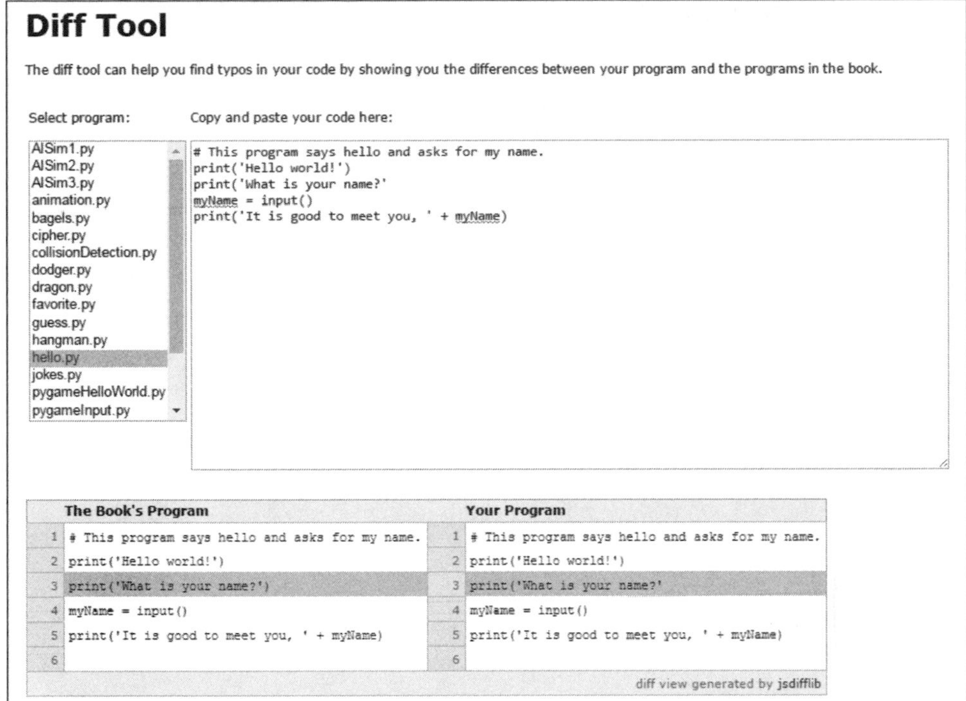
Diff Tool
The diff tool can help you find typos in your code by showing you the differences between your program and the programs in the book.
Select program:
Copy and paste your code here:
AISim1.py
AISim2.py
AISim3.py
animation.py
bagels.py
cipher.py
collisionDetection.py
dodger.py
dragon.py
favorite.py
guess.py
hangman.py
hello.py
jokes.py
pygameHelloWorld.py
pygameInput.py
# This program says hello and asks for my name.
print('Hello world!')
print('What is your name?'
myName = input()
print('It is good to meet you, ' + myName)
The Book's Program
Your Program
1 # This program says hello and asks for my name.
2 print('Hello world!')
3 print('What is your name?')
4 myName = input()
5 print('It is good to meet you, ' + myName)
6
1 # This program says hello and asks for my name.
2 print('Hello world!')
3 print('What is your name?'
4 myName = input()
5 print('It is good to meet you, ' + myName)
6
diff view generated by jsdifflib

Figure 2-6: Using the diff tool at https://www.nostarch.com/inventwithpython#diff

How the Hello World Program Works

Each line of code is an instruction interpreted by Python. These instructions make up the program. A computer program's instructions are like the steps in a recipe. Python completes each instruction in order, beginning from the top of the program and moving downward.

The step where Python is currently working in the program is called the *execution*. When the program starts, the execution is at the first instruction. After executing the instruction, Python moves down to the next instruction.

Let's look at each line of code to see what it's doing. We'll begin with line number 1.

Comments for the Programmer

The first line of the Hello World program is a *comment*:

```
1. # This program says hello and asks for my name.
```

Any text following a hash mark (#) is a comment. Comments are the programmer's notes about what the code does; they are not written for Python but for you, the programmer. Python ignores comments when it runs a program. Programmers usually put a comment at the top of their code to give their program a title. The comment in the Hello World program tells you that the program says hello and asks for your name.

Functions: Mini-Programs Inside Programs

A *function* is kind of like a mini-program inside your program that contains several instructions for Python to execute. The great thing about functions is that you only need to know what they do, not how they do it. Python provides some built-in functions already. We use `print()` and `input()` in the Hello World program.

A *function call* is an instruction that tells Python to run the code inside a function. For example, your program calls the `print()` function to display a string on the screen. The `print()` function takes the string you type between the parentheses as input and displays that text on the screen.

The print() Function

Lines 2 and 3 of the Hello World program are calls to `print()`:

```
2. print('Hello world!')
3. print('What is your name?')
```

A value between the parentheses in a function call is an *argument*. The argument on line 2's `print()` function call is `'Hello world!'`, and the argument on line 3's `print()` function call is `'What is your name?'`. This is called *passing* the argument to the function.

The input() Function

Line 4 is an assignment statement with a variable, `myName`, and a function call, `input()`:

```
4. myName = input()
```

When `input()` is called, the program waits for the user to enter text. The text string that the user enters becomes the value that the function call evaluates to. Function calls can be used in expressions anywhere a value can be used.

The value that the function call evaluates to is called the *return value*. (In fact, "the value a function call returns" means the same thing as "the value a function call evaluates to.") In this case, the return value of the `input()` function is the string that the user entered: their name. If the user enters `Albert`, the `input()` function call evaluates to the string `'Albert'`. The evaluation looks like this:

```
myName = input()
myName = 'Albert'
```

This is how the string value `'Albert'` gets stored in the `myName` variable.

Expressions in Function Calls

The last line in the Hello World program is another `print()` function call:

```
5. print('It is good to meet you, ' + myName)
```

The expression `'It is good to meet you, ' + myName` is between the parentheses of `print()`. Because arguments are always single values, Python will first evaluate this expression and then pass that value as the argument. If `'Albert'` is stored in `myName`, the evaluation looks like this:

```
print('It is good to meet you, ' + myName)
print('It is good to meet you, ' + 'Albert')
print('It is good to meet you, Albert')
```

This is how the program greets the user by name.

The End of the Program

Once the program executes the last line, it *terminates* or *exits*. This means the program stops running. Python forgets all of the values stored in variables, including the string stored in `myName`. If you run the program again and enter a different name, the program will think that is your name:

```
Hello world!
What is your name?
Carolyn
It is good to meet you, Carolyn
```

Remember, the computer does exactly what you program it to do. Computers are dumb and just follow the instructions you give them exactly. The computer doesn't care if you type in your name, someone else's name, or something silly. Type in anything you want. The computer will treat it the same way:

```
Hello world!
What is your name?
poop
It is good to meet you, poop
```

Naming Variables

Giving variables descriptive names makes it easier to understand what a program does. You could have called the `myName` variable `abrahamLincoln` or `nAmE`, and Python would have run the program just the same. But those names don't really tell you much about what information the variable might hold. As Chapter 1 discussed, if you were moving to a new house and you labeled every moving box *Stuff*, that wouldn't be helpful at all! This book's interactive shell examples use variable names like `spam`, `eggs`, and `bacon` because the variable names in these examples don't matter. However, this book's programs all use descriptive names, and so should your programs.

Variable names are *case sensitive*, which means the same variable name in a different case is considered a different variable. So `spam`, `SPAM`, `Spam`, and `sPAM` are four different variables in Python. They each contain their own separate values. It's a bad idea to have differently cased variables in your program. Use descriptive names for your variables instead.

Variable names are usually lowercase. If there's more than one word in the variable name, it's a good idea to capitalize each word after the first. For example, the variable name `whatIHadForBreakfastThisMorning` is much easier to read than `whatihadforbreakfastthismorning`. Capitalizing your variables this way is called *camel case* (because it resembles the humps on a camel's back), and it makes your code more readable. Programmers also prefer using shorter variable names to make code easier to understand: `breakfast` or `foodThisMorning` is more readable than `whatIHadForBreakfastThisMorning`. These are *conventions*—optional but standard ways of doing things in Python programming.

Summary

Once you understand how to use strings and functions, you can start making programs that interact with users. This is important because text is the main way the user and the computer will communicate with each other. The user enters text through the keyboard with the `input()` function, and the computer displays text on the screen with the `print()` function.

Strings are just values of a new data type. All values have a data type, and the data type of a value affects how the `+` operator functions.

Functions are used to carry out complicated instructions in your program. Python has many built-in functions that you'll learn about in this book. Function calls can be used in expressions anywhere a value is used.

The instruction or step in your program where Python is currently working is called the execution. In Chapter 3, you'll learn more about making the execution move in ways other than just straight down the program. Once you learn this, you'll be ready to create games!

3

GUESS THE NUMBER

In this chapter, you're going to make a Guess the Number game. The computer will think of a secret number from 1 to 20 and ask the user to guess it. After each guess, the computer will tell the user whether the number is too high or too low. The user wins if they can guess the number within six tries.

This is a good game to code because it covers many programming concepts in a short program. You'll learn how to convert values to different data types and when you would need to do this. Since this program is a game, from now on we'll call the user the *player*.

TOPICS COVERED IN THIS CHAPTER

- `import` statements
- Modules
- The `randint()` function
- `for` statements
- Blocks
- The `str()`, `int()`, and `float()` functions
- Booleans
- Comparison operators
- Conditions
- The difference between = and ==
- `if` statements
- `break` statements

Sample Run of Guess the Number

Here's what the Guess the Number program looks like to the player when it's run. The player's input is marked in bold.

```
Hello! What is your name?
Albert
Well, Albert, I am thinking of a number between 1 and 20.
Take a guess.
10
Your guess is too high.
Take a guess.
2
Your guess is too low.
Take a guess.
4
Good job, Albert! You guessed my number in 3 guesses!
```

Source Code for Guess the Number

Open a new file editor window by clicking **File ▸ New Window**. In the blank window that appears, enter the source code and save it as *guess.py*. Then run the program by pressing F5.

MAKE SURE YOU'RE
USING PYTHON 3,
NOT PYTHON 2!

When you enter this code into the file editor, be sure to pay attention to the spacing at the front of the lines. Some lines need to be indented four or eight spaces.

If you get errors after entering this code, compare the code you typed to the book's code with the online diff tool at *https://www.nostarch.com/inventwithpython#diff*.

guess.py

```
# This is a Guess the Number game.
import random

guessesTaken = 0

print('Hello! What is your name?')
myName = input()

number = random.randint(1, 20)
print('Well, ' + myName + ', I am thinking of a number between 1 and 20.')

for guessesTaken in range(6):
    print('Take a guess.') # Four spaces in front of "print"
    guess = input()
    guess = int(guess)

    if guess < number:
        print('Your guess is too low.') # Eight spaces in front of "print"

    if guess > number:
        print('Your guess is too high.')

    if guess == number:
        break

if guess == number:
    guessesTaken = str(guessesTaken + 1)
    print('Good job, ' + myName + '! You guessed my number in ' +
      guessesTaken + ' guesses!')

if guess != number:
    number = str(number)
    print('Nope. The number I was thinking of was ' + number + '.')
```

Importing the random Module

Let's take a look at the first two lines of this program:

```
# This is a Guess the Number game.
import random
```

The first line is a comment, which you saw in Chapter 2. Remember that Python will ignore everything after the # character. The comment here just reminds us what this program does.

The second line is an import statement. Remember, statements are instructions that perform some action but don't evaluate to a value like expressions do. You've already seen the assignment statement, which stores a value in a variable.

While Python includes many built-in functions, some functions are written in separate programs called *modules*. You can use these functions by importing their modules into your program with an import statement.

Line 2 imports the random module so that the program can call the randint() function. This function will come up with a random number for the player to guess.

Now that you've imported the random module, you need to set up some variables to store values your program will use later.

Line 4 creates a new variable named guessesTaken:

```
4. guessesTaken = 0
```

You'll store the number of guesses the player has made in this variable. Since the player hasn't made any guesses at this point in the program, store the integer 0 here.

```
6. print('Hello! What is your name?')
7. myName = input()
```

Lines 6 and 7 are the same as the lines in the Hello World program in Chapter 2. Programmers often reuse code from other programs to save themselves work.

Line 6 is a function call to print(). Remember that a function is like a mini-program inside your program. When your program calls a function, it runs this mini-program. The code inside print() displays the string argument you passed it on the screen.

Line 7 lets the player enter their name and stores it in the myName variable. Remember, the string might not really be the player's name; it's just whatever string the player types. Computers are dumb and follow their instructions, no matter what.

Generating Random Numbers with the random.randint() Function

Now that your other variables are set up, you can use the random module's function to set the computer's secret number:

```
9. number = random.randint(1, 20)
```

Line 9 calls a new function named randint() and stores the return value in number. Remember, function calls can be part of expressions because they evaluate to a value.

The `randint()` function is provided by the `random` module, so you must call it with `random.randint()` (don't forget the period!) to tell Python that the function `randint()` is in the `random` module.

`randint()` will return a random integer between (and including) the two integer arguments you pass it. Line 9 passes `1` and `20`, separated by commas, between the parentheses that follow the function name. The random integer that `randint()` returns is stored in a variable named `number`—this is the secret number the player is trying to guess.

Just for a moment, go back to the interactive shell and enter **`import random`** to import the `random` module. Then enter **`random.randint(1, 20)`** to see what the function call evaluates to. It will return an integer between `1` and `20`. Repeat the code again, and the function call will return another integer. The `randint()` function returns a random integer each time, just as rolling a die will result in a random number each time. For example, enter the following into the interactive shell. The results you get when you call the `randint()` function will probably be different (it is random, after all!).

```
>>> import random
>>> random.randint(1, 20)
12
>>> random.randint(1, 20)
18
>>> random.randint(1, 20)
3
>>> random.randint(1, 20)
18
>>> random.randint(1, 20)
7
```

You can also try different ranges of numbers by changing the arguments. For example, enter **`random.randint(1, 4)`** to get only integers between `1` and `4` (including both `1` and `4`). Or try **`random.randint(1000, 2000)`** to get integers between `1000` and `2000`.

Enter this code in the interactive shell and see what numbers you get:

```
>>> random.randint(1, 4)
3
>>> random.randint(1000, 2000)
1294
```

You can change the game's code slightly to make the game behave differently. In our original code, we use an integer between `1` and `20`:

```
 9. number = random.randint(1, 20)
10. print('Well, ' + myName + ', I am thinking of a number between 1 and 20.')
```

Try changing the integer range to `(1, 100)` instead:

```
 9. number = random.randint(1, 100)
10. print('Well, ' + myName + ', I am thinking of a number between 1 and 100.')
```

Now the computer will think of an integer between `1` and `100` instead of `1` and `20`. Changing line 9 will change the range of the random number, but remember to also change line 10 so that the game tells the player the new range instead of the old one.

You can use the `randint()` function whenever you want to add randomness to your games. You'll use randomness in many games. (Think of how many board games use dice.)

Welcoming the Player

After the computer assigns `number` a random integer, it greets the player:

```
10. print('Well, ' + myName + ', I am thinking of a number between 1 and 20.')
```

On line 10, `print()` welcomes the player by name and tells them that the computer is thinking of a random number.

At first glance, it may look like there's more than one string argument in line 10, but examine the line carefully. The `+` operators between the three strings concatenate them into one string. And that one string is the argument passed to `print()`. If you look closely, you'll see that the commas are inside the quotes and part of the strings themselves.

Flow Control Statements

In previous chapters, the program execution started at the top instruction in the program and moved straight down, executing each instruction in order. But with the `for`, `if`, `else`, and `break` statements, you can make the execution loop or skip instructions based on conditions. These kinds of statements are *flow control statements*, since they change the flow of the program execution as it moves around your program.

Using Loops to Repeat Code

Line 12 is a `for` statement, which indicates the beginning of a `for` loop:

```
12. for guessesTaken in range(6):
```

Loops let you execute code over and over again. Line 12 will repeat its code six times. A `for` statement begins with the `for` keyword, followed by a new variable name, the `in` keyword, a call to the `range()` function that specifies the number of loops it should do, and a colon. Let's go over a few additional concepts so that you can work with loops.

Grouping with Blocks

Several lines of code can be grouped together in a *block*. Every line in a block of code begins with at least the number of spaces as the first line in the block. You can tell where a block begins and ends by looking at the number of spaces at the front of the lines. This is the line's *indentation*.

Python programmers typically use four *additional* spaces of indentation to begin a block. Any following line that's indented by that same amount is part of the block. The block ends when there's a line of code with the *same indentation as before* the block started. There can also be blocks within other blocks. Figure 3-1 shows a code diagram with the blocks outlined and numbered.

```
   12. for guessesTaken in range(6):
❶  13. ••••print('Take a guess.')
   14. ••••guess = input()
   15. ••••guess = int(guess)
   16.
   17. ••••if guess < number:
❷  18. ••••••••print('Your guess is too low.')
   19.
   20. ••••if guess > number:
❸  21. ••••••••print('Your guess is too high.')
   22.
   23. ••••if guess == number:
❹  24. ••••••••break
   25.
   26. if guess == number:
```

Figure 3-1: An example of blocks and their indentation. The gray dots represent spaces.

In Figure 3-1, line 12 has no indentation and isn't inside any block. Line 13 has an indentation of four spaces. Since this line is indented more than the previous line, a new block starts here. Every line following this one with the same amount of indentation or more is considered part of block ❶. If Python encounters another line with less indentation than the block's first line, the block has ended. Blank lines are ignored.

Line 18 has an indentation of eight spaces, which starts block ❷. This block is *inside* block ❶. But the next line, line 20, is indented only four spaces. Because the indentation has decreased, you know that line 18's block ❷ has ended, and because line 20 has the same indentation as line 13, you know it's in block ❶.

Line 21 increases the indentation to eight spaces again, so another new block within a block has started: block ❸. At line 23, we exit block ❸, and at line 24 we enter the final block within a block, block ❹. Both block ❶ and block ❹ end on line 24.

Looping with for Statements

The `for` statement marks the beginning of a loop. Loops execute the same code repeatedly. When the execution reaches a `for` statement, it enters the block that follows the `for` statement. After running all the code in this block, the execution moves back to the top of the block to run the code all over again.

Enter the following into the interactive shell:

```
>>> for i in range(3):
    print('Hello! i is set to', i)


Hello! i is set to 0
Hello! i is set to 1
Hello! i is set to 2
```

Notice that after you typed `for i in range(3):` and pressed ENTER, the interactive shell didn't show another `>>>` prompt because it was expecting you to type a block of code. Press ENTER again after the last instruction to tell the interactive shell you are done entering the block of code. (This applies only when you are working in the interactive shell. When writing *.py* files in the file editor, you don't need to insert a blank line.)

Let's look at the `for` loop on line 12 of *guess.py*:

```
12. for guessesTaken in range(6):
13.     print('Take a guess.') # Four spaces in front of "print"
14.     guess = input()
15.     guess = int(guess)
16.
17.     if guess < number:
18.         print('Your guess is too low.') # Eight spaces in front of "print"
19.
20.     if guess > number:
21.         print('Your guess is too high.')
22.
23.     if guess == number:
24.         break
25.
26. if guess == number:
```

In Guess the Number, the `for` block begins at the `for` statement on line 12, and the first line after the `for` block is line 26.

A `for` statement always has a colon (`:`) after the condition. Statements that end with a colon expect a new block on the next line. This is illustrated in Figure 3-2.

```
12. for guessesTaken in range(6):
13.     print('Take a guess.') # Four spaces in front of "print"
14.     guess = input()
15.     guess = int(guess)
16.
17.     if guess < number:
18.         print('Your guess is too low.') # Eight spaces in front of "print"
19.
20.     if guess > number:
21.         print('Your guess is too high.')
22.
23.     if guess == number:
24.         break
25.
26. if guess == number:
```

The execution loops six times.

Figure 3-2: The `for` *loop's flow of execution*

Figure 3-2 shows how the execution flows. The execution will enter the `for` block at line 13 and keep going down. Once the program reaches the end of the `for` block, instead of going down to the next line, the execution loops back up to the start of the `for` block at line 13. It does this six times because of the `range(6)` function call in the `for` statement. Each time the execution goes through the loop is called an *iteration*.

Think of the `for` statement as saying, "Execute the code in the following block a certain number of times."

Getting the Player's Guess

Lines 13 and 14 ask the player to guess what the secret number is and let them enter their guess:

```
13.     print('Take a guess.') # Four spaces in front of "print"
14.     guess = input()
```

That number the player enters is stored in a variable named `guess`.

Converting Values with the int(), float(), and str() Functions

Line 15 calls a new function called `int()`:

```
15.     guess = int(guess)
```

The `int()` function takes one argument and returns the argument's value as an integer.

Enter the following into the interactive shell to see how the `int()` function works:

```
>>> int('42')
42
```

The `int('42')` call will return the integer value `42`.

```
>>> 3 + int('2')
5
```

The `3 + int('2')` line shows an expression that uses the return value of `int()` as part of an expression. It evaluates to the integer value `5`:

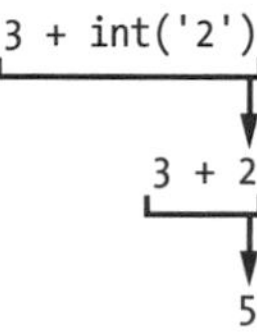

Even though you can pass a string to `int()`, you cannot pass it just any string. Passing `'forty-two'` to `int()` will result in an error:

```
>>> int('forty-two')
Traceback (most recent call last):
  File "<pyshell#5>", line 1, in <module>
    int('forty-two')
ValueError: invalid literal for int() with base 10: 'forty-two'
```

The string you pass to `int()` must be made of numbers.

In Guess the Number, we get the player's number using the `input()` function. Remember, the `input()` function always returns a *string* of text the player entered. If the player types `5`, the `input()` function will return the string value `'5'`, not the integer value `5`. But we'll need to compare the player's number with an integer later, and Python cannot use the < and > comparison operators to compare a string and an integer value:

```
>>> 4 < '5'
Traceback (most recent call last):
  File "<pyshell#0>", line 1, in <module>
    4 < '5'
TypeError: unorderable types: int() < str()
```

Therefore, we need to convert the string into an integer:

```
    guess = input()
    guess = int(guess)
```

On line 14, we assign the guess variable to the string value of whatever number the player typed. Line 15 overwrites the string value in guess with the integer value returned by int(). The code int(guess) returns a new integer value based on the string it was provided, and guess = assigns that new value to guess. This lets the code later in the program compare whether guess is greater than, less than, or equal to the secret number in the number variable.

The float() and str() functions will similarly return float and string versions of the arguments passed to them. Enter the following into the interactive shell:

```
>>> float('42')
42.0
>>> float(42)
42.0
```

When the string '42' or the integer 42 is passed to float(), the float 42.0 is returned.

Now try using the str() function:

```
>>> str(42)
'42'
>>> str(42.0)
'42.0'
```

When the integer 42 is passed to str(), the string '42' is returned. But when the float 42.0 is passed to str(), the string '42.0' is returned.

Using the int(), float(), and str() functions, you can take a value of one data type and return it as a value of a different data type.

The Boolean Data Type

Every value in Python belongs to one data type. The data types that have been introduced so far are integers, floats, strings, and now Booleans. The *Boolean* data type has only two values: True or False. Boolean values must be entered with an uppercase T or F and the rest of the value's name in lowercase.

Boolean values can be stored in variables just like the other data types:

```
>>> spam = True
>>> eggs = False
```

In this example, you set spam to True and eggs to False. Remember to capitalize the first letter.

You will use Boolean values (called *bools* for short) with comparison operators to form conditions. We'll cover comparison operators first and then go over conditions.

Comparison Operators

Comparison operators compare two values and evaluate to a `True` or `False` Boolean value. Table 3-1 lists all of the comparison operators.

Table 3-1: Comparison Operators

Operator	Operation
`<`	Less than
`>`	Greater than
`<=`	Less than or equal to
`>=`	Greater than or equal to
`==`	Equal to
`!=`	Not equal to

You've already read about the `+`, `-`, `*`, and `/` math operators. Like any operator, comparison operators combine with values to form expressions such as `guessesTaken < 6`.

Line 17 of the Guess the Number program uses the less than comparison operator:

```
17.     if guess < number:
```

We'll discuss `if` statements in more detail shortly; for now, let's just look at the expression that follows the `if` keyword (the `guess < number` part). This expression contains two values (the values in the variables `guess` and `number`) connected by an operator (the `<`, or less than, sign).

Checking for True or False with Conditions

A *condition* is an expression that combines two values with a comparison operator (such as `<` or `>`) and evaluates to a Boolean value. A condition is just another name for an expression that evaluates to `True` or `False`. One place we use conditions is in `if` statements.

For example, the condition `guess < number` on line 17 asks, "Is the value stored in `guess` less than the value stored in `number`?" If so, then the condition evaluates to `True`. If not, the condition evaluates to `False`.

Say that `guess` stores the integer `10` and `number` stores the integer `16`. Because `10` is less than `16`, this condition evaluates to the Boolean value of `True`. The evaluation would look like this:

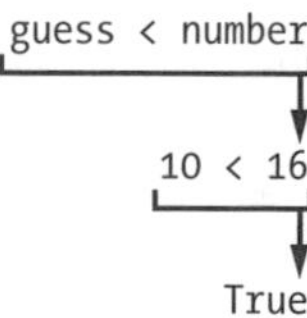

Experimenting with Booleans, Comparison Operators, and Conditions

Enter the following expressions in the interactive shell to see their Boolean results:

```
>>> 0 < 6
True
>>> 6 < 0
False
```

The condition `0 < 6` returns the Boolean value `True` because the number `0` is less than the number `6`. But because `6` isn't less than `0`, the condition `6 < 0` evaluates to `False`.

Notice that `10 < 10` evaluates to `False` because the number `10` isn't smaller than the number `10`:

```
>>> 10 < 10
False
```

The values are the same. If Alice were the same height as Bob, you wouldn't say that Alice is taller than Bob or that Alice is shorter than Bob. Both of those statements would be false.

Now enter these expressions into the interactive shell:

```
>>> 10 == 10
True
>>> 10 == 11
False
>>> 11 == 10
False
>>> 10 != 10
False
```

In this example, `10` is equal to `10`, so `10 == 10` evaluates to `True`. But `10` is not equal to `11`, so `10 == 11` is `False`. Even if the order is flipped, `11` is still not equal to `10`, so `11 == 10` is `False`. Finally, `10` is equal to `10`, so `10 != 10` is `False`.

You can also evaluate string expressions with comparison operators:

```
>>> 'Hello' == 'Hello'
True
>>> 'Goodbye' != 'Hello'
True
>>> 'Hello' == 'HELLO'
False
```

`'Hello'` is equal to `'Hello'`, so `'Hello' == 'Hello'` is `True`. `'Goodbye'` is not equal to `'Hello'`, so `'Goodbye' != 'Hello'` is also `True`.

Notice that the last line evaluates to `False`. Upper- and lowercase letters are not the same in Python, so `'Hello'` is not equal to `'HELLO'`.

String and integer values will never be equal to each other. For example, enter the following into the interactive shell:

```
>>> 42 == 'Hello'
False
>>> 42 != '42'
True
```

In the first example, `42` is an integer and `'Hello'` is a string, so the values are not equal and the expression evaluates to `False`. In the second example, the string `'42'` is still not an integer, so the expression "the integer `42` is not equal to the string `'42'`" evaluates to `True`.

The Difference Between = and ==

Be careful not to confuse the assignment operator, `=`, and the equal to comparison operator, `==`. The equal sign, `=`, is used in assignment statements to store a value to a variable, whereas the double equal sign, `==`, is used in expressions to see whether two values are equal. It's easy to accidentally use one when you mean to use the other.

It might help to remember that both the equal to comparison operator, `==`, and the not equal to comparison operator, `!=`, have two characters.

if Statements

Line 17 is an `if` statement:

```
17.     if guess < number:
18.         print('Your guess is too low.') # Eight spaces in front of "print"
```

The code block following the `if` statement will run if the `if` statement's condition evaluates to `True`. If the condition is `False`, the code in the `if` block is skipped. Using `if` statements, you can make the program run certain code only when you want it to.

Line 17 checks whether the player's guess is less than the computer's secret number. If so, then the execution moves inside the `if` block on line 18 and prints a message telling the player their guess was too low.

Line 20 checks whether the player's guess is greater than the secret number:

```
20.     if guess > number:
21.         print('Your guess is too high.')
```

If this condition is `True`, then the `print()` function call tells the player that their guess is too high.

Leaving Loops Early with the break Statement

The `if` statement on line 23 checks whether the number the player guessed is equal to the secret number. If it is, the program runs the `break` statement on line 24:

```
23.     if guess == number:
24.         break
```

A `break` statement tells the execution to jump immediately out of the `for` block to the first line after the end of the `for` block. The `break` statement is found only inside loops, such as in a `for` block.

Checking Whether the Player Won

The `for` block ends at the next line of code with no indentation, which is line 26:

```
26. if guess == number:
```

The execution leaves the `for` block either because it has looped six times (when the player runs out of guesses) or because the `break` statement on line 24 has executed (when the player guesses the number correctly).

Line 26 checks whether the player guessed correctly. If so, the execution enters the `if` block at line 27:

```
27.     guessesTaken = str(guessesTaken + 1)
28.     print('Good job, ' + myName + '! You guessed my number in ' +
          guessesTaken + ' guesses!')
```

Lines 27 and 28 execute only if the condition in the `if` statement on line 26 is `True` (that is, if the player correctly guessed the computer's number).

Line 27 calls the `str()` function, which returns the string form of `guessesTaken + 1` (since the range function goes from 0 to 5 instead of 1 to 6). Line 28 concatenates strings to tell the player they have won and how many guesses it took. Only string values can concatenate to other strings. This is why line 27 had to change `guessesTaken + 1` to the string form. Otherwise, trying to concatenate a string with an integer would cause Python to display an error.

Checking Whether the Player Lost

If the player runs out of guesses, the execution will go to this line of code:

```
30. if guess != number:
```

Line 30 uses the not equal to comparison operator `!=` to check whether the player's last guess is not equal to the secret number. If this condition evaluates to `True`, the execution moves into the `if` block on line 31.

Lines 31 and 32 are inside the `if` block, executing only if the condition on line 30 is `True`:

```
31.     number = str(number)
32.     print('Nope. The number I was thinking of was ' + number + '.')
```

In this block, the program tells the player what the secret number was. This requires concatenating strings, but `number` stores an integer value. Line 31 overwrites `number` with a string so that it can be concatenated to the `'Nope. The number I was thinking of was '` and `'.'` strings on line 32.

At this point, the execution has reached the end of the code, and the program terminates. Congratulations! You've just programmed your first real game!

You can adjust the game's difficulty by changing the number of guesses the player gets. To give the player only four guesses, change the code on line 12:

```
12. for guessesTaken in range(4):
```

By passing `4` to `range()`, you ensure that the code inside the loop runs only four times instead of six. This makes the game much more difficult. To make the game easier, pass a larger integer to the `range()` function call. This will cause the loop to run a few *more* times and accept *more* guesses from the player.

Summary

Programming is just the action of writing code for programs—that is, creating programs that can be executed by a computer.

When you see someone using a computer program (for example, playing your Guess the Number game), all you see is some text appearing on the screen. The program decides what text to display on the screen (the program's *output*) based on its instructions and on the text that the player typed with the keyboard (the program's *input*). A program is just a collection of instructions that act on the user's input.

There are a few kinds of instructions:

- **Expressions** are values connected by operators. Expressions are all evaluated down to a single value. For example, `2 + 2` evaluates to `4` or `'Hello' + ' ' + 'World'` evaluates to `'Hello World'`. When expressions are next to the `if` and `for` keywords, you can also call them *conditions*.
- **Assignment statements** store values in variables so you can remember the values later in the program.

- **The `if`, `for`, and `break` statements** are flow control statements that can make the execution skip instructions, loop over instructions, or break out of loops. Function calls also change the flow of execution by jumping to the instructions inside of a function.
- **The `print()` and `input()` functions** display text on the screen and get text from the keyboard. Instructions that deal with the *input* and *output* of the program are called *I/O* (pronounced *eye oh*).

That's it—just those four things. Of course, there are many details to be learned about those four types of instructions. In later chapters, you'll read about more data types and operators, more flow control statements, and many other functions that come with Python. There are also different types of I/O beyond text, such as input from the mouse and sound and graphics output.

4

A JOKE-TELLING PROGRAM

This chapter's program tells a few jokes to the user and demonstrates more advanced ways to use strings with the `print()` function. Most of the games in this book will have simple text for input and output. The input is typed on the keyboard by the user, and the output is the text displayed on the screen.

TOPICS COVERED IN THIS CHAPTER

- Escape characters
- Using single quotes and double quotes for strings
- Using `print()`'s `end` keyword parameter to skip newlines

You've already learned how to display simple text output with the print() function. Now let's take a deeper look at how strings and print() work in Python.

Sample Run of Jokes

Here's what the user sees when they run the Jokes program:

```
What do you get when you cross a snowman with a vampire?
Frostbite!

What do dentists call an astronaut's cavity?
A black hole!

Knock knock.
Who's there?
Interrupting cow.
Interrupting cow wh-MOO!
```

Source Code for Jokes

MAKE SURE YOU'RE USING PYTHON 3, NOT PYTHON 2!

Open a new file editor window by clicking **File ▸ New Window**. In the blank window that appears, enter the source code and save it as *jokes.py*. Then run the program by pressing F5.

If you get errors after entering this code, compare the code you typed to the book's code with the online diff tool at *https://www.nostarch.com/inventwithpython#diff*.

jokes.py

```
print('What do you get when you cross a snowman with a vampire?')
input()
print('Frostbite!')
print()
print('What do dentists call an astronaut\'s cavity?')
input()
print('A black hole!')
print()
print('Knock knock.')
input()
print("Who's there?")
input()
print('Interrupting cow.')
input()
print('Interrupting cow wh', end='')
print('-MOO!')
```

How the Code Works

Let's start by looking at the first four lines of code:

```
1. print('What do you get when you cross a snowman with a vampire?')
2. input()
3. print('Frostbite!')
4. print()
```

Lines 1 and 3 use the print() function call to ask and give the answer to the first joke. You don't want the user to immediately read the joke's punchline, so there's a call to the input() function after the first print() instance. The user will read the joke, press ENTER, and then read the punchline.

The user can still type in a string and press ENTER, but this returned string isn't being stored in any variable. The program will just forget about it and move to the next line of code.

The last print() function call doesn't have a string argument. This tells the program to just print a blank line. Blank lines are useful to keep the text from looking crowded.

Escape Characters

Lines 5 to 8 print the question and answer to the next joke:

```
5. print('What do dentists call an astronaut\'s cavity?')
6. input()
7. print('A black hole!')
8. print()
```

On line 5, there's a backslash right before the single quote: \'. (Note that \ is a backslash, and / is a forward slash.) This backslash tells you that the letter right after it is an escape character. An *escape character* lets you print special characters that are difficult or impossible to enter into the source code, such as the single quote in a string value that begins and ends with single quotes.

In this case, if we didn't include the backslash, the single quote in astronaut\'s would be interpreted as the end of the string. But this quote needs to be *part of* the string. The escaped single quote tells Python that it should include the single quote in the string.

But what if you actually want to display a backslash?

Switch from your *jokes.py* program to the interactive shell and enter this print() statement:

```
>>> print('They flew away in a green\teal helicopter.')
They flew away in a green    eal helicopter.
```

This instruction didn't print a backslash because the t in teal was interpreted as an escape character since it came after a backslash. The \t simulates pressing TAB on your keyboard.

This line will give you the correct output:

```
>>> print('They flew away in a green\\teal helicopter.')
They flew away in a green\teal helicopter.
```

This way the \\ is a backslash character, and there is no \t to interpret as TAB.

Table 4-1 is a list of some escape characters in Python, including \n, which is the newline escape character that you have used before.

Table 4-1: Escape Characters

Escape character	What is actually printed
\\	Backslash (\)
\'	Single quote (')
\"	Double quote (")
\n	Newline
\t	Tab

There are a few more escape characters in Python, but these are the characters you will most likely need for creating games.

Single and Double Quotes

While we're still in the interactive shell, let's take a closer look at quotes. Strings don't always have to be between single quotes in Python. You can also put them between double quotes. These two lines print the same thing:

```
>>> print('Hello world')
Hello world
>>> print("Hello world")
Hello world
```

But you cannot mix quotes. This line will give you an error because it uses both quote types at once:

```
>>> print('Hello world")
SyntaxError: EOL while scanning single-quoted string
```

I like to use single quotes so I don't have to hold down SHIFT to type them. They're easier to type, and Python doesn't care either way.

Also, note that just as you need the `\'` to have a single quote in a string surrounded by single quotes, you need the `\"` to have a double quote in a string surrounded by double quotes. Look at this example:

```
>>> print('I asked to borrow Abe\'s car for a week. He said, "Sure."')
I asked to borrow Abe's car for a week. He said, "Sure."
```

You use single quotes to surround the string, so you need to add a backslash before the single quote in `Abe\'s`. But the double quotes in `"Sure."` don't need backslashes. The Python interpreter is smart enough to know that if a string starts with one type of quote, the other type of quote doesn't mean the string is ending.

Now check out another example:

```
>>> print("She said, \"I can't believe you let them borrow your car.\"")
She said, "I can't believe you let them borrow your car."
```

The string is surrounded in double quotes, so you need to add backslashes for all of the double quotes within the string. You don't need to escape the single quote in `can't`.

To summarize, in the single-quote strings, you don't need to escape double quotes but do need to escape single quotes, and in the double-quote strings, you don't need to escape single quotes but do need to escape double quotes.

The print() Function's end Keyword Parameter

Now let's go back to *jokes.py* and take a look at lines 9 to 16:

```
 9. print('Knock knock.')
10. input()
11. print("Who's there?")
12. input()
13. print('Interrupting cow.')
14. input()
15. print('Interrupting cow wh', end='')
16. print('-MOO!')
```

Did you notice the second argument in line 15's `print()` function? Normally, `print()` adds a newline character to the end of the string it prints. This is why a blank `print()` function will just print a newline. But `print()` can optionally have a second parameter: `end`.

Remember that an argument is the value passed in a function call. The blank string passed to `print()` is called a *keyword argument*. The `end` in `end=''` is called a *keyword parameter*. To pass a keyword argument to this keyword parameter, you must type `end=` before it.

When we run this section of code, the output is

```
Knock knock.
Who's there?
Interrupting cow.
Interrupting cow wh-MOO!
```

Because we passed a blank string to the `end` parameter, the `print()` function will add a blank string instead of adding a newline. This is why `'-MOO!'` appears next to the previous line, instead of on its own line. There was no newline after the `'Interrupting cow wh'` string was printed.

Summary

This chapter explores the different ways you can use the `print()` function. Escape characters are used for characters that are difficult to type into the code with the keyboard. If you want to use special characters in a string, you must use a backslash escape character, `\`, followed by another letter for the special character. For example, `\n` would be a newline. If your special character is a backslash itself, you use `\\`.

The `print()` function automatically appends a newline character to the end of a string. Most of the time, this is a helpful shortcut. But sometimes you don't want a newline character. To change this, you can pass a blank string as the keyword argument for `print()`'s `end` keyword parameter. For example, to print `spam` to the screen without a newline character, you would call `print('spam', end='')`.

5

DRAGON REALM

The game you will create in this chapter is called Dragon Realm. The player decides between two caves, which hold either treasure or certain doom.

How to Play Dragon Realm

In this game, the player is in a land full of dragons. The dragons all live in caves with their large piles of collected treasure. Some dragons are friendly and share their treasure. Other dragons are hungry and eat anyone who enters their cave. The player approaches two caves, one with a friendly dragon and the other with a hungry dragon, but doesn't know which dragon is in which cave. The player must choose between the two.

TOPICS COVERED IN THIS CHAPTER

- Flowcharts
- Creating your own functions with the def keyword
- Multiline strings
- while statements
- The and, or, and not Boolean operators
- Truth tables
- The return keyword
- Global and local variable scope
- Parameters and arguments
- The sleep() function

Sample Run of Dragon Realm

Here's what the Dragon Realm game looks like when it's run. The player's input is in bold.

```
You are in a land full of dragons. In front of you,
you see two caves. In one cave, the dragon is friendly
and will share his treasure with you. The other dragon
is greedy and hungry, and will eat you on sight.
Which cave will you go into? (1 or 2)
1
You approach the cave...
It is dark and spooky...
A large dragon jumps out in front of you! He opens his jaws and...
Gobbles you down in one bite!
Do you want to play again? (yes or no)
no
```

Flowchart for Dragon Realm

It often helps to write down everything you want your game or program to do before you start writing code. When you do this, you are *designing the program.*

For example, it may help to draw a flowchart. A *flowchart* is a diagram that shows every possible action that can happen in the game and which actions are connected. Figure 5-1 is a flowchart for Dragon Realm.

To see what happens in the game, put your finger on the START box. Then follow one arrow from that box to another box. Your finger is like the program execution. The program terminates when your finger lands on the END box.

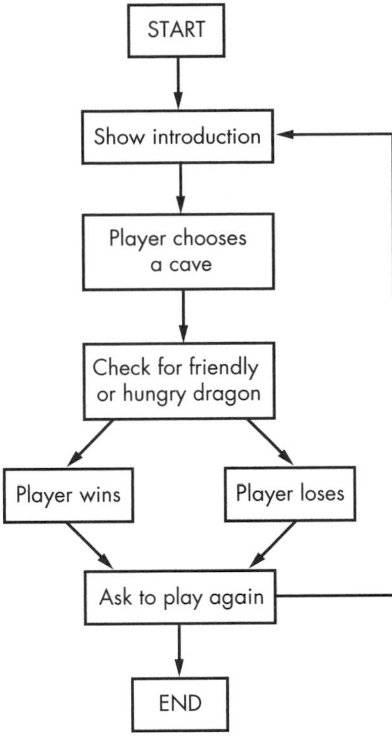

Figure 5-1: Flowchart for the Dragon Realm game

When you get to the "Check for friendly or hungry dragon" box, you can go to the "Player wins" box or the "Player loses" box. At this branching point, the program can go in different directions. Either way, both paths will eventually end up at the "Ask to play again" box.

Source Code for Dragon Realm

Open a new file editor window by clicking **File ▸ New Window**. Enter the source code and save it as *dragon.py*. Then run the program by pressing F5. If you get errors, compare the code you typed to the book's code with the online diff tool at *https://www.nostarch.com/inventwithpython#diff*.

dragon.py

```
import random
import time

def displayIntro():
    print('''You are in a land full of dragons. In front of you,
you see two caves. In one cave, the dragon is friendly
and will share his treasure with you. The other dragon
is greedy and hungry, and will eat you on sight.''')
```

```
 9.     print()
10.
11. def chooseCave():
12.     cave = ''
13.     while cave != '1' and cave != '2':
14.         print('Which cave will you go into? (1 or 2)')
15.         cave = input()
16.
17.     return cave
18.
19. def checkCave(chosenCave):
20.     print('You approach the cave...')
21.     time.sleep(2)
22.     print('It is dark and spooky...')
23.     time.sleep(2)
24.     print('A large dragon jumps out in front of you! He opens his jaws
          and...')
25.     print()
26.     time.sleep(2)
27.
28.     friendlyCave = random.randint(1, 2)
29.
30.     if chosenCave == str(friendlyCave):
31.         print('Gives you his treasure!')
32.     else:
33.         print('Gobbles you down in one bite!')
34.
35. playAgain = 'yes'
36. while playAgain == 'yes' or playAgain == 'y':
37.     displayIntro()
38.     caveNumber = chooseCave()
39.     checkCave(caveNumber)
40.
41.     print('Do you want to play again? (yes or no)')
42.     playAgain = input()
```

Let's look at the source code in more detail.

Importing the random and time Modules

This program imports two modules:

```
1. import random
2. import time
```

The `random` module provides the `randint()` function, which we used in the Guess the Number game from Chapter 3. Line 2 imports the `time` module, which contains time-related functions.

Functions in Dragon Realm

Functions let you run the same code multiple times without having to copy and paste that code over and over again. Instead, you put that code inside a function and call the function whenever you need to. Because you write the code only once in the function, if the function's code has a mistake, you only have to change it in one place in the program.

You've already used a few functions, like `print()`, `input()`, `randint()`, `str()`, and `int()`. Your programs have called these functions to execute the code inside them. In the Dragon Realm game, you'll write your own functions using `def` statements.

def Statements

Line 4 is a `def` statement:

```
4. def displayIntro():
5.     print('''You are in a land full of dragons. In front of you,
6. you see two caves. In one cave, the dragon is friendly
7. and will share his treasure with you. The other dragon
8. is greedy and hungry, and will eat you on sight.''')
9.     print()
```

The `def` statement defines a new function (in this case, the `displayIntro()` function), which you can call later in the program.

Figure 5-2 shows the parts of a `def` statement. It has the `def` keyword followed by a function name with parentheses, and then a colon (:). The block after the `def` statement is called the `def` block.

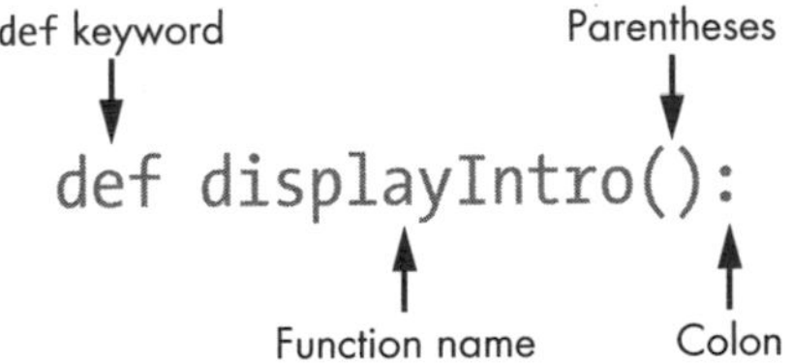

Figure 5-2: Parts of a `def` *statement*

Calling a Function

When you *define* a function, you specify the instructions for it to run in the following block. When you *call* a function, the code inside the `def` block executes. Unless you call the function, the instructions in the `def` block will not execute.

In other words, when the execution reaches a `def` statement, it skips down to the first line after the `def` block. But when a function is called, the execution moves inside of the function to the first line of the `def` block.

For example, look at the call to the displayIntro() function on line 37:

```
37.     displayIntro()
```

Calling this function runs the print() call, which displays the "You are in a land full of dragons . . ." introduction.

Where to Put Function Definitions

A function's def statement and def block must come *before* you call the function, just as you must assign a value to a variable before you use that variable. If you put the function call before the function definition, you'll get an error. Let's look at a short program as an example. Open a new file editor window, enter this code, save it as *example.py*, and run it:

```
sayGoodbye()

def sayGoodbye():
    print('Goodbye!')
```

If you try to run this program, Python will give you an error message that looks like this:

```
Traceback (most recent call last):
  File "C:/Users/Al/AppData/Local/Programs/Python/Python36/example.py",
    line 1, in <module>
    sayGoodbye()
NameError: name 'sayGoodbye' is not defined
```

To fix this error, move the function definition before the function call:

```
def sayGoodbye():
    print('Goodbye!')

sayGoodbye()
```

Now, the function is defined before it is called, so Python will know what sayGoodbye() should do. Otherwise, Python won't have the instructions for sayGoodbye() when it is called and so won't be able to run it.

Multiline Strings

So far, all of the strings in our print() function calls have been on one line and have had one quote character at the start and end. However, if you use three quotes at the start and end of a string, then it can go across several lines. These are *multiline strings*.

Enter the following into the interactive shell to see how multiline strings work:

```
>>> fizz = '''Dear Alice,
I will return to Carol's house at the end of the month.
Your friend,
Bob'''
>>> print(fizz)
Dear Alice,
I will return to Carol's house at the end of the month.
Your friend,
Bob
```

Note the line breaks in the printed string. In a multiline string, the newline characters are included as part of the string. You don't have to use the `\n` escape character or escape quotes as long as you don't use three quotes together. These line breaks make the code easier to read when large amounts of text are involved.

How to Loop with while Statements

Line 11 defines another function called `chooseCave()`:

```
11. def chooseCave():
```

This function's code asks the player which cave they want to go in, either `1` or `2`. We'll need to use a `while` statement to ask the player to choose a cave, which marks the start of a new kind of loop: a `while` loop.

Unlike a `for` loop, which loops a specific number of times, a `while` loop repeats as long as a certain condition is `True`. When the execution reaches a `while` statement, it evaluates the condition next to the `while` keyword. If the condition evaluates to `True`, the execution moves inside the following block, called the `while` block. If the condition evaluates to `False`, the execution moves past the `while` block.

You can think of a `while` statement as being almost the same as an `if` statement. The program execution enters the blocks of both statements if their condition is `True`. But when the condition reaches the end of the block in a `while` loop, it moves back to the `while` statement to recheck the condition.

Look at the `def` block for `chooseCave()` to see a `while` loop in action:

```
12.     cave = ''
13.     while cave != '1' and cave != '2':
```

Line 12 creates a new variable called `cave` and stores a blank string in it. Then a `while` loop begins on line 13. The `chooseCave()` function needs to make sure the player entered 1 or 2 and not something else. A loop here keeps asking the player which cave they choose until they enter one of these two valid responses. This is called *input validation*.

The condition also contains a new operator you haven't seen before: and. Just as - and * are mathematical operators, and == and != are comparison operators, the and operator is a Boolean operator. Let's take a closer look at Boolean operators.

Boolean Operators

Boolean logic deals with things that are either true or false. Boolean operators compare values and evaluate to a single Boolean value.

Think of the sentence "Cats have whiskers and dogs have tails." "Cats have whiskers" is true, and "dogs have tails" is also true, so the entire sentence "Cats have whiskers *and* dogs have tails" is true.

But the sentence "Cats have whiskers and dogs have wings" would be false. Even though "cats have whiskers" is true, dogs don't have wings, so "dogs have wings" is false. In Boolean logic, things can only be entirely true or entirely false. Because of the word *and*, the entire sentence is true only if *both* parts are true. If one or both parts are false, then the entire sentence is false.

The and Operator

The and operator in Python also requires the whole Boolean expression to be True or False. If the Boolean values on both sides of the and keyword are True, then the expression evaluates to True. If either or both of the Boolean values are False, then the expression evaluates to False.

Enter the following expressions with the and operator into the interactive shell:

```
>>> True and True
True
>>> True and False
False
>>> False and True
False
>>> False and False
False
>>> spam = 'Hello'
>>> 10 < 20 and spam == 'Hello'
True
```

The and operator can be used to evaluate any two Boolean expressions. In the last example, 10 < 20 evaluates to True and spam == 'Hello' also evaluates to True, so the two Boolean expressions joined by the and operator evaluate as True.

If you ever forget how a Boolean operator works, you can look at its *truth table*, which shows how every combination of Boolean values evaluates. Table 5-1 shows every combination for the and operator.

Table 5-1: The and Operator's Truth Table

A and B	Evaluates to
`True and True`	`True`
`True and False`	`False`
`False and True`	`False`
`False and False`	`False`

The or Operator

The `or` operator is similar to the `and` operator, except it evaluates to `True` if *either* of the two Boolean values is `True`. The only time the `or` operator evaluates to `False` is if *both* of the Boolean values are `False`.

Now enter the following into the interactive shell:

```
>>> True or True
True
>>> True or False
True
>>> False or True
True
>>> False or False
False
>>> 10 > 20 or 20 > 10
True
```

In the last example, `10` is not greater than `20` but `20` is greater than `10`, so the first expression evaluates to `False` and the second expression evaluates to `True`. Because the second expression is `True`, this whole expression evaluates as `True`.

The `or` operator's truth table is shown in Table 5-2.

Table 5-2: The `or` Operator's Truth Table

A or B	Evaluates to
`True or True`	`True`
`True or False`	`True`
`False or True`	`True`
`False or False`	`False`

The not Operator

Instead of combining two values, the `not` operator works on only one value. The `not` operator evaluates to the opposite Boolean value: `True` expressions evaluate to `False`, and `False` expressions evaluate to `True`.

Enter the following into the interactive shell:

```
>>> not True
False
>>> not False
True
>>> not ('black' == 'white')
True
```

The `not` operator can also be used on any Boolean expression. In the last example, the expression `'black' == 'white'` evaluates to `False`. This is why `not ('black' == 'white')` is `True`.

The `not` operator's truth table is shown in Table 5-3.

Table 5-3: The not Operator's Truth Table

not A	Evaluates to
`not True`	`False`
`not False`	`True`

Evaluating Boolean Operators

Look at line 13 of the Dragon Realm game again:

```
13.     while cave != '1' and cave != '2':
```

The condition has two parts connected by the `and` Boolean operator. The condition is `True` only if both parts are `True`.

The first time the `while` statement's condition is checked, `cave` is set to the blank string, `''`. The blank string is not equal to the string `'1'`, so the left side evaluates to `True`. The blank string is also not equal to the string `'2'`, so the right side evaluates to `True`.

So the condition then turns into `True and True`. Because both values are `True`, the whole condition evaluates to `True`, so the program execution enters the `while` block, where the program will attempt to assign a nonblank value for `cave`.

Line 14 asks the player to choose a cave:

```
13.     while cave != '1' and cave != '2':
14.         print('Which cave will you go into? (1 or 2)')
15.         cave = input()
```

Line 15 lets the player type their response and press ENTER. This response is stored in `cave`. After this code is executed, the execution loops back to the top of the `while` statement and rechecks the condition at line 13.

If the player entered 1 or 2, then cave will be either '1' or '2' (since input() always returns strings). This makes the condition False, and the program execution will continue past the while loop. For example, if the user entered '1', then the evaluation would look like this:

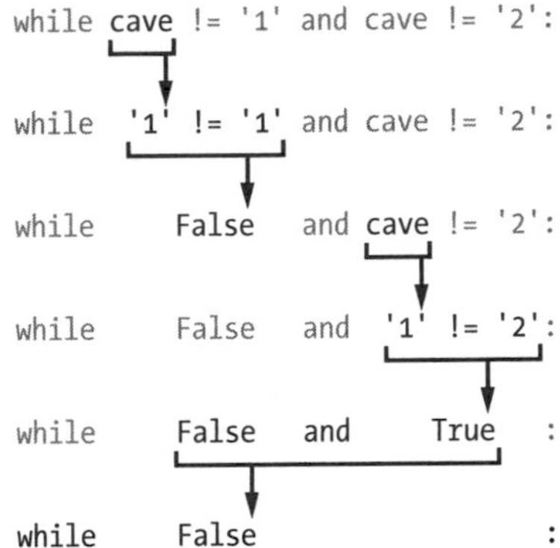

But if the player entered 3 or 4 or HELLO, that response would be invalid. The condition would then be True and would enter the while block to ask the player again. The program keeps asking the player which cave they choose until they enter 1 or 2. This guarantees that once the execution moves on, the cave variable contains a valid response.

Return Values

Line 17 has something new called a return statement:

```
17.     return cave
```

A return statement appears only inside def blocks where a function—in this case, chooseCave()—is defined. Remember how the input() function returns a string value that the player entered? The chooseCave() function will also return a value. Line 17 returns the string that is stored in cave, either '1' or '2'.

Once the return statement executes, the program execution jumps immediately out of the def block (just as the break statement makes the execution jump out of a while block). The program execution moves back to the line with the function call. The function call itself will evaluate to the function's return value.

Skip down to line 38 for a moment where the chooseCave() function is called:

```
38.     caveNumber = chooseCave()
```

On line 38, when the program calls the function chooseCave(), which was defined on line 11, the function call evaluates to the string inside of cave, which is then stored in caveNumber. The while loop inside chooseCave() guarantees that chooseCave() will return only either '1' or '2' as its return value. So caveNumber can have only one of these two values.

Global Scope and Local Scope

There is something special about variables that are created inside functions, like the cave variable in the chooseCave() function on line 12:

```
12.     cave = ''
```

A *local scope* is created whenever a function is called. Any variables assigned in this function exist within the local scope. Think of a *scope* as a container for variables. What makes variables in local scopes special is that they are forgotten when the function returns and they will be re-created if the function is called again. The value of a local variable isn't remembered between function calls.

Variables that are assigned outside of functions exist in the *global scope*. There is only one global scope, and it is created when your program begins. When your program terminates, the global scope is destroyed, and all its variables are forgotten. Otherwise, the next time you ran your program, the variables would remember their values from the last time you ran it.

A variable that exists in a local scope is called a *local variable*, while a variable that exists in the global scope is called a *global variable*. A variable must be one or the other; it cannot be both local and global.

The variable cave is created inside the chooseCave() function. This means it is created in the chooseCave() function's local scope. It will be forgotten when chooseCave() returns and will be re-created if chooseCave() is called a second time.

Local and global variables can have the same name, but they are different variables because they are in different scopes. Let's write a new program to illustrate these concepts:

```
  def bacon():
❶     spam = 99        # Creates a local variable named spam
❷     print(spam)      # Prints 99

❸ spam = 42          # Creates a global variable named spam
❹ print(spam)        # Prints 42
❺ bacon()            # Calls the bacon() function and prints 99
❻ print(spam)        # Prints 42
```

We first make a function called bacon(). In bacon(), we create a variable called spam and assign it 99 ❶. At ❷, we call print() to print this local spam variable, which is 99. At ❸, a global variable called spam is also declared and set to 42. This variable is global because it is outside of all functions.

When the global spam variable is passed to print() at ❹, it prints 42. When the bacon() function is called at ❺, ❶ and ❷ are executed, and the local spam variable is created, set, and then printed. So calling bacon() prints the value 99. After the bacon() function call returns, the local spam variable is forgotten. If we print spam at ❻, we are printing the global variable, so the output there is 42.

When run, this code will output the following:

```
42
99
42
```

Where a variable is created determines what scope it is in. Keep this in mind when writing your programs.

Function Parameters

The next function defined in the Dragon Realm program is named checkCave().

```
def checkCave(chosenCave):
```

Notice the text chosenCave between the parentheses. This is a *parameter*: a local variable that is used by the function's code. When the function is called, the call's arguments are the values assigned to the parameters.

Let's go back to the interactive shell for a moment. Remember that for some function calls, like str() or randint(), you would pass one or more arguments between the parentheses:

```
>>> str(5)
'5'
>>> random.randint(1, 20)
14
>>> len('Hello')
5
```

This example includes a Python function you haven't seen yet: len(). The len() function returns an integer indicating how many characters are in the string passed to it. In this case, it tells us that the string 'Hello' has 5 characters.

You will also pass an argument when you call checkCave(). This argument is stored in a new variable named chosenCave, which is checkCave()'s parameter.

Here is a short program that demonstrates defining a function (sayHello) with a parameter (name):

```
def sayHello(name):
    print('Hello, ' + name + '. Your name has ' + str(len(name)) +
      ' letters.')
```

```
sayHello('Alice')
sayHello('Bob')
spam = 'Carol'
sayHello(spam)
```

When you call `sayHello()` with an argument in the parentheses, the argument is assigned to the `name` parameter, and the code in the function is executed. There's just one line of code in the `sayHello()` function, which is a `print()` function call. Inside the `print()` function call are some strings and the `name` variable, along with a call to the `len()` function. Here, `len()` is used to count the number of characters in `name`. If you run the program, the output looks like this:

```
Hello, Alice. Your name has 5 letters.
Hello, Bob. Your name has 3 letters.
Hello, Carol. Your name has 5 letters.
```

For each call to `sayHello()`, a greeting and the length of the `name` argument are printed. Notice that because the string `'Carol'` is assigned to the `spam` variable, `sayHello(spam)` is equivalent to `sayHello('Carol')`.

Displaying the Game Results

Let's go back to the Dragon Realm game's source code:

```
20.     print('You approach the cave...')
21.     time.sleep(2)
```

The `time` module has a function called `sleep()` that pauses the program. Line 21 passes the integer value `2` so that `time.sleep()` will pause the program for 2 seconds.

```
22.     print('It is dark and spooky...')
23.     time.sleep(2)
```

Here the code prints some more text and waits for another 2 seconds. These short pauses add suspense to the game instead of displaying the text all at once. In Chapter 4's Jokes program, you called the `input()` function to pause until the player pressed ENTER. Here, the player doesn't have to do anything except wait a couple of seconds.

```
24.     print('A large dragon jumps out in front of you! He opens his jaws
          and...')
25.     print()
26.     time.sleep(2)
```

With the suspense building, our program will next determine which cave has the friendly dragon.

Deciding Which Cave Has the Friendly Dragon

Line 28 calls the randint() function, which will randomly return either 1 or 2.

```
28.     friendlyCave = random.randint(1, 2)
```

This integer value is stored in friendlyCave and indicates the cave with the friendly dragon.

```
30.     if chosenCave == str(friendlyCave):
31.         print('Gives you his treasure!')
```

Line 30 checks whether the player's chosen cave in the chosenCave variable ('1' or '2') is equal to the friendly dragon cave.

But the value in friendlyCave is an integer because randint() returns integers. You can't compare strings and integers with the == sign, because they will *never* be equal to each other: '1' is not equal to 1, and '2' is not equal to 2.

So friendlyCave is passed to the str() function, which returns the string value of friendlyCave. Now the values will have the same data type and can be meaningfully compared to each other. We could have also converted chosenCave to an integer value instead. Then line 30 would have looked like this:

```
if int(chosenCave) == friendlyCave:
```

If chosenCave is equal to friendlyCave, the condition evaluates to True, and line 31 tells the player they have won the treasure.

Now we have to add some code to run if the condition is false. Line 32 is an else statement:

```
32.     else:
33.         print('Gobbles you down in one bite!')
```

An else statement can come only after an if block. The else block executes if the if statement's condition is False. Think of this as the program's way of saying, "If this condition is true, then execute the if block or else execute the else block."

In this case, the else statement runs when chosenCave is not equal to friendlyCave. Then, the print() function call on line 33 is run, telling the player that they've been eaten by the dragon.

The Game Loop

The first part of the program defines several functions but doesn't run the code inside of them. Line 35 is where the main part of the program begins because it is the first line that runs:

```
35. playAgain = 'yes'
36. while playAgain == 'yes' or playAgain == 'y':
```

This line is where the main part of the program begins. The previous `def` statements merely defined the functions. They didn't run the code inside of those functions.

Lines 35 and 36 are setting up a loop that contains the rest of the game code. At the end of the game, the player can tell the program whether they want to play again. If they do, the execution enters the `while` loop to run the entire game all over again. If they don't, the `while` statement's condition will be `False`, and the execution will move to the end of the program and terminate.

The first time the execution comes to this `while` statement, line 35 will have just assigned `'yes'` to the `playAgain` variable. That means the condition will be `True` at the start of the program. This guarantees that the execution enters the loop at least once.

Calling the Functions in the Program

Line 37 calls the `displayIntro()` function:

```
37.     displayIntro()
```

This isn't a Python function—it is the function that you defined earlier on line 4. When this function is called, the program execution jumps to the first line in the `displayIntro()` function on line 5. When all the lines in the function have been executed, the execution jumps back to line 37 and continues moving down.

Line 38 also calls a function that you defined:

```
38.     caveNumber = chooseCave()
```

Remember that the `chooseCave()` function lets the player choose the cave they want to enter. When line 17's `return cave` executes, the program execution jumps back to line 38. The `chooseCave()` call then evaluates to the return value, which will be an integer value representing the cave the player chose to enter. This return value is stored in a new variable named `caveNumber`.

Then the program execution moves on to line 39:

```
39.     checkCave(caveNumber)
```

Line 39 calls the `checkCave()` function, passing the value in `caveNumber` as an argument. Not only does the execution jump to line 20, but the value in `caveNumber` is copied to the parameter `chosenCave` inside the `checkCave()` function. This is the function that will display either `'Gives you his treasure!'` or `'Gobbles you down in one bite!'` depending on the cave the player chooses to enter.

Asking the Player to Play Again

Whether the player won or lost, they are asked if they want to play again.

```
41.     print('Do you want to play again? (yes or no)')
42.     playAgain = input()
```

The variable `playAgain` stores what the player types. Line 42 is the last line of the `while` block, so the program jumps back to line 36 to check the `while` loop's condition: `playAgain == 'yes' or playAgain == 'y'`.

If the player enters the string `'yes'` or `'y'`, then the execution enters the loop again at line 37.

If the player enters `'no'` or `'n'` or something silly like `'Abraham Lincoln'`, then the condition is `False`, and the program execution continues to the line after the `while` block. But since there aren't any lines after the `while` block, the program terminates.

One thing to note: the string `'YES'` is not equal to the string `'yes'` since the computer does not consider upper- and lowercase letters the same. If the player entered the string `'YES'`, then the `while` statement's condition would evaluate to `False` and the program would still terminate. Later, the Hangman program will show you how to avoid this problem. (See "The `lower()` and `upper()` String Methods" on page 101.)

You've just completed your second game! In Dragon Realm, you used a lot of what you learned in the Guess the Number game and picked up a few new tricks. If you didn't understand some of the concepts in this program, go over each line of the source code again and try changing the code to see how the program changes.

In Chapter 6, you won't create another game. Instead, you will learn how to use a feature of IDLE called the *debugger*.

Summary

In the Dragon Realm game, you created your own functions. A function is a mini-program within your program. The code inside the function runs when the function is called. By breaking up your code into functions, you can organize your code into shorter and easier-to-understand sections.

Arguments are values copied to the function's parameters when the function is called. The function call itself evaluates to the return value.

You also learned about variable scopes. Variables created inside of a function exist in the local scope, and variables created outside of all functions exist in the global scope. Code in the global scope cannot make use of local variables. If a local variable has the same name as a global variable, Python considers it a separate variable. Assigning new values to the local variable won't change the value in the global variable.

Variable scopes might seem complicated, but they are useful for organizing functions as separate pieces of code from the rest of the program. Because each function has its own local scope, you can be sure that the code in one function won't cause bugs in other functions.

Almost every program has functions because they are so useful. By understanding how functions work, you can save yourself a lot of typing and make bugs easier to fix.

6

USING THE DEBUGGER

If you enter the wrong code, the computer won't give you the right program. A computer program will always do what you tell it to, but what you tell it to do might not be what you actually *want* it to do. These errors are *bugs* in a computer program. Bugs happen when the programmer has not carefully thought about exactly what the program is doing.

TOPICS COVERED IN THIS CHAPTER

- Three types of errors
- IDLE's debugger
- The Go and Quit buttons
- Stepping into, over, and out
- Breakpoints

Types of Bugs

There are three types of bugs that can happen in your program:

Syntax errors This type of bug comes from typos. When the Python interpreter sees a syntax error, it's because your code isn't written in proper Python language. A Python program with even a single syntax error won't run.

Runtime errors These are bugs that happen while the program is running. The program will work up until it reaches the line of code with the error, and then the program will terminate with an error message (this is called *crashing*). The Python interpreter will display a *traceback*: an error message showing the line containing the problem.

Semantic errors These bugs—which are the trickiest to fix—don't crash the program, but they prevent the program from doing what the programmer intended it to do. For example, if the programmer wants the variable `total` to be the *sum* of the values in variables `a`, `b`, and `c` but writes `total = a * b * c`, then the value in `total` will be wrong. This could crash the program later on, but it won't be immediately obvious where the semantic bug happened.

Finding bugs in a program can be hard, if you even notice them at all! When running your program, you might discover that sometimes functions are not called when they are supposed to be, or maybe they are called too many times. You might code the condition for a `while` loop incorrectly, so that it loops the wrong number of times. You might write a loop that never exits, a semantic error known as an *infinite loop*. To stop a program stuck in an infinite loop, you can press CTRL-C in the interactive shell.

In fact, create an infinite loop by entering this code in the interactive shell (remember to press ENTER twice to let the interactive shell know you are done typing in the `while` block):

```
>>> while True:
        print('Press Ctrl-C to stop this infinite loop!!!')
```

Now press and hold down CTRL-C to stop the program. The interactive shell will look like this:

```
Press Ctrl-C to stop this infinite loop!!!
Press Ctrl-C to stop this infinite loop!!!
Press Ctrl-C to stop this infinite loop!!!
Press Ctrl-C to stop this infinite loop!!!
Press Ctrl-C to stop this infinite loop!!!
Traceback (most recent call last):
  File "<pyshell#1>", line 2, in <module>
    print('Press Ctrl-C to stop this infinite loop!!!')
  File "C:\Program Files\Python 3.5\lib\idlelib\PyShell.py", line 1347, in
write
    return self.shell.write(s, self.tags)
KeyboardInterrupt
```

The `while` loop is always `True`, so the program will continue printing the same line forever until it is stopped by the user. In this example, we pressed CTRL-C to stop the infinite loop after the `while` loop had executed five times.

The Debugger

It can be hard to figure out the source of a bug because the lines of code are executed quickly and the values in variables change so often. A *debugger* is a program that lets you step through your code one line at a time in the same order that Python executes each instruction. The debugger also shows you what values are stored in variables at each step.

Starting the Debugger

In IDLE, open the Dragon Realm game you made in Chapter 5. After opening the *dragon.py* file, click the interactive shell and then click **Debug ▸ Debugger** to display the Debug Control window (Figure 6-1).

When the debugger is run, the Debug Control window will look like Figure 6-2. Make sure to select the **Stack**, **Locals**, **Source**, and **Globals** checkboxes.

Now when you run the Dragon Realm game by pressing F5, IDLE's debugger will activate. This is called running a program *under a debugger*. When you run a Python program under the debugger, the program will stop before it executes the first instruction. If you click the file editor's title bar (and you've selected the **Source** checkbox in the Debug Control window), the first instruction is highlighted in gray. The Debug Control window shows the execution is on line 1, which is the `import random` line.

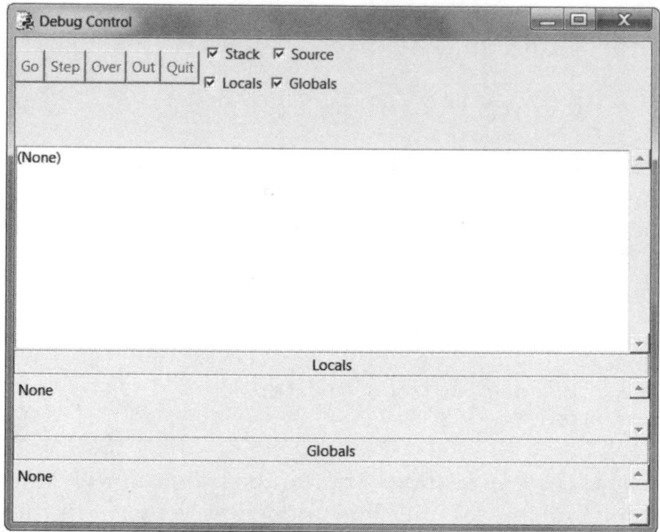

Figure 6-1: The Debug Control window

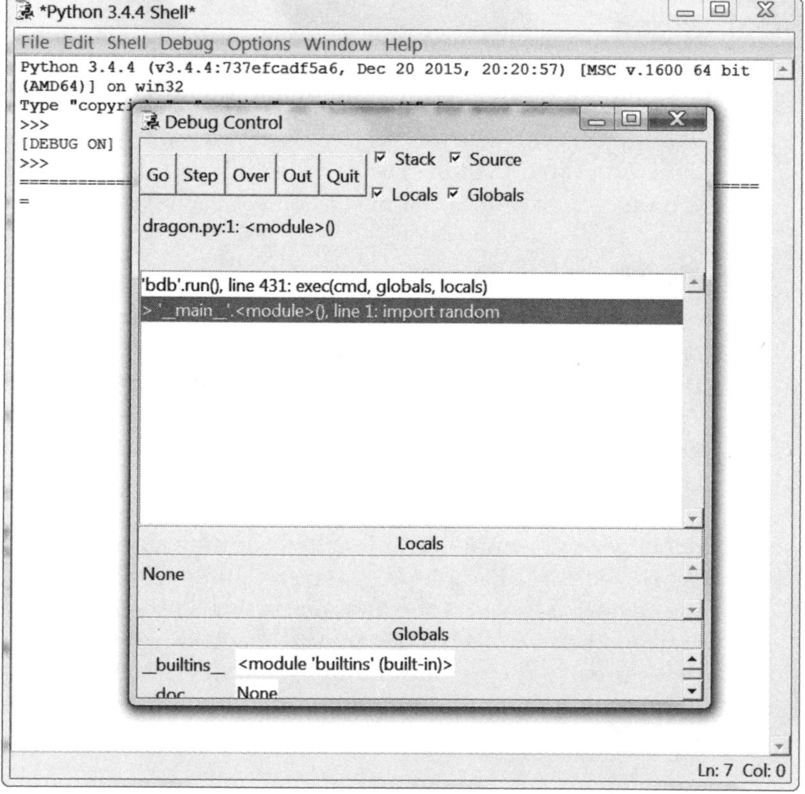

Figure 6-2: Running the Dragon Realm game under the debugger

Stepping Through the Program with the Debugger

The debugger lets you execute one instruction at a time; this process is called *stepping*. Execute a single instruction now by clicking the **Step** button in the Debug Control window. Python will execute the `import random` instruction, and then stop before it executes the next instruction. The Debug Control window shows you what line is *about* to be executed when you click the Step button, so the execution should now be on line 2, the `import time` line. Click the **Quit** button to terminate the program for now.

Here's a summary of what happens when you click the Step button as you run Dragon Realm under a debugger. Press F5 to start running Dragon Realm again and then follow these instructions:

1. Click the **Step** button twice to run the two `import` lines.
2. Click the **Step** button three more times to execute the three `def` statements.
3. Click the **Step** button again to define the `playAgain` variable.
4. Click **Go** to run the rest of the program or click **Quit** to terminate the program.

The debugger skipped line 3 because it's a blank line. Notice you can only step forward with the debugger; you can't go backward.

Globals Area

The *Globals area* in the Debug Control window is where all the global variables are displayed. Remember, global variables are variables created outside of any functions (that is, in the global scope).

The text next to the function names in the Globals area looks like `"<function checkCave at 0x012859B0>"`. The module names also have confusing-looking text next to them, like `"<module 'random' from 'C:\\Python31\\lib\\random.pyc'>"`. You don't need to know what this text means to debug your programs. Just seeing whether the functions and modules are in the Globals area will tell you whether a function has been defined or a module has been imported.

You can also ignore the `__builtins__`, `__doc__`, `__name__`, and other similar lines in the Globals area. (Those are variables that appear in every Python program.)

In the Dragon Realm program, the three `def` statements, which execute and define functions, will appear in the Globals area of the Debug Control window. When the `playAgain` variable is created, it will also show up in the Globals area. Next to the variable name will be the string `'yes'`. The debugger lets you see the values of all the variables in the program as the program runs. This is useful for fixing bugs.

Locals Area

In addition to the Globals area, there is a *Locals area*, which shows you the local scope variables and their values. The Locals area will contain variables only when the program execution is inside of a function. When the execution is in the global scope, this area is blank.

The Go and Quit Buttons

If you get tired of clicking the Step button repeatedly and just want the program to run normally, click the Go button at the top of the Debug Control window. This will tell the program to run normally instead of stepping.

To terminate the program entirely, click the Quit button at the top of the Debug Control window. The program will exit immediately. This is helpful if you must start debugging again from the beginning of the program.

Stepping Into, Over, and Out

Start the Dragon Realm program with the debugger. Keep stepping until the debugger is at line 37. As shown in Figure 6-3, this is the line with `displayIntro()`. When you click Step again, the debugger will jump into this function call and appear on line 5, the first line in the `displayIntro()` function. This kind of stepping, which is what you've been doing so far, is called *stepping into*.

When the execution is paused at line 5, you'll want to stop stepping. If you clicked Step once more, the debugger would step into the `print()` function. The `print()` function is one of Python's built-in functions, so it isn't useful to step through with the debugger. Python's own functions—such as `print()`, `input()`, `str()`, and `randint()`—have been carefully checked for errors. You can assume they're not the parts causing bugs in your program.

You don't want to waste time stepping through the internals of the `print()` function. So, instead of clicking Step to step into the `print()` function's code, click **Over**. This will *step over* the code inside the `print()` function. The code inside `print()` will be executed at normal speed, and then the debugger will pause once the execution returns from `print()`.

Stepping over is a convenient way to skip stepping through code inside a function. The debugger will now be paused at line 38, `caveNumber = chooseCave()`.

Click **Step** again to step into the `chooseCave()` function. Keep stepping through the code until line 15, the `input()` call. The program will wait until you type a response into the interactive shell, just like when you run the program normally. If you try clicking the Step button now, nothing will happen because the program is waiting for a keyboard response.

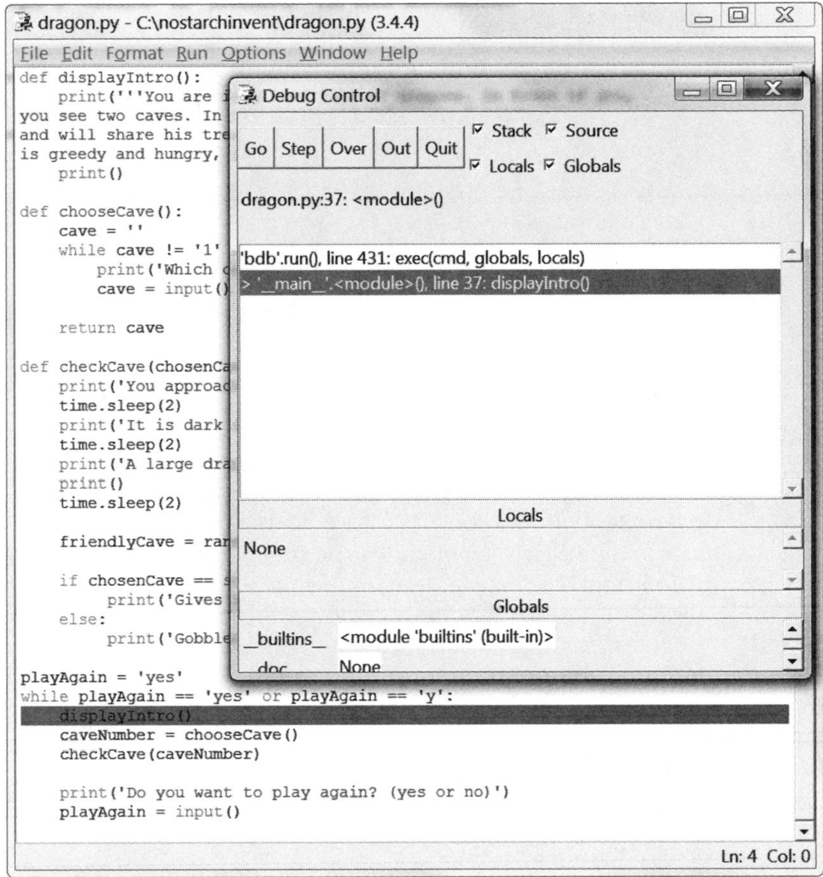

Figure 6-3: Keep stepping until you reach line 37.

Click back to the interactive shell and type which cave you want to enter. The blinking cursor must be on the bottom line in the interactive shell before you can type. Otherwise, the text you type will not appear.

Once you press ENTER, the debugger will continue to step through lines of code again.

Next, click the **Out** button on the Debug Control window. This is called *stepping out* because it will cause the debugger to step over as many lines as it needs to until the execution has returned from the function it is in. After it jumps out, the execution will be on the line after the one that called the function.

If you are not inside a function, clicking Out will cause the debugger to execute all the remaining lines in the program. This is the same behavior that happens when you click the Go button.

Here's a recap of what each button does:

Go Executes the rest of the code as normal, or until it reaches a breakpoint (see "Setting Breakpoints" on page 73).

Step Executes one instruction or one step. If the line is a function call, the debugger will step into the function.

Over Executes one instruction or one step. If the line is a function call, the debugger won't *step into* the function but instead will *step over* the call.

Out Keeps stepping over lines of code until the debugger leaves the function it was in when Out was clicked. This *steps out* of the function.

Quit Immediately terminates the program.

Now that we know how to use the debugger, let's try finding bugs in some programs.

Finding the Bug

The debugger can help you find the cause of bugs in your program. As an example, here is a small program with a bug. The program comes up with a random addition problem for the user to solve. In the interactive shell, click **File ▸ New Window** to open a new file editor window. Enter this program into that window and save it as *buggy.py*.

buggy.py

```
import random
number1 = random.randint(1, 10)
number2 = random.randint(1, 10)
print('What is ' + str(number1) + ' + ' + str(number2) + '?')
answer = input()
if answer == number1 + number2:
    print('Correct!')
else:
    print('Nope! The answer is ' + str(number1 + number2))
```

Type the program exactly as it is shown, even if you can already tell what the bug is. Then run the program by pressing F5. Here's what it might look like when you run the program:

```
What is 5 + 1?
6
Nope! The answer is 6
```

That's a bug! The program doesn't crash, but it's not working correctly. The program says the user is wrong even if they enter the correct answer.

Running the program under a debugger will help find the bug's cause. At the top of the interactive shell, click **Debug ▸ Debugger** to display the Debug Control window. (Make sure you've checked the **Stack**, **Source**, **Locals**, and **Globals** checkboxes.) Then press F5 in the file editor to run the program. This time it will run under the debugger.

The debugger starts at the `import random` line:

```
import random
```

Nothing special happens here, so just click **Step** to execute it. You will see the random module added to the Globals area.

Click **Step** again to run line 2:

```
2. number1 = random.randint(1, 10)
```

A new file editor window will appear with the *random.py* file. You have stepped inside the randint() function inside the random module. You know Python's built-in functions won't be the source of your bugs, so click **Out** to step out of the randint() function and back to your program. Then close the *random.py* file's window. Next time, you can click Over to step over the randint() function instead of stepping into it.

Line 3 is also a randint() function call:

```
3. number2 = random.randint(1, 10)
```

Skip stepping into this code by clicking **Over**.

Line 4 is a print() call to show the player the random numbers:

```
4. print('What is ' + str(number1) + ' + ' + str(number2) + '?')
```

You know what numbers the program will print even before it prints them! Just look at the Globals area of the Debug Control window. You can see the number1 and number2 variables, and next to them are the integer values stored in those variables.

The number1 variable has the value 4 and the number2 variable has the value 8. (Your random numbers will probably be different.) When you click Step, the str() function will concatenate the string version of these integers, and the program will display the string in the print() call with these values. When I ran the debugger, it looked like Figure 6-4.

Click **Step** from line 5 to execute input().

```
5. answer = input()
```

The debugger waits until the player enters a response into the program. Enter the correct answer (in my case, 12) in the interactive shell. The debugger will resume and move down to line 6:

```
6. if answer == number1 + number2:
7.     print('Correct!')
```

Line 6 is an if statement. The condition is that the value in answer must match the sum of number1 and number2. If the condition is True, the debugger will move to line 7. If the condition is False, the debugger will move to line 9. Click **Step** one more time to find out where it goes.

```
8. else:
9.     print('Nope! The answer is ' + str(number1 + number2))
```

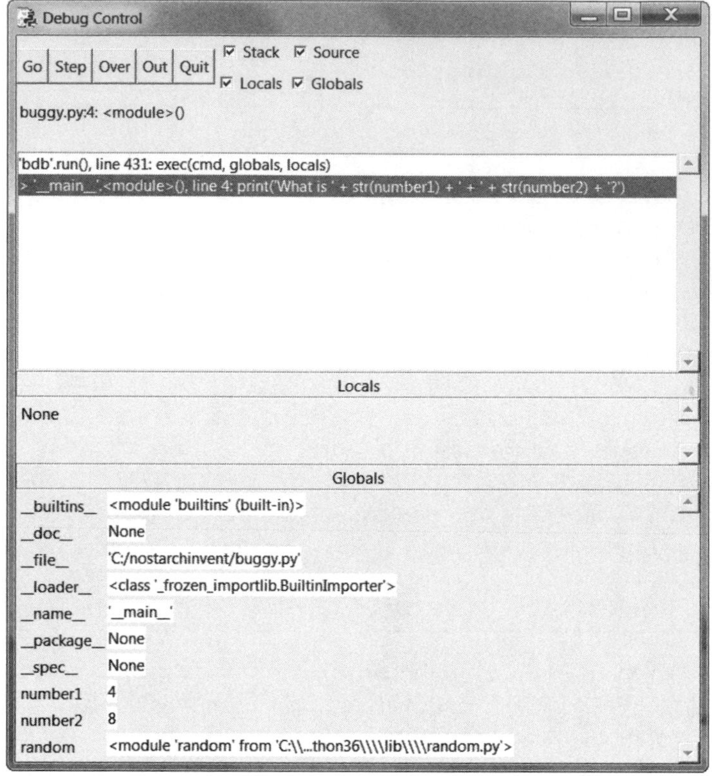

Figure 6-4: `number1` *is set to* `4`*, and* `number2` *is set to* `8`*.*

The debugger is now on line 9! What happened? The condition in the `if` statement must have been `False`. Look at the values for `number1`, `number2`, and `answer`. Notice that `number1` and `number2` are integers, so their sum would have also been an integer. But `answer` is a string.

That means that `answer == number1 + number2` would have evaluated to `'12' == 12`. A string value and an integer value will never be equal to each other, so the condition evaluated to `False`.

That is the bug in the program: the code uses `answer` when it should have used `int(answer)`. Change line 6 to `int(answer) == number1 + number2` and run the program again.

```
What is 2 + 3?
5
Correct!
```

Now the program works correctly. Run it one more time and enter a wrong answer on purpose. You've now debugged this program! Remember, the computer will run your programs exactly as you type them, even if what you type isn't what you intend.

Setting Breakpoints

Stepping through the code one line at a time might still be too slow. Often you'll want the program to run at normal speed until it reaches a certain line. You can set a *breakpoint* on a line when you want the debugger to take control once the execution reaches that line. If you think there's a problem with your code on, say, line 17, just set a breakpoint on that line (or maybe a few lines before that).

When the execution reaches that line, the program will break into the debugger. Then you can step through lines to see what is happening. Clicking Go will execute the program normally until it reaches another breakpoint or the end of the program.

To set a breakpoint on Windows, right-click the line in the file editor and select **Set Breakpoint** from the menu that appears. On OS X, CTRL-click to get to a menu and select **Set Breakpoint**. You can set breakpoints on as many lines as you want. The file editor highlights each breakpoint line in yellow. Figure 6-5 shows an example of what a breakpoint looks like.

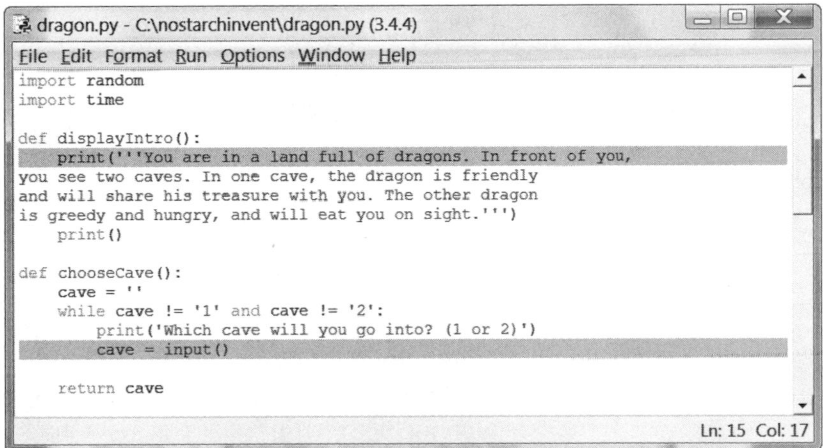

Figure 6-5: The file editor with two breakpoints set

To remove the breakpoint, click the line and select **Clear Breakpoint** from the menu that appears.

Using Breakpoints

Next we'll look at a program that calls `random.randint(0, 1)` to simulate coin flips. If the function returns the integer `1`, that will be heads, and if it returns the integer `0`, that will be tails. The `flips` variable will track how many coin flips have been done. The `heads` variable will track how many came up heads.

The program will do coin flips 1,000 times. This would take a person over an hour to do, but the computer can do it in one second! There's no bug in this program, but the debugger will let us look at the state of the program while it's running. Enter the following code into the file editor and save it as *coinFlips.py*. If you get errors after entering this code, compare the code you typed to the book's code with the online diff tool at *https://www.nostarch.com/inventwithpython#diff*.

coinFlips.py

```
 1. import random
 2. print('I will flip a coin 1000 times. Guess how many times it will come up
      heads. (Press enter to begin)')
 3. input()
 4. flips = 0
 5. heads = 0
 6. while flips < 1000:
 7.     if random.randint(0, 1) == 1:
 8.         heads = heads + 1
 9.     flips = flips + 1
10.
11.     if flips == 900:
12.         print('900 flips and there have been ' + str(heads) + ' heads.')
13.     if flips == 100:
14.         print('At 100 tosses, heads has come up ' + str(heads) + ' times
              so far.')
15.     if flips == 500:
16.         print('Halfway done, and heads has come up ' + str(heads) +
              ' times.')
17.
18. print()
19. print('Out of 1000 coin tosses, heads came up ' + str(heads) + ' times!')
20. print('Were you close?')
```

The program runs pretty fast. It spends more time waiting for the user to press ENTER than doing the coin flips. Let's say you wanted to see it do coin flips one by one. On the interactive shell's window, click **Debug ▸ Debugger** to bring up the Debug Control window. Then press F5 to run the program.

The program starts in the debugger on line 1. Press **Step** three times in the Debug Control window to execute the first three lines (that is, lines 1, 2, and 3). You'll notice the buttons become disabled because `input()` was called and the interactive shell is waiting for the user to type something. Click the interactive shell and press ENTER. (Be sure to click beneath the text in the interactive shell; otherwise, IDLE might not receive your keystrokes.)

You can click Step a few more times, but you'll find that it would take quite a while to get through the entire program. Instead, set a breakpoint on lines 12, 14, and 16 so that the debugger breaks in when `flips` is equal to `900`, `100`, and `500`, respectively. The file editor will highlight these lines as shown in Figure 6-6.

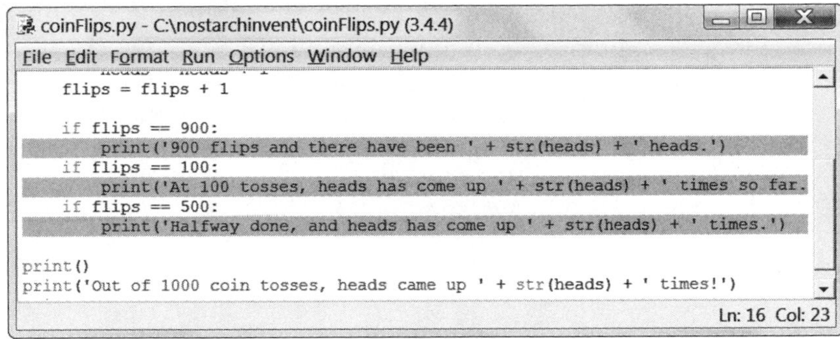

Figure 6-6: Three breakpoints set in coinflips.py

After setting the breakpoints, click **Go** in the Debug Control window. The program will run at normal speed until it reaches the next breakpoint. When `flip` is set to `100`, the condition for the `if` statement on line 13 is `True`. This causes line 14 (where there's a breakpoint set) to execute, which tells the debugger to stop the program and take over. Look at the Globals area of the Debug Control window to see what the values of `flips` and `heads` are.

Click **Go** again and the program will continue until it reaches the next breakpoint on line 16. Again, see how the values in `flips` and `heads` have changed.

Click **Go** again to continue the execution until the next breakpoint is reached, which is on line 12.

Summary

Writing programs is only the first part of programming. The next part is making sure the code you wrote actually works. Debuggers let you step through the code one line at a time. You can examine which lines execute in what order and what values the variables contain. When stepping through line by line is too slow, you can set breakpoints to stop the debugger only at the lines you want.

Using the debugger is a great way to understand what a program is doing. While this book provides explanations of all the game code we use, the debugger can help you find out more on your own.

7

DESIGNING HANGMAN WITH FLOWCHARTS

In this chapter, you'll design a Hangman game. This game is more complicated than our previous games but also more fun. Because the game is advanced, we'll first carefully plan it out by creating a flowchart in this chapter. In Chapter 8, we'll actually write the code for Hangman.

TOPICS COVERED IN THIS CHAPTER

- ASCII art
- Designing a program with flowcharts

How to Play Hangman

Hangman is a game for two people in which one player thinks of a word and then draws a blank line on the page for each letter in the word. The second player then tries to guess letters that might be in the word.

If the second player guesses the letter correctly, the first player writes the letter in the proper blank. But if the second player guesses incorrectly, the first player draws a single body part of a hanging man. The second player has to guess all the letters in the word before the hanging man is completely drawn to win the game.

Sample Run of Hangman

Here is an example of what the player might see when they run the Hangman program you'll write in Chapter 8. The text the player enters is in bold.

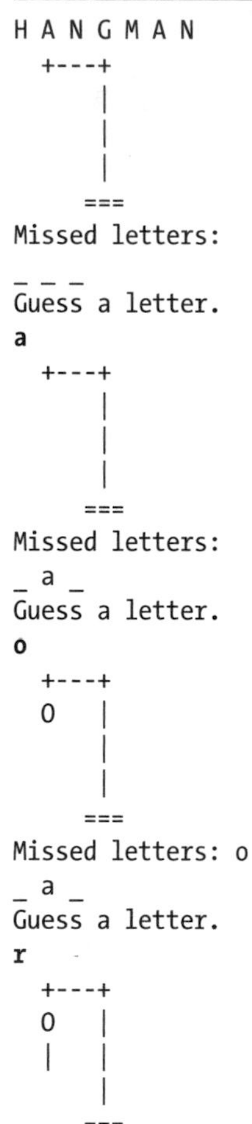

```
H A N G M A N
  +---+
      |
      |
      |
     ===
Missed letters:
_ _ _
Guess a letter.
a
  +---+
      |
      |
      |
     ===
Missed letters:
_ a _
Guess a letter.
o
  +---+
  O   |
      |
      |
     ===
Missed letters: o
_ a _
Guess a letter.
r
  +---+
  O   |
  |   |
      |
     ===
```

```
Missed letters: or
_ a _
Guess a letter.
t
 +---+
 O   |
 |   |
     |
    ===
Missed letters: or
_ a t
Guess a letter.
a
You have already guessed that letter. Choose again.
Guess a letter.
c
Yes! The secret word is "cat"! You have won!
Do you want to play again? (yes or no)
no
```

ASCII Art

The graphics for Hangman are keyboard characters printed on the screen. This type of graphic is called *ASCII art* (pronounced *ask-ee*), which was a sort of precursor to emoji. Here is a cat drawn in ASCII art:

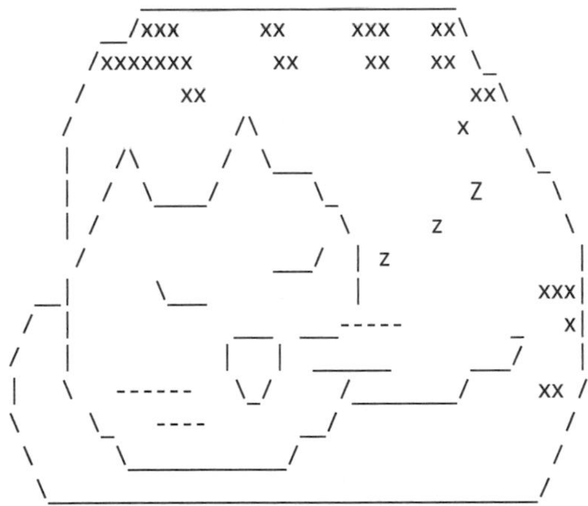

The pictures for the Hangman game will look like this ASCII art:

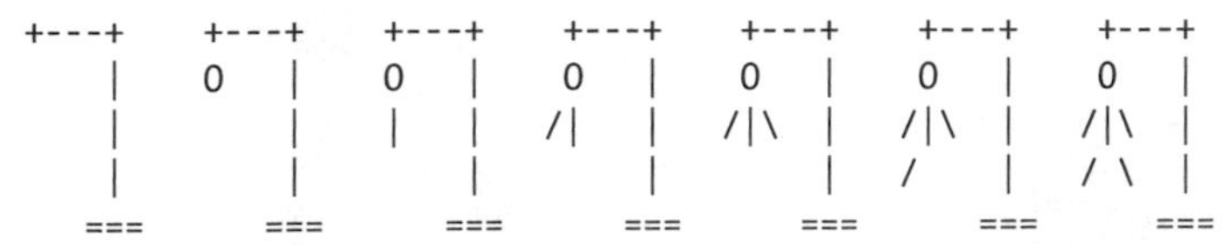

Designing a Program with a Flowchart

This game is a bit more complicated than the ones you've seen so far, so let's take a moment to think about how it's put together. First you'll create a flowchart (like the one in Figure 5-1 on page 47 for the Dragon Realm game) to help visualize what this program will do.

As discussed in Chapter 5, a flowchart is a diagram that shows a series of steps as boxes connected with arrows. Each box represents a step, and the arrows show the possible next steps. Put your finger on the START box of the flowchart and trace through the program by following the arrows to other boxes until you get to the END box. You can only move from one box to another in the direction of the arrow. You can never go backward unless there's an arrow going back, like in the "Player already guessed this letter" box.

Figure 7-1 is a complete flowchart for Hangman.

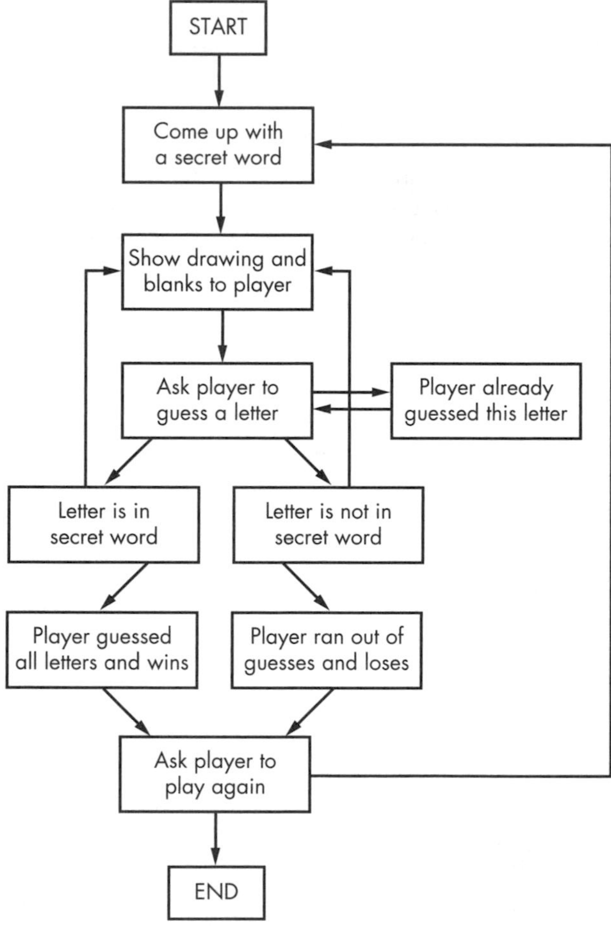

Figure 7-1: The complete flowchart for the Hangman game

Of course, you don't *have* to make a flowchart; you could just start writing code. But often once you start programming, you'll think of things that must be added or changed. You may end up having to delete a lot of your code, which would be a waste of effort. To avoid this, it's best to plan how the program will work before you start writing it.

Creating the Flowchart

Your flowcharts don't have to look like the one in Figure 7-1. As long as *you* understand your flowchart, it will be helpful when you start coding. You can begin making a flowchart with just a START and an END box, as shown in Figure 7-2.

Now think about what happens when you play Hangman. First, the computer thinks of a secret word. Then the player guesses letters. Add boxes for these events, as shown in Figure 7-3. The new boxes in each flowchart have a dashed outline.

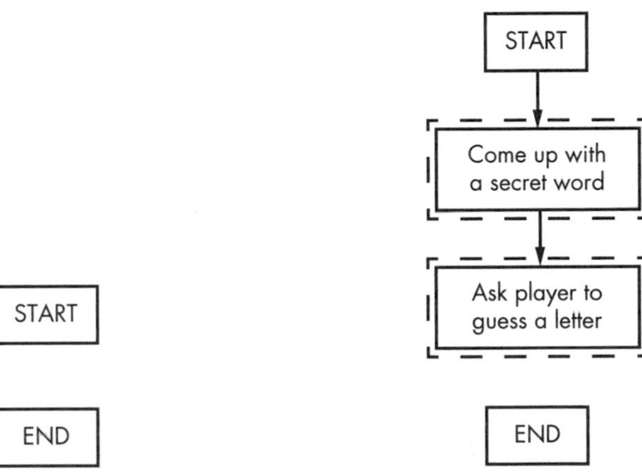

Figure 7-2: Begin your flowchart with a START and an END box.

Figure 7-3: Draw the first two steps of Hangman as boxes with descriptions.

But the game doesn't end after the player guesses a letter. The program needs to check whether that letter is in the secret word.

Branching from a Flowchart Box

There are two possibilities: the letter is either in the word or not. You'll add two new boxes to the flowchart, one for each case. This creates a branch in the flowchart, as shown in Figure 7-4.

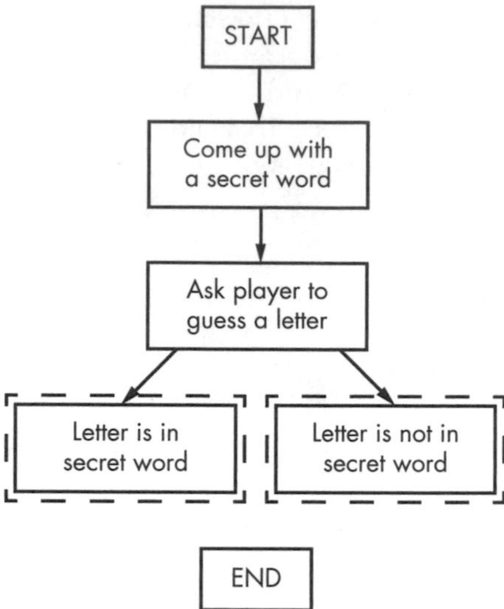

Figure 7-4: The branch has two arrows going to separate boxes.

If the letter is in the secret word, check whether the player has guessed all the letters and won the game. If the letter isn't in the secret word, check whether the hanging man is complete and the player has lost. Add boxes for those cases too.

The flowchart now looks like Figure 7-5.

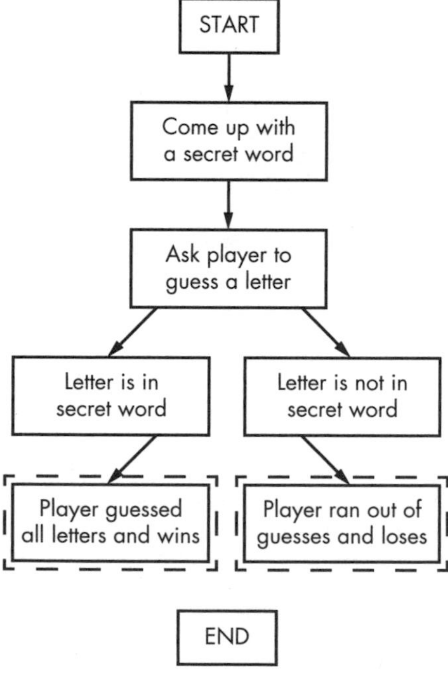

Figure 7-5: After the branch, the steps continue on their separate paths.

You don't need an arrow from the "Letter is in secret word" box to the "Player ran out of guesses and loses" box, because it's impossible for the player to lose if they have just guessed correctly. It's also impossible for the player to win if they have just guessed incorrectly, so you don't need to draw an arrow for that either.

Ending or Restarting the Game

Once the player has won or lost, ask them if they want to play again with a new secret word. If the player doesn't want to play again, the program ends; otherwise, the program continues and thinks up a new secret word. This is shown in Figure 7-6.

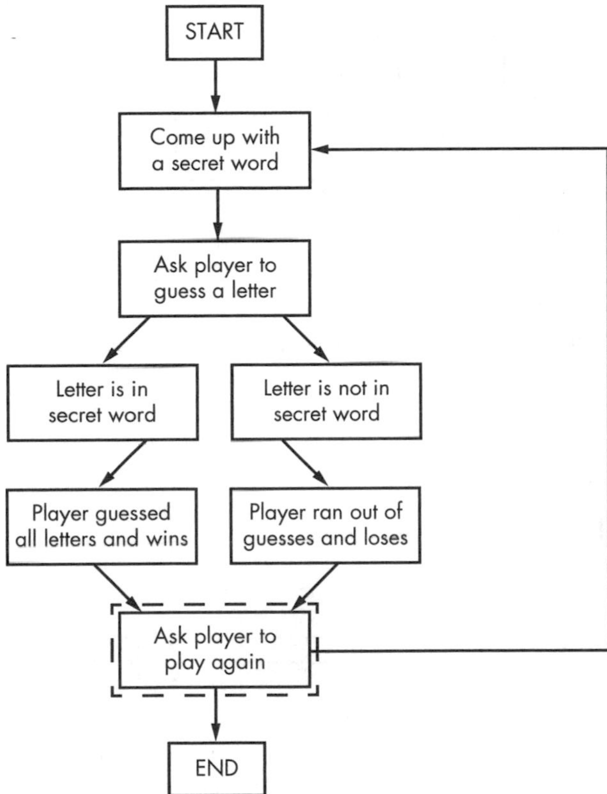

Figure 7-6: The flowchart branches after asking the player to play again.

Guessing Again

The flowchart looks mostly complete now, but we're still missing a few things. For one, the player doesn't guess a letter just once; they keep guessing letters until they win or lose. Draw two new arrows, as shown in Figure 7-7.

What if the player guesses the same letter again? Rather than counting this letter again, allow them to guess a different letter. This new box is shown in Figure 7-8.

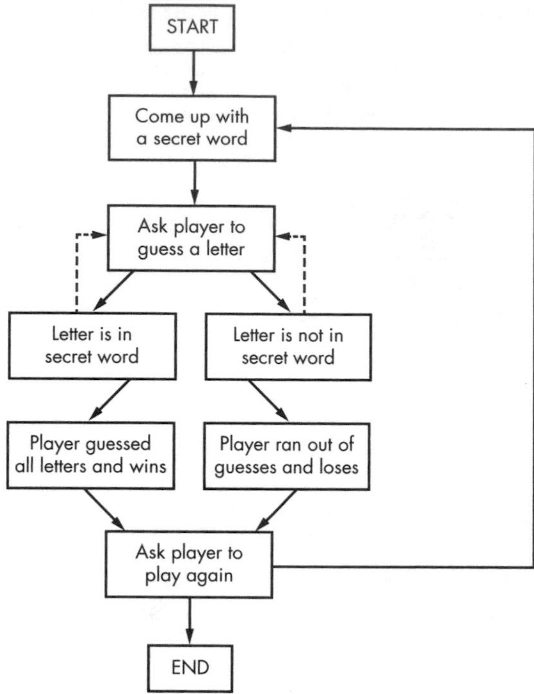

Figure 7-7: The dashed arrows show the player can guess again.

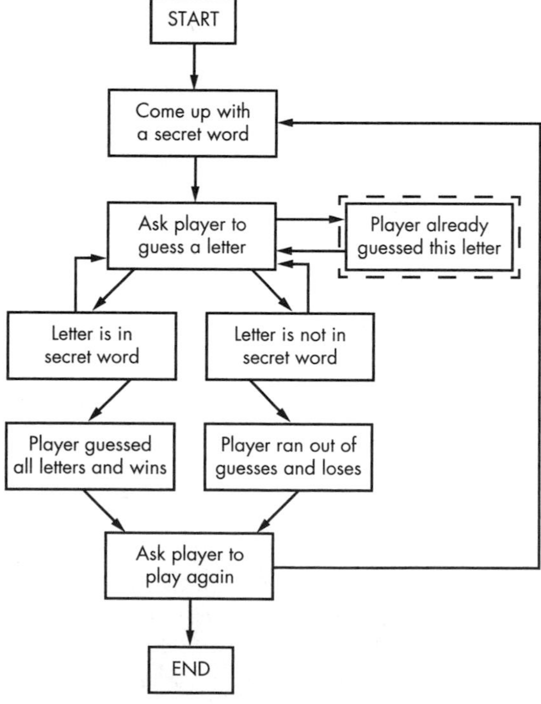

Figure 7-8: Add a step in case the player guesses a letter they already guessed.

If the player guesses the same letter twice, the flowchart leads back to the "Ask player to guess a letter" box.

Offering Feedback to the Player

The player needs to know how they're doing in the game. The program should show them the hanging man drawing and the secret word (with blanks for the letters they haven't guessed yet). These visuals will let them see how close they are to winning or losing the game.

This information is updated every time the player guesses a letter. Add a "Show drawing and blanks to player" box to the flowchart between the "Come up with a secret word" box and the "Ask player to guess a letter" box, as shown in Figure 7-9.

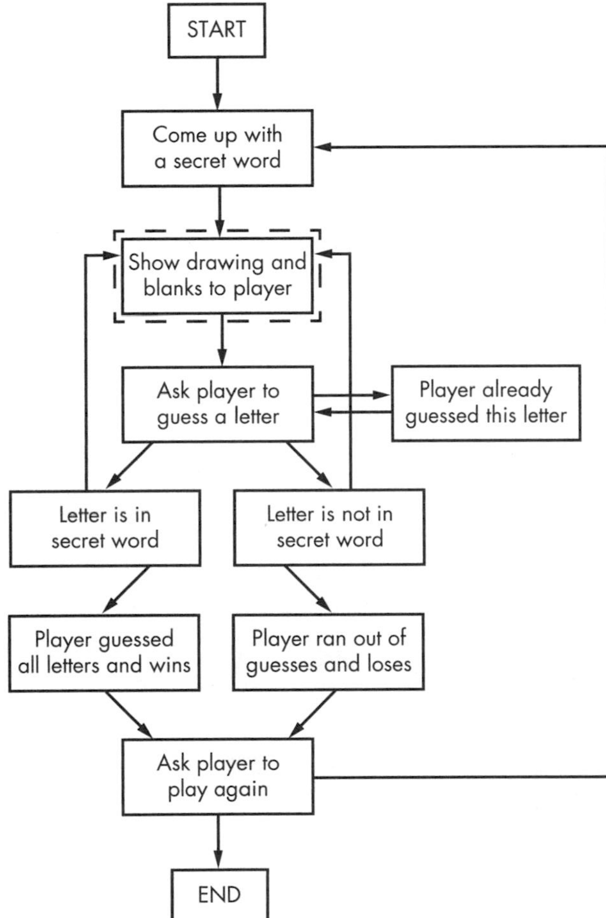

Figure 7-9: Add a "Show drawing and blanks to player" box to give the player feedback.

That looks good! This flowchart completely maps out the order of everything that can happen in the Hangman game. When you design your own games, a flowchart can help you remember everything you need to code.

Summary

It may seem like a lot of work to sketch out a flowchart about the program first. After all, people want to play games, not look at flowcharts! But it is much easier to make changes and identify problems by thinking about how the program works *before* writing the code for it.

If you jump in to write the code first, you may discover problems that require you to change the code you've already written, wasting time and effort. And every time you change your code, you risk creating new bugs by changing too little or too much. It is much more efficient to know what you want to build before you build it. Now that we have a flowchart, let's create the Hangman program in Chapter 8!

8

WRITING THE HANGMAN CODE

This chapter's game introduces many new concepts, but don't worry: you'll experiment with them in the interactive shell before actually programming the game. You'll learn about *methods*, which are functions attached to values. You'll also learn about a new data type called a *list*. Once you understand these concepts, it will be much easier to program Hangman.

TOPICS COVERED IN THIS CHAPTER

- Lists
- The `in` operator
- Methods
- The `split()`, `lower()`, `upper()`, `startswith()`, and `endswith()` string methods
- `elif` statements

Source Code for Hangman

This chapter's game is a bit longer than the previous games, but much of it is the ASCII art for the hanging man pictures. Enter the following into the file editor and save it as *hangman.py*. If you get errors after entering the following code, compare the code you typed to the book's code with the online diff tool at *https://www.nostarch.com/inventwithpython#diff*.

MAKE SURE YOU'RE USING PYTHON 3, NOT PYTHON 2!

hangman.py

```
import random
HANGMAN_PICS = ['''
  +---+
      |
      |
      |
     ===''', '''
  +---+
  O   |
      |
      |
     ===''', '''
  +---+
  O   |
  |   |
      |
     ===''', '''
  +---+
  O   |
 /|   |
      |
     ===''', '''
  +---+
  O   |
 /|\  |
      |
```

```
     ===''', '''
  +---+
  O   |
 /|\  |
 /    |
     ===''', '''
  +---+
  O   |
 /|\  |
 / \  |
     ===''']
words = 'ant baboon badger bat bear beaver camel cat clam cobra cougar coyote crow deer dog donkey duck eagle ferret fox frog goat goose hawk lion lizard llama mole monkey moose mouse mule newt otter owl panda parrot pigeon python rabbit ram rat raven rhino salmon seal shark sheep skunk sloth snake spider stork swan tiger toad trout turkey turtle weasel whale wolf wombat zebra'.split()

def getRandomWord(wordList):
    # This function returns a random string from the passed list of strings.
    wordIndex = random.randint(0, len(wordList) - 1)
    return wordList[wordIndex]

def displayBoard(missedLetters, correctLetters, secretWord):
    print(HANGMAN_PICS[len(missedLetters)])
    print()

    print('Missed letters:', end=' ')
    for letter in missedLetters:
        print(letter, end=' ')
    print()

    blanks = '_' * len(secretWord)

    for i in range(len(secretWord)): # Replace blanks with correctly guessed letters.
        if secretWord[i] in correctLetters:
            blanks = blanks[:i] + secretWord[i] + blanks[i+1:]

    for letter in blanks: # Show the secret word with spaces in between each letter.
        print(letter, end=' ')
    print()

def getGuess(alreadyGuessed):
    # Returns the letter the player entered. This function makes sure the player entered a single letter and not something else.
    while True:
        print('Guess a letter.')
        guess = input()
        guess = guess.lower()
        if len(guess) != 1:
            print('Please enter a single letter.')
```

```
        elif guess in alreadyGuessed:
            print('You have already guessed that letter. Choose again.')
        elif guess not in 'abcdefghijklmnopqrstuvwxyz':
            print('Please enter a LETTER.')
        else:
            return guess

def playAgain():
    # This function returns True if the player wants to play again;
      otherwise, it returns False.
    print('Do you want to play again? (yes or no)')
    return input().lower().startswith('y')


print('H A N G M A N')
missedLetters = ''
correctLetters = ''
secretWord = getRandomWord(words)
gameIsDone = False

while True:
    displayBoard(missedLetters, correctLetters, secretWord)

    # Let the player enter a letter.
    guess = getGuess(missedLetters + correctLetters)

    if guess in secretWord:
        correctLetters = correctLetters + guess

        # Check if the player has won.
        foundAllLetters = True
        for i in range(len(secretWord)):
            if secretWord[i] not in correctLetters:
                foundAllLetters = False
                break
        if foundAllLetters:
            print('Yes! The secret word is "' + secretWord +
              '"! You have won!')
            gameIsDone = True
    else:
        missedLetters = missedLetters + guess

        # Check if player has guessed too many times and lost.
        if len(missedLetters) == len(HANGMAN_PICS) - 1:
            displayBoard(missedLetters, correctLetters, secretWord)
            print('You have run out of guesses!\nAfter ' +
              str(len(missedLetters)) + ' missed guesses and ' +
              str(len(correctLetters)) + ' correct guesses,
              the word was "' + secretWord + '"')
            gameIsDone = True

```

```
    # Ask the player if they want to play again (but only if the game is done).
    if gameIsDone:
        if playAgain():
            missedLetters = ''
            correctLetters = ''
            gameIsDone = False
            secretWord = getRandomWord(words)
        else:
            break
```

Importing the random Module

The Hangman program randomly selects a secret word for the player to guess from a list of words. The `random` module will provide this ability, so line 1 imports it.

```
1. import random
```

But the `HANGMAN_PICS` variable on line 2 looks a little different from the variables we've seen so far. In order to understand what this code means, we need to learn about a few more concepts.

Constant Variables

Lines 2 to 37 are one long assignment statement for the `HANGMAN_PICS` variable.

```
 2. HANGMAN_PICS = ['''
 3.   +---+
 4.       |
 5.       |
 6.       |
 7.      ===''', '''
--snip--
37.      ===''']
```

The `HANGMAN_PICS` variable's name is in all uppercase letters. This is the programming convention for constant variables. *Constants* are variables meant to have values that never change from their first assignment statement. Although you can change the value in `HANGMAN_PICS` just as you can for any other variable, the all-uppercase name reminds you not to do so.

As with all conventions, you don't *have* to follow this one. But doing so makes it easier for other programmers to read your code. They'll know that `HANGMAN_PICS` will always have the value it was assigned from lines 2 to 37.

The Lists Data Type

HANGMAN_PICS contains several multiline strings. It can do this because it's a list. Lists have a list value that can contain several other values. Enter this into the interactive shell:

```
>>> animals = ['aardvark', 'anteater', 'antelope', 'albert']
>>> animals
['aardvark', 'anteater', 'antelope', 'albert']
```

The list value in animals contains four values. List values begin with a left square bracket, [, and end with a right square bracket,]. This is like how strings begin and end in quotation marks.

Commas separate the individual values inside of a list. These values are also called *items*. Each item in HANGMAN_PICS is a multiline string.

Lists let you store several values without using a variable for each one. Without lists, the code would look like this:

```
>>> animals1 = 'aardvark'
>>> animals2 = 'anteater'
>>> animals3 = 'antelope'
>>> animals4 = 'albert'
```

This code would be hard to manage if you had hundreds or thousands of strings. But a list can easily contain any number of values.

Accessing Items with Indexes

You can access an item inside a list by adding square brackets to the end of the list variable with a number between them. The number between the square brackets is the *index*. In Python, the index of the first item in a list is 0. The second item is at index 1, the third item is at index 2, and so on. Because the indexes begin at 0 and not 1, we say that Python lists are *zero indexed*.

While we're still in the interactive shell and working with the animals list, enter **animals[0]**, **animals[1]**, **animals[2]**, and **animals[3]** to see how they evaluate:

```
>>> animals[0]
'aardvark'
>>> animals[1]
'anteater'
>>> animals[2]
'antelope'
>>> animals[3]
'albert'
```

Notice that the first value in the list, 'aardvark', is stored in index 0 and not index 1. Each item in the list is numbered in order starting from 0.

Using the square brackets, you can treat items in the list just like any other value. For example, enter **animals[0] + animals[2]** into the interactive shell:

```
>>> animals[0] + animals[2]
'aardvarkantelope'
```

Both variables at indexes 0 and 2 of animals are strings, so the values are concatenated. The evaluation looks like this:

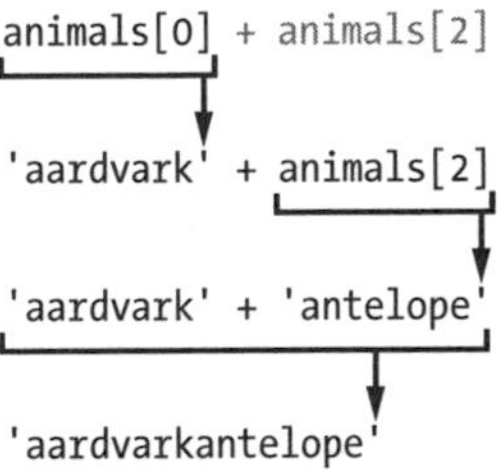

Out-of-Range Indexes and IndexError

If you try accessing an index that is too high to be in the list, you'll get an IndexError that will crash your program. To see an example of this error, enter the following into the interactive shell:

```
>>> animals = ['aardvark', 'anteater', 'antelope', 'albert']
>>> animals[9999]
Traceback (most recent call last):
  File "", line 1, in
    animals[9999]
IndexError: list index out of range
```

Because there is no value at index 9999, you get an error.

Changing List Items with Index Assignment

You can also change the value of an item in a list using *index assignment*. Enter the following into the interactive shell:

```
>>> animals = ['aardvark', 'anteater', 'antelope', 'albert']
>>> animals[1] = 'ANTEATER'
>>> animals
['aardvark', 'ANTEATER', 'antelope', 'albert']
```

The new 'ANTEATER' string overwrites the second item in the animals list. So typing animals[1] by itself evaluates to the list's current second item, but using it on the left side of an assignment operator assigns a new value to the list's second item.

List Concatenation

You can join several lists into one list using the + operator, just as you can with strings. Doing so is called *list concatenation*. To see this in action, enter the following into the interactive shell:

```
>>> [1, 2, 3, 4] + ['apples', 'oranges'] + ['Alice', 'Bob']
[1, 2, 3, 4, 'apples', 'oranges', 'Alice', 'Bob']
```

['apples'] + ['oranges'] will evaluate to ['apples', 'oranges']. But ['apples'] + 'oranges' will result in an error. You can't add a list value and a string value with the + operator. If you want to add values to the end of a list without using list concatenation, use the append() method (described in "The reverse() and append() List Methods" on page 95).

The in Operator

The in operator can tell you whether a value is in a list or not. Expressions that use the in operator return a Boolean value: True if the value is in the list and False if it isn't. Enter the following into the interactive shell:

```
>>> animals = ['aardvark', 'anteater', 'antelope', 'albert']
>>> 'antelope' in animals
True
>>> 'ant' in animals
False
```

The expression 'antelope' in animals returns True because the string 'antelope' is one of the values in the animals list. It is located at index 2. But when you enter the expression 'ant' in animals, it returns False because the string 'ant' doesn't exist in the list.

The in operator also works for strings, checking whether one string exists in another. Enter the following into the interactive shell:

```
>>> 'hello' in 'Alice said hello to Bob.'
True
```

Storing a list of multiline strings in the HANGMAN_PICS variable covered a lot of concepts. For example, you saw that lists are useful for storing multiple values in a single variable. You also learned some techniques for working with lists, such as index assignment and list concatenation. Methods are another new concept you'll learn how to use in the Hangman game; we'll explore them next.

Calling Methods

A *method* is a function attached to a value. To call a method, you must attach it to a specific value using a period. Python has many useful methods, and we'll use some of them in the Hangman program.

But first, let's look at some list and string methods.

The reverse() and append() List Methods

The list data type has a couple of methods you'll probably use a lot: `reverse()` and `append()`. The `reverse()` method will reverse the order of the items in the list. Try entering `spam = [1, 2, 3, 4, 5, 6, 'meow', 'woof']`, and then `spam.reverse()` to reverse the list. Then enter `spam` to view the contents of the variable.

```
>>> spam = [1, 2, 3, 4, 5, 6, 'meow', 'woof']
>>> spam.reverse()
>>> spam
['woof', 'meow', 6, 5, 4, 3, 2, 1]
```

The most common list method you'll use is `append()`. This method will add the value you pass as an argument to the end of the list. Try entering the following into the interactive shell:

```
>>> eggs = []
>>> eggs.append('hovercraft')
>>> eggs
['hovercraft']
>>> eggs.append('eels')
>>> eggs
['hovercraft', 'eels']
```

These methods do change the lists they are called on. They don't return a new list. We say that these methods change the list *in place.*

The split() String Method

The string data type has a `split()` method, which returns a list of strings made from a string that has been split. Try using the `split()` method by entering the following into the interactive shell:

```
>>> sentence = input()
My very energetic mother just served us nachos.
>>> sentence.split()
['My', 'very', 'energetic', 'mother', 'just', 'served', 'us', 'nachos.']
```

The result is a list of eight strings, one string for each word in the original string. The splitting occurs wherever there is a space in the string. The spaces are not included in any of the items in the list.

Line 38 of the Hangman program also uses the `split()` method, as shown next. The code is long, but it's really just a simple assignment statement that has one long string of words separated by spaces, with a `split()` method call at the end. The `split()` method evaluates to a list with each word in the string as a single list item.

```
38. words = 'ant baboon badger bat bear beaver camel cat clam cobra cougar
       coyote crow deer dog donkey duck eagle ferret fox frog goat goose hawk
       lion lizard llama mole monkey moose mouse mule newt otter owl panda
       parrot pigeon python rabbit ram rat raven rhino salmon seal shark sheep
       skunk sloth snake spider stork swan tiger toad trout turkey turtle
       weasel whale wolf wombat zebra'.split()
```

It's easier to write this program using `split()`. If you created a list to begin with, you would have to type `['ant', 'baboon', 'badger'`, and so on, with quotes and commas for every word.

You can also add your own words to the string on line 38 or remove any you don't want to be in the game. Just make sure that spaces separate the words.

Getting a Secret Word from the Word List

Line 40 defines the `getRandomWord()` function. A list argument will be passed for its `wordList` parameter. This function will return a single secret word from the list in `wordList`.

```
40. def getRandomWord(wordList):
41.     # This function returns a random string from the passed list of
          strings.
42.     wordIndex = random.randint(0, len(wordList) - 1)
43.     return wordList[wordIndex]
```

In line 42, we store a random index for this list in the `wordIndex` variable by calling `randint()` with two arguments. The first argument is `0` (for the first possible index), and the second is the value that the expression `len(wordList) - 1` evaluates to (for the last possible index in a `wordList`).

Remember that list indexes start at `0`, not `1`. If you have a list of three items, the index of the first item is `0`, the index of the second item is `1`, and the index of the third item is `2`. The length of this list is 3, but index `3` would be after the last index. This is why line 42 subtracts `1` from the length of `wordList`. The code on line 42 will work no matter what the size of `wordList` is. Now you can add or remove strings in `wordList` if you like.

The `wordIndex` variable will be set to a random index for the list passed as the `wordList` parameter. Line 43 will return the element in `wordList` at the integer stored in `wordIndex`.

Let's pretend `['apple', 'orange', grape']` was passed as the argument to `getRandomWord()` and that `randint(0, 2)` returned the integer `2`. That would mean that line 43 would evaluate to `return wordList[2]`, and then evaluate to `return 'grape'`. This is how `getRandomWord()` returns a random string in `wordList`.

So the input to `getRandomWord()` is a list of strings, and the return value output is a randomly selected string from that list. In the Hangman game, this is how a secret word is selected for the player to guess.

Displaying the Board to the Player

Next, you need a function to print the Hangman board on the screen. It should also display how many letters the player has correctly (and incorrectly) guessed.

```
45. def displayBoard(missedLetters, correctLetters, secretWord):
46.     print(HANGMAN_PICS[len(missedLetters)])
47.     print()
```

This code defines a new function named `displayBoard()`. This function has three parameters:

`missedLetters` A string of the letters the player has guessed that are not in the secret word

`correctLetters` A string of the letters the player has guessed that are in the secret word

`secretWord` A string of the secret word that the player is trying to guess

The first `print()` function call will display the board. The global variable `HANGMAN_PICS` has a list of strings for each possible board. (Remember that global variables can be read from inside a function.) `HANGMAN_PICS[0]` shows an empty gallows, `HANGMAN_PICS[1]` shows the head (when the player misses one letter), `HANGMAN_PICS[2]` shows the head and body (when the player misses two letters), and so on until `HANGMAN_PICS[6]`, which shows the full hanging man.

The number of letters in `missedLetters` will reflect how many incorrect guesses the player has made. Call `len(missedLetters)` to find out this number. So, if `missedLetters` is `'aetr'`, then `len('aetr')` will return `4`. Printing `HANGMAN_PICS[4]` will display the appropriate hanging man picture for four misses. This is what `HANGMAN_PICS[len(missedLetters)]` on line 46 evaluates to.

Line 49 prints the string `'Missed letters:'` with a space character at the end instead of a newline:

```
49.     print('Missed letters:', end=' ')
50.     for letter in missedLetters:
51.         print(letter, end=' ')
52.     print()
```

The `for` loop on line 50 will iterate over each character in the string `missedLetters` and print it on the screen. Remember that `end=' '` will replace the newline character that is printed after the string with a single space character. For example, if `missedLetters` were `'ajtw'`, this `for` loop would display `a j t w`.

The rest of the `displayBoard()` function (lines 54 to 62) displays the missed letters and creates the string of the secret word with all of the not-yet-guessed letters as blanks. It does this using the `range()` function and list slicing.

The list() and range() Functions

When called with one argument, range() will return a range object of integers from 0 up to (but not including) the argument. This range object is used in for loops but can also be converted to the more familiar list data type with the list() function. Enter list(range(10)) into the interactive shell:

```
>>> list(range(10))
[0, 1, 2, 3, 4, 5, 6, 7, 8, 9]
>>> list('Hello')
['H', 'e', 'l', 'l', 'o']
```

The list() function is similar to the str() or int() functions. It takes the value it's passed and returns a list. It's easy to generate huge lists with the range() function. For example, enter **list(range(10000))** into the interactive shell:

```
>>> list(range(10000))
[0, 1, 2, 3, 4, 5, 6, 7, 8, 9, 10, 11, 12, 13, 14, 15,...
      --snip--
...9989, 9990, 9991, 9992, 9993, 9994, 9995, 9996, 9997, 9998, 9999]
```

The list is so huge, it won't even fit onto the screen. But you can store the list in a variable:

```
>>> spam = list(range(10000))
```

If you pass two integer arguments to range(), the range object it returns is from the first integer argument up to (but not including) the second integer argument. Next enter **list(range(10, 20))** into the interactive shell as follows:

```
>>> list(range(10, 20))
[10, 11, 12, 13, 14, 15, 16, 17, 18, 19]
```

As you can see, our list only goes up to 19 and does not include 20.

List and String Slicing

List slicing creates a new list value using a subset of another list's items. To slice a list, specify two indexes (the beginning and end) with a colon in the square brackets after the list name. For example, enter the following into the interactive shell:

```
>>> spam = ['apples', 'bananas', 'carrots', 'dates']
>>> spam[1:3]
['bananas', 'carrots']
```

The expression spam[1:3] evaluates to a list with items in spam from index 1 up to (but not including) index 3.

If you leave out the first index, Python will automatically think you want index 0 for the first index:

```
>>> spam = ['apples', 'bananas', 'carrots', 'dates']
>>> spam[:2]
['apples', 'bananas']
```

If you leave out the second index, Python will automatically think you want the rest of the list:

```
>>> spam = ['apples', 'bananas', 'carrots', 'dates']
>>> spam[2:]
['carrots', 'dates']
```

You can also use slices with strings in the same way you use them with lists. Each character in the string is like an item in the list. Enter the following into the interactive shell:

```
>>> myName = 'Zophie the Fat Cat'
>>> myName[4:12]
'ie the F'
>>> myName[:10]
'Zophie the'
>>> myName[7:]
'the Fat Cat'
```

The next part of the Hangman code uses slicing.

Displaying the Secret Word with Blanks

Now you want to print the secret word, but with blank lines for the letters that haven't been guessed. You can use the underscore character (_) for this. First create a string with nothing but one underscore for each letter in the secret word. Then replace the blanks for each letter in `correctLetters`.

So if the secret word were `'otter'`, then the blanked-out string would be `'_____'` (five underscores). If `correctLetters` were the string `'rt'`, you would change the string to `'_tt_r'`. Lines 54 to 58 are the part of the code that does that:

```
54.     blanks = '_' * len(secretWord)
55.
56.     for i in range(len(secretWord)): # Replace blanks with correctly
          guessed letters.
57.         if secretWord[i] in correctLetters:
58.             blanks = blanks[:i] + secretWord[i] + blanks[i+1:]
```

Line 54 creates the `blanks` variable full of underscores using string replication. Remember that the `*` operator can be used on a string and an integer, so the expression `'_' * 5` evaluates to `'_____'`. This will ensure that `blanks` has the same number of underscores as `secretWord` has letters.

Line 56 has a for loop that goes through each letter in secretWord and replaces the underscore with the actual letter if it exists in correctLetters.

Let's take another look at the previous example, where the value of secretWord is 'otter' and the value in correctLetters is 'tr'. You would want the string '_tt_r' displayed to the player. Let's figure out how to create this string.

Line 56's len(secretWord) call would return 5. The range(len(secretWord)) call becomes range(5), which makes the for loop iterate over 0, 1, 2, 3, and 4.

Because the value of i will take on each value in [0, 1, 2, 3, 4], the code in the for loop looks like this:

```
if secretWord[0] in correctLetters:
    blanks = blanks[:0] + secretWord[0] + blanks[1:]

if secretWord[1] in correctLetters:
    blanks = blanks[:1] + secretWord[1] + blanks[2:]
--snip--
```

We're showing only the first two iterations of the for loop, but starting with 0, i will take the value of each number in the range. In the first iteration, i takes the value 0, so the if statement checks whether the letter in secretWord at index 0 is in correctLetters. The loop does this for every letter in the secretWord, one letter at a time.

If you are confused about the value of something like secretWord[0] or blanks[3:], look at Figure 8-1. It shows the value of the secretWord and blanks variables and the index for each letter in the string.

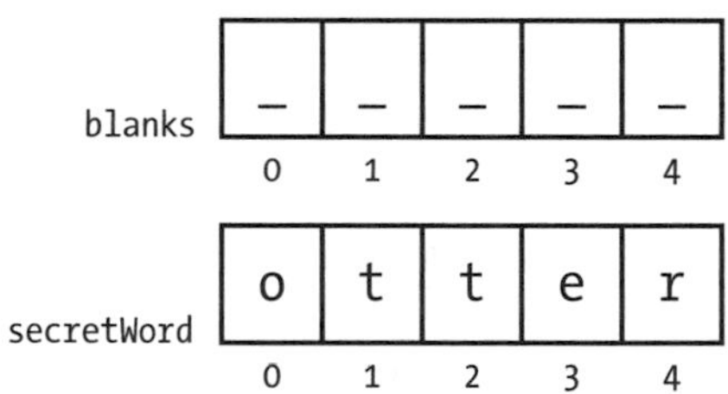

Figure 8-1: The indexes of the blanks and secretWord strings

If you replace the list slices and the list indexes with the values they represent, the loop code looks like this:

```
if 'o' in 'tr': # False
    blanks = '' + 'o' + '____' # This line is skipped.
--snip--
if 'r' in 'tr': # True
    blanks = '_tt_' + 'r' + '' # This line is executed.

# blanks now has the value '_tt_r'.
```

The preceding code examples all do the *same thing* when `secretWord` is `'otter'` and `correctLetters` is `'tr'`. The next few lines of code print the new value of `blanks` with spaces between each letter:

```
60.     for letter in blanks: # Show the secret word with spaces in between each letter.
61.         print(letter, end=' ')
62.     print()
```

Notice that the `for` loop on line 60 doesn't call the `range()` function. Instead of iterating on the range object this function call would return, it iterates on the string value in the `blanks` variable. On each iteration, the `letter` variable takes on a new character from the `'otter'` string in `blanks`.

The printed output after the spaces are added would be `'_ t t _ r'`.

Getting the Player's Guess

The `getGuess()` function will be called so that the player can enter a letter to guess. The function returns the letter the player guessed as a string. Further, `getGuess()` will make sure that the player types a valid letter before it returns from the function.

```
def getGuess(alreadyGuessed):
    # Returns the letter the player entered. This function makes sure the player entered a single letter and not something else.
```

A string of the letters the player has guessed is passed as the argument for the `alreadyGuessed` parameter. Then the `getGuess()` function asks the player to guess a single letter. This single letter will be `getGuess()`'s return value. Now, because Python is case sensitive, we need to make sure the player's guess is a lowercase letter so we can check it against the secret word. That's where the `lower()` method comes in.

The lower() and upper() String Methods

Enter **`'Hello world!'.lower()`** into the interactive shell to see an example of the `lower()` method:

```
>>> 'Hello world!'.lower()
'hello world!'
```

The `lower()` method returns a string with all the characters in lowercase. There is also an `upper()` method for strings, which returns a string with all the characters in uppercase. Try it out by entering **`'Hello world!'.upper()`** into the interactive shell:

```
>>> 'Hello world!'.upper()
'HELLO WORLD!'
```

Because the upper() method returns a string, you can also call a method on that string.

Now enter this into the interactive shell:

```
>>> 'Hello world!'.upper().lower()
'hello world!'
```

'Hello world!'.upper() evaluates to the string 'HELLO WORLD!', and then the string's lower() method is called. This returns the string 'hello world!', which is the final value in the evaluation:

```
'Hello world!'.upper().lower()
          'HELLO WORLD!'.lower()
                    'hello world!'
```

The order is important. 'Hello world!'.lower().upper() isn't the same as 'Hello world!'.upper().lower():

```
>>> 'Hello world!'.lower().upper()
'HELLO WORLD!'
```

That evaluation looks like this:

```
'Hello world!'.lower().upper()
          'hello world!'.upper()
                    'HELLO WORLD!'
```

If a string is stored in a variable, you can also call a string method on that variable:

```
>>> spam = 'Hello world!'
>>> spam.upper()
'HELLO WORLD!'
```

This code does not change the value in spam. The spam variable will still contain 'Hello world!'.

Going back to the Hangman program, we use lower() when we ask for the player's guess:

```
    while True:
        print('Guess a letter.')
        guess = input()
        guess = guess.lower()
```

Now, even if the player enters an uppercase letter as a guess, the getGuess() function will return a lowercase letter.

Leaving the while Loop

Line 66's `while` loop will keep asking the player for a letter until they enter a single letter that hasn't been guessed previously.

The condition for the `while` loop is simply the Boolean value `True`. That means the only way the execution will ever leave this loop is by executing a `break` statement, which leaves the loop, or a `return` statement, which leaves not just the loop but the entire function.

The code inside the loop asks the player to enter a letter, which is stored in the variable `guess`. If the player entered an uppercase letter, it would be overwritten with a lowercase letter on line 69.

elif Statements

The next part of the Hangman program uses `elif` statements. You can think of `elif` or "else-if" statements as saying, "If this is true, do this. Or else if this next condition is true, do that. Or else if none of them is true, do this last thing." Take a look at the following code:

```
if catName == 'Fuzzball':
    print('Your cat is fuzzy.')
elif catName == 'Spots':
    print('Your cat is spotted.')
else:
    print('Your cat is not fuzzy or spotted.')
```

If the `catName` variable is equal to the string `'Fuzzball'`, then the `if` statement's condition is `True` and the `if` block tells the user that their cat is fuzzy. However, if this condition is `False`, then Python tries the `elif` statement's condition next. If `catName` is `'Spots'`, then the string `'Your cat is spotted.'` is printed to the screen. If both are `False`, then the code tells the user their cat isn't fuzzy or spotted.

You can have as many `elif` statements as you want:

```
if catName == 'Fuzzball':
    print('Your cat is fuzzy.')
elif catName == 'Spots':
    print('Your cat is spotted.')
elif catName == 'Chubs':
    print('Your cat is chubby.')
elif catName == 'Puff':
    print('Your cat is puffy.')
else:
    print('Your cat is neither fuzzy nor spotted nor chubby nor puffy.')
```

When one of the `elif` conditions is `True`, its code is executed, and then the execution jumps to the first line past the `else` block. So *one, and only one,* of the blocks in the `if-elif-else` statements will be executed. You can also leave off the `else` block if you don't need one and just have `if-elif` statements.

Making Sure the Player Entered a Valid Guess

The guess variable contains the player's letter guess. The program needs to make sure they entered a valid guess: one, and only one, letter that has not yet been guessed. If they didn't, the execution will loop back and ask them for a letter again.

```
70.         if len(guess) != 1:
71.             print('Please enter a single letter.')
72.         elif guess in alreadyGuessed:
73.             print('You have already guessed that letter. Choose again.')
74.         elif guess not in 'abcdefghijklmnopqrstuvwxyz':
75.             print('Please enter a LETTER.')
76.         else:
77.             return guess
```

Line 70's condition checks whether guess is not one character long, line 72's condition checks whether guess already exists inside the alreadyGuessed variable, and line 74's condition checks whether guess is not a letter in the standard English alphabet. If any of these conditions are True, the game prompts the player to enter a new guess.

If all of these conditions are False, then the else statement's block executes, and getGuess() returns the value in guess on line 77.

Remember, only one of the blocks in an if-elif-else statement will be executed.

Asking the Player to Play Again

The playAgain() function has just a print() function call and a return statement:

```
def playAgain():
    # This function returns True if the player wants to play again;
      otherwise, it returns False.
    print('Do you want to play again? (yes or no)')
    return input().lower().startswith('y')
```

The return statement has an expression that looks complicated, but you can break it down. Here's a step-by-step look at how Python evaluates this expression if the user enters YES:

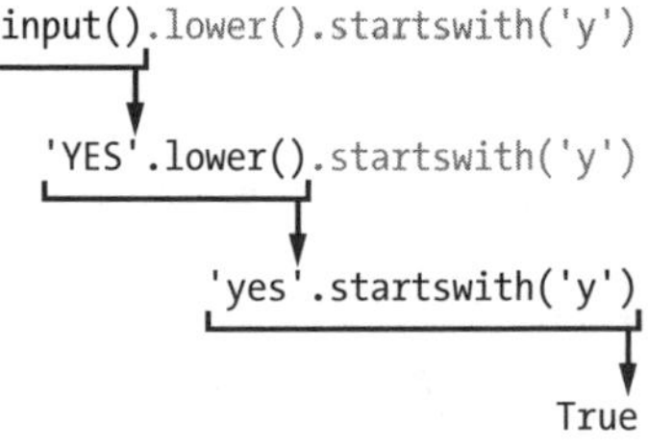

The point of the playAgain() function is to let the player enter yes or no to tell the program if they want to play another round of Hangman. The player should be able to type YES, yes, Y, or anything else that begins with a y in order to mean "yes." If the player enters YES, then the return value of input() is the string 'YES'. And 'YES'.lower() returns the lowercase version of the attached string. So the return value of 'YES'.lower() is 'yes'.

But there's the second method call, startswith('y'). This function returns True if the associated string begins with the string parameter between the parentheses and False if it doesn't. The return value of 'yes'.startswith('y') is True.

That's it—you evaluated this expression! It lets the player enter a response, sets the response in lowercase, checks whether it begins with the letter y, and then returns True if it does and False if it doesn't.

On a side note, there's also an endswith(*someString*) string method that will return True if the string ends with the string in *someString* and False if it doesn't. endswith() is sort of like the opposite of startswith().

Review of the Hangman Functions

That's all the functions we're creating for this game! Let's review them:

getRandomWord(wordList) Takes a list of strings passed to it and returns one string from it. That is how a word is chosen for the player to guess.

displayBoard(missedLetters, correctLetters, secretWord) Shows the current state of the board, including how much of the secret word the player has guessed so far and the wrong letters the player has guessed. This function needs three parameters passed to it to work correctly. correctLetters and missedLetters are strings made up of the letters that the player has guessed that are in and not in the secret word, respectively. And secretWord is the secret word the player is trying to guess. This function has no return value.

getGuess(alreadyGuessed) Takes a string of letters the player has already guessed and will keep asking the player for a letter that isn't in alreadyGuessed. This function returns the string of the valid letter the player guessed.

playAgain() Asks if the player wants to play another round of Hangman. This function returns True if the player does, False if they don't.

After the functions, the code for the main part of the program begins at line 85. Everything up to this point has been just function definitions and a large assignment statement for HANGMAN_PICS.

The Game Loop

The main part of the Hangman program displays the name of the game, sets up some variables, and executes a while loop. This section walks through the remainder of the program step by step.

```
85. print('H A N G M A N')
86. missedLetters = ''
87. correctLetters = ''
88. secretWord = getRandomWord(words)
89. gameIsDone = False
```

Line 85 is the first `print()` call that executes when the game is run. It displays the title of the game. Next, blank strings are assigned to the variables `missedLetters` and `correctLetters` since the player hasn't guessed any missed or correct letters yet.

The `getRandomWord(words)` call at line 88 will evaluate to a randomly selected word from the `words` list.

Line 89 sets `gameIsDone` to `False`. The code will set `gameIsDone` to `True` when it wants to signal that the game is over and ask the player whether they want to play again.

Calling the displayBoard() Function

The remainder of the program consists of a `while` loop. The loop's condition is always `True`, which means it will loop forever until it encounters a `break` statement. (This happens later on line 126.)

```
91. while True:
92.     displayBoard(missedLetters, correctLetters, secretWord)
```

Line 92 calls the `displayBoard()` function, passing it the three variables set on lines 86, 87, and 88. Based on how many letters the player has correctly guessed and missed, this function displays the appropriate Hangman board to the player.

Letting the Player Enter Their Guess

Next the `getGuess()` function is called so the player can enter their guess.

```
94.     # Let the player enter a letter.
95.     guess = getGuess(missedLetters + correctLetters)
```

The `getGuess()` function requires an `alreadyGuessed` parameter so it can check whether the player enters a letter they've already guessed. Line 95 concatenates the strings in the `missedLetters` and `correctLetters` variables and passes the result as the argument for the `alreadyGuessed` parameter.

Checking Whether the Letter Is in the Secret Word

If the `guess` string exists in `secretWord`, then this code concatenates `guess` to the end of the `correctLetters` string:

```
97.     if guess in secretWord:
98.         correctLetters = correctLetters + guess
```

This string will be the new value of correctLetters.

Checking Whether the Player Won

How does the program know whether the player has guessed every letter in the secret word? Well, correctLetters has each letter that the player correctly guessed, and secretWord is the secret word itself. But you can't simply check whether correctLetters == secretWord. If secretWord were the string 'otter' and correctLetters were the string 'orte', then correctLetters == secretWord would be False even though the player *has* guessed each letter in the secret word.

The only way you can be sure the player has won is to iterate over each letter in secretWord and see if it exists in correctLetters. If, and only if, every letter in secretWord exists in correctLetters has the player won.

```
100.         # Check if the player has won.
101.         foundAllLetters = True
102.         for i in range(len(secretWord)):
103.             if secretWord[i] not in correctLetters:
104.                 foundAllLetters = False
105.                 break
```

If you find a letter in secretWord that doesn't exist in correctLetters, you know that the player has *not* guessed all the letters. The new variable foundAllLetters is set to True on line 101 before the loop begins. The loop starts out assuming that all the letters in the secret word have been found. But the loop's code on line 104 will change foundAllLetters to False the first time it finds a letter in secretWord that isn't in correctLetters.

If all the letters in the secret word have been found, the player is told they have won, and gameIsDone is set to True:

```
106.         if foundAllLetters:
107.             print('Yes! The secret word is "' + secretWord +
                   '"! You have won!')
108.             gameIsDone = True
```

Handling an Incorrect Guess

Line 109 is the start of the else block.

```
109.     else:
110.         missedLetters = missedLetters + guess
```

Remember, the code in this block will execute if the condition was False. But which condition? To find out, point your finger at the start of the else keyword and move it straight up. You'll see that the else keyword's indentation is the same as the if keyword's indentation on line 97:

```
 97.     if guess in secretWord:
--snip--
```

```
109.     else:
110.         missedLetters = missedLetters + guess
```

So if the condition on line 97 (`guess in secretWord`) were `False`, then the execution would move into this else block.

Wrongly guessed letters are concatenated to the `missedLetters` string on line 110. This is like what line 98 did for letters the player guessed correctly.

Checking Whether the Player Lost

Each time the player guesses incorrectly, the code concatenates the wrong letter to the string in `missedLetters`. So the length of `missedLetters`—or, in code, `len(missedLetters)`—is also the number of wrong guesses.

```
112.         # Check if player has guessed too many times and lost.
113.         if len(missedLetters) == len(HANGMAN_PICS) - 1:
114.             displayBoard(missedLetters, correctLetters, secretWord)
115.             print('You have run out of guesses!\nAfter ' +
                   str(len(missedLetters)) + ' missed guesses and ' +
                   str(len(correctLetters)) + ' correct guesses,
                   the word was "' + secretWord + '"')
116.             gameIsDone = True
```

The `HANGMAN_PICS` list has seven ASCII art strings. So when the length of the `missedLetters` string is equal to `len(HANGMAN_PICS) - 1` (that is, `6`), the player has run out of guesses. You know the player has lost because the hanging man picture will be finished. Remember, `HANGMAN_PICS[0]` is the first item in the list, and `HANGMAN_PICS[6]` is the last one.

Line 115 prints the secret word, and line 116 sets the `gameIsDone` variable to `True`.

```
118.     # Ask the player if they want to play again (but only if the game is
           done).
119.     if gameIsDone:
120.         if playAgain():
121.             missedLetters = ''
122.             correctLetters = ''
123.             gameIsDone = False
124.             secretWord = getRandomWord(words)
```

Ending or Resetting the Game

Whether the player won or lost after guessing their letter, the game should ask the player if they want to play again. The `playAgain()` function handles getting a yes or no from the player, so it is called on line 120.

If the player does want to play again, the values in `missedLetters` and `correctLetters` must be reset to blank strings, `gameIsDone` reset to `False`, and a new secret word stored in `secretWord`. This way, when the execution loops back to the beginning of the `while` loop on line 91, the board will be reset to a fresh game.

If the player didn't enter something that began with y when asked whether they wanted to play again, then line 120's condition would be False, and the else block would execute:

```
125.        else:
126.            break
```

The break statement causes the execution to jump to the first instruction after the loop. But because there are no more instructions after the loop, the program terminates.

Summary

Hangman has been our most advanced game yet, and you've learned several new concepts while making it. As your games get more and more complex, it's a good idea to sketch out a flowchart of what should happen in your program.

Lists are values that can contain other values. Methods are functions attached to a value. Lists have an append() method. Strings have lower(), upper(), split(), startswith(), and endswith() methods. You'll learn about many more data types and methods in the rest of this book.

The elif statement lets you add an "or else-if" clause to the middle of your if-else statements.

9

EXTENDING HANGMAN

Now that you've created a basic Hangman game, let's look at some ways you can extend it with new features. In this chapter, you'll add multiple word sets for the computer to draw from and the ability to change the game's difficulty level.

TOPICS COVERED IN THIS CHAPTER

- The dictionary data type
- Key-value pairs
- The `keys()` and `values()` dictionary methods
- Multiple variable assignment

Adding More Guesses

After you've played Hangman a few times, you might think that six guesses isn't enough for the player to get many of the words. You can easily give them more guesses by adding more multiline strings to the `HANGMAN_PICS` list.

Save your *hangman.py* program as *hangman2.py*. Then add the following instructions on line 37 and after to extend the list that contains the hanging man ASCII art:

```
37.      ===''', '''
38.   +---+
39.  [O   |
40.  /|\  |
41.  / \  |
42.      ===''', '''
43.   +---+
44.  [O]  |
45.  /|\  |
46.  / \  |
47.      ===''']
```

This code adds two new multiline strings to the `HANGMAN_PICS` list, one with the hanging man's left ear drawn, and the other with both ears drawn. Because the program will tell the player they have lost based on `len(missedLetters) == len(HANGMAN_PICS) - 1`, this is the only change you need to make. The rest of the program works with the new `HANGMAN_PICS` list just fine.

The Dictionary Data Type

In the first version of the Hangman program, we used an animal word list, but you could change the list of words on line 48. Instead of animals, you could have colors:

```
48. words = 'red orange yellow green blue indigo violet white black brown'
      .split()
```

Or shapes:

```
48. words = 'square triangle rectangle circle ellipse rhombus trapezoid
      chevron pentagon hexagon septagon octagon'.split()
```

Or fruits:

```
48. words = 'apple orange lemon lime pear watermelon grape grapefruit cherry
      banana cantaloupe mango strawberry tomato'.split()
```

With some modification, you can even change the code so that the Hangman game uses sets of words, such as animals, colors, shapes, or fruits. The program can tell the player which set the secret word is from.

To make this change, you'll need a new data type called a *dictionary*. A dictionary is a collection of values like a list. But instead of accessing the items in the dictionary with an integer index, you can access them with an index of any data type. For dictionaries, these indexes are called *keys*.

Dictionaries use { and } (curly brackets) instead of [and] (square brackets). Enter the following into the interactive shell:

```
>>> spam = {'hello':'Hello there, how are you?', 4:'bacon', 'eggs':9999 }
```

The values between the curly brackets are *key-value pairs*. The keys are on the left of the colon and the key's values are on the right. You can access the values like items in lists by using the key. To see an example, enter the following into the interactive shell:

```
>>> spam = {'hello':'Hello there, how are you?', 4:'bacon', 'eggs':9999}
>>> spam['hello']
'Hello there, how are you?'
>>> spam[4]
'bacon'
>>> spam['eggs']
9999
```

Instead of putting an integer between the square brackets, you can use, say, a string key. In the `spam` dictionary, I used both the integer `4` and the string `'eggs'` as keys.

Getting the Size of Dictionaries with len()

You can get the number of key-value pairs in a dictionary with the `len()` function. For example, enter the following into the interactive shell:

```
>>> stuff = {'hello':'Hello there, how are you?', 4:'bacon', 'spam':9999}
>>> len(stuff)
3
```

The `len()` function will return an integer value for the number of key-value pairs, which in this case is `3`.

The Difference Between Dictionaries and Lists

One difference between dictionaries and lists is that dictionaries can have keys of any data type, as you've seen. But remember, because `0` and `'0'` are different values, they will be different keys. Enter this into the interactive shell:

```
>>> spam = {'0':'a string', 0:'an integer'}
>>> spam[0]
'an integer'
>>> spam['0']
'a string'
```

You can also loop over both lists and the keys in dictionaries using a `for` loop. To see how this works, enter the following into the interactive shell:

```
>>> favorites = {'fruit':'apples', 'animal':'cats', 'number':42}
>>> for k in favorites:
        print(k)
fruit
number
animal
>>> for k in favorites:
        print(favorites[k])
apples
42
cats
```

The keys and values may have printed in a different order for you because, unlike lists, dictionaries are unordered. The first item in a list named `listStuff` would be `listStuff[0]`. But there's no first item in a dictionary, because dictionaries do not have any sort of order. In this code, Python just chooses an order based on how it stores the dictionary in memory, which is not guaranteed to always be the same.

Enter the following into the interactive shell:

```
>>> favorites1 = {'fruit':'apples', 'number':42, 'animal':'cats'}
>>> favorites2 = {'animal':'cats',  'number':42, 'fruit':'apples'}
>>> favorites1 == favorites2
True
```

The expression `favorites1 == favorites2` evaluates to `True` because dictionaries are unordered and considered equal if they have the same key-value pairs in them. Meanwhile, lists are ordered, so two lists with the same values in a different order are not equal to each other. To see the difference, enter this into the interactive shell:

```
>>> listFavs1 = ['apples', 'cats', 42]
>>> listFavs2 = ['cats', 42, 'apples']
>>> listFavs1 == listFavs2
False
```

The expression `listFavs1 == listFavs2` evaluates to `False` because the lists' contents are ordered differently.

The keys() and values() Dictionary Methods

Dictionaries have two useful methods, `keys()` and `values()`. These will return values of a type called `dict_keys` and `dict_values`, respectively. Much like range objects, list forms of those data types are returned by `list()`.

Enter the following into the interactive shell:

```
>>> favorites = {'fruit':'apples', 'animal':'cats', 'number':42}
>>> list(favorites.keys())
['fruit', 'number', 'animal']
>>> list(favorites.values())
['apples', 42, 'cats']
```

Using `list()` with the `keys()` or `values()` methods, you can get a list of just the keys or just the values of a dictionary.

Using Dictionaries of Words in Hangman

Let's change the code in the new Hangman game to support different sets of secret words. First, replace the value assigned to `words` with a dictionary whose keys are strings and values are lists of strings. The string method `split()` will return a list of strings with one word each.

```
48. words = {'Colors':'red orange yellow green blue indigo violet white black
        brown'.split(),
49. 'Shapes':'square triangle rectangle circle ellipse rhombus trapezoid
        chevron pentagon hexagon septagon octagon'.split(),
50. 'Fruits':'apple orange lemon lime pear watermelon grape grapefruit cherry
        banana cantaloupe mango strawberry tomato'.split(),
51. 'Animals':'bat bear beaver cat cougar crab deer dog donkey duck eagle
        fish frog goat leech lion lizard monkey moose mouse otter owl panda
        python rabbit rat shark sheep skunk squid tiger turkey turtle weasel
        whale wolf wombat zebra'.split()}
```

Lines 48 to 51 are still just one assignment statement. The instruction doesn't end until the final curly bracket on line 51.

Randomly Choosing from a List

The `choice()` function in the `random` module takes a list argument and returns a random value from it. This is similar to what the previous `getRandomWord()` function did. You'll use `choice()` in the new version of the `getRandomWord()` function.

To see how the `choice()` function works, enter the following into the interactive shell:

```
>>> import random
>>> random.choice(['cat', 'dog', 'mouse'])
'mouse'
>>> random.choice(['cat', 'dog', 'mouse'])
'cat'
```

Just as the `randint()` function returns a random integer each time, the `choice()` function returns a random value from the list.

Change the getRandomWord() function so that its parameter will be a dictionary of lists of strings, instead of just a list of strings. Here is what the function originally looked like:

```
def getRandomWord(wordList):
    # This function returns a random string from the passed list of
      strings.
    wordIndex = random.randint(0, len(wordList) - 1)
    return wordList[wordIndex]
```

Change the code in this function so that it looks like this:

```
53. def getRandomWord(wordDict):
54.     # This function returns a random string from the passed dictionary of
          lists of strings and its key.
55.     # First, randomly select a key from the dictionary:
56.     wordKey = random.choice(list(wordDict.keys()))
57.
58.     # Second, randomly select a word from the key's list in the
          dictionary:
59.     wordIndex = random.randint(0, len(wordDict[wordKey]) - 1)
60.
61.     return [wordDict[wordKey][wordIndex], wordKey]
```

We've changed the name of the wordList parameter to wordDict to be more descriptive. Now instead of choosing a random word from a list of strings, first the function chooses a random key in the wordDict dictionary by calling random.choice(). And instead of returning the string wordList[wordIndex], the function returns a list with two items. The first item is wordDict[wordKey][wordIndex]. The second item is wordKey.

The wordDict[wordKey][wordIndex] expression on line 61 may look complicated, but it's just an expression you can evaluate one step at a time like anything else. First, imagine that wordKey has the value 'Fruits' and wordIndex has the value 5. Here is how wordDict[wordKey][wordIndex] would evaluate:

```
wordDict[wordKey][wordIndex]
            ↓
wordDict['Fruits'][wordIndex]
            ↓
['apple', 'orange', 'lemon', 'lime', 'pear', 'watermelon', 'grape', 'grapefruit',
'cherry', 'banana', 'cantaloupe', 'mango', 'strawberry', 'tomato'][wordIndex]
            ↓
['apple', 'orange', 'lemon', 'lime', 'pear', 'watermelon', 'grape', 'grapefruit',
'cherry', 'banana', 'cantaloupe', 'mango', 'strawberry', 'tomato'][5]
            ↓
        'watermelon'
```

In this case, the item in the list this function returns would be the string `'watermelon'`. (Remember that indexes start at `0`, so `[5]` refers to the sixth item in the list, not the fifth.)

Because the `getRandomWord()` function now returns a list of two items instead of a string, `secretWord` will be assigned a list, not a string. You can assign these two items into two separate variables using multiple assignment, which we'll cover in "Multiple Assignment" on page 118.

Deleting Items from Lists

A `del` statement will delete an item at a certain index from a list. Because `del` is a statement, not a function or an operator, it doesn't have parentheses or evaluate to a return value. To try it out, enter the following into the interactive shell:

```
>>> animals = ['aardvark', 'anteater', 'antelope', 'albert']
>>> del animals[1]
>>> animals
['aardvark', 'antelope', 'albert']
```

Notice that when you deleted the item at index `1`, the item that used to be at index `2` became the new value at index `1`; the item that used to be at index `3` became the new value at index `2`; and so on. Everything above the deleted item moved down one index.

You can type `del animals[1]` again and again to keep deleting items from the list:

```
>>> animals = ['aardvark', 'anteater', 'antelope', 'albert']
>>> del animals[1]
>>> animals
['aardvark', 'antelope', 'albert']
>>> del animals[1]
>>> animals
['aardvark', 'albert']
>>> del animals[1]
>>> animals
['aardvark']
```

The length of the `HANGMAN_PICS` list is also the number of guesses the player gets. By deleting strings from this list, you can reduce the number of guesses and make the game harder.

Add the following lines of code to your program between the lines `print('H A N G M A N')` and `missedLetters = ''`:

```
print('H A N G M A N')

difficulty = 'X'
while difficulty not in 'EMH':
    print('Enter difficulty: E - Easy, M - Medium, H - Hard')
    difficulty = input().upper()
```

```
if difficulty == 'M':
    del HANGMAN_PICS[8]
    del HANGMAN_PICS[7]
if difficulty == 'H':
    del HANGMAN_PICS[8]
    del HANGMAN_PICS[7]
    del HANGMAN_PICS[5]
    del HANGMAN_PICS[3]

missedLetters = ''
```

This code deletes items from the `HANGMAN_PICS` list, making it shorter depending on the difficulty level selected. As the difficulty level increases, more items are deleted from the `HANGMAN_PICS` list, resulting in fewer guesses. The rest of the code in the Hangman game uses the length of this list to tell when the player has run out of guesses.

Multiple Assignment

Multiple assignment is a shortcut to assign multiple variables in one line of code. To use multiple assignment, separate your variables with commas and assign them to a list of values. For example, enter the following into the interactive shell:

```
>>> spam, eggs, ham = ['apples', 'cats', 42]
>>> spam
'apples'
>>> eggs
'cats'
>>> ham
42
```

The preceding example is equivalent to the following assignment statements:

```
>>> spam = ['apples', 'cats', 42][0]
>>> eggs = ['apples', 'cats', 42][1]
>>> ham = ['apples', 'cats', 42][2]
```

You must put the same number of variables on the left side of the `=` assignment operator as there are items in the list on the right side. Python will automatically assign the value of the first item in the list to the first variable, the second item's value to the second variable, and so on. If you don't have the same number of variables and items, the Python interpreter will give you an error, like so:

```
>>> spam, eggs, ham, bacon = ['apples', 'cats', 42, 10, 'hello']
Traceback (most recent call last):
```

```
  File "<pyshell#8>", line 1, in <module>
    spam, eggs, ham, bacon = ['apples', 'cats', 42, 10, 'hello']
ValueError: too many values to unpack

>>> spam, eggs, ham, bacon = ['apples', 'cats']
Traceback (most recent call last):
  File "<pyshell#9>", line 1, in <module>
    spam, eggs, ham, bacon = ['apples', 'cats']
ValueError: need more than 2 values to unpack
```

Change lines 120 and 157 of the Hangman code to use multiple assignment with the return value of `getRandomWord()`:

```
119. correctLetters = ''
120. secretWord, secretSet = getRandomWord(words)
121. gameIsDone = False
--snip--
156.                gameIsDone = False
157.                secretWord, secretSet = getRandomWord(words)
158.            else:
159.                break
```

Line 120 assigns the two returned values from `getRandomWord(words)` to `secretWord` and `secretSet`. Line 157 does this again if the player chooses to play another game.

Printing the Word Category for the Player

The last change you'll make is to tell the player which set of words they're trying to guess. This way, the player will know if the secret word is an animal, color, shape, or fruit. Here is the original code:

```
while True:
    displayBoard(missedLetters, correctLetters, secretWord)
```

In your new version of Hangman, add line 124 so your program looks like this:

```
123. while True:
124.     print('The secret word is in the set: ' + secretSet)
125.     displayBoard(missedLetters, correctLetters, secretWord)
```

Now you're done with the changes to the Hangman program. Instead of just a single list of strings, the secret word is chosen from many different lists of strings. The program also tells the player which set of words the secret word is from. Try playing this new version. You can easily change the `words` dictionary starting on line 48 to include more sets of words.

Summary

We're done with Hangman! You learned some new concepts when you added the extra features in this chapter. Even after you've finished writing a game, you can always add more features as you learn more about Python programming.

Dictionaries are similar to lists except that they can use any type of value for an index, not just integers. The indexes in dictionaries are called keys. Multiple assignment is a shortcut to assign multiple variables the values in a list.

Hangman was fairly advanced compared to the previous games in this book. But at this point, you know most of the basic concepts in writing programs: variables, loops, functions, and data types such as lists and dictionaries. The later programs in this book will still be a challenge to master, but you've finished the steepest part of the climb!

10

TIC-TAC-TOE

This chapter features a Tic-Tac-Toe game. Tic-Tac-Toe is normally played with two people. One player is *X* and the other player is *O*. Players take turns placing their *X* or *O*. If a player gets three of their marks on the board in a row, column, or diagonal, they win. When the board fills up with neither player winning, the game ends in a draw.

This chapter doesn't introduce many new programming concepts. The user will play against a simple artificial intelligence, which we will write using our existing programming knowledge. An *artificial intelligence (AI)* is a computer program that can intelligently respond to the player's moves. The AI that plays Tic-Tac-Toe isn't complicated; it's really just a few lines of code.

Let's get started by looking at a sample run of the program. The player makes their move by entering the number of the space they want to take. To help us remember which index in the list is for which space, we'll number the board like a keyboard's number pad, as shown in Figure 10-1.

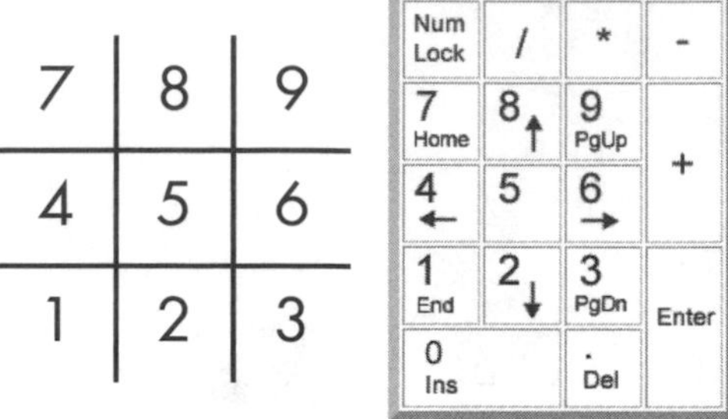

Figure 10-1: The board is numbered like the keyboard's number pad.

> **TOPICS COVERED IN THIS CHAPTER**
>
> - Artificial intelligence
> - List references
> - Short-circuit evaluation
> - The `None` value

Sample Run of Tic-Tac-Toe

Here's what the user sees when they run the Tic-Tac-Toe program. The text the player enters is in bold.

```
Welcome to Tic-Tac-Toe!
Do you want to be X or O?
X
The computer will go first.
O| |
-+-+-
 | |
-+-+-
 | |
What is your next move? (1-9)
3
O| |
-+-+-
 | |
-+-+-
O| |X

What is your next move? (1-9)
4
```

```
O| |O
-+-+-
X| |
-+-+-
O| |X
What is your next move? (1-9)
5
O|O|O
-+-+-
X|X|
-+-+-
O| |X
The computer has beaten you! You lose.
Do you want to play again? (yes or no)
no
```

Source Code for Tic-Tac-Toe

MAKE SURE YOU'RE
USING PYTHON 3,
NOT PYTHON 2!

In a new file, enter the following source code and save it as *tictactoe.py*. Then run the game by pressing F5. If you get errors, compare the code you typed to the book's code with the online diff tool at *https://www.nostarch.com/inventwithpython#diff*.

tictactoe.py

```
# Tic-Tac-Toe

import random

def drawBoard(board):
    # This function prints out the board that it was passed.

    # "board" is a list of 10 strings representing the board (ignore index 0).
    print(board[7] + '|' + board[8] + '|' + board[9])
    print('-+-+-')
    print(board[4] + '|' + board[5] + '|' + board[6])
    print('-+-+-')
    print(board[1] + '|' + board[2] + '|' + board[3])

def inputPlayerLetter():
    # Lets the player type which letter they want to be.
    # Returns a list with the player's letter as the first item and the computer's letter as the second.
    letter = ''
    while not (letter == 'X' or letter == 'O'):
        print('Do you want to be X or O?')
        letter = input().upper()

```

```
    # The first element in the list is the player's letter; the second is the computer's letter.
    if letter == 'X':
        return ['X', 'O']
    else:
        return ['O', 'X']

def whoGoesFirst():
    # Randomly choose which player goes first.
    if random.randint(0, 1) == 0:
        return 'computer'
    else:
        return 'player'

def makeMove(board, letter, move):
    board[move] = letter

def isWinner(bo, le):
    # Given a board and a player's letter, this function returns True if that player has won.
    # We use "bo" instead of "board" and "le" instead of "letter" so we don't have to type as much.
    return ((bo[7] == le and bo[8] == le and bo[9] == le) or # Across the top
    (bo[4] == le and bo[5] == le and bo[6] == le) or # Across the middle
    (bo[1] == le and bo[2] == le and bo[3] == le) or # Across the bottom
    (bo[7] == le and bo[4] == le and bo[1] == le) or # Down the left side
    (bo[8] == le and bo[5] == le and bo[2] == le) or # Down the middle
    (bo[9] == le and bo[6] == le and bo[3] == le) or # Down the right side
    (bo[7] == le and bo[5] == le and bo[3] == le) or # Diagonal
    (bo[9] == le and bo[5] == le and bo[1] == le)) # Diagonal

def getBoardCopy(board):
    # Make a copy of the board list and return it.
    boardCopy = []
    for i in board:
        boardCopy.append(i)
    return boardCopy

def isSpaceFree(board, move):
    # Return True if the passed move is free on the passed board.
    return board[move] == ' '

def getPlayerMove(board):
    # Let the player enter their move.
    move = ' '
    while move not in '1 2 3 4 5 6 7 8 9'.split() or not isSpaceFree(board, int(move)):
        print('What is your next move? (1-9)')
        move = input()
    return int(move)

def chooseRandomMoveFromList(board, movesList):
    # Returns a valid move from the passed list on the passed board.
```

```
    # Returns None if there is no valid move.
    possibleMoves = []
    for i in movesList:
        if isSpaceFree(board, i):
            possibleMoves.append(i)

    if len(possibleMoves) != 0:
        return random.choice(possibleMoves)
    else:
        return None

def getComputerMove(board, computerLetter):
    # Given a board and the computer's letter, determine where to move and return that move.
    if computerLetter == 'X':
        playerLetter = 'O'
    else:
        playerLetter = 'X'

    # Here is the algorithm for our Tic-Tac-Toe AI:
    # First, check if we can win in the next move.
    for i in range(1, 10):
        boardCopy = getBoardCopy(board)
        if isSpaceFree(boardCopy, i):
            makeMove(boardCopy, computerLetter, i)
            if isWinner(boardCopy, computerLetter):
                return i

    # Check if the player could win on their next move and block them.
    for i in range(1, 10):
        boardCopy = getBoardCopy(board)
        if isSpaceFree(boardCopy, i):
            makeMove(boardCopy, playerLetter, i)
            if isWinner(boardCopy, playerLetter):
                return i

    # Try to take one of the corners, if they are free.
    move = chooseRandomMoveFromList(board, [1, 3, 7, 9])
    if move != None:
        return move

    # Try to take the center, if it is free.
    if isSpaceFree(board, 5):
        return 5

    # Move on one of the sides.
    return chooseRandomMoveFromList(board, [2, 4, 6, 8])

def isBoardFull(board):
    # Return True if every space on the board has been taken. Otherwise, return False.
    for i in range(1, 10):
        if isSpaceFree(board, i):
            return False
    return True
```

```
print('Welcome to Tic-Tac-Toe!')

while True:
    # Reset the board.
    theBoard = [' '] * 10
    playerLetter, computerLetter = inputPlayerLetter()
    turn = whoGoesFirst()
    print('The ' + turn + ' will go first.')
    gameIsPlaying = True

    while gameIsPlaying:
        if turn == 'player':
            # Player's turn
            drawBoard(theBoard)
            move = getPlayerMove(theBoard)
            makeMove(theBoard, playerLetter, move)

            if isWinner(theBoard, playerLetter):
                drawBoard(theBoard)
                print('Hooray! You have won the game!')
                gameIsPlaying = False
            else:
                if isBoardFull(theBoard):
                    drawBoard(theBoard)
                    print('The game is a tie!')
                    break
                else:
                    turn = 'computer'

        else:
            # Computer's turn
            move = getComputerMove(theBoard, computerLetter)
            makeMove(theBoard, computerLetter, move)

            if isWinner(theBoard, computerLetter):
                drawBoard(theBoard)
                print('The computer has beaten you! You lose.')
                gameIsPlaying = False
            else:
                if isBoardFull(theBoard):
                    drawBoard(theBoard)
                    print('The game is a tie!')
                    break
                else:
                    turn = 'player'

    print('Do you want to play again? (yes or no)')
    if not input().lower().startswith('y'):
        break
```

Designing the Program

Figure 10-2 shows a flowchart of the Tic-Tac-Toe program. The program starts by asking the player to choose their letter, *X* or *O*. Who takes the first turn is randomly chosen. Then the player and computer take turns making moves.

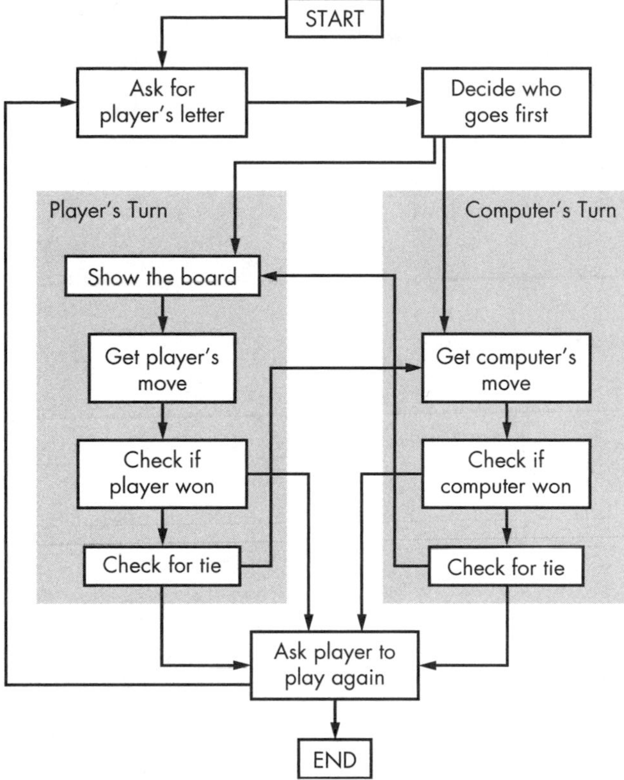

Figure 10-2: Flowchart for Tic-Tac-Toe

The boxes on the left side of the flowchart show what happens during the player's turn, and the ones on the right side show what happens during the computer's turn. After the player or computer makes a move, the program checks whether they won or caused a tie, and then the game switches turns. After the game is over, the program asks the player if they want to play again.

Representing the Board as Data

First, you must figure out how to represent the board as data in a variable. On paper, the Tic-Tac-Toe board is drawn as a pair of horizontal lines and a pair of vertical lines, with an *X*, *O*, or empty space in each of the nine spaces.

In the program, the Tic-Tac-Toe board is represented as a list of strings like the ASCII art of Hangman. Each string represents one of the nine spaces on the board. The strings are either `'X'` for the *X* player, `'O'` for the *O* player, or a single space `' '` for a blank space.

Remember that we're laying out our board like a number pad on a keyboard. So if a list with 10 strings was stored in a variable named `board`, then `board[7]` would be the top-left space on the board, `board[8]` would be the top-middle space, `board[9]` would be the top-right space, and so on. The program ignores the string at index `0` in the list. The player will enter a number from 1 to 9 to tell the game which space they want to move on.

Strategizing with the Game AI

The AI needs to be able to look at the board and decide which types of spaces it will move on. To be clear, we will label three types of spaces on the Tic-Tac-Toe board: corners, sides, and the center. The chart in Figure 10-3 shows what each space is.

The AI's strategy for playing Tic-Tac-Toe will follow a simple *algorithm*—a finite series of instructions to compute a result. A single program can make use of several different algorithms. An algorithm can be represented with a flowchart. The Tic-Tac-Toe AI's algorithm will compute the best move to make, as shown in Figure 10-4.

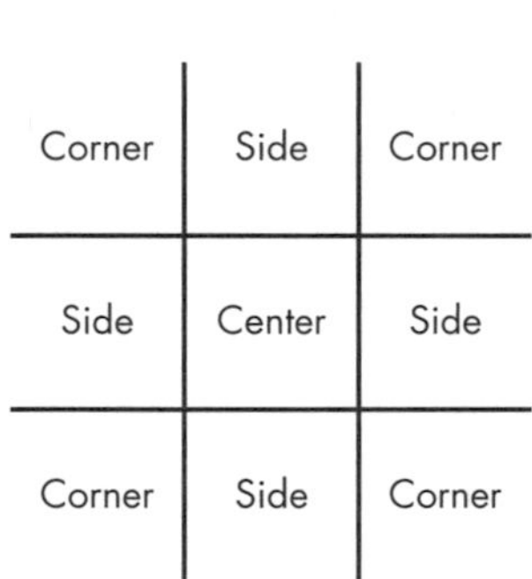

Figure 10-3: Locations of the side, corner, and center spaces

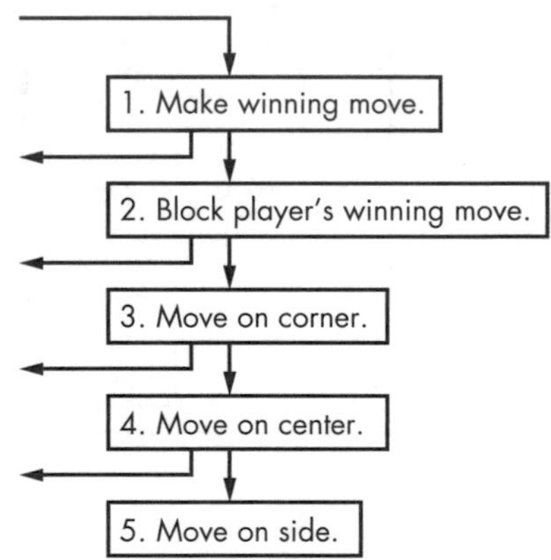

Figure 10-4: The boxes represent the five steps of the "Get computer's move" algorithm. The arrows pointing to the left go to the "Check if computer won" box.

The AI's algorithm has the following steps:

1. See if there's a move the computer can make that will win the game. If there is, make that move. Otherwise, go to step 2.
2. See if there's a move the player can make that will cause the computer to lose the game. If there is, move there to block the player. Otherwise, go to step 3.
3. Check if any of the corner spaces (spaces 1, 3, 7, or 9) are free. If so, move there. If no corner space is free, go to step 4.

4. Check if the center is free. If so, move there. If it isn't, go to step 5.
5. Move on any of the side spaces (spaces 2, 4, 6, or 8). There are no more steps because the side spaces are all that's left if the execution reaches step 5.

This all takes place in the Get computer's move box on the flowchart in Figure 10-2. You could add this information to the flowchart with the boxes in Figure 10-4.

This algorithm is implemented in `getComputerMove()` and the other functions that `getComputerMove()` calls.

Importing the random Module

The first couple of lines are made up of a comment and a line importing the `random` module so that you can call the `randint()` function later on:

```
# Tic-Tac-Toe

import random
```

You've seen both these concepts before, so let's move on to the next part of the program.

Printing the Board on the Screen

In the next part of the code, we define a function to draw the board:

```
def drawBoard(board):
    # This function prints out the board that it was passed.

    # "board" is a list of 10 strings representing the board (ignore index 0).
    print(board[7] + '|' + board[8] + '|' + board[9])
    print('-+-+-')
    print(board[4] + '|' + board[5] + '|' + board[6])
    print('-+-+-')
    print(board[1] + '|' + board[2] + '|' + board[3])
```

The `drawBoard()` function prints the game board represented by the `board` parameter. Remember that the board is represented as a list of 10 strings, where the string at index `1` is the mark on space 1 on the Tic-Tac-Toe board, and so on. The string at index `0` is ignored. Many of the game's functions work by passing a list of 10 strings as the board.

Be sure to get the spacing right in the strings; otherwise, the board will look funny when printed on the screen. Here are some example calls (with an argument for `board`) to `drawBoard()` and what the function would print.

```
>>> drawBoard([' ', ' ', ' ', ' ', 'X', 'O', ' ', 'X', ' ', 'O'])
X| |
-+-+-
X|O|
-+-+-
 | |
>>> drawBoard([' ', ' ', ' ', ' ', ' ', ' ', ' ', ' ', ' ', ' '])
 | |
-+-+-
 | |
-+-+-
 | |
```

The program takes each string and places it on the board in number order according to the keyboard number pad from Figure 10-1, so the first three strings are the bottom row of the board, the next three strings are the middle, and the last three strings are the top.

Letting the Player Choose X or O

Next, we'll define a function to assign *X* or *O* to the player:

```
def inputPlayerLetter():
    # Lets the player enter which letter they want to be.
    # Returns a list with the player's letter as the first item and the
      computer's letter as the second.
    letter = ''
    while not (letter == 'X' or letter == 'O'):
        print('Do you want to be X or O?')
        letter = input().upper()
```

The `inputPlayerLetter()` function asks whether the player wants to be *X* or *O*. The `while` loop's condition contains parentheses, which means the expression inside the parentheses is evaluated first. If the `letter` variable was set to `'X'`, the expression would evaluate like this:

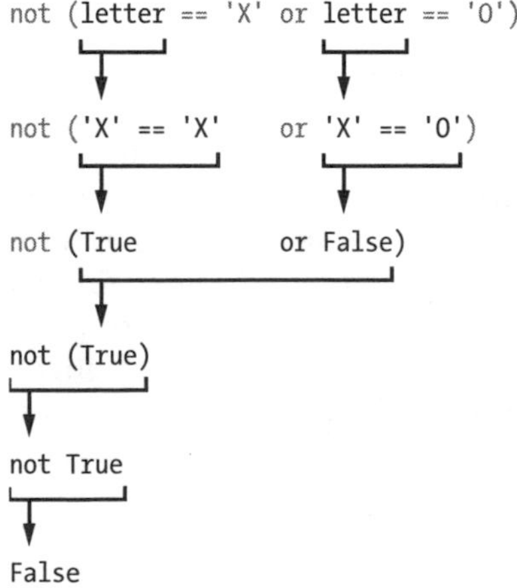

If letter has the value 'X' or 'O', then the loop's condition is False and lets the program execution continue past the while block. If the condition is True, the program will keep asking the player to choose a letter until the player enters an *X* or *O*. Line 21 automatically changes the string returned by the call to input() to uppercase letters with the upper() string method.

The next function returns a list with two items:

```
23.     # The first element in the list is the player's letter; the second is
          the computer's letter.
24.     if letter == 'X':
25.         return ['X', 'O']
26.     else:
27.         return ['O', 'X']
```

The first item (the string at index 0) is the player's letter, and the second item (the string at index 1) is the computer's letter. The if and else statements choose the appropriate list to return.

Deciding Who Goes First

Next we create a function that uses randint() to choose whether the player or computer plays first:

```
29. def whoGoesFirst():
30.     # Randomly choose which player goes first.
31.     if random.randint(0, 1) == 0:
32.         return 'computer'
33.     else:
34.         return 'player'
```

The whoGoesFirst() function does a virtual coin flip to determine whether the computer or the player goes first. The coin flip is done with a call to random.randint(0, 1). There is a 50 percent chance the function returns 0 and a 50 percent chance the function returns 1. If this function call returns a 0, the whoGoesFirst() function returns the string 'computer'. Otherwise, the function returns the string 'player'. The code that calls this function will use the return value to determine who will make the first move of the game.

Placing a Mark on the Board

The makeMove() function is simple:

```
36. def makeMove(board, letter, move):
37.     board[move] = letter
```

The parameters are board, letter, and move. The variable board is the list with 10 strings that represents the state of the board. The variable letter is the player's letter (either 'X' or 'O'). The variable move is the place on the board where that player wants to go (which is an integer from 1 to 9).

But wait—in line 37, this code seems to change one of the items in the board list to the value in letter. Because this code is in a function, though, the board parameter will be forgotten when the function returns. So shouldn't the change to board be forgotten as well?

Actually, this isn't the case, because lists are special when you pass them as arguments to functions. You are actually passing a *reference* to the list, not the list itself. Let's learn about the difference between lists and references to lists.

List References

Enter the following into the interactive shell:

```
>>> spam = 42
>>> cheese = spam
>>> spam = 100
>>> spam
100
>>> cheese
42
```

These results make sense from what you know so far. You assign 42 to the spam variable, then assign the value in spam to the variable cheese. When you later overwrite spam to 100, this doesn't affect the value in cheese. This is because spam and cheese are different variables that store different values.

But lists don't work this way. When you assign a list to a variable, you are actually assigning a list reference to the variable. A *reference* is a value that points to the location where some bit of data is stored. Let's look at some code that will make this easier to understand. Enter this into the interactive shell:

```
❶ >>> spam = [0, 1, 2, 3, 4, 5]
❷ >>> cheese = spam
❸ >>> cheese[1] = 'Hello!'
>>> spam
[0, 'Hello!', 2, 3, 4, 5]
>>> cheese
[0, 'Hello!', 2, 3, 4, 5]
```

The code only changed the cheese list, but it seems that both the cheese and spam lists have changed. This is because the spam variable doesn't contain the list value itself but rather a reference to the list, as shown in Figure 10-5. The list itself is not contained in any variable but rather exists outside of them.

```
❶ spam = [0, 1, 2, 3, 4, 5]
```

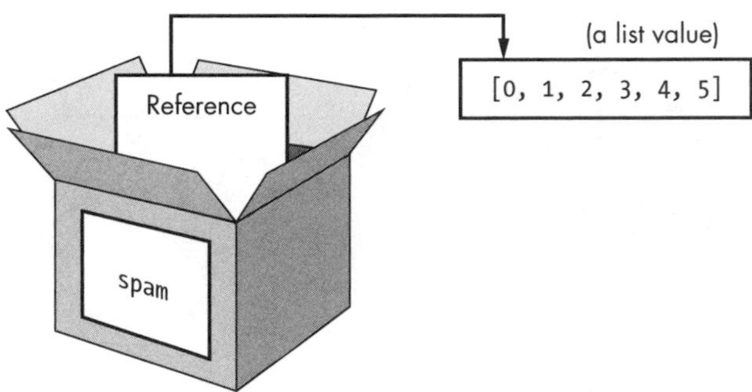

Figure 10-5: The spam *list created at ❶. Variables don't store lists but rather references to lists.*

Notice that `cheese = spam` copies the *list reference* in `spam` to `cheese` ❷, instead of copying the list value itself. Now both `spam` and `cheese` store a reference that refers to the same list value. But there is only one list because the list itself wasn't copied. Figure 10-6 shows this copying.

```
❷ cheese = spam
```

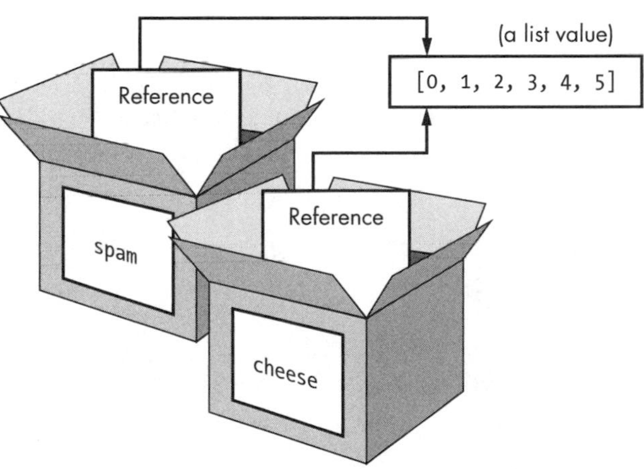

Figure 10-6: The spam *and* cheese *variables store two references to the same list.*

So the `cheese[1] = 'Hello!'` line at ❸ changes the same list that `spam` refers to. This is why `spam` returns the same list value that `cheese` does. They both have references that refer to the same list, as shown in Figure 10-7.

❸ cheese[1] = 'Hello'

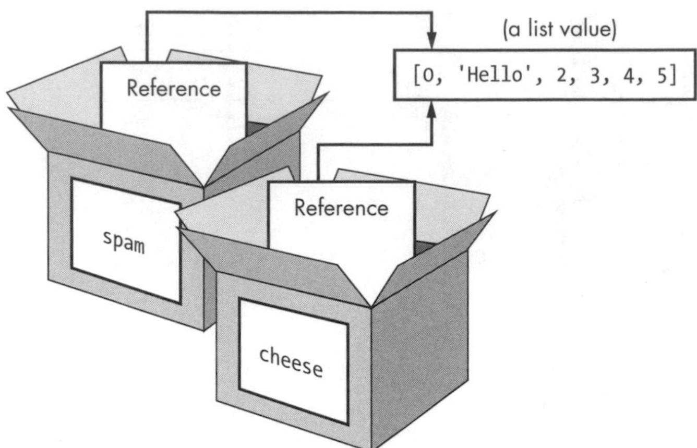

Figure 10-7: Changing the list changes all variables with references to that list.

If you want spam and cheese to store two different lists, you have to create two lists instead of copying a reference:

```
>>> spam = [0, 1, 2, 3, 4, 5]
>>> cheese = [0, 1, 2, 3, 4, 5]
```

In the preceding example, spam and cheese store two different lists (even though these lists are identical in content). Now if you modify one of the lists, it won't affect the other because spam and cheese have references to two different lists:

```
>>> spam = [0, 1, 2, 3, 4, 5]
>>> cheese = [0, 1, 2, 3, 4, 5]
>>> cheese[1] = 'Hello!'
>>> spam
[0, 1, 2, 3, 4, 5]
>>> cheese
[0, 'Hello!', 2, 3, 4, 5]
```

Figure 10-8 shows how the variables and list values are set up in this example.

Dictionaries work the same way. Variables don't store dictionaries; they store *references* to dictionaries.

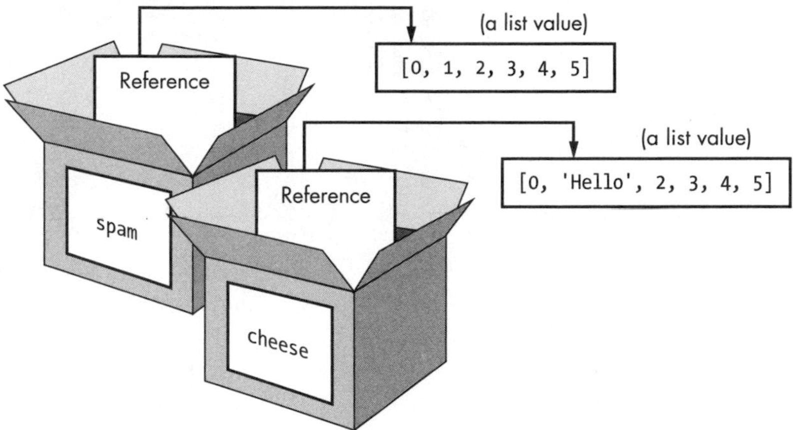

Figure 10-8: The spam and cheese variables now each store references to two different lists.

Using List References in makeMove()

Let's go back to the `makeMove()` function:

```
36. def makeMove(board, letter, move):
37.     board[move] = letter
```

When a list value is passed for the `board` parameter, the function's local variable is really a copy of the reference to the list, not a copy of the list itself. So any changes to `board` in this function will also be made to the original list. Even though `board` is a local variable, the `makeMove()` function modifies the original list.

The `letter` and `move` parameters are copies of the string and integer values that you pass. Since they are copies of values, if you modify `letter` or `move` in this function, the original variables you used when you called `makeMove()` aren't modified.

Checking Whether the Player Won

Lines 42 to 49 in the `isWinner()` function are actually one long `return` statement:

```
39. def isWinner(bo, le):
40.     # Given a board and a player's letter, this function returns True if
          that player has won.
41.     # We use "bo" instead of "board" and "le" instead of "letter" so we
          don't have to type as much.
42.     return ((bo[7] == le and bo[8] == le and bo[9] == le) or # Across the
          top
```

```
43.     (bo[4] == le and bo[5] == le and bo[6] == le) or # Across the middle
44.     (bo[1] == le and bo[2] == le and bo[3] == le) or # Across the bottom
45.     (bo[7] == le and bo[4] == le and bo[1] == le) or # Down the left side
46.     (bo[8] == le and bo[5] == le and bo[2] == le) or # Down the middle
47.     (bo[9] == le and bo[6] == le and bo[3] == le) or # Down the right
          side
48.     (bo[7] == le and bo[5] == le and bo[3] == le) or # Diagonal
49.     (bo[9] == le and bo[5] == le and bo[1] == le)) # Diagonal
```

The bo and le names are shortcuts for the board and letter parameters. These shorter names mean you have less to type in this function. Remember, Python doesn't care what you name your variables.

There are eight possible ways to win at Tic-Tac-Toe: you can have a line across the top, middle, or bottom rows; you can have a line down the left, middle, or right columns; or you can have a line across either of the two diagonals.

Each line of the condition checks whether the three spaces for a given line are equal to the letter provided (combined with the and operator). You combine each line using the or operator to check for the eight different ways to win. This means only one of the eight ways must be True in order for us to say that the player who owns the letter in le is the winner.

Let's pretend that le is 'O' and bo is [' ', 'O', 'O', 'O', ' ', 'X', ' ', 'X', ' ', ' ']. The board would look like this:

```
X| |
-+-+-
 |X|
-+-+-
O|O|O
```

Here is how the expression after the return keyword on line 42 would evaluate. First Python replaces the variables bo and le with the values in each variable:

```
return (('X' == 'O' and ' ' == 'O' and ' ' == 'O') or
(' ' == 'O' and 'X' == 'O' and ' ' == 'O') or
('O' == 'O' and 'O' == 'O' and 'O' == 'O') or
('X' == 'O' and ' ' == 'O' and 'O' == 'O') or
(' ' == 'O' and 'X' == 'O' and 'O' == 'O') or
(' ' == 'O' and ' ' == 'O' and 'O' == 'O') or
('X' == 'O' and 'X' == 'O' and 'O' == 'O') or
(' ' == 'O' and 'X' == 'O' and 'O' == 'O'))
```

Next, Python evaluates all those == comparisons inside the parentheses to Boolean values:

```
return ((False and False and False) or
(False and False and False) or
(True and True and True) or
(False and False and True) or
(False and False and True) or
```

```
(False and False and True) or
(False and False and True) or
(False and False and True))
```

Then the Python interpreter evaluates all the expressions inside the parentheses:

```
return ((False) or
(False) or
(True) or
(False) or
(False) or
(False) or
(False) or
(False))
```

Since now there's only one value inside each of the inner parentheses, you can get rid of them:

```
return (False or
False or
True or
False or
False or
False or
False or
False)
```

Now Python evaluates the expression connected by all those `or` operators:

```
return (True)
```

Once again, get rid of the parentheses, and you are left with one value:

```
return True
```

So given those values for `bo` and `le`, the expression would evaluate to `True`. This is how the program can tell if one of the players has won the game.

Duplicating the Board Data

The `getBoardCopy()` function allows you to easily make a copy of a given 10-string list that represents a Tic-Tac-Toe board in the game.

```
def getBoardCopy(board):
    # Make a copy of the board list and return it.
    boardCopy = []
    for i in board:
        boardCopy.append(i)
    return boardCopy
```

When the AI algorithm is planning its moves, it will sometimes need to make modifications to a temporary copy of the board without changing the actual board. In those cases, we call this function to make a copy of the board's list. The new list is created on line 53.

Right now, the list stored in boardCopy is just an empty list. The for loop will iterate over the board parameter, appending a copy of the string values in the actual board to the duplicate board. After the getBoardCopy() function builds up a copy of the actual board, it returns a reference to this new board in boardCopy, not to the original one in board.

Checking Whether a Space on the Board Is Free

Given a Tic-Tac-Toe board and a possible move, the simple isSpaceFree() function returns whether that move is available or not:

```
58. def isSpaceFree(board, move):
59.     # Return True if the passed move is free on the passed board.
60.     return board[move] == ' '
```

Remember that free spaces in the board lists are marked as a single-space string. If the item at the space's index is not equal to ' ', then the space is taken.

Letting the Player Enter a Move

The getPlayerMove() function asks the player to enter the number for the space they want to move on:

```
62. def getPlayerMove(board):
63.     # Let the player enter their move.
64.     move = ' '
65.     while move not in '1 2 3 4 5 6 7 8 9'.split() or not
          isSpaceFree(board, int(move)):
66.         print('What is your next move? (1-9)')
67.         move = input()
68.     return int(move)
```

The condition on line 65 is True if either of the expressions on the left or right side of the or operator is True. The loop makes sure the execution doesn't continue until the player has entered an integer between 1 and 9. It also checks that the space entered isn't already taken, given the Tic-Tac-Toe board passed to the function for the board parameter. The two lines of code inside the while loop simply ask the player to enter a number from 1 to 9.

The expression on the left side checks whether the player's move is equal to '1', '2', '3', and so on up to '9' by creating a list with these strings (with the split() method) and checking whether move is in this list. In this expression, '1 2 3 4 5 6 7 8 9'.split() evaluates to ['1', '2', '3', '4', '5', '6', '7', '8', '9'], but the former is easier to type.

The expression on the right side checks whether the move the player entered is a free space on the board by calling `isSpaceFree()`. Remember that `isSpaceFree()` returns `True` if the move you pass is available on the board. Note that `isSpaceFree()` expects an integer for `move`, so the `int()` function returns an integer form of `move`.

The `not` operators are added to both sides so that the condition is `True` when either of these requirements is unfulfilled. This causes the loop to ask the player again and again for a number until they enter a proper move.

Finally, line 68 returns the integer form of whatever move the player entered. `input()` returns strings, so the `int()` function is called to return an integer form of the string.

Short-Circuit Evaluation

You may have noticed there's a possible problem in the `getPlayerMove()` function. What if the player entered `'Z'` or some other noninteger string? The expression `move not in '1 2 3 4 5 6 7 8 9'.split()` on the left side of `or` would return `False` as expected, and then Python would evaluate the expression on the right side of the `or` operator.

But calling `int('Z')` would cause Python to give an error, because the `int()` function can take only strings of number characters like `'9'` or `'0'`, not strings like `'Z'`.

To see an example of this kind of error, enter the following into the interactive shell:

```
>>> int('42')
42
>>> int('Z')
Traceback (most recent call last):
  File "<pyshell#3>", line 1, in <module>
    int('Z')
ValueError: invalid literal for int() with base 10: 'Z'
```

But when you play the Tic-Tac-Toe game and try entering `'Z'` for your move, this error doesn't happen. This is because the `while` loop's condition is being short-circuited.

Short-circuiting means that an expression evaluates only part of the way, since the rest of the expression doesn't change what the expression evaluates to. Here's a short program that gives a good example of short-circuiting. Enter the following into the interactive shell:

```
>>> def ReturnsTrue():
        print('ReturnsTrue() was called.')
        return True
>>> def ReturnsFalse():
        print('ReturnsFalse() was called.')
        return False
```

```
>>> ReturnsTrue()
ReturnsTrue() was called.
True
>>> ReturnsFalse()
ReturnsFalse() was called.
False
```

When `ReturnsTrue()` is called, it prints `'ReturnsTrue() was called.'` and then also displays the return value of `ReturnsTrue()`. The same goes for `ReturnsFalse()`.

Now enter the following into the interactive shell:

```
>>> ReturnsFalse() or ReturnsTrue()
ReturnsFalse() was called.
ReturnsTrue() was called.
True
>>> ReturnsTrue() or ReturnsFalse()
ReturnsTrue() was called.
True
```

The first part makes sense: the expression `ReturnsFalse() or ReturnsTrue()` calls both of the functions, so you see both of the printed messages.

But the second expression only shows `'ReturnsTrue() was called.'`, not `'ReturnsFalse() was called.'`. This is because Python didn't call `ReturnsFalse()` at all. Since the left side of the `or` operator is `True`, it doesn't matter what `ReturnsFalse()` returns, so Python doesn't bother calling it. The evaluation was short-circuited.

The same applies for the `and` operator. Now enter the following into the interactive shell:

```
>>> ReturnsTrue() and ReturnsTrue()
ReturnsTrue() was called.
ReturnsTrue() was called.
True
>>> ReturnsFalse() and ReturnsFalse()
ReturnsFalse() was called.
False
```

Again, if the left side of the `and` operator is `False`, then the entire expression is `False`. It doesn't matter whether the right side of `and` is `True` or `False`, so Python doesn't bother evaluating it. Both `False and True` and `False and False` evaluate to `False`, so Python short-circuits the evaluation.

Let's return to lines 65 to 68 of the Tic-Tac-Toe program:

```
65.     while move not in '1 2 3 4 5 6 7 8 9'.split() or not
          isSpaceFree(board, int(move)):
66.         print('What is your next move? (1-9)')
67.         move = input()
68.     return int(move)
```

Since the part of the condition on the left side of the or operator (move not in '1 2 3 4 5 6 7 8 9'.split()) evaluates to True, the Python interpreter knows that the entire expression will evaluate to True. It doesn't matter if the expression on the right side of or evaluates to True or False, because only one value on either side of the or operator needs to be True for the whole expression to be True.

So Python stops checking the rest of the expression and doesn't even bother evaluating the not isSpaceFree(board, int(move)) part. This means the int() and the isSpaceFree() functions are never called as long as move not in '1 2 3 4 5 6 7 8 9'.split() is True.

This works out well for the program, because if the right side of the condition is True, then move isn't a string of a single-digit number. That would cause int() to give us an error. But if move not in '1 2 3 4 5 6 7 8 9'.split() evaluates to True, Python short-circuits not isSpaceFree(board, int(move)) and int(move) is not called.

Choosing a Move from a List of Moves

Now let's look at the chooseRandomMoveFromList() function, which is useful for the AI code later in the program:

```
def chooseRandomMoveFromList(board, movesList):
    # Returns a valid move from the passed list on the passed board.
    # Returns None if there is no valid move.
    possibleMoves = []
    for i in movesList:
        if isSpaceFree(board, i):
            possibleMoves.append(i)
```

Remember that the board parameter is a list of strings that represents a Tic-Tac-Toe board. The second parameter, movesList, is a list of integers of possible spaces from which to choose. For example, if movesList is [1, 3, 7, 9], that means chooseRandomMoveFromList() should return the integer for one of the corner spaces.

However, chooseRandomMoveFromList() first checks that the space is valid to make a move on. The possibleMoves list starts as a blank list. The for loop then iterates over movesList. The moves that cause isSpaceFree() to return True are added to possibleMoves with the append() method.

At this point, the possibleMoves list has all of the moves that were in movesList that are also free spaces. The program then checks whether the list is empty:

```
    if len(possibleMoves) != 0:
        return random.choice(possibleMoves)
    else:
        return None
```

If the list isn't empty, then there's at least one possible move that can be made on the board.

But this list could be empty. For example, if `movesList` was `[1, 3, 7, 9]` but the board represented by the `board` parameter had all the corner spaces already taken, the `possibleMoves` list would be `[]`. In that case, `len(possibleMoves)` evaluates to `0`, and the function returns the value `None`.

The None Value

The `None` value represents the lack of a value. `None` is the only value of the data type `NoneType`. You might use the `None` value when you need a value that means "does not exist" or "none of the above."

For example, say you had a variable named `quizAnswer` that holds the user's answer to some true/false pop quiz question. The variable could hold `True` or `False` for the user's answer. But if the user didn't answer the question, you wouldn't want to set `quizAnswer` to `True` or `False`, because then it would look like the user answered the question. Instead, you could set `quizAnswer` to `None` if the user skipped the question.

As a side note, `None` is not displayed in the interactive shell like other values are:

```
>>> 2 + 2
4
>>> 'This is a string value.'
'This is a string value.'
>>> None
>>>
```

The values of the first two expressions are printed as output on the next line, but `None` has no value, so it is not printed.

Functions that don't seem to return anything actually return the `None` value. For example, `print()` returns `None`:

```
>>> spam = print('Hello world!')
Hello world!
>>> spam == None
True
```

Here we assigned `print('Hello world!')` to `spam`. The `print()` function, like all functions, has a return value. Even though `print()` prints an output, the function call returns `None`. IDLE doesn't show `None` in the interactive shell, but you can tell `spam` is set to `None` because `spam == None` evaluates as `True`.

Creating the Computer's AI

The `getComputerMove()` function contains the AI's code:

```
def getComputerMove(board, computerLetter):
    # Given a board and the computer's letter, determine where to move
      and return that move.
```

```
    if computerLetter == 'X':
        playerLetter = 'O'
    else:
        playerLetter = 'X'
```

The first argument is a Tic-Tac-Toe board for the `board` parameter. The second argument is the letter the computer uses—either `'X'` or `'O'` in the `computerLetter` parameter. The first few lines simply assign the other letter to a variable named `playerLetter`. This way, the same code can be used whether the computer is *X* or *O*.

Remember how the Tic-Tac-Toe AI algorithm works:

1. See if there's a move the computer can make that will win the game. If there is, take that move. Otherwise, go to step 2.
2. See if there's a move the player can make that will cause the computer to lose the game. If there is, the computer should move there to block the player. Otherwise, go to step 3.
3. Check if any of the corners (spaces 1, 3, 7, or 9) are free. If no corner space is free, go to step 4.
4. Check if the center is free. If so, move there. If it isn't, go to step 5.
5. Move on any of the sides (spaces 2, 4, 6, or 8). There are no more steps, because the side spaces are the only spaces left if the execution has reached this step.

The function will return an integer from `1` to `9` representing the computer's move. Let's walk through how each of these steps is implemented in the code.

Checking Whether the Computer Can Win in One Move

Before anything else, if the computer can win in the next move, it should make that winning move immediately.

```
90.     # Here is the algorithm for our Tic-Tac-Toe AI:
91.     # First, check if we can win in the next move.
92.     for i in range(1, 10):
93.         boardCopy = getBoardCopy(board)
94.         if isSpaceFree(boardCopy, i):
95.             makeMove(boardCopy, computerLetter, i)
96.             if isWinner(boardCopy, computerLetter):
97.                 return i
```

The `for` loop that starts on line 92 iterates over every possible move from 1 to 9. The code inside the loop simulates what would happen if the computer made that move.

The first line in the loop (line 93) makes a copy of the `board` list. This is so the simulated move inside the loop doesn't modify the real Tic-Tac-Toe board stored in the `board` variable. The `getBoardCopy()` returns an identical but separate board list value.

Line 94 checks whether the space is free and, if so, simulates making the move on the copy of the board. If this move results in the computer winning, the function returns that move's integer.

If none of the spaces results in winning, the loop ends, and the program execution continues to line 100.

Checking Whether the Player Can Win in One Move

Next, the code will simulate the human player moving on each of the spaces:

```
 99.     # Check if the player could win on their next move and block them.
100.     for i in range(1, 10):
101.         boardCopy = getBoardCopy(board)
102.         if isSpaceFree(boardCopy, i):
103.             makeMove(boardCopy, playerLetter, i)
104.             if isWinner(boardCopy, playerLetter):
105.                 return i
```

The code is similar to the loop on line 92 except the player's letter is put on the board copy. If the `isWinner()` function shows that the player would win with a move, then the computer will return that same move to block this from happening.

If the human player cannot win in one more move, the `for` loop finishes, and the execution continues to line 108.

Checking the Corner, Center, and Side Spaces (in That Order)

If the computer can't make a winning move and doesn't need to block the player's move, it will move to a corner, center, or side space, depending on the spaces available.

The computer first tries to move to one of the corner spaces:

```
107.     # Try to take one of the corners, if they are free.
108.     move = chooseRandomMoveFromList(board, [1, 3, 7, 9])
109.     if move != None:
110.         return move
```

The call to the `chooseRandomMoveFromList()` function with the list `[1, 3, 7, 9]` ensures that the function returns the integer for one of the corner spaces: 1, 3, 7, or 9.

If all the corner spaces are taken, the `chooseRandomMoveFromList()` function returns `None`, and the execution moves on to line 113:

```
112.     # Try to take the center, if it is free.
113.     if isSpaceFree(board, 5):
114.         return 5
```

If none of the corners is available, line 114 moves on the center space if it is free. If the center space isn't free, the execution moves on to line 117:

```
116.     # Move on one of the sides.
117.     return chooseRandomMoveFromList(board, [2, 4, 6, 8])
```

This code also makes a call to `chooseRandomMoveFromList()`, except you pass it a list of the side spaces:`[2, 4, 6, 8]`. This function won't return `None` because the side spaces are the only spaces that can possibly be left. This ends the `getComputerMove()` function and the AI algorithm.

Checking Whether the Board Is Full

The last function is `isBoardFull()`:

```
119. def isBoardFull(board):
120.     # Return True if every space on the board has been taken. Otherwise,
           return False.
121.     for i in range(1, 10):
122.         if isSpaceFree(board, i):
123.             return False
124.     return True
```

This function returns `True` if the 10-string list in the `board` argument it was passed has an `'X'` or `'O'` in every index (except for index `0`, which is ignored). The `for` loop lets us check indexes `1` through `9` on the `board` list. As soon as it finds a free space on the board (that is, when `isSpaceFree(board, i)` returns `True`), the `isBoardFull()` function will return `False`.

If the execution manages to go through every iteration of the loop, then none of the spaces is free. Line 124 will then execute `return True`.

The Game Loop

Line 127 is the first line that isn't inside of a function, so it's the first line of code that executes when you run this program.

```
127. print('Welcome to Tic-Tac-Toe!')
```

This line greets the player before the game starts. The program then enters a `while` loop at line 129:

```
129. while True:
130.     # Reset the board.
131.     theBoard = [' '] * 10
```

The `while` loop keeps looping until the execution encounters a `break` statement. Line 131 sets up the main Tic-Tac-Toe board in a variable named `theBoard`. The board starts empty, which we represent with a list of 10 single space strings.Rather than type out this full list, line 131 uses list replication. It's shorter to type `[' '] * 10` than `[' ', ' ', ' ', ' ', ' ', ' ', ' ', ' ', ' ', ' ']`.

Choosing the Player's Mark and Who Goes First

Next, the `inputPlayerLetter()` function lets the player enter whether they want to be the *X* or *O*:

```
132.     playerLetter, computerLetter = inputPlayerLetter()
```

The function returns a two-string list, either `['X', 'O']` or `['O', 'X']`. We use multiple assignment to set `playerLetter` to the first item in the returned list and `computerLetter` to the second.

From there, the `whoGoesFirst()` function randomly decides who goes first, returning either the string `'player'` or the string `'computer'`, and then line 134 tells the player who will go first:

```
133.     turn = whoGoesFirst()
134.     print('The ' + turn + ' will go first.')
135.     gameIsPlaying = True
```

The `gameIsPlaying` variable keeps track of whether the game is still being played or if someone has won or tied.

Running the Player's Turn

Line 137's loop will keep going back and forth between the code for the player's turn and the computer's turn, as long as `gameIsPlaying` is set to `True`:

```
137.     while gameIsPlaying:
138.         if turn == 'player':
139.             # Player's turn
140.             drawBoard(theBoard)
141.             move = getPlayerMove(theBoard)
142.             makeMove(theBoard, playerLetter, move)
```

The `turn` variable was originally set to either `'player'` or `'computer'` by the `whoGoesFirst()` call on line 133. If `turn` equals `'computer'`, then line 138's condition is `False`, and the execution jumps to line 156.

But if line 138 evaluates to `True`, line 140 calls `drawBoard()` and passes the `theBoard` variable to print the Tic-Tac-Toe board on the screen. Then `getPlayerMove()` lets the player enter their move (and also makes sure it is a valid move). The `makeMove()` function adds the player's *X* or *O* to `theBoard`.

Now that the player has made their move, the program should check whether they have won the game:

```
144.         if isWinner(theBoard, playerLetter):
145.             drawBoard(theBoard)
146.             print('Hooray! You have won the game!')
147.             gameIsPlaying = False
```

If the isWinner() function returns True, the if block's code displays the winning board and prints a message telling the player they have won. The gameIsPlaying variable is also set to False so that the execution doesn't continue on to the computer's turn.

If the player didn't win with their last move, maybe their move filled up the entire board and tied the game. The program checks that condition next with an else statement:

```
148.         else:
149.             if isBoardFull(theBoard):
150.                 drawBoard(theBoard)
151.                 print('The game is a tie!')
152.                 break
```

In this else block, the isBoardFull() function returns True if there are no more moves to make. In that case, the if block starting at line 149 displays the tied board and tells the player a tie has occurred. The execution then breaks out of the while loop and jumps to line 173.

If the player hasn't won or tied the game, the program enters another else statement:

```
153.             else:
154.                 turn = 'computer'
```

Line 154 sets the turn variable to 'computer' so that the program will execute the code for the computer's turn on the next iteration.

Running the Computer's Turn

If the turn variable wasn't 'player' for the condition on line 138, then it must be the computer's turn. The code in this else block is similar to the code for the player's turn:

```
156.     else:
157.         # Computer's turn
158.         move = getComputerMove(theBoard, computerLetter)
159.         makeMove(theBoard, computerLetter, move)
160.
161.         if isWinner(theBoard, computerLetter):
162.             drawBoard(theBoard)
163.             print('The computer has beaten you! You lose.')
164.             gameIsPlaying = False
```

```
165.            else:
166.                if isBoardFull(theBoard):
167.                    drawBoard(theBoard)
168.                    print('The game is a tie!')
169.                    break
170.                else:
171.                    turn = 'player'
```

Lines 157 to 171 are almost identical to the code for the player's turn on lines 139 to 154. The only difference is that this code uses the computer's letter and calls `getComputerMove()`.

If the game isn't won or tied, line 171 sets `turn` to the player's turn. There are no more lines of code inside the `while` loop, so the execution jumps back to the `while` statement on line 137.

Asking the Player to Play Again

Finally, the program asks the player if they want to play another game:

```
173.    print('Do you want to play again? (yes or no)')
174.    if not input().lower().startswith('y'):
175.        break
```

Lines 173 to 175 are executed immediately after the `while` block started by the `while` statement on line 137. `gameIsPlaying` is set to `False` when the game has ended, so at this point the game asks the player if they want to play again.

The `not input().lower().startswith('y')` expression will be `True` if the player enters anything that doesn't start with a `'y'`. In that case, the `break` statement executes. That breaks the execution out of the `while` loop that was started on line 129. But since there are no more lines of code after that `while` block, the program terminates and the game ends.

Summary

Creating a program with AI comes down to carefully considering all the possible situations the AI can encounter and how it should respond in each of those situations. The Tic-Tac-Toe AI is simple because not as many moves are possible in Tic-Tac-Toe as in a game like chess or checkers.

Our computer AI checks for any possible winning moves. Otherwise, it checks whether it must block the player's move. Then the AI simply chooses any available corner space, then the center space, then the side spaces. This is a simple algorithm for the computer to follow.

The key to implementing our AI is to make copies of the board data and simulate moves on the copy. That way, the AI code can see whether a move results in a win or loss. Then the AI can make that move on the real board. This type of simulation is effective at predicting what is or isn't a good move.

11

THE BAGELS DEDUCTION GAME

Bagels is a deduction game in which the player tries to guess a random three-digit number (with no repeating digits) generated by the computer. After each guess, the computer gives the player three types of clues:

Bagels None of the three digits guessed is in the secret number.

Pico One of the digits is in the secret number, but the guess has the digit in the wrong place.

Fermi The guess has a correct digit in the correct place.

The computer can give multiple clues, which are sorted in alphabetical order. If the secret number is 456 and the player's guess is 546, the clues would be "fermi pico pico." The "fermi" is from the 6 and "pico pico" are from the 4 and 5.

In this chapter, you'll learn a few new methods and functions that come with Python. You'll also learn about augmented assignment operators and string interpolation. While they don't let you do anything you couldn't do before, they are nice shortcuts to make coding easier.

TOPICS COVERED IN THIS CHAPTER

- The `random.shuffle()` function
- Augmented assignment operators, `+=`, `-=`, `*=`, `/=`
- The `sort()` list method
- The `join()` string method
- String interpolation
- The conversion specifier `%s`
- Nested loops

Sample Run of Bagels

Here's what the user sees when they run the Bagels program. The text the player enters is shown in bold.

```
I am thinking of a 3-digit number. Try to guess what it is.
The clues I give are...
When I say:    That means:
  Bagels       None of the digits is correct.
  Pico         One digit is correct but in the wrong position.
  Fermi        One digit is correct and in the right position.
I have thought up a number. You have 10 guesses to get it.
Guess #1:
123
Fermi
Guess #2:
453
Pico
Guess #3:
425
Fermi
Guess #4:
326
Bagels
Guess #5:
489
Bagels
Guess #6:
075
Fermi Fermi
Guess #7:
015
Fermi Pico
Guess #8:
175
```

```
You got it!
Do you want to play again? (yes or no)
no
```

Source Code for Bagels

MAKE SURE YOU'RE USING PYTHON 3, NOT PYTHON 2!

In a new file, enter the following source code and save it as *bagels.py*. Then run the game by pressing F5. If you get errors, compare the code you typed to the book's code with the online diff tool at *https://www.nostarch.com/inventwithpython#diff*.

bagels.py

```
import random

NUM_DIGITS = 3
MAX_GUESS = 10

def getSecretNum():
    # Returns a string of unique random digits that is NUM_DIGITS long.
    numbers = list(range(10))
    random.shuffle(numbers)
    secretNum = ''
    for i in range(NUM_DIGITS):
        secretNum += str(numbers[i])
    return secretNum

def getClues(guess, secretNum):
    # Returns a string with the Pico, Fermi, & Bagels clues to the user.
    if guess == secretNum:
        return 'You got it!'

    clues = []
    for i in range(len(guess)):
        if guess[i] == secretNum[i]:
            clues.append('Fermi')
        elif guess[i] in secretNum:
            clues.append('Pico')
    if len(clues) == 0:
        return 'Bagels'

    clues.sort()
    return ' '.join(clues)

def isOnlyDigits(num):
    # Returns True if num is a string of only digits. Otherwise, returns False.
    if num == '':
        return False
```

```
    for i in num:
        if i not in '0 1 2 3 4 5 6 7 8 9'.split():
            return False

    return True


print('I am thinking of a %s-digit number. Try to guess what it is.' % (NUM_DIGITS))
print('The clues I give are...')
print('When I say:    That means:')
print('  Bagels       None of the digits is correct.')
print('  Pico         One digit is correct but in the wrong position.')
print('  Fermi        One digit is correct and in the right position.')

while True:
    secretNum = getSecretNum()
    print('I have thought up a number. You have %s guesses to get it.' % (MAX_GUESS))

    guessesTaken = 1
    while guessesTaken <= MAX_GUESS:
        guess = ''
        while len(guess) != NUM_DIGITS or not isOnlyDigits(guess):
            print('Guess #%s: ' % (guessesTaken))
            guess = input()

        print(getClues(guess, secretNum))
        guessesTaken += 1

        if guess == secretNum:
            break
        if guessesTaken > MAX_GUESS:
            print('You ran out of guesses. The answer was %s.' % (secretNum))

    print('Do you want to play again? (yes or no)')
    if not input().lower().startswith('y'):
        break
```

Flowchart for Bagels

The flowchart in Figure 11-1 describes what happens in this game and the order in which each step can happen.

The flowchart for Bagels is pretty simple. The computer generates a secret number, the player tries to guess that number, and the computer gives the player clues based on their guess. This happens over and over again until the player either wins or loses. After the game finishes, whether the player won or not, the computer asks the player whether they want to play again.

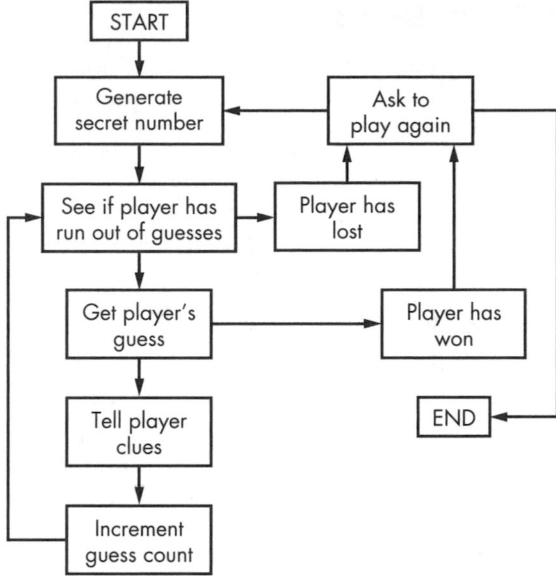

Figure 11-1: Flowchart for the Bagels game

Importing random and Defining getSecretNum()

At the start of the program, we'll import the `random` module and set up some global variables. Then we'll define a function named `getSecretNum()`.

```
1. import random
2.
3. NUM_DIGITS = 3
4. MAX_GUESS = 10
5.
6. def getSecretNum():
7.     # Returns a string of unique random digits that is NUM_DIGITS long.
```

Instead of using the integer `3` for the number of digits in the answer, we use the constant variable `NUM_DIGITS`. The same goes for the number of guesses the player gets; we use the constant variable `MAX_GUESS` instead of the integer `10`. Now it will be easy to change the number of guesses or secret number digits. Just change the values at line 3 or 4, and the rest of the program will still work without any more changes.

The `getSecretNum()` function generates a secret number that contains only unique digits. The Bagels game is much more fun if you don't have duplicate digits in the secret number, such as `'244'` or `'333'`. We'll use some new Python functions to make this happen in `getSecretNum()`.

Shuffling a Unique Set of Digits

The first two lines of getSecretNum() shuffle a set of nonrepeating numbers:

```
8.      numbers = list(range(10))
9.      random.shuffle(numbers)
```

Line 8's list(range(10)) evaluates to [0, 1, 2, 3, 4, 5, 6, 7, 8, 9], so the numbers variable contains a list of all 10 digits.

Changing List Item Order with the random.shuffle() Function

The random.shuffle() function randomly changes the order of a list's items (in this case, the list of digits). This function doesn't return a value but rather modifies the list you pass it *in place*. This is similar to the way the makeMove() function in Chapter 10's Tic-Tac-Toe game modified the list it was passed in place, rather than returning a new list with the change. This is why you do *not* write code like numbers = random.shuffle(numbers).

Try experimenting with the shuffle() function by entering the following code into the interactive shell:

```
>>> import random
>>> spam = list(range(10))
>>> print(spam)
[0, 1, 2, 3, 4, 5, 6, 7, 8, 9]
>>> random.shuffle(spam)
>>> print(spam)
[3, 0, 5, 9, 6, 8, 2, 4, 1, 7]
>>> random.shuffle(spam)
>>> print(spam)
[9, 8, 3, 5, 4, 7, 1, 2, 0, 6]
```

Each time random.shuffle() is called on spam, the items in the spam list are shuffled. You'll see how we use the shuffle() function to make a secret number next.

Getting the Secret Number from the Shuffled Digits

The secret number will be a string of the first NUM_DIGITS digits of the shuffled list of integers:

```
10.     secretNum = ''
11.     for i in range(NUM_DIGITS):
12.         secretNum += str(numbers[i])
13.     return secretNum
```

The secretNum variable starts out as a blank string. The for loop on line 11 iterates NUM_DIGITS number of times. On each iteration through the loop, the integer at index i is pulled from the shuffled list, converted to a string, and concatenated to the end of secretNum.

For example, if numbers refers to the list [9, 8, 3, 5, 4, 7, 1, 2, 0, 6], then on the first iteration, numbers[0] (that is, 9) will be passed to str(); this returns '9', which is concatenated to the end of secretNum. On the second iteration, the same happens with numbers[1] (that is, 8), and on the third iteration the same happens with numbers[2] (that is, 3). The final value of secretNum that is returned is '983'.

Notice that secretNum in this function contains a string, not an integer. This may seem odd, but remember that you cannot concatenate integers. The expression 9 + 8 + 3 evaluates to 20, but what you want is '9' + '8' + '3', which evaluates to '983'.

Augmented Assignment Operators

The += operator on line 12 is one of the *augmented assignment operators*. Normally, if you want to add or concatenate a value to a variable, you use code that looks like this:

```
>>> spam = 42
>>> spam = spam + 10
>>> spam
52
>>> eggs = 'Hello '
>>> eggs = eggs + 'world!'
>>> eggs
'Hello world!'
```

The augmented assignment operators are shortcuts that free you from retyping the variable name. The following code does the same thing as the previous code:

```
>>> spam = 42
>>> spam += 10       # The same as spam = spam + 10
>>> spam
52
>>> eggs = 'Hello '
>>> eggs += 'world!' # The same as eggs = eggs + 'world!'
>>> eggs
'Hello world!'
```

There are other augmented assignment operators as well. Enter the following into the interactive shell:

```
>>> spam = 42
>>> spam -= 2
>>> spam
40
```

The statement spam -= 2 is the same as the statement spam = spam - 2, so the expression evaluates to spam = 42 - 2 and then to spam = 40.

There are augmented assignment operators for multiplication and division, too:

```
>>> spam *= 3
>>> spam
120
>>> spam /= 10
>>> spam
12.0
```

The statement `spam *= 3` is the same as `spam = spam * 3`. So, since `spam` was set equal to `40` earlier, the full expression would be `spam = 40 * 3`, which evaluates to `120`. The expression `spam /= 10` is the same as `spam = spam / 10`, and `spam = 120 / 10` evaluates to `12.0`. Notice that `spam` becomes a floating point number after it's divided.

Calculating the Clues to Give

The `getClues()` function will return a string with fermi, pico, and bagels clues depending on the `guess` and `secretNum` parameters.

```
15. def getClues(guess, secretNum):
16.     # Returns a string with the Pico, Fermi, & Bagels clues to the user.
17.     if guess == secretNum:
18.         return 'You got it!'
19.
20.     clues = []
21.     for i in range(len(guess)):
22.         if guess[i] == secretNum[i]:
23.             clues.append('Fermi')
24.         elif guess[i] in secretNum:
25.             clues.append('Pico')
```

The most obvious step is to check whether the guess is the same as the secret number, which we do in line 17. In that case, line 18 returns `'You got it!'`.

If the guess isn't the same as the secret number, the program must figure out what clues to give the player. The list in `clues` will start empty and have `'Fermi'` and `'Pico'` strings added as needed.

The program does this by looping through each possible index in `guess` and `secretNum`. The strings in both variables will be the same length, so line 21 could have used either `len(guess)` or `len(secretNum)` and worked the same. As the value of `i` changes from `0` to `1` to `2`, and so on, line 22 checks whether the first, second, third, and so on character of `guess` is the same as the character in the corresponding index of `secretNum`. If so, line 23 adds the string `'Fermi'` to `clues`.

Otherwise, line 24 checks whether the number at the ith position in guess exists anywhere in secretNum. If so, you know that the number is somewhere in the secret number but not in the same position. In that case, line 25 then adds 'Pico' to clues.

If the clues list is empty after the loop, then you know that there are no correct digits at all in guess:

```
26.     if len(clues) == 0:
27.         return 'Bagels'
```

In this case, line 27 returns the string 'Bagels' as the only clue.

The sort() List Method

Lists have a method named sort() that arranges the list items in alphabetical or numerical order. When the sort() method is called, it doesn't return a sorted list but rather sorts the list in place. This is just like how the shuffle() method works.

You would never want to use return spam.sort() because that would return the value None. Instead you want a separate line, spam.sort(), and then the line return spam.

Enter the following into the interactive shell:

```
>>> spam = ['cat', 'dog', 'bat', 'anteater']
>>> spam.sort()
>>> spam
['anteater', 'bat', 'cat', 'dog']
>>> spam = [9, 8, 3, 5.5, 5, 7, 1, 2.1, 0, 6]
>>> spam.sort()
>>> spam
[0, 1, 2.1, 3, 5, 5.5, 6, 7, 8, 9]
```

When we sort a list of strings, the strings are returned in alphabetical order, but when we sort a list of numbers, the numbers are returned in numerical order.

On line 29, we use sort() on clues:

```
29.     clues.sort()
```

The reason you want to sort the clue list alphabetically is to get rid of extra information that would help the player guess the secret number more easily. If clues was ['Pico', 'Fermi', 'Pico'], that would tell the player that the center digit of the guess is in the correct position. Since the other two clues are both Pico, the player would know that all they have to do to get the secret number is swap the first and third digits.

If the clues are always sorted in alphabetical order, the player can't be sure which number the Fermi clue refers to. This makes the game harder and more fun to play.

The join() String Method

The join() string method returns a list of strings as a single string joined together.

```
30.     return ' '.join(clues)
```

The string that the method is called on (on line 30, this is a single space, ' ') appears between each string in the list. To see an example, enter the following into the interactive shell:

```
>>> ' '.join(['My', 'name', 'is', 'Zophie'])
'My name is Zophie'
>>> ', '.join(['Life', 'the Universe', 'and Everything'])
'Life, the Universe, and Everything'
```

So the string that is returned on line 30 is each string in clue combined with a single space between each string. The join() string method is sort of like the opposite of the split() string method. While split() returns a list from a split-up string, join() returns a string from a combined list.

Checking Whether a String Has Only Numbers

The isOnlyDigits() function helps determine whether the player entered a valid guess:

```
32. def isOnlyDigits(num):
33.     # Returns True if num is a string of only digits. Otherwise, returns
          False.
34.     if num == '':
35.         return False
```

Line 34 first checks whether num is the blank string and, if so, returns False. The for loop then iterates over each character in the string num:

```
37.     for i in num:
38.         if i not in '0 1 2 3 4 5 6 7 8 9'.split():
39.             return False
40.
41.     return True
```

The value of i will have a single character on each iteration. Inside the for block, the code checks whether i exists in the list returned by '0 1 2 3 4 5 6 7 8 9'.split(). (The return value from split() is equivalent to ['0', '1',

'2', '3', '4', '5', '6', '7', '8', '9'].) If i doesn't exist in that list, you know there's a nondigit character in num. In that case, line 39 returns False.

But if the execution continues past the for loop, then you know that every character in num is a digit. In that case, line 41 returns True.

Starting the Game

After all of the function definitions, line 44 is the actual start of the program:

```
44. print('I am thinking of a %s-digit number. Try to guess what it is.' %
      (NUM_DIGITS))
45. print('The clues I give are...')
46. print('When I say:    That means:')
47. print('  Bagels       None of the digits is correct.')
48. print('  Pico         One digit is correct but in the wrong position.')
49. print('  Fermi        One digit is correct and in the right position.')
```

The print() function calls tell the player the rules of the game and what the pico, fermi, and bagels clues mean. Line 44's print() call has % (NUM_DIGITS) added to the end and %s inside the string. This is a technique known as *string interpolation*.

String Interpolation

String interpolation, also known as *string formatting*, is a coding shortcut. Normally, if you want to use the string values inside variables in another string, you have to use the + concatenation operator:

```
>>> name = 'Alice'
>>> event = 'party'
>>> location = 'the pool'
>>> day = 'Saturday'
>>> time = '6:00pm'
>>> print('Hello, ' + name + '. Will you go to the ' + event + ' at ' +
location + ' this ' + day + ' at ' + time + '?')
Hello, Alice. Will you go to the party at the pool this Saturday at 6:00pm?
```

As you can see, it can be time-consuming to type a line that concatenates several strings. Instead, you can use string interpolation, which lets you put placeholders like %s into the string. These placeholders are called *conversion specifiers*. Once you've put in the conversion specifiers, you can put all the variable names at the end of the string. Each %s is replaced with a variable at the end of the line, in the order in which you entered the variable. For example, the following code does the same thing as the previous code:

```
>>> name = 'Alice'
>>> event = 'party'
>>> location = 'the pool'
>>> day = 'Saturday'
```

```
>>> time = '6:00pm'
>>> print('Hello, %s. Will you go to the %s at %s this %s at %s?' % (name,
event, location, day, time))
Hello, Alice. Will you go to the party at the pool this Saturday at 6:00pm?
```

Notice that the first variable name is used for the first %s, the second variable for the second %s, and so on. You must have the same number of %s conversion specifiers as you have variables.

Another benefit of using string interpolation instead of string concatenation is that interpolation works with any data type, not just strings. All values are automatically converted to the string data type. If you concatenated an integer to a string, you'd get this error:

```
>>> spam = 42
>>> print('Spam == ' + spam)
Traceback (most recent call last):
  File "<stdin>", line 1, in <module>
TypeError: Can't convert 'int' object to str implicitly
```

String concatenation can only combine two strings, but spam is an integer. You would have to remember to put str(spam) instead of spam.

Now enter this into the interactive shell:

```
>>> spam = 42
>>> print('Spam is %s' % (spam))
Spam is 42
```

With string interpolation, this conversion to strings is done for you.

The Game Loop

Line 51 is an infinite while loop that has a condition of True, so it will loop forever until a break statement is executed:

```
51. while True:
52.     secretNum = getSecretNum()
53.     print('I have thought up a number. You have %s guesses to get it.' %
          (MAX_GUESS))
54.
55.     guessesTaken = 1
56.     while guessesTaken <= MAX_GUESS:
```

Inside the infinite loop, you get a secret number from the getSecretNum() function. This secret number is assigned to secretNum. Remember, the value in secretNum is a string, not an integer.

Line 53 tells the player how many digits are in the secret number by using string interpolation instead of string concatenation. Line 55 sets the variable guessesTaken to 1 to mark this is as the first guess. Then line 56 has a new while loop that loops as long as the player has guesses left. In code, this is when guessesTaken is less than or equal to MAX_GUESS.

Notice that the while loop on line 56 is inside another while loop that started on line 51. These loops inside loops are called *nested loops*. Any break or continue statements, such as the break statement on line 66, will only break or continue out of the innermost loop, not any of the outer loops.

Getting the Player's Guess

The guess variable holds the player's guess returned from input(). The code keeps looping and asking the player for a guess until they enter a valid guess:

```
57.         guess = ''
58.         while len(guess) != NUM_DIGITS or not isOnlyDigits(guess):
59.             print('Guess #%s: ' % (guessesTaken))
60.             guess = input()
```

A valid guess has only digits and the same number of digits as the secret number. The while loop that starts on line 58 checks for the validity of the guess.

The guess variable is set to the blank string on line 57, so the while loop's condition on line 58 is False the first time it is checked, ensuring the execution enters the loop starting on line 59.

Getting the Clues for the Player's Guess

After execution gets past the while loop that started on line 58, guess contains a valid guess. Now the program passes guess and secretNum to the getClues() function:

```
62.         print(getClues(guess, secretNum))
63.         guessesTaken += 1
```

It returns a string of the clues, which are displayed to the player on line 62. Line 63 increments guessesTaken using the augmented assignment operator for addition.

Checking Whether the Player Won or Lost

Now we figure out if the player won or lost the game:

```
65.         if guess == secretNum:
66.             break
67.         if guessesTaken > MAX_GUESS:
68.             print('You ran out of guesses. The answer was %s.' %
                  (secretNum))
```

If guess is the same value as secretNum, the player has correctly guessed the secret number, and line 66 breaks out of the while loop that was started on line 56. If not, then execution continues to line 67, where the program checks whether the player ran out of guesses.

If the player still has more guesses, execution jumps back to the `while` loop on line 56, where it lets the player have another guess. If the player runs out of guesses (or the program breaks out of the loop with the `break` statement on line 66), execution proceeds past the loop and to line 70.

Asking the Player to Play Again

Line 70 asks the player whether they want to play again:

```
70.     print('Do you want to play again? (yes or no)')
71.     if not input().lower().startswith('y'):
72.         break
```

The player's response is returned by `input()`, has the `lower()` method called on it, and then the `startswith()` method called on that to check if the player's response begins with a `y`. If it doesn't, the program breaks out of the `while` loop that started on line 51. Since there's no more code after this loop, the program terminates.

If the response does begin with `y`, the program does not execute the `break` statement and execution jumps back to line 51. The program then generates a new secret number so the player can play a new game.

Summary

Bagels is a simple game to program but can be difficult to win. But if you keep playing, you'll eventually discover better ways to guess using the clues the game gives you. This is much like how you'll get better at programming the more you keep at it.

This chapter introduced a few new functions and methods—`shuffle()`, `sort()`, and `join()`—along with a couple of handy shortcuts. Augmented assignment operators require less typing when you want to change a variable's relative value; for example, `spam = spam + 1` can be shortened to `spam += 1`. With string interpolation, you can make your code much more readable by placing `%s` (called a *conversion specifier*) inside the string instead of using many string concatenation operations.

In Chapter 12, we won't be doing any programming, but the concepts—Cartesian coordinates and negative numbers—will be necessary for the games in the later chapters of the book. These math concepts are used not only in the Sonar Treasure Hunt, Reversegam, and Dodger games we will be making but also in many other games. Even if you already know about these concepts, give Chapter 12 a brief read to refresh yourself.

12

THE CARTESIAN COORDINATE SYSTEM

This chapter goes over some simple mathematical concepts you will use in the rest of this book. In two-dimensional (2D) games, the graphics on the screen can move left or right and up or down. These games need a way to translate a place on the screen into integers the program can deal with.

This is where the *Cartesian coordinate system* comes in. *Coordinates* are numbers that represent a specific point on the screen. These numbers can be stored as integers in your program's variables.

TOPICS COVERED IN THIS CHAPTER

- Cartesian coordinate systems
- The x-axis and y-axis
- Negative numbers
- Pixels
- The commutative property of addition
- Absolute values and the abs() function

Grids and Cartesian Coordinates

A common way to refer to specific places on a chessboard is by marking each row and column with letters and numbers. Figure 12-1 shows a chessboard that has each row and column marked.

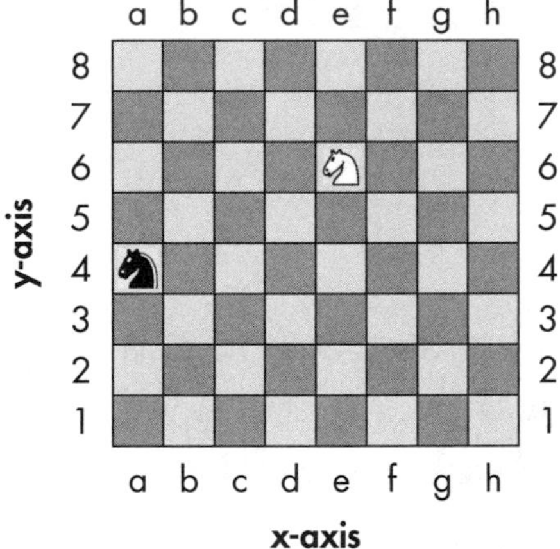

Figure 12-1: A sample chessboard with a black knight at (a, 4) and a white knight at (e, 6)

A coordinate for a space on the chessboard is a combination of a row and a column. In chess, the knight piece looks like a horse head. The white knight in Figure 12-1 is located at the point (e, 6) since it is in column e and row 6, and the black knight is located at point (a, 4) because it is in column a and row 4.

You can think of a chessboard as a Cartesian coordinate system. By using a row label and column label, you can give a coordinate that is for one—and only one—space on the board. If you've learned about Cartesian coordinate systems in math class, you may know that numbers are used for both the rows and columns. A chessboard using numerical coordinates would look like Figure 12-2.

The numbers going left and right along the columns are part of the *x-axis*. The numbers going up and down along the rows are part of the *y-axis*. Coordinates are always described with the x-coordinate first, followed by the y-coordinate. In Figure 12-2, the x-coordinate for the white knight is 5 and the y-coordinate is 6, so the white knight is located at the coordinates (5, 6) and not (6, 5). Similarly, the black knight is located at the coordinate (1, 4), not (4, 1), since the black knight's x-coordinate is 1 and its y-coordinate is 4.

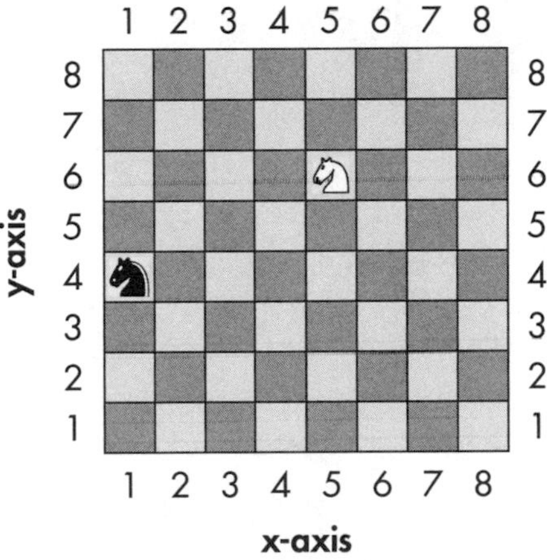

Figure 12-2: The same chessboard but with numeric coordinates for both rows and columns

Notice that for the black knight to move to the white knight's position, the black knight must move two spaces up and four spaces to the right. But you don't need to look at the board to figure this out. If you know the white knight is located at (5, 6) and the black knight is located at (1, 4), you can use subtraction to figure out this information.

Subtract the black knight's x-coordinate from the white knight's x-coordinate: 5 – 1 = 4. The black knight has to move along the x-axis by four spaces. Now subtract the black knight's y-coordinate from the white knight's y-coordinate: 6 – 4 = 2. The black knight has to move along the y-axis by two spaces.

By doing some math with the coordinate numbers, you can figure out the distances between two coordinates.

Negative Numbers

Cartesian coordinates also use *negative numbers*—numbers that are less than zero. A minus sign in front of a number shows it is negative: –1 is less than 0. And –2 is less than –1. But 0 itself isn't positive or negative. In Figure 12-3, you can see the positive numbers increasing to the right and the negative numbers decreasing to the left on a number line.

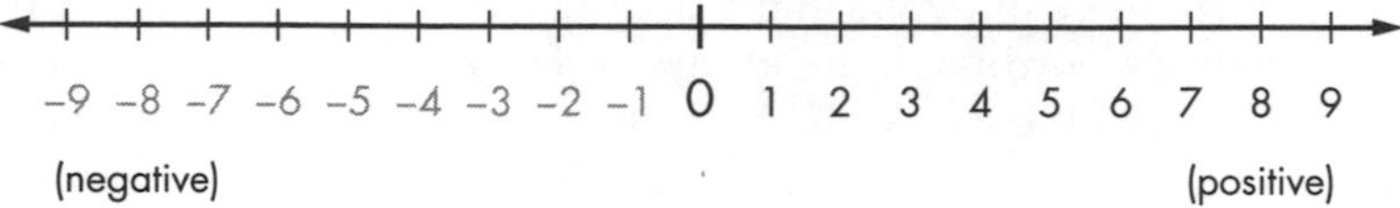

Figure 12-3: A number line with positive and negative numbers

The number line is useful to see subtraction and addition. You can think of the expression 5 + 3 as the white knight starting at position 5 and moving 3 spaces to the right. As you can see in Figure 12-4, the white knight ends up at position 8. This makes sense, because 5 + 3 is 8.

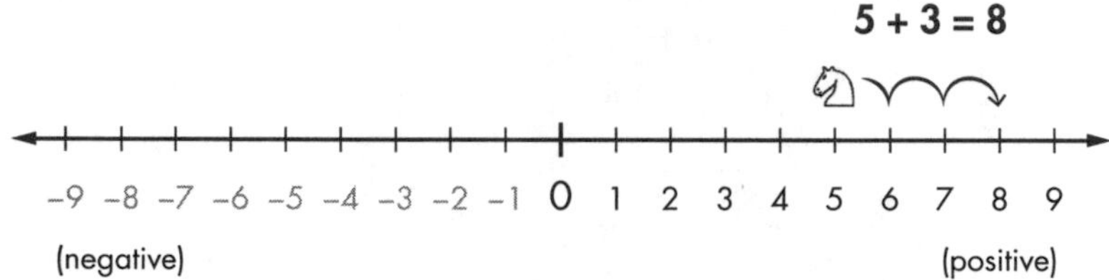

Figure 12-4: Moving the white knight to the right adds to the coordinate.

You subtract by moving the white knight to the left. So if the expression is 5 – 6, the white knight starts at position 5 and moves 6 spaces to the left, as shown in Figure 12-5.

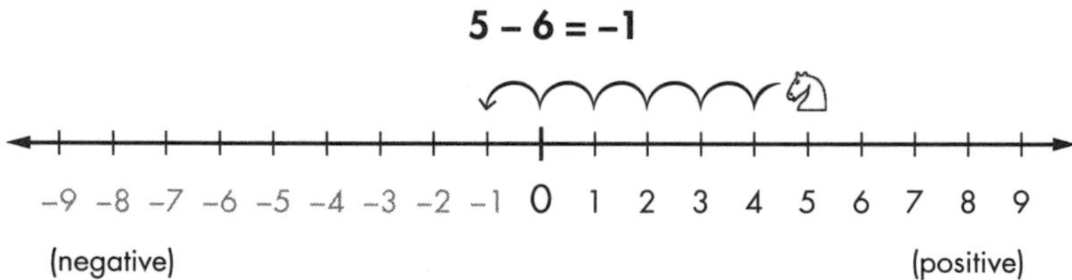

Figure 12-5: Moving the white knight to the left subtracts from the coordinate.

The white knight ends up at position –1. That means 5 – 6 equals –1.

If you add or subtract a negative number, the white knight moves in the *opposite* direction than it does with positive numbers. If you add a negative number, the knight moves to the *left*. If you subtract a negative number, the knight moves to the *right*. The expression –1 – (–4) would be equal to 3, as shown in Figure 12-6. Notice that –1 – (–4) has the same answer as –1 + 4.

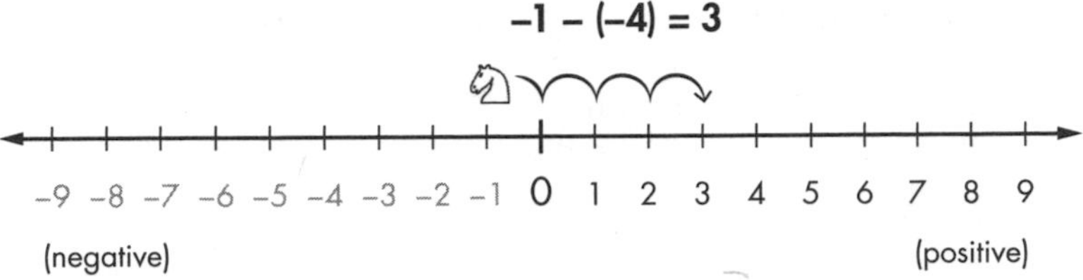

Figure 12-6: The knight starts at −6 and moves to the right by 4 spaces.

You can think of the x-axis as a number line. Add another number line going up and down for the y-axis. If you put these two number lines together, you have a Cartesian coordinate system like the one in Figure 12-7.

Adding a positive number (or subtracting a negative number) would move the knight up on the y-axis or to the right on the x-axis, and subtracting a positive number (or adding a negative number) would move the knight down on the y-axis or to the left on the x-axis.

The (0, 0) coordinate at the center is called the *origin*. You may have used a coordinate system like this in your math class. As you're about to see, coordinate systems like these have a lot of little tricks you can use to make figuring out coordinates easier.

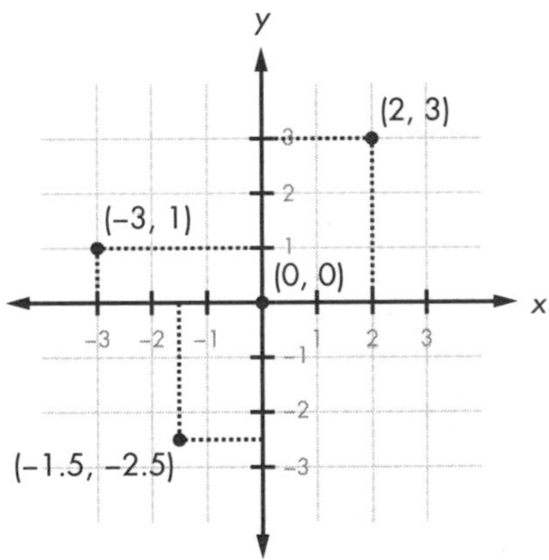

Figure 12-7: Putting two number lines together creates a Cartesian coordinate system.

The Coordinate System of a Computer Screen

Your computer screen is made up of *pixels*, the smallest dot of color a screen can show. It's common for computer screens to use a coordinate system that has the origin (0, 0) at the top-left corner and that increases going down and to the right. You can see this in Figure 12-8, which shows a laptop with a screen resolution that is 1,920 pixels wide and 1,080 pixels tall.

There are no negative coordinates. Most computer graphics use this coordinate system for pixels on the screen, and you will use it in this book's games. For programming, it's important to know how coordinate systems work—both the kind used for mathematics and the kind used for computer screens.

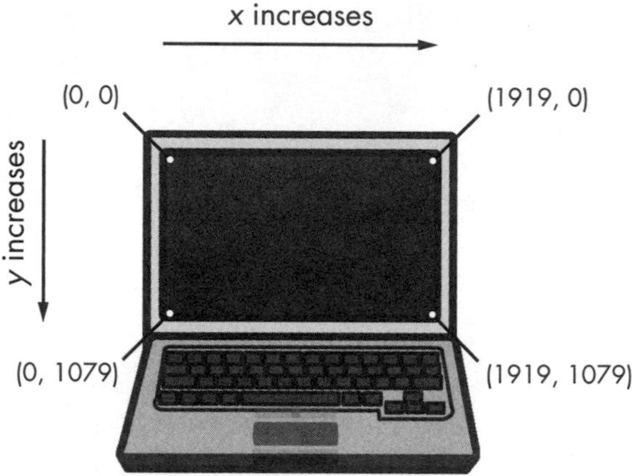

Figure 12-8: The Cartesian coordinate system on a computer screen

Math Tricks

Subtracting and adding negative numbers is easy when you have a number line in front of you. It can also be easy without a number line. Here are three tricks to help you add and subtract negative numbers by yourself.

Trick 1: A Minus Eats the Plus Sign on Its Left

When you see a minus sign with a plus sign on the left, you can replace the plus sign with a minus sign. Imagine the minus sign "eating" the plus sign to its left. The answer is still the same, because adding a negative value is the same as subtracting a positive value. So 4 + –2 and 4 – 2 both evaluate to 2, as you can see here:

4 + –2

↓

4 – 2

↓

2

Trick 2: Two Minuses Combine into a Plus

When you see the two minus signs next to each other without a number between them, they can combine into a plus sign. The answer is still the same, because subtracting a negative value is the same as adding a positive value:

Trick 3: Two Numbers Being Added Can Swap Places

You can always swap the numbers in addition. This is the *commutative property of addition*. That means that doing a swap like 6 + 4 to 4 + 6 will not change the answer, as you can see when you count the boxes in Figure 12-9.

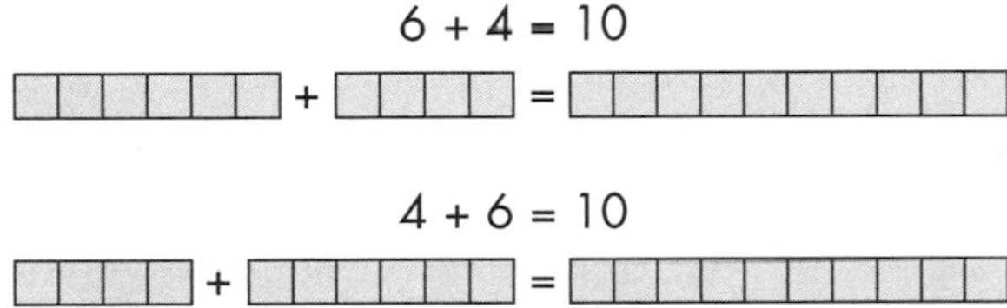

Figure 12-9: The commutative property of addition lets you swap numbers.

Say you are adding a negative number and a positive number, like –6 + 8. Because you are adding numbers, you can swap the order of the numbers without changing the answer. This means –6 + 8 is the same as 8 + –6. Then when you look at 8 + –6, you see that the minus sign can eat the plus sign to its left, and the problem becomes 8 – 6 = 2, as you can see here:

–6 + 8

Swap the order of the addition.

8 + –6

The minus sign eats the plus sign on its left.

8 – 6

2

You've rearranged the problem so that it's easier to solve without using a calculator or computer.

Absolute Values and the abs() Function

A number's *absolute value* is the number without the minus sign in front of it. Therefore, positive numbers do not change, but negative numbers become positive. For example, the absolute value of –4 is 4. The absolute value of –7 is 7. The absolute value of 5 (which is already positive) is just 5.

You can figure out the distance between two objects by subtracting their positions and taking the absolute value of the difference. Imagine that the white knight is at position 4 and the black knight is at position –2. The distance would be 6, since 4 – –2 is 6, and the absolute value of 6 is 6.

It works no matter what the order of the numbers is. For example, –2 – 4 (that is, negative two minus four) is –6, and the absolute value of –6 is also 6.

Python's `abs()` function returns the absolute value of an integer. Enter the following into the interactive shell:

```
>>> abs(-5)
5
>>> abs(42)
42
>>> abs(-10.5)
10.5
```

The absolute value of `-5` is `5`. The absolute value of a positive number is just the number, so the absolute value of `42` is `42`. Even numbers with decimals have an absolute value, so the absolute value of `-10.5` is `10.5`.

Summary

Most programming doesn't require understanding a lot of math. Up until this chapter, we've been getting by with simple addition and multiplication.

Cartesian coordinate systems are needed to describe where a certain position is located in a two-dimensional area. Coordinates have two numbers: the x-coordinate and the y-coordinate. The x-axis runs left and right, and the y-axis runs up and down. On a computer screen, the origin is in the top-left corner and the coordinates increase going right and downward.

The three math tricks you learned in this chapter make it easy to add positive and negative integers. The first trick is that a minus sign will eat the plus sign on its left. The second trick is that two minuses next to each other will combine into a plus sign. The third trick is that you can swap the position of the numbers you are adding.

The rest of the games in this book use these concepts because they have two-dimensional areas in them. All graphical games require understanding how Cartesian coordinates work.

13

SONAR TREASURE HUNT

The Sonar Treasure Hunt game in this chapter is the first to make use of the Cartesian coordinate system that you learned about in Chapter 12. This game also uses data structures, which is just a fancy way of saying it has list values that contain other lists and similar complex variables. As the games you program become more complicated, you'll need to organize your data into data structures.

In this chapter's game, the player drops sonar devices at various places in the ocean to locate sunken treasure chests. *Sonar* is a technology that ships use to locate objects under the sea. The sonar devices in this game tell the player how far away the closest treasure chest is, but not in what direction. But by placing multiple sonar devices, the player can figure out the location of the treasure chest.

TOPICS COVERED IN THIS CHAPTER

- Data structures
- The Pythagorean theorem
- The `remove()` list method
- The `isdigit()` string method
- The `sys.exit()` function

There are 3 chests to collect, and the player has only 20 sonar devices to use to find them. Imagine that you couldn't see the treasure chest in Figure 13-1. Because each sonar device can find only the distance from the chest, not the chest's direction, the treasure could be anywhere on the ring around the sonar device.

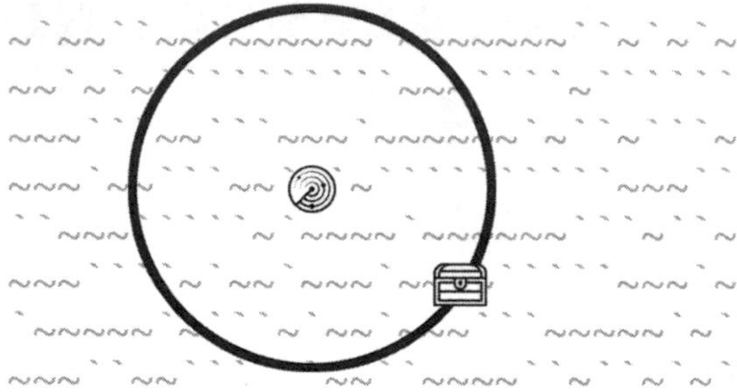

Figure 13-1: The sonar device's ring touches the (hidden) treasure chest.

But multiple sonar devices working together can narrow down the chest's location to the exact coordinates where the rings intersect (see Figure 13-2).

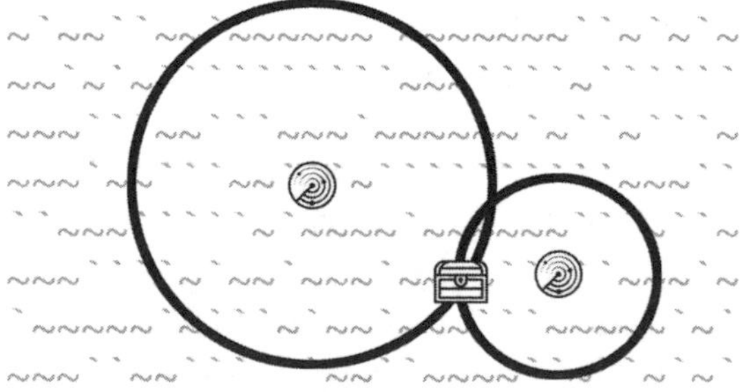

Figure 13-2: Combining multiple rings shows where treasure chests could be hidden.

Sample Run of Sonar Treasure Hunt

Here's what the user sees when they run the Sonar Treasure Hunt program. The text the player enters is shown in bold.

```
S O N A R !

Would you like to view the instructions? (yes/no)
no
             1         2         3         4         5
   012345678901234567890123456789012345678901234567890123456789

 0 ~`~``~``~``~`~`~```~`~``````~```~`~~~`~~```~~`~~~~~`~~`~~~~` 0
 1 ~~~~~`~~~~~````~``~~```~``~`~`~`~``~~```~~~`~`~```~~~~`~`~~` 1
 2 ```~````~``~`~`~~~``~~`````~~``~``~``~~```~~``~~`~~~````~~`~ 2
 3 `````~~``````~`~~~~~```~~``~~~`~`~~~~~~````~`~```~~~``~```~` 3
 4 ~~~`~~~`~`~~~``~~~`~`~``~~~~``~~~~``~~~~`~`~``~~```~``~~`~`~ 4
 5 `~``~````~`~`~~``~~~~``````~```~~~~`````````~``~~~`~~``~~``` 5
 6 ~`~```~~`~~```~````````~~```~```~~~~``~~~`~`~~`~``~~~`~~`~`` 6
 7 ~`~~~```~``~```~`~```~~~~~~~`~~`~`~~~~``~```~~~`~```~``~``~` 7
 8 `~``~~`~`~~`~~`~~``~```~````~`~```~``~````~~~````~~``~~``~~` 8
 9 ~`~``~~````~~```~`~~```~~`~``~`~~``~`~`~~~~`~`~~`~`~```~~``` 9
10 `~~~~~~`~``~``~~~``~``~~~~`~``~```~`~~``~~~~~~``````~~`~``~~ 10
11 ~``~~~````~`~~`~~~`~~~``~```````~`~``~~~~````~~~``````~`~`~~ 11
12 ~~~~~``~`~````~```~`~`~`~~`~~`~``~~~~~~~`~~```~~``~~`~~~~``` 12
13 `~~```~~`````````~~~`~~~``~~~~~~~~`~~``~~`~```~`~~````~~~``~ 13
14 ```~``~`~`~``~``~`~``~`~``~~```~`~~~``~~``~```~`~~`~```````~ 14

   012345678901234567890123456789012345678901234567890123456789
             1         2         3         4         5
You have 20 sonar device(s) left. 3 treasure chest(s) remaining.
Where do you want to drop the next sonar device? (0-59 0-14) (or type quit)
25 5
             1         2         3         4         5
   012345678901234567890123456789012345678901234567890123456789

 0 ~`~``~``~``~`~`~```~`~``````~```~`~~~`~~```~~`~~~~~`~~`~~~~` 0
 1 ~~~~~`~~~~~````~``~~```~``~`~`~`~``~~```~~~`~`~```~~~~`~`~~` 1
 2 ```~````~``~`~`~~~``~~`````~~``~``~``~~```~~``~~`~~~````~~`~ 2
 3 `````~~``````~`~~~~~```~~``~~~`~`~~~~~~````~`~```~~~``~```~` 3
 4 ~~~`~~~`~`~~~``~~~`~`~``~~~~``~~~~``~~~~`~`~``~~```~``~~`~`~ 4
 5 `~``~````~`~`~~``~~~~````5`~```~~~~`````````~``~~~`~~``~~``` 5
 6 ~`~```~~`~~```~````````~~```~```~~~~``~~~`~`~~`~``~~~`~~`~`` 6
 7 ~`~~~```~``~```~`~```~~~~~~~`~~`~`~~~~``~```~~~`~```~``~``~` 7
 8 `~``~~`~`~~`~~`~~``~```~````~`~```~``~````~~~````~~``~~``~~` 8
 9 ~`~``~~````~~```~`~~```~~`~``~`~~``~`~`~~~~`~`~~`~`~```~~``` 9
10 `~~~~~~`~``~``~~~``~``~~~~`~``~```~`~~``~~~~~~``````~~`~``~~ 10
11 ~``~~~````~`~~`~~~`~~~``~```````~`~``~~~~````~~~``````~`~`~~ 11
12 ~~~~~``~`~````~```~`~`~`~~`~~`~``~~~~~~~`~~```~~``~~`~~~~``` 12
13 `~~```~~`````````~~~`~~~``~~~~~~~~`~~``~~`~```~`~~````~~~``~ 13
14 ```~``~`~`~``~``~`~``~`~``~~```~`~~~``~~``~```~`~~`~```````~ 14

   012345678901234567890123456789012345678901234567890123456789
             1         2         3         4         5
```

```
Treasure detected at a distance of 5 from the sonar device.
You have 19 sonar device(s) left. 3 treasure chest(s) remaining.
Where do you want to drop the next sonar device? (0-59 0-14) (or type quit)
30 5
             1         2         3         4         5
   012345678901234567890123456789012345678901234567890123456789

 0 ~`~``~``~``~`~`~```~`~```````~``~`~~~`~~```~~`~~~~~`~~`~~~~` 0
 1 ~~~~~`~~~~~````~``~~```~``~`~`~`~``~~```~~~`~`~```~~~~`~`~~` 1
 2 ```~````~``~`~`~~~``~~`````~~``~``~``~~```~~``~~`~~~````~~`~ 2
 3 `````~~``````~`~~~~~```~~``~~~`~`~~~~~~`````~`~```~~~``~``~` 3
 4 ~~~`~~~`~`~~~``~~~`~`~``~~~~``~~~~``~~~~`~`~``~~```~``~~`~`~ 4
 5 `~``~````~`~`~~``~~~~````5`~``3~~~~````````~``~~~`~~``~~```` 5
 6 ~`~```~~`~~```~````````~~```~```~~~~``~~~`~`~~`~``~~~`~~`~`` 6
 7 ~`~~~```~``~```~`~```~~~~~~~`~~`~`~~~~``~```~~~`~```~``~``~` 7
 8 `~``~~`~`~~`~~`~~``~```~````~`~```~``~````~~~```~~``~~```~~` 8
 9 ~`~``~~````~~```~`~~```~~`~``~`~~``~`~`~~~~`~`~~`~`~```~~``` 9
10 `~~~~~~`~``~``~~~``~``~~~~`~``~```~`~~``~~~~~~``````~~`~``~~ 10
11 ~``~~~````~`~~`~~~`~~~``~```````~`~``~~~~````~~~``````~`~`~~ 11
12 ~~~~~``~`~````~```~`~`~`~~`~~`~``~~~~~~~`~~``~~``~~`~~~~~``` 12
13 `~~```~~````````~~~`~~~```~~~~~~~~`~~``~~`~```~`~~````~~~``~ 13
14 ```~``~`~`~``~```~`~``~`~``~~```~`~~~``~~``~```~`~~`~``````~ 14

   012345678901234567890123456789012345678901234567890123456789
             1         2         3         4         5
Treasure detected at a distance of 3 from the sonar device.
You have 18 sonar device(s) left. 3 treasure chest(s) remaining.
Where do you want to drop the next sonar device? (0-59 0-14) (or type quit)
25 10
             1         2         3         4         5
   012345678901234567890123456789012345678901234567890123456789

 0 ~`~``~``~``~`~`~```~`~```````~``~`~~~`~~```~~`~~~~~`~~`~~~~` 0
 1 ~~~~~`~~~~~````~``~~```~``~`~`~`~``~~```~~~`~`~```~~~~`~`~~` 1
 2 ```~````~``~`~`~~~``~~`````~~``~``~``~~```~~``~~`~~~````~~`~ 2
 3 `````~~``````~`~~~~~```~~``~~~`~`~~~~~~`````~`~```~~~``~``~` 3
 4 ~~~`~~~`~`~~~``~~~`~`~``~~~~``~~~~``~~~~`~`~``~~```~``~~`~`~ 4
 5 `~``~````~`~`~~``~~~~````5`~``3~~~~````````~``~~~`~~``~~```` 5
 6 ~`~```~~`~~```~````````~~```~```~~~~``~~~`~`~~`~``~~~`~~`~`` 6
 7 ~`~~~```~``~```~`~```~~~~~~~`~~`~`~~~~``~```~~~`~```~``~``~` 7
 8 `~``~~`~`~~`~~`~~``~```~````~`~```~``~````~~~```~~``~~```~~` 8
 9 ~`~``~~````~~```~`~~```~~`~``~`~~``~`~`~~~~`~`~~`~`~```~~``` 9
10 `~~~~~~`~``~``~~~``~``~~~4`~``~```~`~~``~~~~~~``````~~`~``~~ 10
11 ~``~~~````~`~~`~~~`~~~``~```````~`~``~~~~````~~~``````~`~`~~ 11
12 ~~~~~``~`~````~```~`~`~`~~`~~`~``~~~~~~~`~~``~~``~~`~~~~~``` 12
13 `~~```~~````````~~~`~~~```~~~~~~~~`~~``~~`~```~`~~````~~~``~ 13
14 ```~``~`~`~``~```~`~``~`~``~~```~`~~~``~~``~```~`~~`~``````~ 14

   012345678901234567890123456789012345678901234567890123456789
             1         2         3         4         5
Treasure detected at a distance of 4 from the sonar device.
You have 17 sonar device(s) left. 3 treasure chest(s) remaining.
Where do you want to drop the next sonar device? (0-59 0-14) (or type quit)
29 8
```

```
             1         2         3         4         5
   012345678901234567890123456789012345678901234567890123456789

 0 ~`~``~``~``~`~`~```~`~``````~```~`~~~`~~```~~`~~~~~`~~`~~~~` 0
 1 ~~~~~`~~~~~````~``~~```~``~`~`~`~``~~```~~~`~`~```~~~~`~`~~` 1
 2 ```~````~``~`~`~~~`~~`````~~`~``~``~~```~~``~~`~~~`````~~`~ 2
 3 `````~~``````~`~~~~~```~~``~~~`~`~~~~~~`````~`~```~~~```~``~` 3
 4 ~~~`~~~`~`~~~``~~~`~`~``~~~~``~~~~``~~~~`~`~``~~```~``~~`~`~ 4
 5 `~``~````~`~`~~``~~~~````X`~``X~~~~````````~``~~~`~~``~~```` 5
 6 ~`~```~~`~~```~``````````~~```~```~~~~``~~~`~`~~`~``~~~`~~`~`` 6
 7 ~`~~~```~``~```~`~```~~~~~~~`~~`~`~~~~``~```~~~`~```~``~``~` 7
 8 `~``~~`~`~~`~~`~~``~```~````~X~```~``~````~~~````~~``~~``~~` 8
 9 ~`~``~~````~~```~`~~```~~`~``~`~~``~`~`~~~~`~`~~`~`~````~~``` 9
10 `~~~~~~`~``~``~~~``~``~~~X`~``~```~`~~``~~~~~~``````~~`~``~~ 10
11 ~``~~~````~`~~`~~~`~~~``~```````~`~``~~~~````~~~``````~`~`~~ 11
12 ~~~~~``~`~````~````~`~`~`~~`~~`~``~~~~~~~`~~```~~``~~`~~~~``` 12
13 `~~````~~``````````~~~`~~~```~~~~~~~~`~~``~~`~```~`~~````~~~``~ 13
14 ```~``~`~`~``~```~`~``~`~``~~```~`~~~``~~``~```~`~~`~``````~ 14

   012345678901234567890123456789012345678901234567890123456789
             1         2         3         4         5
You have found a sunken treasure chest!
You have 16 sonar device(s) left. 2 treasure chest(s) remaining.
Where do you want to drop the next sonar device? (0-59 0-14) (or type quit)
--snip--
```

Source Code for Sonar Treasure Hunt

MAKE SURE YOU'RE
USING PYTHON 3,
NOT PYTHON 2!

Enter the following source code in a new file and save the file as *sonar.py*. Then run it by pressing F5 (or FN-F5 on OS X). If you get errors after entering this code, compare the code you typed to the book's code with the online diff tool at *https://www.nostarch.com/inventwithpython#diff*.

sonar.py

```
# Sonar Treasure Hunt

import random
import sys
import math

def getNewBoard():
    # Create a new 60x15 board data structure.
    board = []
    for x in range(60): # The main list is a list of 60 lists.
        board.append([])
        for y in range(15): # Each list in the main list has
          15 single-character strings.
```

```
            # Use different characters for the ocean to make it more readable.
            if random.randint(0, 1) == 0:
                board[x].append('~')
            else:
                board[x].append('`')
    return board

def drawBoard(board):
    # Draw the board data structure.
    tensDigitsLine = '    ' # Initial space for the numbers down the left side of the board
    for i in range(1, 6):
        tensDigitsLine += (' ' * 9) + str(i)

    # Print the numbers across the top of the board.
    print(tensDigitsLine)
    print('   ' + ('0123456789' * 6))
    print()

    # Print each of the 15 rows.
    for row in range(15):
        # Single-digit numbers need to be padded with an extra space.
        if row < 10:
            extraSpace = ' '
        else:
            extraSpace = ''

        # Create the string for this row on the board.
        boardRow = ''
        for column in range(60):
            boardRow += board[column][row]

        print('%s%s %s %s' % (extraSpace, row, boardRow, row))

    # Print the numbers across the bottom of the board.
    print()
    print('   ' + ('0123456789' * 6))
    print(tensDigitsLine)

def getRandomChests(numChests):
    # Create a list of chest data structures (two-item lists of x, y int coordinates).
    chests = []
    while len(chests) < numChests:
        newChest = [random.randint(0, 59), random.randint(0, 14)]
        if newChest not in chests: # Make sure a chest is not already here.
            chests.append(newChest)
    return chests

def isOnBoard(x, y):
    # Return True if the coordinates are on the board; otherwise, return False.
    return x >= 0 and x <= 59 and y >= 0 and y <= 14
```

```

def makeMove(board, chests, x, y):
    # Change the board data structure with a sonar device character. Remove treasure chests from the chests list as they are found.
    # Return False if this is an invalid move.
    # Otherwise, return the string of the result of this move.
    smallestDistance = 100 # Any chest will be closer than 100.
    for cx, cy in chests:
        distance = math.sqrt((cx - x) * (cx - x) + (cy - y) * (cy - y))

        if distance < smallestDistance: # We want the closest treasure chest.
            smallestDistance = distance

    smallestDistance = round(smallestDistance)

    if smallestDistance == 0:
        # xy is directly on a treasure chest!
        chests.remove([x, y])
        return 'You have found a sunken treasure chest!'
    else:
        if smallestDistance < 10:
            board[x][y] = str(smallestDistance)
            return 'Treasure detected at a distance of %s from the sonar device.' % (smallestDistance)
        else:
            board[x][y] = 'X'
            return 'Sonar did not detect anything. All treasure chests out of range.'

def enterPlayerMove(previousMoves):
    # Let the player enter their move. Return a two-item list of int xy coordinates.
    print('Where do you want to drop the next sonar device? (0-59 0-14) (or type quit)')
    while True:
        move = input()
        if move.lower() == 'quit':
            print('Thanks for playing!')
            sys.exit()

        move = move.split()
        if len(move) == 2 and move[0].isdigit() and move[1].isdigit() and isOnBoard(int(move[0]), int(move[1])):
            if [int(move[0]), int(move[1])] in previousMoves:
                print('You already moved there.')
                continue
            return [int(move[0]), int(move[1])]

        print('Enter a number from 0 to 59, a space, then a number from 0 to 14.')

def showInstructions():
    print('''Instructions:
```

```
You are the captain of the Simon, a treasure-hunting ship. Your current mission
is to use sonar devices to find three sunken treasure chests at the bottom of
the ocean. But you only have cheap sonar that finds distance, not direction.

Enter the coordinates to drop a sonar device. The ocean map will be marked with
how far away the nearest chest is, or an X if it is beyond the sonar device's
range. For example, the C marks are where chests are. The sonar device shows a
3 because the closest chest is 3 spaces away.

              1         2         3
    012345678901234567890123456789012

  0 ~~~~`~```~`~``~~~``~`~~``~~~``~`~ 0
  1 ~`~`~``~~`~```~~~```~~`~`~~~`~~~~ 1
  2 `~`C``3`~~~~`C`~~~~`````~~``~~~`` 2
  3 ````````~~~`````~~~`~`````~`~``~` 3
  4 ~`~~~~`~~`~~`C`~``~~`~~~`~```~``~ 4

    012345678901234567890123456789012
              1         2         3
(In the real game, the chests are not visible in the ocean.)

Press enter to continue...''')
    input()

    print('''When you drop a sonar device directly on a chest, you retrieve it and the other
sonar devices update to show how far away the next nearest chest is. The chests
are beyond the range of the sonar device on the left, so it shows an X.

              1         2         3
    012345678901234567890123456789012

  0 ~~~~`~```~`~``~~~``~`~~``~~~``~`~ 0
  1 ~`~`~``~~`~```~~~```~~`~`~~~`~~~~ 1
  2 `~`X``7`~~~~`C`~~~~`````~~``~~~`` 2
  3 ````````~~~`````~~~`~`````~`~``~` 3
  4 ~`~~~~`~~`~~`C`~``~~`~~~`~```~``~ 4

    012345678901234567890123456789012
              1         2         3

The treasure chests don't move around. Sonar devices can detect treasure chests
up to a distance of 9 spaces. Try to collect all 3 chests before running out of
sonar devices. Good luck!

```

```
Press enter to continue...''')
    input()



print('S O N A R !')
print()
print('Would you like to view the instructions? (yes/no)')
if input().lower().startswith('y'):
    showInstructions()

while True:
    # Game setup
    sonarDevices = 20
    theBoard = getNewBoard()
    theChests = getRandomChests(3)
    drawBoard(theBoard)
    previousMoves = []

    while sonarDevices > 0:
        # Show sonar device and chest statuses.
        print('You have %s sonar device(s) left. %s treasure chest(s) remaining.' % (sonarDevices, len(theChests)))

        x, y = enterPlayerMove(previousMoves)
        previousMoves.append([x, y]) # We must track all moves so that sonar devices can be updated.

        moveResult = makeMove(theBoard, theChests, x, y)
        if moveResult == False:
            continue
        else:
            if moveResult == 'You have found a sunken treasure chest!':
                # Update all the sonar devices currently on the map.
                for x, y in previousMoves:
                    makeMove(theBoard, theChests, x, y)
            drawBoard(theBoard)
            print(moveResult)

        if len(theChests) == 0:
            print('You have found all the sunken treasure chests! Congratulations and good game!')
            break

        sonarDevices -= 1

    if sonarDevices == 0:
        print('We\'ve run out of sonar devices! Now we have to turn the ship around and head')
        print('for home with treasure chests still out there! Game over.')
        print('    The remaining chests were here:')
        for x, y in theChests:
            print('    %s, %s' % (x, y))

```

```
    print('Do you want to play again? (yes or no)')
    if not input().lower().startswith('y'):
        sys.exit()
```

Designing the Program

Before trying to understand the source code, play the game a few times to learn what is going on. The Sonar Treasure Hunt game uses lists of lists and other complicated variables, called *data structures*. Data structures store arrangements of values to represent something. For example, in Chapter 10, a Tic-Tac-Toe board data structure was a list of strings. The string represented an *X*, an *O*, or an empty space, and the index of the string in the list represented the space on the board. The Sonar Treasure Hunt game will have similar data structures for the locations of treasure chests and sonar devices.

Importing the random, sys, and math Modules

At the start of the program, we import the `random`, `sys`, and `math` modules:

```
# Sonar Treasure Hunt

import random
import sys
import math
```

The `sys` module contains the `exit()` function, which terminates the program immediately. None of the lines of code after the `sys.exit()` call will run; the program just stops as though it has reached the end. This function is used later in the program.

The `math` module contains the `sqrt()` function, which is used to find the square root of a number. The math behind square roots is explained the "Finding the Closest Treasure Chest" on page 186.

Creating a New Game Board

The start of each new game requires a new `board` data structure, which is created by `getNewBoard()`. The Sonar Treasure Hunt game board is an ASCII art ocean with x- and y-coordinates around it.

When we use the `board` data structure, we want to be able to access its coordinate system in the same way we access Cartesian coordinates. To do that, we'll use a list of lists to call each coordinate on the board like this: `board[x][y]`. The x-coordinate comes before the y-coordinate—to get the string at coordinate (26, 12), you access `board[26][12]`, not `board[12][26]`.

```
 7. def getNewBoard():
 8.     # Create a new 60x15 board data structure.
 9.     board = []
10.     for x in range(60): # The main list is a list of 60 lists.
11.         board.append([])
12.         for y in range(15): # Each list in the main list has
              15 single-character strings.
13.             # Use different characters for the ocean to make it more
                  readable.
14.             if random.randint(0, 1) == 0:
15.                 board[x].append('~')
16.             else:
17.                 board[x].append('`')
```

The board data structure is a list of lists of strings. The first list represents the x-coordinate. Since the game's board is 60 characters across, this first list needs to contain 60 lists. At line 10, we create a for loop that will append 60 blank lists to it.

But board is more than just a list of 60 blank lists. Each of the 60 lists represents an x-coordinate of the game board. There are 15 rows in the board, so each of these 60 lists must contain 15 strings. Line 12 is another for loop that adds 15 single-character strings that represent the ocean.

The ocean will be a bunch of randomly chosen '~' and '`' strings. The tilde (~) and backtick (`) characters—located next to the 1 key on your keyboard—will be used for the ocean waves. To determine which character to use, lines 14 to 17 apply this logic: if the return value of random.randint() is 0, add the '~' string; otherwise, add the '`' string. This will give the ocean a random, choppy look.

For a smaller example, if board were set to [['~', '~', '`'], [['~', '~', '`'], [['~', '~', '`'], ['~', '`', '`'], ['`', '~', '`']] then the board it drew would look like this:

```
~~~~`
~~~`~
`````
```

Finally, the function returns the value in the board variable on line 18:

```
18.     return board
```

Drawing the Game Board

Next we'll define the drawBoard() method that we call whenever we actually draw a new board:

```
20. def drawBoard(board):
```
```

The full game board with coordinates along the edges looks like this:

```
             1         2         3         4         5
   012345678901234567890123456789012345678901234567890123456789
 0 ~~~`~``~~~``~~~~``~`~`~`~`~~`~~~`~~`~``````~~`~``~`~~```~`~` 0
 1 `~`~````~~``~`~```~```~```~`~~~``~~`~~~``````~`~``~~``~~`~~` 1
 2 ```~~~~`~`~~```~~~``~````~~`~`~~`~`~`~```~~`~``~~`~`~~~~~~`~ 2
 3 ~~~~`~~~``~```~``~~`~`~~`~`~~``~`````~`~`````~```~`~`~`~`````~ 3
 4 ~```~~~~~`~~````~~~~```~~~`~`~`~````~`~~`~`~~``~~`~``~`~``~~ 4
 5 `~```~`~`~~`~~~```~~``~````````~~``~`~`~~~~`~~``~~~~~~`~````~~` 5
 6 ``~~`~~`~``~``````~````~~``~`~~~~`~~```~~~``~`~`~~``~~~```~~~ 6
 7 ``~``~~~~~~```~`~```~~~``~`~``~`~~~~~~````````~~~`~~`~~`~~`~~ 7
 8 ~~`~`~~```~``~~``~~~``~~`~`~~`~`~```~```~~~```~~~~~~`~`~~~~` 8
 9 ```~```~`~~~`~~```~``~``~~~```~`````~```~`~~`~~~~~`~``~~~~~``` 9
10 `~~~~```~`~`````~`~`~~``~`~~~~`~``~``~```~~````````~`~``~````` 10
11 ~~`~`~~`~``~`~~~```````````````````~~`````~`~~``~`~~~~`~~~`~~`~ 11
12 ~~`~~~~```~~~`````~~``~`~`~~``````~`~~``~`````````~~``~~~`~~`~ 12
13 `~````````~~``~`~~~```~~~~```~~`~`~~~`~`````````~~`~````~``~`~~~~ 13
14 ~~~``~````~``````~~`~`~``~~`~``~`~~`~`~``~`~``~~``~`~``~```~~~ 14
   012345678901234567890123456789012345678901234567890123456789
             1         2         3         4         5
```

The drawing in the `drawBoard()` function has four steps:

1. Create a string variable of the line with 1, 2, 3, 4, and 5 spaced out with wide gaps. These numbers mark the coordinates for 10, 20, 30, 40, and 50 on the x-axis.
2. Use that string to display the x-axis coordinates along the top of the screen.
3. Print each row of the ocean along with the y-axis coordinates on both sides of the screen.
4. Print the x-axis again at the bottom. Having coordinates on all sides makes it easier to see where to place a sonar device.

Drawing the X-Coordinates Along the Top of the Board

The first part of `drawBoard()` prints the x-axis at the top of the board. Because we want each part of the board to be even, each coordinate label can take up only one character space. When the coordinate numbering reaches 10, there are two digits for each number, so we put the digits in the tens place on a separate line, as shown in Figure 13-3. The x-axis is organized so that the first line shows the tens-place digits and the second line shows the ones-place digits.

```
+++++++++++++1+++++++++2+++++++++3          # First line
+++0123456789012345678901234567890123456789  # Second line

+0 ~`~``~``~``~`~`~```~`~```````~```~`~~~`~~ 0 # Third line
```

Figure 13-3: The spacing used for printing the top of the game board

Lines 22 to 24 create the string for the first line of the board, which is the tens-place part of the x-axis:

```
21.     # Draw the board data structure.
22.     tensDigitsLine = '    ' # Initial space for the numbers down the left
          side of the board
23.     for i in range(1, 6):
24.         tensDigitsLine += (' ' * 9) + str(i)
```

The numbers marking the tens position on the first line all have 9 spaces between them, and there are 13 spaces in front of the `1`. Lines 22 to 24 create a string with this line and store it in a variable named `tensDigitsLine`:

```
26.     # Print the numbers across the top of the board.
27.     print(tensDigitsLine)
28.     print('   ' + ('0123456789' * 6))
29.     print()
```

To print the numbers across the top of the game board, first print the contents of the `tensDigitsLine` variable. Then, on the next line, print three spaces (so that this row lines up correctly), and then print the string `'0123456789'` six times: `('0123456789' * 6)`.

Drawing the Ocean

Lines 32 to 44 print each row of the ocean waves, including the numbers down the sides to label the y-axis:

```
31.     # Print each of the 15 rows.
32.     for row in range(15):
33.         # Single-digit numbers need to be padded with an extra space.
34.         if row < 10:
35.             extraSpace = ' '
36.         else:
37.             extraSpace = ''
```

The `for` loop prints rows 0 to 14, along with the row numbers on either side of the board.

But we have the same problem that we had with the x-axis. Numbers with only one digit (such as 0, 1, 2, and so on) take up only one space when printed, but numbers with two digits (such as 10, 11, and 12) take up two spaces. The rows won't line up if the coordinates have different sizes. The board would look like this:

```
8 ~~`~`~~```~``~~``~~~``~~`~`~~`~`~```~```~~~```~~~~~~`~`~~~~` 8
9 ```~``~`~~~`~~```~`~``~~~```~```~```~`~~`~~~~~`~``~~~~~``` 9
10 `~~~~```~`~````~`~`~~``~`~~~~`~``~``~```~~````````~`~``~````` 10
11 ~~`~`~~`~``~`~~~`````````````````~~`````~`~~``~`~~~~`~~~`~~`~ 11
```

The solution is easy: add a space in front of all the single-digit numbers. Lines 34 to 37 set the variable extraSpace to either a space or an empty string. The extraSpace variable is always printed, but it has a space character only for single-digit row numbers. Otherwise, it is an empty string. This way, all of the rows will line up when you print them.

Printing a Row in the Ocean

The board parameter is a data structure for the entire ocean's waves. Lines 39 to 44 read the board variable and print a single row:

```
39.     # Create the string for this row on the board.
40.     boardRow = ''
41.     for column in range(60):
42.         boardRow += board[column][row]
43.
44.     print('%s%s %s %s' % (extraSpace, row, boardRow, row))
```

At line 40, boardRow starts as a blank string. The for loop on line 32 sets the row variable for the current row of ocean waves to print. Inside this loop on line 41 is another for loop that iterates over each column of the current row. We make boardRow by concatenating board[column][row] in this loop, which means concatenating board[0][row], board[1][row], board[2][row], and so on up to board[59][row]. This is because the row contains 60 characters, from index 0 to index 59.

The for loop on line 41 iterates over integers 0 to 59. On each iteration, the next character in the board data structure is copied to the end of boardRow. By the time the loop is done, boardRow has the row's complete ASCII art waves. The string in boardRow is then printed along with the row numbers on line 44.

Drawing the X-Coordinates Along the Bottom of the Board

Lines 46 to 49 are similar to lines 26 to 29:

```
46.     # Print the numbers across the bottom of the board.
47.     print()
48.     print('    ' + ('0123456789' * 6))
49.     print(tensDigitsLine)
```

These lines print the x-coordinates at the bottom of the board.

Creating the Random Treasure Chests

The game randomly decides where the hidden treasure chests are. The treasure chests are represented as a list of lists of two integers. These two integers are the x- and y-coordinates of a single chest. For example, if the chest data structure were [[2, 2], [2, 4], [10, 0]], then this would mean there were three treasure chests, one at (2, 2), another at (2, 4), and a third at (10, 0).

The getRandomChests() function creates a certain number of chest data structures at randomly assigned coordinates:

```
51. def getRandomChests(numChests):
52.     # Create a list of chest data structures (two-item lists of x, y int coordinates).
53.     chests = []
54.     while len(chests) < numChests:
55.         newChest = [random.randint(0, 59), random.randint(0, 14)]
56.         if newChest not in chests: # Make sure a chest is not already here.
57.             chests.append(newChest)
58.     return chests
```

The numChests parameter tells the function how many treasure chests to generate. Line 54's while loop will iterate until all of the chests have been assigned coordinates. Two random integers are selected for the coordinates on line 55. The x-coordinate can be anywhere from 0 to 59, and the y-coordinate can be anywhere from 0 to 14. The [random.randint(0, 59), random.randint(0, 14)] expression will evaluate to a list value like [2, 2] or [2, 4] or [10, 0]. If these coordinates do not already exist in the chests list, they are appended to chests on line 57.

Determining Whether a Move Is Valid

When the player enters the x- and y-coordinates for where they want to drop a sonar device, we need to make sure that the numbers are valid. As mentioned before, there are two conditions for a move to be valid: the x-coordinate must be between 0 and 59, and the y-coordinate must be between 0 and 14.

The isOnBoard() function uses a simple expression with and operators to combine these conditions into one expression and to ensure that each part of the expression is True:

```
def isOnBoard(x, y):
    # Return True if the coordinates are on the board; otherwise, return False.
    return x >= 0 and x <= 59 and y >= 0 and y <= 14
```

Because we are using the and Boolean operator, if even one of the coordinates is invalid, then the entire expression evaluates to False.

Placing a Move on the Board

In the Sonar Treasure Hunt game, the game board is updated to display a number that represents each sonar device's distance to the closest treasure chest. So when the player makes a move by giving the program an x- and y-coordinate, the board changes based on the positions of the treasure chests.

```
def makeMove(board, chests, x, y):
    # Change the board data structure with a sonar device character.
      Remove treasure chests from the chests list as they are found.
    # Return False if this is an invalid move.
    # Otherwise, return the string of the result of this move.
```

The `makeMove()` function takes four parameters: the game board's data structure, the treasure chest's data structure, the x-coordinate, and the y-coordinate. The `makeMove()` function will return a string value describing what happened in response to the move:

- If the coordinates land directly on a treasure chest, `makeMove()` returns `'You have found a sunken treasure chest!'`.
- If the coordinates are within a distance of 9 or less of a chest, `makeMove()` returns `'Treasure detected at a distance of %s from the sonar device.'` (where `%s` is replaced with the integer distance).
- Otherwise, `makeMove()` will return `'Sonar did not detect anything. All treasure chests out of range.'`.

Given the coordinates of where the player wants to drop the sonar device and a list of x- and y-coordinates for the treasure chests, you'll need an algorithm to find out which treasure chest is closest.

Finding the Closest Treasure Chest

Lines 68 to 75 are an algorithm to determine which treasure chest is closest to the sonar device.

```
68.     smallestDistance = 100 # Any chest will be closer than 100.
69.     for cx, cy in chests:
70.         distance = math.sqrt((cx - x) * (cx - x) + (cy - y) * (cy - y))
71.
72.         if distance < smallestDistance: # We want the closest treasure
              chest.
73.             smallestDistance = distance
```

The `x` and `y` parameters are integers (say, `3` and `5`), and together they represent the location on the game board where the player guessed. The `chests` variable will have a value such as `[[5, 0], [0, 2], [4, 2]]`, which represents the locations of three treasure chests. Figure 13-4 illustrates this value.

To find the distance between the sonar device and a treasure chest, we'll need to do some math to find the distance between two x- and y-coordinates. Let's say we place a sonar device at (3, 5) and want to find the distance to the treasure chest at (4, 2).

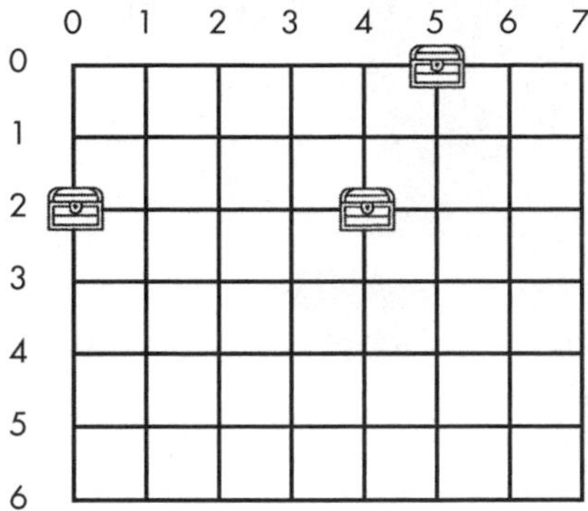

Figure 13-4: The treasure chests represented by `[[5, 0], [0, 2], [4, 2]]`

To find the distance between two sets of x- and y-coordinates, we'll use the *Pythagorean theorem.* This theorem applies to *right triangles*—triangles where one corner is 90 degrees, the same kind of corner you find in a rectangle. The Pythagorean theorem says that the diagonal side of the triangle can be calculated from the lengths of the horizontal and vertical sides. Figure 13-5 shows a right triangle drawn between the sonar device at (3, 5) and the treasure chest at (4, 2).

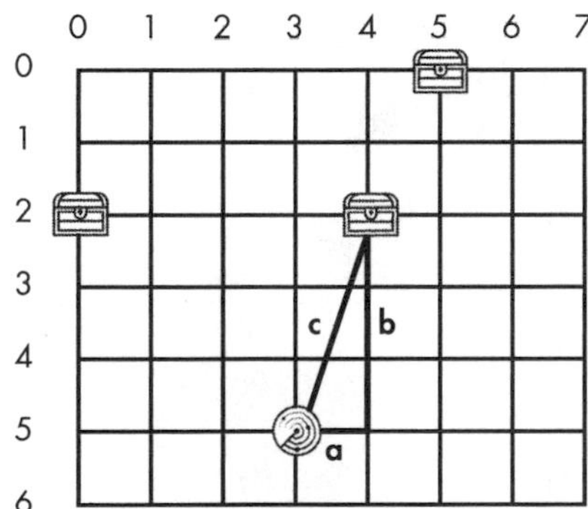

Figure 13-5: The board with a right triangle drawn over the sonar device and a treasure chest

The Pythagorean theorem is $a^2 + b^2 = c^2$, in which a is the length of the horizontal side, b is the length of the vertical side, and c is the length of the diagonal side, or *hypotenuse.* These lengths are *squared,* which means that number is multiplied by itself. "Unsquaring" a number is called finding the number's *square root,* as we'll have to do to get c from c^2.

Let's use the Pythagorean theorem to find the distance between the sonar device at (3, 5) and chest at (4, 2):

1. To find *a*, subtract the second x-coordinate, 4, from the first x-coordinate, 3: 3 – 4 = –1.
2. To find a^2, multiply *a* by *a*: –1 × –1 = 1. (A negative number times a negative number is always a positive number.)
3. To find *b*, subtract the second y-coordinate, 2, from the first y-coordinate, 5: 5 – 2 = 3.
4. To find b^2, multiply *b* by *b*: 3 × 3 = 9.
5. To find c^2, add a^2 and b^2: 1 + 9 = 10.
6. To get *c* from c^2, you need to find the square root of c^2.

The `math` module that we imported on line 5 has a square root function named `sqrt()`. Enter the following into the interactive shell:

```
>>> import math
>>> math.sqrt(10)
3.1622776601683795
>>> 3.1622776601683795 * 3.1622776601683795
10.000000000000002
```

Notice that multiplying a square root by itself produces the square number. (The extra `2` at the end of the `10` is from an unavoidable slight imprecision in the `sqrt()` function.)

By passing c^2 to `sqrt()`, we can tell that the sonar device is 3.16 units away from the treasure chest. The game will round this down to 3.

Let's look at lines 68 to 70 again:

```
68.     smallestDistance = 100 # Any chest will be closer than 100.
69.     for cx, cy in chests:
70.         distance = math.sqrt((cx - x) * (cx - x) + (cy - y) * (cy - y))
```

The code inside line 69's `for` loop calculates the distance of each chest. Line 68 gives `smallestDistance` the impossibly long distance of `100` at the beginning of the loop so that at least one of the treasure chests you find will be put into `smallestDistance` in line 73. Since `cx - x` represents the horizontal distance *a* between the chest and sonar device, `(cx - x) * (cx - x)` is the a^2 of our Pythagorean theorem calculation. It is added to `(cy - y) * (cy - y)`, the b^2. This sum is c^2 and is passed to `sqrt()` to get the distance between the chest and sonar device.

We want to find the distance between the sonar device and the closest chest, so if this distance is less than the smallest distance, it is saved as the new smallest distance on line 73:

```
72.         if distance < smallestDistance: # We want the closest treasure chest.
73.             smallestDistance = distance
```

By the time the for loop has finished, you know that smallestDistance holds the shortest distance between the sonar device and all of the treasure chests in the game.

Removing Values with the remove() List Method

The remove() list method removes the first occurrence of a value matching the passed-in argument. For example, enter the following into the interactive shell:

```
>>> x = [42, 5, 10, 42, 15, 42]
>>> x.remove(10)
>>> x
[42, 5, 42, 15, 42]
```

The 10 value has been removed from the x list.

Now enter the following into the interactive shell:

```
>>> x = [42, 5, 10, 42, 15, 42]
>>> x.remove(42)
>>> x
[5, 10, 42, 15, 42]
```

Notice that only the first 42 value was removed and the second and third ones are still there. The remove() method removes the first, and only the first, occurrence of the value you pass it.

If you try to remove a value that isn't in the list, you'll get an error:

```
>>> x = [5, 42]
>>> x.remove(10)
Traceback (most recent call last):
  File "<stdin>", line 1, in <module>
ValueError: list.remove(x): x not in list
```

Like the append() method, the remove() method is called on a list and does not return a list. You want to use code like x.remove(42), not x = x.remove(42).

Let's go back to finding the distances between sonar devices and treasure chests in the game. The only time that smallestDistance is equal to 0 is when the sonar device's x- and y-coordinates are the same as a treasure chest's x- and y-coordinates. This means the player has correctly guessed the location of a treasure chest.

```
    if smallestDistance == 0:
        # xy is directly on a treasure chest!
        chests.remove([x, y])
        return 'You have found a sunken treasure chest!'
```

When this happens, the program removes this chest's two-integer list from the chests data structure with the remove() list method. Then the function returns 'You have found a sunken treasure chest!'.

But if smallestDistance is not 0, the player didn't guess an exact location of a treasure chest, and the else block starting on line 81 executes:

```
81.     else:
82.         if smallestDistance < 10:
83.             board[x][y] = str(smallestDistance)
84.             return 'Treasure detected at a distance of %s from the sonar
                  device.' % (smallestDistance)
85.         else:
86.             board[x][y] = 'X'
87.             return 'Sonar did not detect anything. All treasure chests
                  out of range.'
```

If the sonar device's distance to a treasure chest is less than 10, line 83 marks the board with the string version of smallestDistance. If not, the board is marked with an 'X'. This way, the player knows how close each sonar device is to a treasure chest. If the player sees a 0, they know they're way off.

Getting the Player's Move

The enterPlayerMove() function collects the x- and y-coordinates of the player's next move:

```
89. def enterPlayerMove(previousMoves):
90.     # Let the player enter their move. Return a two-item list of int
          xy coordinates.
91.     print('Where do you want to drop the next sonar device? (0-59 0-14)
          (or type quit)')
92.     while True:
93.         move = input()
94.         if move.lower() == 'quit':
95.             print('Thanks for playing!')
96.             sys.exit()
```

The previousMoves parameter is a list of two-integer lists of the previous places the player put a sonar device. This information will be used so that the player cannot place a sonar device somewhere they have already put one.

The while loop will keep asking the player for their next move until they enter coordinates for a place that doesn't already have a sonar device. The player can also enter 'quit' to quit the game. In that case, line 96 calls the sys.exit() function to terminate the program immediately.

Assuming the player has not entered 'quit', the code checks that the input is two integers separated by a space. Line 98 calls the split() method on move as the new value of move:

```
98.         move = move.split()
99.         if len(move) == 2 and move[0].isdigit() and move[1].isdigit() and
              isOnBoard(int(move[0]), int(move[1])):
100.            if [int(move[0]), int(move[1])] in previousMoves:
101.                print('You already moved there.')
102.                continue
103.            return [int(move[0]), int(move[1])]
```

```
104.
105.        print('Enter a number from 0 to 59, a space, then a number from
              0 to 14.')
```

If the player typed in a value like '1 2 3', then the list returned by split() would be ['1', '2', '3']. In that case, the expression len(move) == 2 would be False (the list in move should be only two numbers because it represents a coordinate), and the entire expression would evaluate immediately to False. Python doesn't check the rest of the expression because of short-circuiting (which was described in "Short-Circuit Evaluation" on page 139).

If the list's length is 2, then the two values will be at indexes move[0] and move[1]. To check whether those values are numeric digits (like '2' or '17'), you could use a function like isOnlyDigits() from "Checking Whether a String Has Only Numbers" on page 158. But Python already has a method that does this.

The string method isdigit() returns True if the string consists solely of numbers. Otherwise, it returns False. Enter the following into the interactive shell:

```
>>> '42'.isdigit()
True
>>> 'forty'.isdigit()
False
>>> ''.isdigit()
False
>>> 'hello'.isdigit()
False
>>> x = '10'
>>> x.isdigit()
True
```

Both move[0].isdigit() and move[1].isdigit() must be True for the whole condition to be True. The final part of line 99's condition calls the isOnBoard() function to check whether the x- and y-coordinates exist on the board.

If the entire condition is True, line 100 checks whether the move exists in the previousMoves list. If it does, then line 102's continue statement causes the execution to go back to the start of the while loop at line 92 and then ask for the player's move again. If it doesn't, line 103 returns a two-integer list of the x- and y-coordinates.

Printing the Game Instructions for the Player

The showInstructions() function is a couple of print() calls that print multiline strings:

```
107. def showInstructions():
108.     print('''Instructions:
109. You are the captain of the Simon, a treasure-hunting ship. Your current
         mission
```

```
--snip--
Press enter to continue...''')
    input()
```

The `input()` function gives the player a chance to press ENTER before printing the next string. This is because the IDLE window can show only so much text at a time, and we don't want the player to have to scroll up to read the beginning of the text. After the player presses ENTER, the function returns to the line that called the function.

The Game Loop

Now that we've entered all the functions that our game will call, let's enter the main part of the game. The first thing the player sees after running the program is the game title printed by line 159. This is the main part of the program, which begins by offering the player instructions and then setting up the variables the game will use.

```
159. print('S O N A R !')
160. print()
161. print('Would you like to view the instructions? (yes/no)')
162. if input().lower().startswith('y'):
163.     showInstructions()
164.
165. while True:
166.     # Game setup
167.     sonarDevices = 20
168.     theBoard = getNewBoard()
169.     theChests = getRandomChests(3)
170.     drawBoard(theBoard)
171.     previousMoves = []
```

The expression `input().lower().startswith('y')` lets the player request the instructions, and it evaluates to `True` if the player enters a string that begins with `'y'` or `'Y'`. For example:

```
input().lower().startswith('y')
    ↓
'Y'.lower().startswith('y')
    ↓
'y'.startswith('y')
    ↓
True
```

If this condition is `True`, `showInstructions()` is called on line 163. Otherwise, the game begins.

Several variables are set up on lines 167 to 171; these are described in Table 13-1.

Table 13-1: Variables Used in the Main Game Loop

Variable	Description
sonarDevices	The number of sonar devices (and turns) the player has left.
theBoard	The board data structure used for this game.
theChests	The list of chest data structures. getRandomChests() returns a list of three treasure chests at random places on the board.
previousMoves	A list of all the x and y moves the player has made in the game.

We're going to use these variables soon, so make sure to review their descriptions before moving on!

Displaying the Game Status for the Player

Line 173's while loop executes as long as the player has sonar devices remaining and prints a message telling them how many sonar devices and treasure chests are left:

```
173.     while sonarDevices > 0:
174.         # Show sonar device and chest statuses.
175.         print('You have %s sonar device(s) left. %s treasure chest(s)
               remaining.' % (sonarDevices, len(theChests)))
```

After printing how many devices are left, the while loop continues to execute.

Handling the Player's Move

Line 177 is still part of the while loop and uses multiple assignment to assign the x and y variables to the two-item list representing the player's move coordinates returned by enterPlayerMove(). We'll pass in previousMoves so that enterPlayerMove()'s code can ensure the player doesn't repeat a previous move.

```
177.         x, y = enterPlayerMove(previousMoves)
178.         previousMoves.append([x, y]) # We must track all moves so that
               sonar devices can be updated.
179.
180.         moveResult = makeMove(theBoard, theChests, x, y)
181.         if moveResult == False:
182.             continue
```

The x and y variables are then appended to the end of the previousMoves list. The previousMoves variable is a list of x- and y-coordinates of each move the player makes in this game. This list is used later in the program on lines 177 and 186.

The x, y, theBoard, and theChests variables are all passed to the makeMove() function at line 180. This function makes the necessary modifications to place a sonar device on the board.

If makeMove() returns False, then there was a problem with the x and y values passed to it. The continue statement sends the execution back to the start of the while loop on line 173 to ask the player for x- and y-coordinates again.

Finding a Sunken Treasure Chest

If makeMove() doesn't return False, it returns a string of the results of that move. If this string is 'You have found a sunken treasure chest!', then all the sonar devices on the board should update to detect the *next* closest treasure chest on the board:

```
183.         else:
184.             if moveResult == 'You have found a sunken treasure chest!':
185.                 # Update all the sonar devices currently on the map.
186.                 for x, y in previousMoves:
187.                     makeMove(theBoard, theChests, x, y)
188.             drawBoard(theBoard)
189.             print(moveResult)
```

The x- and y-coordinates of all the sonar devices are in previousMoves. By iterating over previousMoves on line 186, you can pass all of these x- and y-coordinates to the makeMove() function again to redraw the values on the board. Because the program doesn't print any new text here, the player doesn't realize the program is redoing all of the previous moves. It just appears that the board updates itself.

Checking Whether the Player Won

Remember that the makeMove() function modifies the theChests list you sent it. Because theChests is a list, any changes made to it inside the function will persist after execution returns from the function. The makeMove() function removes items from theChests when treasure chests are found, so eventually (if the player keeps guessing correctly) all of the treasure chests will have been removed. (Remember, by "treasure chest" we mean the two-item lists of the x- and y-coordinates inside the theChests list.)

```
191.         if len(theChests) == 0:
192.             print('You have found all the sunken treasure chests!
                   Congratulations and good game!')
193.             break
```

When all the treasure chests have been found on the board and removed from theChests, the theChests list will have a length of 0. When that happens, the code displays a congratulatory message to the player and then executes a break statement to break out of this while loop. Execution will then move to line 197, the first line after the while block.

Checking Whether the Player Lost

Line 195 is the last line of the while loop that started on line 173.

```
195.         sonarDevices -= 1
```

The program decrements the sonarDevices variable because the player has used one sonar device. If the player keeps missing the treasure chests, eventually sonarDevices will be reduced to 0. After this line, execution jumps back up to line 173 so it can reevaluate the while statement's condition (which is sonarDevices > 0).

If sonarDevices is 0, then the condition will be False and execution will continue outside the while block on line 197. But until then, the condition will remain True and the player can keep making guesses:

```
197.     if sonarDevices == 0:
198.         print('We\'ve run out of sonar devices! Now we have to turn the
               ship around and head')
199.         print('for home with treasure chests still out there! Game
               over.')
200.         print('    The remaining chests were here:')
201.         for x, y in theChests:
202.             print('    %s, %s' % (x, y))
```

Line 197 is the first line outside the while loop. When the execution reaches this point, the game is over. If sonarDevices is 0, you know the player ran out of sonar devices before finding all the chests and lost.

Lines 198 to 200 will tell the player they've lost. The for loop on line 201 will go through the treasure chests remaining in theChests and display their location so the player can see where the treasure chests were lurking.

Terminating the Program with the sys.exit() Function

Win or lose, the program lets the player decide whether they want to keep playing. If the player does not enter 'yes' or 'Y' or enters some other string that doesn't begin with the letter *y*, then not input().lower().startswith('y') evaluates to True and the sys.exit() function is executed. This causes the program to terminate.

```
204.     print('Do you want to play again? (yes or no)')
205.     if not input().lower().startswith('y'):
206.         sys.exit()
```

Otherwise, execution jumps back to the beginning of the while loop on line 165 and a new game begins.

Summary

Remember how our Tic-Tac-Toe game numbered the spaces on the Tic-Tac-Toe board 1 through 9? This sort of coordinate system might have been okay for a board with fewer than 10 spaces. But the Sonar Treasure Hunt board has 900 spaces! The Cartesian coordinate system we learned about in Chapter 12 really makes all these spaces manageable, especially when our game needs to find the distance between two points on the board.

Locations in games that use a Cartesian coordinate system can be stored in a list of lists in which the first index is the x-coordinate and the second index is the y-coordinate. This makes it easy to access a coordinate using `board[x][y]`.

These data structures (such as the ones used for the ocean and treasure chest locations) make it possible to represent complex concepts as data, and your game programs become mostly about modifying these data structures.

In the next chapter, we'll represent letters as numbers. By representing text as numbers, we can perform math operations on them to encrypt or decrypt secret messages.

14

CAESAR CIPHER

The program in this chapter isn't really a game, but it is fun nevertheless. The program will convert normal English into a secret code. It can also convert secret codes back into regular English. Only someone who knows the key to the secret codes will be able to understand the messages.

Because this program manipulates text to convert it into secret messages, you'll learn several new functions and methods for manipulating strings. You'll also learn how programs can do math with text strings just as they can with numbers.

TOPICS COVERED IN THIS CHAPTER

- Cryptography and ciphers
- Ciphertext, plaintext, keys, and symbols
- Encrypting and decrypting
- The Caesar cipher
- The `find()` string method
- Cryptanalysis
- The brute-force technique

Cryptography and Encryption

The science of writing secret codes is called *cryptography*. For thousands of years, cryptography has made it possible to send secret messages that only the sender and recipient could read, even if someone captured the messenger and read the coded message. A secret code system is called a *cipher*. The cipher used by the program in this chapter is called the *Caesar cipher*.

In cryptography, we call the message that we want to keep secret the *plaintext*. Let's say we have a plaintext message that looks like this:

```
There is a clue behind the bookshelf.
```

Converting the plaintext into the encoded message is called *encrypting* the plaintext. The plaintext is encrypted into the *ciphertext*. The ciphertext looks like random letters, so we can't understand what the original plaintext was just by looking at the ciphertext. Here is the previous example encrypted into ciphertext:

```
aolyl pz h jsBl ilopuk Aol ivvrzolsm.
```

If you know the cipher used to encrypt the message, you can *decrypt* the ciphertext back to the plaintext. (Decryption is the opposite of encryption.)

Many ciphers use *keys*, which are secret values that let you decrypt ciphertext that was encrypted with a specific cipher. Think of the cipher as being like a door lock. You can only unlock it with a particular key.

If you're interested in writing cryptography programs, you can read my book *Hacking Secret Ciphers with Python*. It's free to download from *http://inventwithpython.com/hacking/*.

How the Caesar Cipher Works

The Caesar cipher was one of the earliest ciphers ever invented. In this cipher, you encrypt a message by replacing each letter in it with a "shifted" letter. In cryptography, the encrypted letters are called *symbols* because they can be letters, numbers, or any other signs. If you shift the letter A by one space, you get the letter B. If you shift the letter A by two spaces, you get the letter C. Figure 14-1 shows some letters shifted by three spaces.

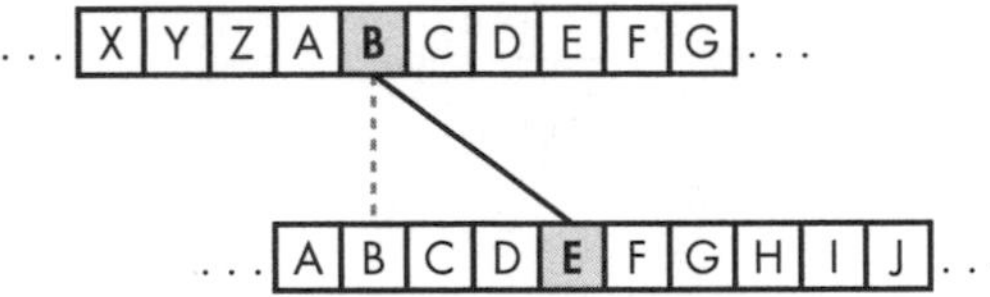

Figure 14-1: A Caesar cipher shifting letters by three spaces. Here, B becomes E.

To get each shifted letter, draw a row of boxes with each letter of the alphabet. Then draw a second row of boxes under it, but start your letters a certain number of spaces over. When you get to the end of the plaintext alphabet, wrap back around to A. Figure 14-2 shows an example with the letters shifted by three spaces.

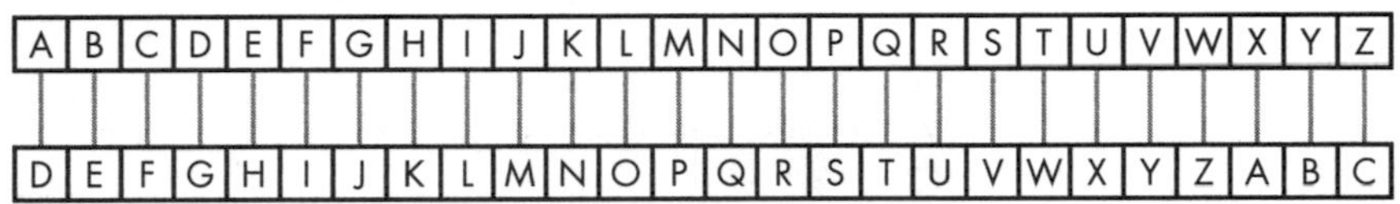

Figure 14-2: The entire alphabet shifted by three spaces

The number of spaces you shift your letters (between 1 and 26) is the key in the Caesar cipher. Unless you know the key (the number used to encrypt the message), you won't be able to decrypt the secret code. The example in Figure 14-2 shows the letter translations for the key 3.

NOTE *While there are 26 possible keys, encrypting your message with 26 will result in a ciphertext that is exactly the same as the plaintext!*

If you encrypt the plaintext word HOWDY with a key of 3, then:

- The letter H becomes K.
- The letter O becomes R.
- The letter W becomes Z.
- The letter D becomes G.
- The letter Y becomes B.

So, the ciphertext of HOWDY with the key 3 becomes KRZGB. To decrypt KRZGB with the key 3, we go from the bottom boxes back to the top.

If you would like to include lowercase letters as distinct from uppercase letters, then add another 26 boxes to the ones you already have and fill them with the 26 lowercase letters. Now with a key of 3, the letter Y becomes b, as shown in Figure 14-3.

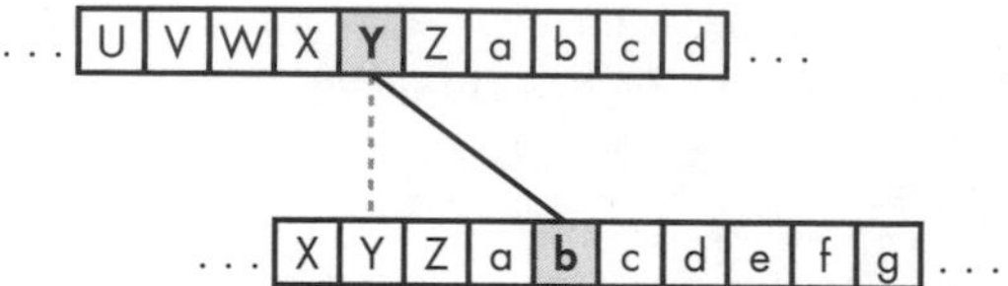

Figure 14-3: The entire alphabet, now including lowercase letters, shifted by three spaces

The cipher works the same way as it did with just uppercase letters. In fact, if you want to use letters from another language's alphabet, you can write boxes with those letters to create your cipher.

Sample Run of Caesar Cipher

Here is a sample run of the Caesar Cipher program encrypting a message:

```
Do you wish to encrypt or decrypt a message?
encrypt
Enter your message:
The sky above the port was the color of television, tuned to a dead channel.
Enter the key number (1-52)
13
Your translated text is:
gur FxL noBIr Gur CBEG JnF Gur pByBE Bs GryrIvFvBA, GHArq GB n qrnq punAAry.
```

Now run the program and decrypt the text that you just encrypted:

```
Do you wish to encrypt or decrypt a message?
decrypt
Enter your message:
gur FxL noBIr Gur CBEG JnF Gur pByBE Bs GryrIvFvBA, GHArq GB n qrnq punAAry.
Enter the key number (1-52)
13
Your translated text is:
The sky above the port was the color of television, tuned to a dead channel.
```

If you do not decrypt with the correct key, the text will not decrypt properly:

```
Do you wish to encrypt or decrypt a message?
decrypt
Enter your message:
gur FxL noBIr Gur CBEG JnF Gur pByBE Bs GryrIvFvBA, GHArq GB n qrnq punAAry.
Enter the key number (1-52)
15
```

```
Your translated text is:
Rfc qiw YZmtc rfc nmpr uYq rfc amjmp md rcjctgqgml, rslcb rm Y bcYb afYllcj.
```

Source Code for Caesar Cipher

MAKE SURE YOU'RE USING PYTHON 3, NOT PYTHON 2!

Enter this source code for the Caesar Cipher program and then save the file as *cipher.py*. If you get errors after entering this code, compare the code you typed to the book's code with the online diff tool at *https://www.nostarch.com/inventwithpython#diff*.

cipher.py

```
# Caesar Cipher
SYMBOLS = 'ABCDEFGHIJKLMNOPQRSTUVWXYZabcdefghijklmnopqrstuvwxyz'
MAX_KEY_SIZE = len(SYMBOLS)

def getMode():
    while True:
        print('Do you wish to encrypt or decrypt a message?')
        mode = input().lower()
        if mode in ['encrypt', 'e', 'decrypt', 'd']:
            return mode
        else:
            print('Enter either "encrypt" or "e" or "decrypt" or "d".')

def getMessage():
    print('Enter your message:')
    return input()

def getKey():
    key = 0
    while True:
        print('Enter the key number (1-%s)' % (MAX_KEY_SIZE))
        key = int(input())
        if (key >= 1 and key <= MAX_KEY_SIZE):
            return key

def getTranslatedMessage(mode, message, key):
    if mode[0] == 'd':
        key = -key
    translated = ''

    for symbol in message:
        symbolIndex = SYMBOLS.find(symbol)
        if symbolIndex == -1: # Symbol not found in SYMBOLS.
            # Just add this symbol without any change.
            translated += symbol
        else:
            # Encrypt or decrypt.
            symbolIndex += key
```

```
            if symbolIndex >= len(SYMBOLS):
                symbolIndex -= len(SYMBOLS)
            elif symbolIndex < 0:
                symbolIndex += len(SYMBOLS)

            translated += SYMBOLS[symbolIndex]
    return translated

mode = getMode()
message = getMessage()
key = getKey()
print('Your translated text is:')
print(getTranslatedMessage(mode, message, key))
```

Setting the Maximum Key Length

The encryption and decryption processes are the reverse of each other, but they share much of the same code. Let's look at how each line works:

```
# Caesar Cipher
SYMBOLS = 'ABCDEFGHIJKLMNOPQRSTUVWXYZabcdefghijklmnopqrstuvwxyz'
MAX_KEY_SIZE = len(SYMBOLS)
```

`MAX_KEY_SIZE` is a constant that stores the length of `SYMBOLS` (`52`). This constant reminds us that in this program, the key used in the cipher should always be between 1 and 52.

Deciding to Encrypt or Decrypt the Message

The `getMode()` function lets the user decide whether they want to use the program's encryption or decryption mode:

```
 5. def getMode():
 6.     while True:
 7.         print('Do you wish to encrypt or decrypt a message?')
 8.         mode = input().lower()
 9.         if mode in ['encrypt', 'e', 'decrypt', 'd']:
10.             return mode
11.         else:
12.             print('Enter either "encrypt" or "e" or "decrypt" or "d".')
```

Line 8 calls `input()` to let the user enter the mode they want. The `lower()` method is then called on this string to return a lowercase version of the string. The value returned from `input().lower()` is stored in `mode`. The `if` statement's condition checks whether the string stored in `mode` exists in the `['encrypt', 'e', 'decrypt', 'd']` list.

This function will return the string in `mode` as long as `mode` is equal to `'encrypt'`, `'e'`, `'decrypt'`, or `'d'`. Therefore, `getMode()` will return the string `mode`. If the user types something that is not `'encrypt'`, `'e'`, `'decrypt'`, or `'d'`, then the `while` loop will ask them again.

Getting the Message from the Player

The getMessage() function simply gets the message to encrypt or decrypt from the user and returns it:

```
def getMessage():
    print('Enter your message:')
    return input()
```

The call for input() is combined with return so that we use only one line instead of two.

Getting the Key from the Player

The getKey() function lets the player enter the key they will use to encrypt or decrypt the message:

```
18. def getKey():
19.     key = 0
20.     while True:
21.         print('Enter the key number (1-%s)' % (MAX_KEY_SIZE))
22.         key = int(input())
23.         if (key >= 1 and key <= MAX_KEY_SIZE):
24.             return key
```

The while loop ensures that the function keeps looping until the user enters a valid key. A valid key here is one between the integer values 1 and 52 (remember that MAX_KEY_SIZE is 52 because there are 52 characters in the SYMBOLS variable). The getKey() function then returns this key. Line 22 sets key to the integer version of what the user entered, so getKey() returns an integer.

Encrypting or Decrypting the Message

The getTranslatedMessage() function does the actual encrypting and decrypting:

```
def getTranslatedMessage(mode, message, key):
    if mode[0] == 'd':
        key = -key
    translated = ''
```

It has three parameters:

mode This sets the function to encryption mode or decryption mode.

message This is the plaintext (or ciphertext) to be encrypted (or decrypted).

key This is the key that is used in this cipher.

Line 27 checks whether the first letter in the `mode` variable is the string `'d'`. If so, then the program is in decryption mode. The only difference between decryption and encryption mode is that in decryption mode, the key is set to the negative version of itself. For example, if `key` is the integer `22`, then decryption mode sets it to `-22`. The reason is explained in "Encrypting or Decrypting Each Letter" on page 205.

The `translated` variable will contain the string of the result: either the ciphertext (if you are encrypting) or the plaintext (if you are decrypting). It starts as a blank string and has encrypted or decrypted characters concatenated to the end of it. Before we can start concatenating the characters to `translated`, however, we need to encrypt or decrypt the text, which we'll do in the rest of `getTranslatedMessage()`.

Finding Passed Strings with the find() String Method

In order to shift the letters around to do the encryption or decryption, we first need to convert them into numbers. The number for each letter in the `SYMBOLS` string will be the index where it appears. Since the letter A is at `SYMBOLS[0]`, the number `0` will represent the capital A. If we wanted to encrypt this with the key 3, we would simply use 0 + 3 to get the index of the encrypted letter: `SYMBOLS[3]` or `'D'`.

We'll use the `find()` string method, which finds the first occurrence of a passed string in the string on which the method is called. Enter the following in the interactive shell:

```
>>> 'Hello world!'.find('H')
0
>>> 'Hello world!'.find('o')
4
>>> 'Hello world!'.find('ell')
1
```

`'Hello world!'.find('H')` returns `0` because the `'H'` is found at the first index of the string `'Hello world!'`. Remember, indexes start at `0`, not `1`. The code `'Hello world!'.find('o')` returns `4` because the lowercase `'o'` is first found at the end of `'Hello'`. The `find()` method stops looking after the first occurrence, so the second `'o'` in `'world'` doesn't matter. You can also find strings with more than one character. The string `'ell'` is found starting at index `1`.

If the passed string cannot be found, the `find()` method returns `-1`:

```
>>> 'Hello world!'.find('xyz')
-1
```

Let's go back to the Caesar Cipher program. Line 31 is a `for` loop that iterates on each character in the `message` string:

```
31.     for symbol in message:
32.         symbolIndex = SYMBOLS.find(symbol)
33.         if symbolIndex == -1: # Symbol not found in SYMBOLS.
```

```
34.             # Just add this symbol without any change.
35.             translated += symbol
```

The `find()` method is used on line 32 to get the index of the string in `symbol`. If `find()` returns `-1`, the character in `symbol` will just be added to `translated` without any change. This means that any characters that aren't part of the alphabet, such as commas and periods, won't be changed.

Encrypting or Decrypting Each Letter

Once you've found a letter's index number, adding the key to the number will perform the shift and give you the index for the encrypted letter.

Line 38 does this addition to get the encrypted (or decrypted) letter.

```
37.             # Encrypt or decrypt.
38.             symbolIndex += key
```

Remember that on line 28, we made the integer in `key` negative for decryption. The code that adds the key will now subtract it, since adding a negative number is the same as subtraction.

However, if this addition (or subtraction, if `key` is negative) causes `symbolIndex` to go past the last index of `SYMBOLS`, we'll need to wrap around to the beginning of the list at `0`. This is handled by the `if` statement starting at line 40:

```
40.             if symbolIndex >= len(SYMBOLS):
41.                 symbolIndex -= len(SYMBOLS)
42.             elif symbolIndex < 0:
43.                 symbolIndex += len(SYMBOLS)
44.
45.             translated += SYMBOLS[symbolIndex]
```

Line 40 checks whether `symbolIndex` has gone past the last index by comparing it to the length of the `SYMBOLS` string. If it has, line 41 subtracts the length of `SYMBOLS` from `symbolIndex`. If `symbolIndex` is now negative, then the index needs to wrap around to the other side of the `SYMBOLS` string. Line 42 checks whether the value of `symbolIndex` is negative after adding the decryption key. If so, line 43 adds the length of `SYMBOLS` to `symbolIndex`.

The `symbolIndex` variable now contains the index of the correctly encrypted or decrypted symbol. `SYMBOLS[symbolIndex]` will point to the character for this index, and this character is added to the end of `translated` on line 45.

The execution loops back to line 31 to repeat this for the next character in `message`. Once the loop is done, the function returns the encrypted (or decrypted) string in `translated` on line 46:

```
46.     return translated
```

The last line in the `getTranslatedMessage()` function returns the `translated` string.

Starting the Program

The start of the program calls each of the three functions defined previously to get the mode, message, and key from the user:

```
mode = getMode()
message = getMessage()
key = getKey()
print('Your translated text is:')
print(getTranslatedMessage(mode, message, key))
```

These three values are passed to getTranslatedMessage(), whose return value (the translated string) is printed to the user.

EXPANDING THE SYMBOLS

If you want to encrypt numbers, spaces, and punctuation marks, just add them to the SYMBOLS string on line 2. For example, you could have your cipher program encrypt numbers, spaces, and punctuation marks by changing line 2 to the following:

```
2. SYMBOLS = 'ABCDEFGHIJKLMNOPQRSTUVWXYZabcdefghijklmnopqrstuvwxyz 123
     4567890!@#$%^&*()'
```

Note that the SYMBOLS string has a space character after the lowercase z.

If you wanted, you could add even more characters to this list. And you don't need to change the rest of your program, since all the lines of code that need the character list just use the SYMBOLS constant.

Just make sure that each character appears only once in the string. Also, you'll need to decrypt your message with the same SYMBOLS string that it was encrypted with.

The Brute-Force Technique

That's the entire Caesar cipher. However, while this cipher may fool some people who don't understand cryptography, it won't keep a message secret from someone who knows *cryptanalysis*. While cryptography is the science of making codes, cryptanalysis is the science of breaking codes.

The whole point of cryptography is to make sure that if someone else gets their hands on the encrypted message, they cannot figure out the original text. Let's pretend we are the code breaker and all we have is this encrypted text:

```
LwCjBA uiG vwB jm xtmiAivB, jCB kmzBiqvBG qA ijACzl.
```

Brute-forcing is the technique of trying every possible key until you find the correct one. Because there are only 52 possible keys, it would be easy for a cryptanalyst to write a hacking program that decrypts with every possible key. Then they could look for the key that decrypts to plain English. Let's add a brute-force feature to the program.

Adding the Brute-Force Mode

First, change lines 7, 9, and 12—which are in the `getMode()` function—to look like the following (the changes are in bold):

```
 5. def getMode():
 6.     while True:
 7.         print('Do you wish to encrypt or decrypt or brute-force a
              message?')
 8.         mode = input().lower()
 9.         if mode in ['encrypt', 'e', 'decrypt', 'd', 'brute', 'b']:
10.             return mode
11.         else:
12.             print('Enter either "encrypt" or "e" or "decrypt" or "d" or
                  "brute" or "b".')
```

This code will let the user select brute force as a mode.

Next, make the following changes to the main part of the program:

```
mode = getMode()
message = getMessage()
if mode[0] != 'b':
    key = getKey()
print('Your translated text is:')
if mode[0] != 'b':
    print(getTranslatedMessage(mode, message, key))
else:
    for key in range(1, MAX_KEY_SIZE + 1):
        print(key, getTranslatedMessage('decrypt', message, key))
```

If the user is not in brute-force mode, they are asked for a key, the original `getTranslatedMessage()` call is made, and the translated string is printed.

However, if the user is in brute-force mode, then the `getTranslatedMessage()` loop iterates from `1` all the way up to `MAX_KEY_SIZE` (which is `52`). Remember that the `range()` function returns a list of integers up to, but not including, the second parameter, which is why we add `+ 1`. The program will then print every possible translation of the message (including the key number used in the translation). Here is a sample run of this modified program:

```
Do you wish to encrypt or decrypt or brute-force a message?
brute
Enter your message:
LwCjBA uiG vwB jm xtmiAivB, jCB kmzBiqvBG qA ijACzl.
```

```
Your translated text is:
1 KvBiAz thF uvA il wslhzhuA, iBA jlyAhpuAF pz hizByk.
2 JuAhzy sgE tuz hk vrkgygtz, hAz ikxzgotzE oy ghyAxj.
3 Itzgyx rfD sty gj uqjfxfsy, gzy hjwyfnsyD nx fgxzwi.
4 Hsyfxw qeC rsx fi tpiewerx, fyx givxemrxC mw efwyvh.
5 Grxewv pdB qrw eh sohdvdqw, exw fhuwdlqwB lv devxug.
6 Fqwdvu ocA pqv dg rngcucpv, dwv egtvckpvA ku cduwtf.
7 Epvcut nbz opu cf qmfbtbou, cvu dfsubjouz jt bctvse.
8 Doubts may not be pleasant, but certainty is absurd.
9 Cntasr lZx mns ad okdZrZms, ats bdqsZhmsx hr Zartqc.
10 BmsZrq kYw lmr Zc njcYqYlr, Zsr acprYglrw gq YZqspb.
11 AlrYqp jXv klq Yb mibXpXkq, Yrq ZboqXfkqv fp XYproa.
12 zkqXpo iWu jkp Xa lhaWoWjp, Xqp YanpWejpu eo WXoqnZ.
--snip--
```

After looking over each row, you can see that the eighth message isn't nonsense but plain English! The cryptanalyst can deduce that the original key for this encrypted text must have been 8. This brute-force method would have been difficult to do back in the days of Julius Caesar and the Roman Empire, but today we have computers that can quickly go through millions or even billions of keys in a short time.

Summary

Computers are good at doing math. When we create a system to translate some piece of information into numbers (as we do with text and ordinals or with space and coordinate systems), computer programs can process these numbers quickly and efficiently. A large part of writing a program is figuring out how to represent the information you want to manipulate as values that Python can understand.

While our Caesar Cipher program can encrypt messages that will keep them secret from people who have to figure them out with pencil and paper, the program won't keep them secret from people who know how to get computers to process information. (Our brute-force mode proves this.)

In Chapter 15, we'll create Reversegam (also known as Reversi or Othello). The AI that plays this game is much more advanced than the AI that played Tic-Tac-Toe in Chapter 10. In fact, it's so good that most of the time you won't be able to beat it!

15

THE REVERSEGAM GAME

In this chapter, we'll make Reversegam, also known as Reversi or Othello. This two-player board game is played on a grid, so we'll use a Cartesian coordinate system with x- and y-coordinates. Our version of the game will have a computer AI that is more advanced than our Tic-Tac-Toe AI from Chapter 10. In fact, this AI is so good that it will probably beat you almost every time you play. (I lose whenever I play against it!)

TOPICS COVERED IN THIS CHAPTER

- How to play Reversegam
- The `bool()` function
- Simulating moves on a Reversegam board
- Programming a Reversegam AI

How to Play Reversegam

Reversegam has an 8×8 board and tiles that are black on one side and white on the other (our game will use *O*s and *X*s instead). The starting board looks like Figure 15-1.

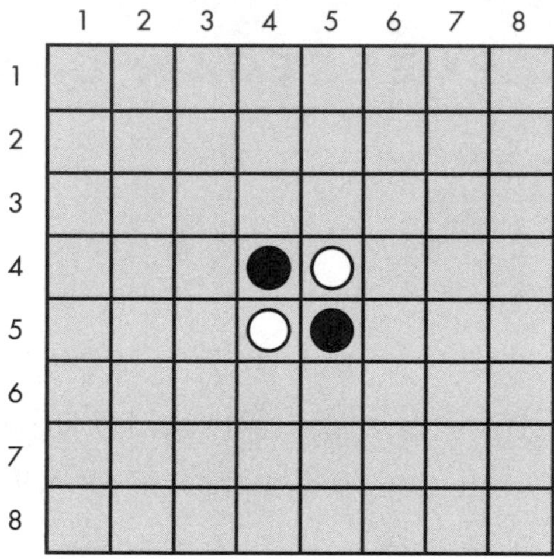

Figure 15-1: The starting Reversegam board has two white tiles and two black tiles.

Two players take turns placing tiles of their chosen color—black or white—on the board. When a player places a tile on the board, any of the opponent's tiles that are between the new tile and the other tiles of the player's color are flipped. For example, when the white player places a new white tile on space (5, 6), as in Figure 15-2, the black tile at (5, 5) is between two white tiles, so it will flip to white, as in Figure 15-3. The goal of the game is to end with more tiles of your color than your opponent's color.

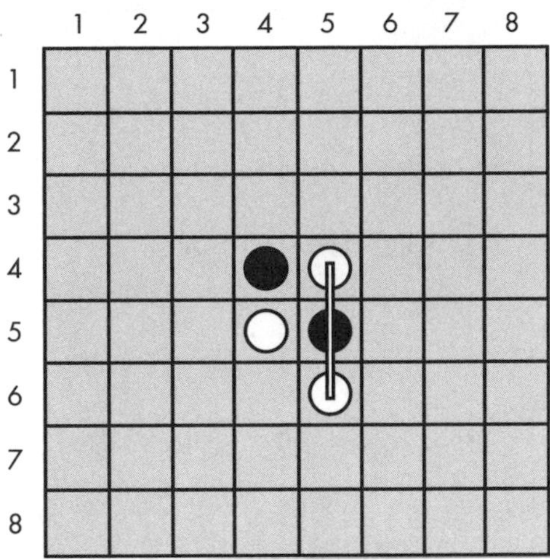

Figure 15-2: White places a new tile.

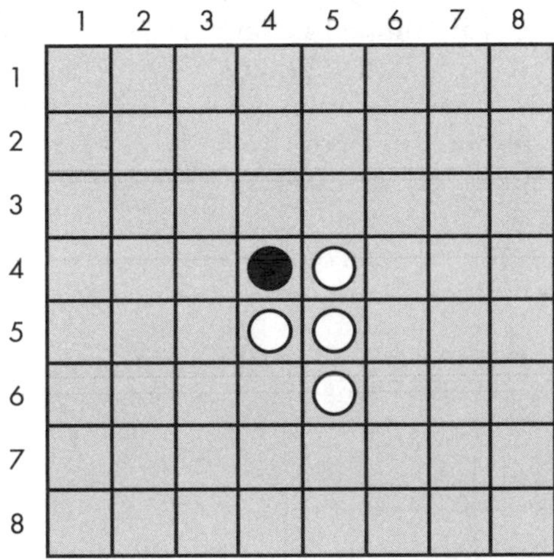

Figure 15-3: White's move has caused one of black's tiles to flip.

Black could make a similar move next, placing a black tile on (4, 6), which would flip the white tile at (4, 5). This results in a board that looks like Figure 15-4.

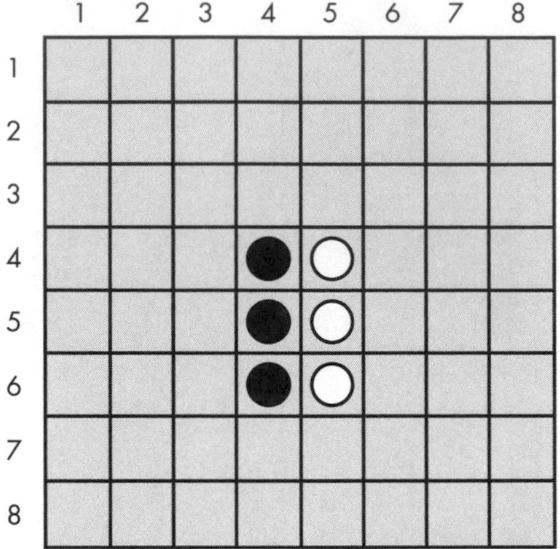

Figure 15-4: Black has placed a new tile, flipping one of white's tiles.

Tiles in all directions are flipped as long as they are between the player's new tile and an existing tile of that color. In Figure 15-5, white places a tile at (3, 6) and flips black tiles in two directions (marked by the lines). The result is shown in Figure 15-6.

Each player can quickly flip many tiles on the board in one or two moves. Players must always make a move that flips at least one tile. The game ends when either a player can't make a move or the board is completely full. The player with the most tiles of their color wins.

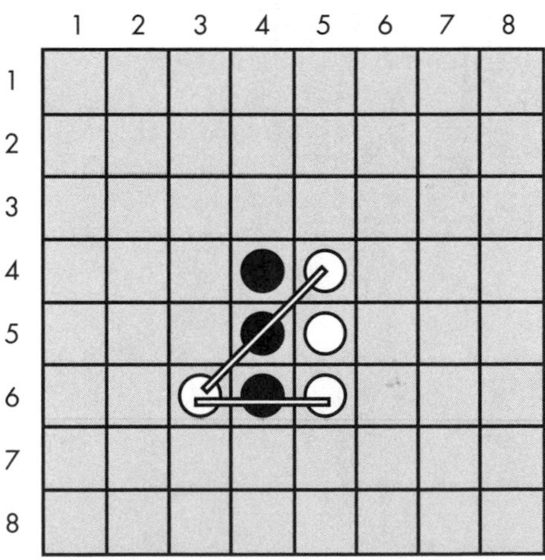

Figure 15-5: White's second move at (3, 6) will flip two of black's tiles.

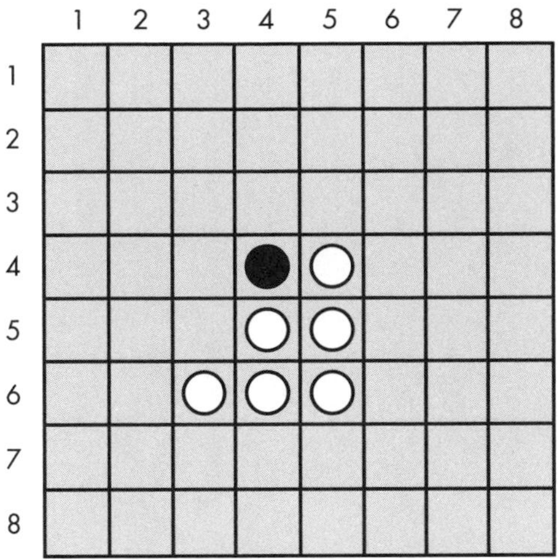

Figure 15-6: The board after white's second move.

The AI we make for this game will look for any corner moves on the board it can take. If there are no corner moves available, the computer will select the move that claims the most tiles.

Sample Run of Reversegam

Here's what the user sees when they run the Reversegam program. The text entered by the player is bold.

```
Welcome to Reversegam!
Do you want to be X or O?
x
The player will go first.
  12345678
 +--------+
1|        |1
2|        |2
3|        |3
4|   XO   |4
5|   OX   |5
6|        |6
7|        |7
8|        |8
 +--------+
  12345678
You: 2 points. Computer: 2 points.
Enter your move, "quit" to end the game, or "hints" to toggle hints.
53
```

```
  12345678
 +--------+
1|        |1
2|        |2
3|    X   |3
4|   XX   |4
5|   OX   |5
6|        |6
7|        |7
8|        |8
 +--------+
  12345678
You: 4 points. Computer: 1 points.
Press Enter to see the computer's move.

--snip--

  12345678
 +--------+
1|OOOOOOOO|1
2|OXXXOOOO|2
3|OXOOOOOO|3
4|OXXOXXOX|4
5|OXXOOXOX|5
6|OXXXXOOX|6
7|OOXXOOOO|7
8|OOXOOOOO|8
 +--------+
  12345678
X scored 21 points. O scored 43 points.
You lost. The computer beat you by 22 points.
Do you want to play again? (yes or no)
no
```

As you can see, the AI was pretty good at beating me, 43 to 21. To help the player out, we'll program the game to provide hints. The player can type `hints` as their move, which will toggle the hints mode on and off. When hints mode is on, all the possible moves the player can make will show up on the board as periods (.), like this:

```
  12345678
 +--------+
1|        |1
2|   .    |2
3|  XO.   |3
4|   XOX  |4
5|   OOO  |5
6|   . .  |6
7|        |7
8|        |8
 +--------+
  12345678
```

As you can see, the player can move on (4, 2), (5, 3), (4, 6), or (6, 6) based on the hints shown on this board.

Source Code for Reversegam

MAKE SURE YOU'RE
USING PYTHON 3,
NOT PYTHON 2!

Reversegam is a mammoth program compared to our previous games. It's nearly 300 lines long! But don't worry: many of these are comments or blank lines to space out the code and make it more readable.

As with our other programs, we'll first create several functions to carry out Reversegam-related tasks that the main section will call. Roughly the first 250 lines of code are for these helper functions, and the last 30 lines of code implement the Reversegam game itself.

If you get errors after entering this code, compare your code to the book's code with the online diff tool at *https://www.nostarch.com/inventwithpython#diff*.

reversegam.py

```
# Reversegam: a clone of Othello/Reversi
import random
import sys
WIDTH = 8  # Board is 8 spaces wide.
HEIGHT = 8 # Board is 8 spaces tall.
def drawBoard(board):
    # Print the board passed to this function. Return None.
    print('  12345678')
    print(' +--------+')
    for y in range(HEIGHT):
        print('%s|' % (y+1), end='')
        for x in range(WIDTH):
            print(board[x][y], end='')
        print('|%s' % (y+1))
    print(' +--------+')
    print('  12345678')

def getNewBoard():
    # Create a brand-new, blank board data structure.
    board = []
    for i in range(WIDTH):
        board.append([' ', ' ', ' ', ' ', ' ', ' ', ' ', ' '])
    return board

def isValidMove(board, tile, xstart, ystart):
    # Return False if the player's move on space xstart, ystart is invalid.
    # If it is a valid move, return a list of spaces that would become the player's if they made a move here.
    if board[xstart][ystart] != ' ' or not isOnBoard(xstart, ystart):
        return False
```

```

    if tile == 'X':
        otherTile = 'O'
    else:
        otherTile = 'X'

    tilesToFlip = []
    for xdirection, ydirection in [[0, 1], [1, 1], [1, 0], [1, -1], [0, -1], [-1, -1], [-1, 0], [-1, 1]]:
        x, y = xstart, ystart
        x += xdirection # First step in the x direction
        y += ydirection # First step in the y direction
        while isOnBoard(x, y) and board[x][y] == otherTile:
            # Keep moving in this x & y direction.
            x += xdirection
            y += ydirection
            if isOnBoard(x, y) and board[x][y] == tile:
                # There are pieces to flip over. Go in the reverse direction until we reach the original space, noting all the tiles along the way.
                while True:
                    x -= xdirection
                    y -= ydirection
                    if x == xstart and y == ystart:
                        break
                    tilesToFlip.append([x, y])

    if len(tilesToFlip) == 0: # If no tiles were flipped, this is not a valid move.
        return False
    return tilesToFlip

def isOnBoard(x, y):
    # Return True if the coordinates are located on the board.
    return x >= 0 and x <= WIDTH - 1 and y >= 0 and y <= HEIGHT - 1

def getBoardWithValidMoves(board, tile):
    # Return a new board with periods marking the valid moves the player can make.
    boardCopy = getBoardCopy(board)

    for x, y in getValidMoves(boardCopy, tile):
        boardCopy[x][y] = '.'
    return boardCopy

def getValidMoves(board, tile):
    # Return a list of [x,y] lists of valid moves for the given player on the given board.
    validMoves = []
    for x in range(WIDTH):
        for y in range(HEIGHT):
            if isValidMove(board, tile, x, y) != False:
                validMoves.append([x, y])
    return validMoves

```

```
def getScoreOfBoard(board):
    # Determine the score by counting the tiles. Return a dictionary with keys 'X' and 'O'.
    xscore = 0
    oscore = 0
    for x in range(WIDTH):
        for y in range(HEIGHT):
            if board[x][y] == 'X':
                xscore += 1
            if board[x][y] == 'O':
                oscore += 1
    return {'X':xscore, 'O':oscore}

def enterPlayerTile():
    # Let the player enter which tile they want to be.
    # Return a list with the player's tile as the first item and the computer's tile as the second.
    tile = ''
    while not (tile == 'X' or tile == 'O'):
        print('Do you want to be X or O?')
        tile = input().upper()

    # The first element in the list is the player's tile, and the second is the computer's tile.
    if tile == 'X':
        return ['X', 'O']
    else:
        return ['O', 'X']

def whoGoesFirst():
    # Randomly choose who goes first.
    if random.randint(0, 1) == 0:
        return 'computer'
    else:
        return 'player'

def makeMove(board, tile, xstart, ystart):
    # Place the tile on the board at xstart, ystart and flip any of the opponent's pieces.
    # Return False if this is an invalid move; True if it is valid.
    tilesToFlip = isValidMove(board, tile, xstart, ystart)

    if tilesToFlip == False:
        return False

    board[xstart][ystart] = tile
    for x, y in tilesToFlip:
        board[x][y] = tile
    return True

def getBoardCopy(board):
    # Make a duplicate of the board list and return it.
    boardCopy = getNewBoard()

```

```
    for x in range(WIDTH):
        for y in range(HEIGHT):
            boardCopy[x][y] = board[x][y]

    return boardCopy

def isOnCorner(x, y):
    # Return True if the position is in one of the four corners.
    return (x == 0 or x == WIDTH - 1) and (y == 0 or y == HEIGHT - 1)

def getPlayerMove(board, playerTile):
    # Let the player enter their move.
    # Return the move as [x, y] (or return the strings 'hints' or 'quit').
    DIGITS1TO8 = '1 2 3 4 5 6 7 8'.split()
    while True:
        print('Enter your move, "quit" to end the game, or "hints" to toggle hints.')
        move = input().lower()
        if move == 'quit' or move == 'hints':
            return move

        if len(move) == 2 and move[0] in DIGITS1TO8 and move[1] in DIGITS1TO8:
            x = int(move[0]) - 1
            y = int(move[1]) - 1
            if isValidMove(board, playerTile, x, y) == False:
                continue
            else:
                break
        else:
            print('That is not a valid move. Enter the column (1-8) and then the row (1-8).')
            print('For example, 81 will move on the top-right corner.')

    return [x, y]

def getComputerMove(board, computerTile):
    # Given a board and the computer's tile, determine where to
    # move and return that move as an [x, y] list.
    possibleMoves = getValidMoves(board, computerTile)
    random.shuffle(possibleMoves) # Randomize the order of the moves.

    # Always go for a corner if available.
    for x, y in possibleMoves:
        if isOnCorner(x, y):
            return [x, y]

    # Find the highest-scoring move possible.
    bestScore = -1
    for x, y in possibleMoves:
        boardCopy = getBoardCopy(board)
        makeMove(boardCopy, computerTile, x, y)
        score = getScoreOfBoard(boardCopy)[computerTile]
        if score > bestScore:
```

```
                bestMove = [x, y]
                bestScore = score
    return bestMove

def printScore(board, playerTile, computerTile):
    scores = getScoreOfBoard(board)
    print('You: %s points. Computer: %s points.' % (scores[playerTile],
      scores[computerTile]))

def playGame(playerTile, computerTile):
    showHints = False
    turn = whoGoesFirst()
    print('The ' + turn + ' will go first.')

    # Clear the board and place starting pieces.
    board = getNewBoard()
    board[3][3] = 'X'
    board[3][4] = 'O'
    board[4][3] = 'O'
    board[4][4] = 'X'

    while True:
        playerValidMoves = getValidMoves(board, playerTile)
        computerValidMoves = getValidMoves(board, computerTile)

        if playerValidMoves == [] and computerValidMoves == []:
            return board # No one can move, so end the game.

        elif turn == 'player': # Player's turn
            if playerValidMoves != []:
                if showHints:
                    validMovesBoard = getBoardWithValidMoves(board,
                      playerTile)
                    drawBoard(validMovesBoard)
                else:
                    drawBoard(board)
                printScore(board, playerTile, computerTile)

                move = getPlayerMove(board, playerTile)
                if move == 'quit':
                    print('Thanks for playing!')
                    sys.exit() # Terminate the program.
                elif move == 'hints':
                    showHints = not showHints
                    continue
                else:
                    makeMove(board, playerTile, move[0], move[1])
            turn = 'computer'

        elif turn == 'computer': # Computer's turn
            if computerValidMoves != []:
                drawBoard(board)
                printScore(board, playerTile, computerTile)

                input('Press Enter to see the computer\'s move.')
```

```
                move = getComputerMove(board, computerTile)
                makeMove(board, computerTile, move[0], move[1])
            turn = 'player'



print('Welcome to Reversegam!')

playerTile, computerTile = enterPlayerTile()

while True:
    finalBoard = playGame(playerTile, computerTile)

    # Display the final score.
    drawBoard(finalBoard)
    scores = getScoreOfBoard(finalBoard)
    print('X scored %s points. O scored %s points.' % (scores['X'], scores['O']))
    if scores[playerTile] > scores[computerTile]:
        print('You beat the computer by %s points! Congratulations!' % (scores[playerTile] - scores[computerTile]))
    elif scores[playerTile] < scores[computerTile]:
        print('You lost. The computer beat you by %s points.' % (scores[computerTile] - scores[playerTile]))
    else:
        print('The game was a tie!')

    print('Do you want to play again? (yes or no)')
    if not input().lower().startswith('y'):
        break
```

Importing Modules and Setting Up Constants

As with our other games, we begin this program by importing modules:

```
1. # Reversegam: a clone of Othello/Reversi
2. import random
3. import sys
4. WIDTH = 8  # Board is 8 spaces wide.
5. HEIGHT = 8 # Board is 8 spaces tall.
```

Line 2 imports the `random` module for its `randint()` and `choice()` functions. Line 3 imports the sys module for its exit() function.

Lines 4 and 5 set two constants, `WIDTH` and `HEIGHT`, which are used to set up the game board.

The Game Board Data Structure

Let's figure out the board's data structure. This data structure is a list of lists, just like the one in Chapter 13's Sonar Treasure Hunt game. The list of lists is created so that `board[x][y]` will represent the character on the space located at position x on the x-axis (going left/right) and position y on the y-axis (going up/down).

This character can either be a ' ' (a space representing an empty position), a '.' (a period representing a possible move in hints mode), or an 'X' or 'O' (letters representing tiles). Whenever you see a parameter named board, it is meant to be this kind of list-of-lists data structure.

It is important to note that while the x- and y-coordinates for the game board will range from 1 to 8, the indexes of the list data structure will range from 0 to 7. Our code will need to make slight adjustments to account for this.

Drawing the Board Data Structure on the Screen

The board data structure is just a Python list value, but we need a nicer way to present it on the screen. The drawBoard() function takes a board data structure and displays it on the screen so the player knows where tiles are placed:

```
 6. def drawBoard(board):
 7.     # Print the board passed to this function. Return None.
 8.     print('  12345678')
 9.     print(' +--------+')
10.     for y in range(HEIGHT):
11.         print('%s|' % (y+1), end='')
12.         for x in range(WIDTH):
13.             print(board[x][y], end='')
14.         print('|%s' % (y+1))
15.     print(' +--------+')
16.     print('  12345678')
```

The drawBoard() function prints the current game board based on the data structure in board.

Line 8 is the first print() function call executed for each board, and it prints the labels for the x-axis along the top of the board. Line 9 prints the top horizontal line of the board. The for loop on line 10 will loop eight times, once for each row. Line 11 prints the label for the y-axis on the left side of the board, and it has an end='' keyword argument to print nothing instead of a new line.

This is so that another loop on line 12 (which also loops eight times, once for each column in the row) prints each position along with an X, O, ., or blank space depending on what's stored in board[x][y]. Line 13's print() function call inside this loop also has an end='' keyword argument so that the newline character is not printed. That will produce a single line on the screen that looks like '1|XXXXXXXX|1' (if each of the board[x][y] values were an 'X').

After the inner loop is done, the print() function calls on lines 15 and 16 to print the bottom horizontal line and x-axis labels.

When the for loop on line 13 prints the row eight times, it forms the entire board:

```
  12345678
 +--------+
1|XXXXXXXX|1
2|XXXXXXXX|2
3|XXXXXXXX|3
4|XXXXXXXX|4
5|XXXXXXXX|5
6|XXXXXXXX|6
7|XXXXXXXX|7
8|XXXXXXXX|8
 +--------+
  12345678
```

Of course, instead of X, some of the spaces on the board will be the other player's mark (O), a period (.) if hints mode is turned on, or a space for empty positions.

Creating a Fresh Board Data Structure

The drawBoard() function will display a board data structure on the screen, but we need a way to create these board data structures as well. The getNewBoard() function returns a list of eight lists, with each list containing eight ' ' strings that will represent a blank board with no moves:

```
18. def getNewBoard():
19.     # Create a brand-new, blank board data structure.
20.     board = []
21.     for i in range(WIDTH):
22.         board.append([' ', ' ', ' ', ' ', ' ', ' ', ' ', ' '])
23.     return board
```

Line 20 creates the list that contains the inner lists. The for loop adds eight inner lists inside this list. These inner lists have eight strings to represent eight empty spaces on the board. Together, this code creates a board with 64 empty spaces—a blank Reversegam board.

Checking Whether a Move Is Valid

Given the board's data structure, the player's tile, and the x- and y-coordinates for the player's move, the isValidMove() function should return True if the Reversegam game rules allow a move on those coordinates, and False if they don't. For a move to be valid, it must be on the board and also flip at least one of the opponent's tiles.

This function uses several x- and y-coordinates on the board, so the xstart and ystart variables keep track of the x- and y-coordinates of the original move.

```
25. def isValidMove(board, tile, xstart, ystart):
26.     # Return False if the player's move on space xstart, ystart is invalid.
27.     # If it is a valid move, return a list of spaces that would become the player's if they made a move here.
28.     if board[xstart][ystart] != ' ' or not isOnBoard(xstart, ystart):
29.         return False
30.
31.     if tile == 'X':
32.         otherTile = 'O'
33.     else:
34.         otherTile = 'X'
35.
36.     tilesToFlip = []
```

Line 28 checks whether the x- and y-coordinates are on the game board and whether the space is empty using the `isOnBoard()` function (which we'll define later in the program). This function makes sure both the x- and y-coordinates are between `0` and the `WIDTH` or `HEIGHT` of the board minus `1`.

The player's tile (either the human player or the computer player) is in `tile`, but this function will need to know the opponent's tile. If the player's tile is `X`, then obviously the opponent's tile is `O`, and vice versa. We use the `if-else` statement on lines 31 to 34 for this.

Finally, if the given x- and y-coordinate is a valid move, `isValidMove()` returns a list of all the opponent's tiles that would be flipped by this move. We create a new empty list, `tilesToFlip`, that we'll use to store all the tile coordinates.

Checking Each of the Eight Directions

In order for a move to be valid, it needs to flip at least one of the opponent's tiles by sandwiching the current player's new tile with one of the player's old tiles. That means that the new tile must be next to one of the opponent's tiles.

The `for` loop on line 37 iterates through a list of lists that represents the directions the program will check for an opponent's tile:

```
37.     for xdirection, ydirection in [[0, 1], [1, 1], [1, 0], [1, -1], [0, -1], [-1, -1], [-1, 0], [-1, 1]]:
```

The game board is a Cartesian coordinate system with x- and y-directions. There are eight directions to check: up, down, left, right, and the four diagonal directions. Each of the eight two-item lists in the list on line 37 is used for checking one of these directions. The program checks a direction by adding the first value in the two-item list to the x-coordinate and the second value to the y-coordinate.

Because the x-coordinates increase as you go to the right, you can check the right direction by adding `1` to the x-coordinate. So the `[1, 0]` list adds `1` to the x-coordinate and `0` to the y-coordinate. Checking the left direction is the opposite: you would subtract `1` (that is, add `-1`) from the x-coordinate.

But to check diagonally, you need to add to or subtract from both coordinates. For example, adding `1` to the x-coordinate and adding `-1` to the y-coordinate would result in checking the up-right diagonal direction.

Figure 15-7 shows a diagram to make it easier to remember which two-item list represents which direction.

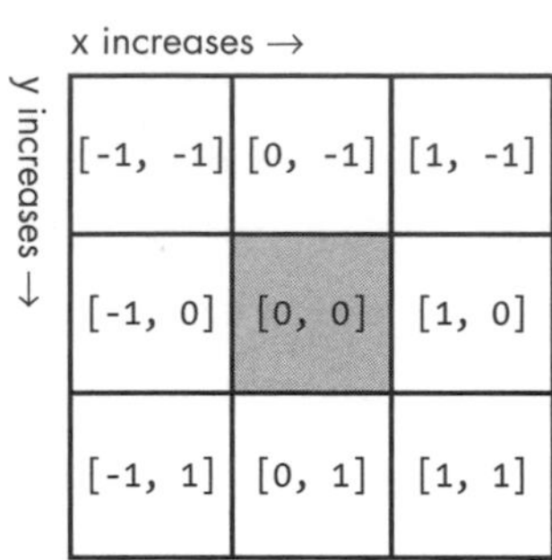

Figure 15-7: Each two-item list represents one of the eight directions.

The `for` loop at line 37 iterates through each of the two-item lists so that each direction is checked. Inside the `for` loop, the `x` and `y` variables are set to the same values as `xstart` and `ystart`, respectively, using multiple assignment at line 38. The `xdirection` and `ydirection` variables are set to the values in one of the two-item lists and change the `x` and `y` variables according to the direction being checked in that iteration of the `for` loop:

```
37.     for xdirection, ydirection in [[0, 1], [1, 1], [1, 0], [1, -1],
          [0, -1], [-1, -1], [-1, 0], [-1, 1]]:
38.         x, y = xstart, ystart
39.         x += xdirection # First step in the x direction
40.         y += ydirection # First step in the y direction
```

The `xstart` and `ystart` variables will stay the same so that the program can remember which space it originally started from.

Remember, for a move to be valid, it must be both on the board and next to one of the other player's tiles. (Otherwise, there aren't any of the opponent's tiles to flip, and a move must flip over at least one tile to be valid.) Line 41 checks this condition, and if it isn't `True`, the execution goes back to the `for` statement to check the next direction.

```
41.         while isOnBoard(x, y) and board[x][y] == otherTile:
42.             # Keep moving in this x & y direction.
43.             x += xdirection
44.             y += ydirection
```

But if the first space checked does have the opponent's tile, then the program should check for more of the opponent's tiles in that direction until it reaches one of the player's tiles or the end of the board. The next tile in the same direction is checked by using `xdirection` and `ydirection` again to make `x` and `y` the next coordinates to check. So the program changes `x` and `y` on lines 43 and 44.

Finding Out Whether There Are Tiles to Flip Over

Next, we check whether there are adjacent tiles that can be flipped over.

```
45.             if isOnBoard(x, y) and board[x][y] == tile:
46.                 # There are pieces to flip over. Go in the reverse
                      direction until we reach the original space, noting all
                      the tiles along the way.
47.                 while True:
48.                     x -= xdirection
49.                     y -= ydirection
50.                     if x == xstart and y == ystart:
51.                         break
52.                     tilesToFlip.append([x, y])
```

The `if` statement on line 45 checks whether a coordinate is occupied by the player's own tile. This tile will mark the end of the sandwich made by the player's tiles surrounding the opponent's tiles. We also need to record the coordinates of all of the opponent's tiles that should be flipped.

The `while` loop moves `x` and `y` in reverse on lines 48 and 49. Until `x` and `y` are back to the original `xstart` and `ystart` position, `xdirection` and `ydirection` are subtracted from `x` and `y`, and each `x` and `y` position is appended to the `tilesToFlip` list. When `x` and `y` have reached the `xstart` and `ystart` position, line 51 breaks the execution out of the loop. Since the original `xstart` and `ystart` position is an empty space (we ensured this was the case on lines 28 and 29), the condition for line 41's `while` loop will be `False`. The program moves on to line 37, and the `for` loop checks the next direction.

The `for` loop does this in all eight directions. After that loop is done, the `tilesToFlip` list will contain the x- and y-coordinates of all our opponent's tiles that would be flipped if the player moved on `xstart`, `ystart`. Remember, the `isValidMove()` function is only checking whether the original move was valid; it doesn't actually permanently change the data structure of the game board.

If none of the eight directions ended up flipping at least one of the opponent's tiles, then `tilesToFlip` will be an empty list:

```
54.     if len(tilesToFlip) == 0: # If no tiles were flipped, this is not a
          valid move.
55.         return False
56.     return tilesToFlip
```

This is a sign that this move is not valid and `isValidMove()` should return `False`. Otherwise, `isValidMove()` returns `tilesToFlip`.

Checking for Valid Coordinates

The `isOnBoard()` function is called from `isValidMove()`. It does a simple check to see whether given x- and y-coordinates are on the board. For example, an x-coordinate of `4` and a y-coordinate of `9999` would not be on the board since y-coordinates only go up to `7`, which is equal to `WIDTH - 1` or `HEIGHT - 1`.

```
58. def isOnBoard(x, y):
59.     # Return True if the coordinates are located on the board.
60.     return x >= 0 and x <= WIDTH - 1 and y >= 0 and y <= HEIGHT - 1
```

Calling this function is shorthand for the Boolean expression on line 72 that checks whether both x and y are between 0 and the WIDTH or HEIGHT subtracted by 1, which is 7.

Getting a List with All Valid Moves

Now let's create a hints mode that displays a board with all possible moves marked on it. The getBoardWithValidMoves() function returns a game board data structure that has periods (.) for all spaces that are valid moves:

```
62. def getBoardWithValidMoves(board, tile):
63.     # Return a new board with periods marking the valid moves the player
          can make.
64.     boardCopy = getBoardCopy(board)
65.
66.     for x, y in getValidMoves(boardCopy, tile):
67.         boardCopy[x][y] = '.'
68.     return boardCopy
```

This function creates a duplicate game board data structure called boardCopy (returned by getBoardCopy() on line 64) instead of modifying the one passed to it in the board parameter. Line 66 calls getValidMoves() to get a list of x- and y-coordinates with all the legal moves the player could make. The board copy is marked with periods in those spaces and returned.

The getValidMoves() function returns a list of two-item lists. The two-item lists hold the x- and y-coordinates for all valid moves of the tile given to it for the board data structure in the board parameter:

```
70. def getValidMoves(board, tile):
71.     # Return a list of [x,y] lists of valid moves for the given player
          on the given board.
72.     validMoves = []
73.     for x in range(WIDTH):
74.         for y in range(HEIGHT):
75.             if isValidMove(board, tile, x, y) != False:
76.                 validMoves.append([x, y])
77.     return validMoves
```

This function uses nested loops (on lines 73 and 74) to check every x- and y-coordinate (all 64 of them) by calling isValidMove() on that space and checking whether it returns False or a list of possible moves (in which case the move is valid). Each valid x- and y-coordinate is appended to the list in validMoves.

Calling the bool() Function

You may have noticed that the program checks whether `isValidMove()` on line 75 returns `False` even though this function returns a list. To understand how this works, you need to learn a bit more about Booleans and the `bool()` function.

The `bool()` function is similar to the `int()` and `str()` functions. It returns the Boolean value form of the value passed to it.

Most data types have one value that is considered the `False` value for that data type. Every other value is considered `True`. For example, the integer `0`, the floating-point number `0.0`, an empty string, an empty list, and an empty dictionary are all considered to be `False` when used as the condition for an `if` or loop statement. All other values are `True`. Enter the following into the interactive shell:

```
>>> bool(0)
False
>>> bool(0.0)
False
>>> bool('')
False
>>> bool([])
False
>>> bool({})
False
>>> bool(1)
True
>>> bool('Hello')
True
>>> bool([1, 2, 3, 4, 5])
True
>>> bool({'spam':'cheese', 'fizz':'buzz'})
True
```

Conditions are automatically interpreted as Boolean values. This is why the condition on line 75 works correctly. The call to the `isValidMove()` function either returns the Boolean value `False` or a nonempty list.

If you imagine that the entire condition is placed inside a call to `bool()`, then line 75's condition `False` becomes `bool(False)` (which, of course, evaluates to `False`). And a condition of a nonempty list placed as the parameter to `bool()` will return `True`.

Getting the Score of the Game Board

The `getScoreOfBoard()` function uses nested `for` loops to check all 64 positions on the board and see which player's tile (if any) is on them:

```
79. def getScoreOfBoard(board):
80.     # Determine the score by counting the tiles. Return a dictionary
          with keys 'X' and 'O'.
```

```
81.     xscore = 0
82.     oscore = 0
83.     for x in range(WIDTH):
84.         for y in range(HEIGHT):
85.             if board[x][y] == 'X':
86.                 xscore += 1
87.             if board[x][y] == 'O':
88.                 oscore += 1
89.     return {'X':xscore, 'O':oscore}
```

For each X tile, the code increments xscore on line 86. For each O tile, the code increments oscore on line 88. The function then returns xscore and oscore in a dictionary.

Getting the Player's Tile Choice

The enterPlayerTile() function asks the player which tile they want to be, either *X* or *O*:

```
def enterPlayerTile():
    # Let the player enter which tile they want to be.
    # Return a list with the player's tile as the first item and the computer's tile as the second.
    tile = ''
    while not (tile == 'X' or tile == 'O'):
        print('Do you want to be X or O?')
        tile = input().upper()

    # The first element in the list is the player's tile, and the second is the computer's tile.
    if tile == 'X':
        return ['X', 'O']
    else:
        return ['O', 'X']
```

The for loop will keep looping until the player enters X or O in either upper- or lowercase. The enterPlayerTile() function then returns a two-item list, where the player's tile choice is the first item and the computer's tile is the second. Later, line 241 calls enterPlayerTile() and uses multiple assignment to put these two returned items in two variables.

Determining Who Goes First

The whoGoesFirst() function randomly selects who goes first and returns either the string 'computer' or the string 'player':

```
def whoGoesFirst():
    # Randomly choose who goes first.
    if random.randint(0, 1) == 0:
        return 'computer'
```

```
109.     else:
110.         return 'player'
```

Placing a Tile on the Board

The makeMove() function is called when a player wants to place a tile on the board and flip the other tiles according to the rules of Reversegam:

```
112. def makeMove(board, tile, xstart, ystart):
113.     # Place the tile on the board at xstart, ystart and flip any of the
           opponent's pieces.
114.     # Return False if this is an invalid move; True if it is valid.
115.     tilesToFlip = isValidMove(board, tile, xstart, ystart)
```

This function modifies in place the board data structure that is passed. Changes made to the board variable (because it is a list reference) will be made to the global scope.

Most of the work is done by isValidMove() on line 115, which returns a list of x- and y-coordinates (in a two-item list) of tiles that need to be flipped. Remember, if the xstart and ystart arguments point to an invalid move, isValidMove() will return the Boolean value False, which is checked for by line 117:

```
117.     if tilesToFlip == False:
118.         return False
119.
120.     board[xstart][ystart] = tile
121.     for x, y in tilesToFlip:
122.         board[x][y] = tile
123.     return True
```

If the return value of isValidMove() (now stored in tilesToFlip) is False, then makeMove() will also return False on line 118.

Otherwise, isValidMove() returns a list of spaces on the board to put down the tiles (the 'X' or 'O' string in tile). Line 120 sets the space that the player has moved on. Line 121 for loop sets all the tiles that are in tilesToFlip.

Copying the Board Data Structure

The getBoardCopy() function is different from getNewBoard(). The getNewBoard() function creates a blank game board data structure that has only empty spaces and the four starting tiles. getBoardCopy() creates a blank game board data structure but then copies all of the positions in the board parameter with a nested loop. The AI uses the getBoardCopy() function so it can make changes to the game board copy without changing the real game board. This technique was also used by the Tic-Tac-Toe program in Chapter 10.

```
def getBoardCopy(board):
    # Make a duplicate of the board list and return it.
    boardCopy = getNewBoard()

    for x in range(WIDTH):
        for y in range(HEIGHT):
            boardCopy[x][y] = board[x][y]

    return boardCopy
```

A call to getNewBoard() sets up boardCopy as a fresh game board data structure. Then the two nested for loops copy each of the 64 tiles from board to the duplicate board data structure in boardCopy.

Determining Whether a Space Is on a Corner

The isOnCorner() function returns True if the coordinates are on a corner space at coordinates (0, 0), (7, 0), (0, 7), or (7, 7):

```
def isOnCorner(x, y):
    # Return True if the position is in one of the four corners.
    return (x == 0 or x == WIDTH - 1) and (y == 0 or y == HEIGHT - 1)
```

Otherwise, isOnCorner() returns False. We'll use this function later for the AI.

Getting the Player's Move

The getPlayerMove() function is called to let the player enter the coordinates of their next move (and check whether the move is valid). The player can also enter hints to turn hints mode on (if it is off) or off (if it is on). Finally, the player can enter quit to quit the game.

```
def getPlayerMove(board, playerTile):
    # Let the player enter their move.
    # Return the move as [x, y] (or return the strings 'hints' or 'quit').
    DIGITS1TO8 = '1 2 3 4 5 6 7 8'.split()
```

The DIGITS1TO8 constant variable is the list ['1', '2', '3', '4', '5', '6', '7', '8']. The getPlayerMove() function uses DIGITS1TO8 a couple times, and this constant is more readable than the full list value. You can't use the isdigit() method because that would allow 0 and 9 to be entered, which are not valid coordinates on the 8×8 board.

The while loop keeps looping until the player types in a valid move:

```
    while True:
        print('Enter your move, "quit" to end the game, or "hints" to toggle hints.')
```

```
145.         move = input().lower()
146.         if move == 'quit' or move == 'hints':
147.             return move
```

Line 146 checks whether the player wants to quit or toggle hints mode, and line 147 returns the string `'quit'` or `'hints'`, respectively. The `lower()` method is called on the string returned by `input()` so the player can type `HINTS` or `Quit` and still have the command understood.

The code that called `getPlayerMove()` will handle what to do if the player wants to quit or toggle hints mode. If the player enters coordinates to move on, the `if` statement on line 149 checks whether the move is valid:

```
149.         if len(move) == 2 and move[0] in DIGITS1TO8 and move[1] in
               DIGITS1TO8:
150.             x = int(move[0]) - 1
151.             y = int(move[1]) - 1
152.             if isValidMove(board, playerTile, x, y) == False:
153.                 continue
154.             else:
155.                 break
```

The game expects that the player has entered the x- and y-coordinates of their move as two numbers without anything between them. Line 149 first checks that the size of the string the player typed in is `2`. After that, it also checks that both `move[0]` (the first character in the string) and `move[1]` (the second character in the string) are strings that exist in `DIGITS1TO8`.

Remember that the game board data structures have indexes from 0 to 7, not 1 to 8. The code prints 1 to 8 when the board is displayed in `drawBoard()` because nonprogrammers are used to numbers beginning at 1 instead of 0. So to convert the strings in `move[0]` and `move[1]` to integers, lines 150 and 151 subtract 1 from `x` and `y`.

Even if the player has entered a correct move, the code needs to check that the move is allowed by the rules of Reversegam. This is done by the `isValidMove()` function, which is passed the game board data structure, the player's tile, and the x- and y-coordinates of the move.

If `isValidMove()` returns `False`, line 153 `continue` statement executes. The execution then goes back to the beginning of the `while` loop and asks the player for a valid move again. Otherwise, the player did enter a valid move, and the execution needs to break out of the `while` loop.

If the `if` statement's condition on line 149 was `False`, then the player didn't enter a valid move. Lines 157 and 158 instruct them on how to correctly enter moves:

```
156.         else:
157.             print('That is not a valid move. Enter the column (1-8) and
                   then the row (1-8).')
158.             print('For example, 81 will move on the top-right corner.')
```

Afterward, the execution moves back to the `while` statement on line 143, because line 158 is not only the last line in the `else` block but also the last line in the while block. The while loop will keep looping until the player enters a valid move. If the player enters x- and y-coordinates, line 160 will execute:

```
160.         return [x, y]
```

Finally, if line 160 executes, getPlayerMove() returns a two-item list with the x- and y-coordinates of the player's valid move.

Getting the Computer's Move

The getComputerMove() function is where the AI algorithm is implemented:

```
162. def getComputerMove(board, computerTile):
163.     # Given a board and the computer's tile, determine where to
164.     # move and return that move as an [x, y] list.
165.     possibleMoves = getValidMoves(board, computerTile)
```

Normally you use the results from getValidMoves() for hints mode, which will print . on the board to show the player all the potential moves they can make. But if getValidMoves() is called with the computer AI's tile (in computerTile), it will also find all the possible moves that the *computer* can make. The AI will select the best move from this list.

First, the random.shuffle() function will randomize the order of moves in the possibleMoves list:

```
166.     random.shuffle(possibleMoves) # Randomize the order of the moves.
```

We want to shuffle the possibleMoves list because it will make the AI less predictable; otherwise, the player could just memorize the moves needed to win because the computer's responses would always be the same. Let's look at the algorithm.

Strategizing with Corner Moves

Corner moves are a good idea in Reversegam because once a tile has been placed on a corner, it can never be flipped over. Line 169 loops through every move in possibleMoves. If any of them is on the corner, the program will return that space as the computer's move:

```
168.     # Always go for a corner if available.
169.     for x, y in possibleMoves:
170.         if isOnCorner(x, y):
171.             return [x, y]
```

Since possibleMoves is a list of two-item lists, we'll use multiple assignment in the for loop to set x and y. If possibleMoves contains multiple corner moves, the first one is always used. But since possibleMoves was shuffled on line 166, which corner move is first in the list is random.

Getting a List of the Highest-Scoring Moves

If there are no corner moves, the program will loop through the entire list of possible moves and find out which results in the highest score. Then bestMove is set to the highest-scoring move the code has found so far, and bestScore is set to the best move's score. This is repeated until the highest-scoring possible move is found.

```
173.     # Find the highest-scoring move possible.
174.     bestScore = -1
175.     for x, y in possibleMoves:
176.         boardCopy = getBoardCopy(board)
177.         makeMove(boardCopy, computerTile, x, y)
178.         score = getScoreOfBoard(boardCopy)[computerTile]
179.         if score > bestScore:
180.             bestMove = [x, y]
181.             bestScore = score
182.     return bestMove
```

Line 174 first sets bestScore to -1 so that the first move the code checks will be set to the first bestMove. This guarantees that bestMove is set to one of the moves from possibleMoves when it returns.

On line 175, the for loop sets x and y to every move in possibleMoves. Before simulating a move, line 176 makes a duplicate game board data structure by calling getBoardCopy(). You'll want a copy you can modify without changing the real game board data structure stored in the board variable.

Then line 177 calls makeMove(), passing the duplicate board (stored in boardCopy) instead of the real board. This will simulate what would happen on the real board if that move were made. The makeMove() function will handle placing the computer's tile and flipping the player's tiles on the duplicate board.

Line 178 calls getScoreOfBoard() with the duplicate board, which returns a dictionary where the keys are 'X' and 'O', and the values are the scores. When the code in the loop finds a move that scores higher than bestScore, lines 179 to 181 will store that move and score as the new values in bestMove and bestScore. After possibleMoves has been fully iterated through, bestMove is returned.

For example, say that getScoreOfBoard() returns the dictionary {'X':22, 'O':8} and computerTile is 'X'. Then getScoreOfBoard(boardCopy)[computerTile] would evaluate to {'X':22, 'O':8}['X'], which would then evaluate to 22. If 22 is larger than bestScore, bestScore is set to 22, and bestMove is set to the current x and y values.

By the time this for loop is finished, you can be sure that bestScore is the highest possible score a move can get, and that move is stored in bestMove.

Even though the code always chooses the first in the list of these tied moves, the choice appears random because the list order was shuffled on line 166. This ensures that the AI won't be predictable when there's more than one best move.

Printing the Scores to the Screen

The printScore() function calls the getScoreOfBoard() function and then prints the player's and computer's scores:

```
def printScore(board, playerTile, computerTile):
    scores = getScoreOfBoard(board)
    print('You: %s points. Computer: %s points.' % (scores[playerTile],
      scores[computerTile]))
```

Remember that getScoreOfBoard() returns a dictionary with the keys 'X' and 'O' and values of the scores for the *X* and *O* players.

That's all the functions for the Reversegam game. The code in the playGame() function implements the actual game and calls these functions as needed.

Starting the Game

The playGame() function calls the previous functions we've written to play a single game:

```
188. def playGame(playerTile, computerTile):
189.     showHints = False
190.     turn = whoGoesFirst()
191.     print('The ' + turn + ' will go first.')
192.
193.     # Clear the board and place starting pieces.
194.     board = getNewBoard()
195.     board[3][3] = 'X'
196.     board[3][4] = 'O'
197.     board[4][3] = 'O'
198.     board[4][4] = 'X'
```

The playGame() function is passed 'X' or 'O' strings for playerTile and computerTile. The player to go first is determined by line 190. The turn variable contains the string 'computer' or 'player' to keep track of whose turn it is. Line 194 creates a blank board data structure, while lines 195 to 198 set up the initial four tiles on the board. The game is now ready to begin.

Checking for a Stalemate

Before getting the player's or computer's turn, we need to check whether it is even possible for either of them to move. If not, then the game is at a stalemate and should end. (If only one side has no valid moves, the turn skips to the other player.)

```
    while True:
        playerValidMoves = getValidMoves(board, playerTile)
        computerValidMoves = getValidMoves(board, computerTile)

```

```
204.         if playerValidMoves == [] and computerValidMoves == []:
205.             return board # No one can move, so end the game.
```

Line 200 is the main loop for running the player's and computer's turns. As long as this loop keeps looping, the game will continue. But before running these turns, lines 201 and 202 check whether either side can make a move by getting a list of valid moves. If both of these lists are empty, then neither player can make a move. Line 205 exits the `playGame()` function by returning the final board, ending the game.

Running the Player's Turn

If the game is not in a stalemate, the program determines whether it is the player's turn by checking whether `turn` is set to the string `'player'`:

```
207.         elif turn == 'player': # Player's turn
208.             if playerValidMoves != []:
209.                 if showHints:
210.                     validMovesBoard = getBoardWithValidMoves(board,
                           playerTile)
211.                     drawBoard(validMovesBoard)
212.                 else:
213.                     drawBoard(board)
214.                 printScore(board, playerTile, computerTile)
```

Line 207 begins an `elif` block containing the code that runs if it is the player's turn. (The `elif` block that starts on line 227 contains the code for the computer's turn.)

All of this code will run only if the player has a valid move, which line 208 determines by checking that `playerValidMoves` is not empty. We display the board on the screen by calling `drawBoard()` on line 211 or 213.

If hints mode is on (that is, `showHints` is `True`), then the board data structure should display `.` on every valid space the player could move, which is accomplished with the `getBoardWithValidMoves()` function. It is passed a game board data structure and returns a copy that also contains periods (`.`). Line 211 passes this board to the `drawBoard()` function.

If hints mode is off, then line 213 passes `board` to `drawBoard()` instead.

After printing the game board to the player, you also want to print the current score by calling `printScore()` on line 214.

Next, the player needs to enter their move. The `getPlayerMove()` function handles this, and its return value is a two-item list of the x- and y-coordinates of the player's move:

```
216.                 move = getPlayerMove(board, playerTile)
```

When we defined `getPlayerMove()`, we already made sure that the player's move is valid.

The getPlayerMove() function may have returned the strings 'quit' or 'hints' instead of a move on the board. Lines 217 to 222 handle these cases:

```
217.             if move == 'quit':
218.                 print('Thanks for playing!')
219.                 sys.exit() # Terminate the program.
220.             elif move == 'hints':
221.                 showHints = not showHints
222.                 continue
223.             else:
224.                 makeMove(board, playerTile, move[0], move[1])
225.         turn = 'computer'
```

If the player entered quit for their move, then getPlayerMove() would return the string 'quit'. In that case, line 219 calls sys.exit() to terminate the program.

If the player entered hints for their move, then getPlayerMove() would return the string 'hints'. In that case, you want to turn hints mode on (if it was off) or off (if it was on).

The showHints = not showHints assignment statement on line 221 handles both of these cases, because not False evaluates to True and not True evaluates to False. Then the continue statement moves the execution to the start of the loop (turn has not changed, so it will still be the player's turn).

Otherwise, if the player didn't quit or toggle hints mode, line 224 calls makeMove() to make the player's move on the board.

Finally, line 225 sets turn to 'computer'. The flow of execution skips the else block and reaches the end of the while block, so execution jumps back to the while statement on line 200. This time, however, it will be the computer's turn.

Running the Computer's Turn

If the turn variable contains the string 'computer', then the code for the computer's turn will run. It is similar to the code for the player's turn, with a few changes:

```
227.     elif turn == 'computer': # Computer's turn
228.         if computerValidMoves != []:
229.             drawBoard(board)
230.             printScore(board, playerTile, computerTile)
231.
232.             input('Press Enter to see the computer\'s move.')
233.             move = getComputerMove(board, computerTile)
234.             makeMove(board, computerTile, move[0], move[1])
```

After printing the board with drawBoard(), the program also prints the current score with a call to printScore() on line 230.

Line 232 calls input() to pause the script so the player can look at the board. This is much like how input() was used to pause the Jokes program in Chapter 4. Instead of using a print() call to print a string before a call to input(), you can do the same thing by passing the string to print to input().

After the player has looked at the board and pressed ENTER, line 233 calls getComputerMove() to get the x- and y-coordinates of the computer's next move. These coordinates are stored in variables x and y using multiple assignment.

Finally, x and y, along with the game board data structure and the computer's tile, are passed to the makeMove() function. This places the computer's tile on the game board in board to reflect the computer's move. Line 233 call to getComputerMove() got the computer's move (and stored it in variables x and y). The call to makeMove() on line 234 makes the move on the board.

Next, line 235 sets the turn variable to 'player':

```
235.             turn = 'player'
```

There is no more code in the while block after line 235, so the execution loops back to the while statement on line 200.

The Game Loop

That's all the functions we'll make for Reversegam. Starting at line 239, the main part of the program runs a game by calling playGame(), but it also displays the final score and asks the player whether they want to play again:

```
239. print('Welcome to Reversegam!')
240.
241. playerTile, computerTile = enterPlayerTile()
```

The program starts by welcoming the player on line 239 and asking them whether they want to be *X* or *O*. Line 241 uses the multiple assignment trick to set playerTile and computerTile to the two values returned by enterPlayerTile().

The while loop on line 243 runs each game:

```
243. while True:
244.     finalBoard = playGame(playerTile, computerTile)
245.
246.     # Display the final score.
247.     drawBoard(finalBoard)
248.     scores = getScoreOfBoard(finalBoard)
249.     print('X scored %s points. O scored %s points.' % (scores['X'],
           scores['O']))
250.     if scores[playerTile] > scores[computerTile]:
251.         print('You beat the computer by %s points! Congratulations!' %
               (scores[playerTile] - scores[computerTile]))
```

```
252.     elif scores[playerTile] < scores[computerTile]:
253.         print('You lost. The computer beat you by %s points.' %
               (scores[computerTile] - scores[playerTile]))
254.     else:
255.         print('The game was a tie!')
```

It begins by calling `playGame()`. This function call does not return until the game is finished. The board data structure returned by `playGame()` will be passed to `getScoreOfBoard()` to count the *X* and *O* tiles to determine the final score. Line 249 displays this final score.

If there are more of the player's tiles than the computer's, line 251 congratulates the player for winning. If the computer won, line 253 tells the player that they lost. Otherwise, line 255 tells the player the game was a tie.

Asking the Player to Play Again

After the game is finished, the player is asked whether they want to play again:

```
257.     print('Do you want to play again? (yes or no)')
258.     if not input().lower().startswith('y'):
259.         break
```

If the player does not type a reply that begins with the letter *y*, such as `yes` or `YES` or `Y`, then the condition on line 258 evaluates to `True`, and line 259 breaks out of the `while` loop that started on line 243, which ends the game. Otherwise, this `while` loop naturally loops, and `playGame()` is called again to begin the next game.

Summary

The Reversegam AI may seem almost unbeatable, but this isn't because the computer is smarter than we are; it's just much faster! The strategy it follows is simple: move on the corner if you can, and otherwise make the move that will flip over the most tiles. A human could do that, but it would be time-consuming to figure out how many tiles would be flipped for every possible valid move. For the computer, calculating this number is simple.

This game is similar to Sonar Treasure Hunt because it makes use of a grid for a board. It is also like the Tic-Tac-Toe game because there's an AI that plans out the best move for the computer to make. This chapter introduced only one new concept: that empty lists, blank strings, and the integer `0` all evaluate to `False` in the context of a condition. Other than that, this game used programming concepts you already knew!

In Chapter 16, you'll learn how to make AIs play computer games against each other.

16

REVERSEGAM AI SIMULATION

The Reversegam AI algorithm from Chapter 15 is simple, but it beats me almost every time I play it. Because the computer can process instructions quickly, it can easily check each possible position on the board and select the highest-scoring move. It would take me a long time to find the best move this way.

The Reversegam program had two functions, `getPlayerMove()` and `getComputerMove()`, which both returned the move selected as a two-item list in the format `[x, y]`. Both functions also had the same parameters, the game board data structure and one type of tile, but the returned moves came from different sources—either the player or the Reversegam algorithm.

What happens when we replace the call to `getPlayerMove()` with a call to `getComputerMove()`? Then the player never has to enter a move; it is decided for them. The computer is playing against itself!

In this chapter, we'll make three new programs in which the computer plays against itself, each based on the Reversegam program in Chapter 15:

- Simulation 1: *AISim1.py* will make changes to *reversegam.py*.
- Simulation 2: *AISim2.py* will make changes to *AISim1.py*.
- Simulation 3: *AISim3.py* will make changes to *AISim2.py*.

The small changes from one program to the next will show you how to turn a "player versus computer" game into a "computer versus computer" simulation. The final program, *AISim3.py*, shares most of its code with *reversegam.py* but serves quite a different purpose. The simulation doesn't let us play Reversegam but teaches us more about the game itself.

You can either type in these changes yourself or download them from the book's website at *https://www.nostarch.com/inventwithpython/*.

TOPICS COVERED IN THIS CHAPTER

- Simulations
- Percentages
- Integer division
- The `round()` function
- Computer-versus-computer games

Making the Computer Play Against Itself

Our *AISim1.py* program will have a few simple changes so that the computer plays against itself. Both the `getPlayerMove()` and `getComputerMove()` functions take a board data structure and the player's tile, and then return the move to make. This is why `getComputerMove()` can replace `getPlayerMove()` and the program still works. In the *AISim1.py* program, the `getComputerMove()` function is being called for both the `X` and `O` players.

We also make the program stop printing the game board for moves that are made. Since a human can't read the game boards as fast as a computer makes moves, it isn't useful to print every move, so we just print the final board at the end of the game.

These are just minimal changes to the program, so it will still say things like `The player will go first.` even though the computer is playing as both the computer and the player.

Sample Run of Simulation 1

Here's what the user sees when they run the *AISim1.py* program. The text entered by the player is bold.

```
Welcome to Reversegam!
The computer will go first.
  12345678
 +--------+
1|XXXXXXXX|1
2|OXXXXXXX|2
3|XOXXOXXX|3
4|XXOOXOOX|4
5|XXOOXXXX|5
6|XXOXOXXX|6
7|XXXOXOXX|7
8|XXXXXXXX|8
 +--------+
  12345678
X scored 51 points. O scored 13 points.
You beat the computer by 38 points! Congratulations!
Do you want to play again? (yes or no)
no
```

Source Code for Simulation 1

Save the old *reversegam.py* file as *AISim1.py* as follows:

1. Select **File ▸ Save As**.
2. Save this file as *AISim1.py* so that you can make changes without affecting *reversegam.py*. (At this point, *reversegam.py* and *AISim1.py* still have the same code.)
3. Make changes to *AISim1.py* and save that file to keep any changes. (*AISim1.py* will have the new changes, and *reversegam.py* will have the original, unchanged code.)

This process will create a copy of our Reversegam source code as a new file that you can make changes to, while leaving the original Reversegam game the same (you may want to play it again to test it). For example, change line 216 in *AISim1.py* to the following (the change is in bold):

```
216.                move = getComputerMove(board, playerTile)
```

Now run the program. Notice that the game still asks whether you want to be *X* or *O*, but it won't ask you to enter any moves. When you replace the `getPlayerMove()` function with the `getComputerMove()` function, you no longer call any code that takes this input from the player. The player still presses ENTER after the original computer's moves (because of the `input('Press Enter to see the computer\'s move.')` on line 232), but the game plays itself!

MAKE SURE YOU'RE
USING PYTHON 3,
NOT PYTHON 2!

Let's make some other changes to *AISim1.py*. Change the following bolded lines. The changes start at line 209. Most of these changes are simply *commenting out* code, which means turning the code into a comment so it won't run.

If you get errors after typing in this code, compare the code you typed to the book's code with the online diff tool at *https://www.nostarch.com/inventwithpython#diff*.

AISim1.py

```
207.         elif turn == 'player': # Player's turn
208.             if playerValidMoves != []:
209.                 #if showHints:
210.                 #     validMovesBoard = getBoardWithValidMoves(board,
                           playerTile)
211.                 #     drawBoard(validMovesBoard)
212.                 #else:
213.                 #     drawBoard(board)
214.                 #printScore(board, playerTile, computerTile)
215.
216.                 move = getComputerMove(board, playerTile)
217.                 #if move == 'quit':
218.                 #     print('Thanks for playing!')
219.                 #     sys.exit() # Terminate the program.
220.                 #elif move == 'hints':
221.                 #     showHints = not showHints
222.                 #     continue
223.                 #else:
224.                 makeMove(board, playerTile, move[0], move[1])
225.             turn = 'computer'
226.
227.         elif turn == 'computer': # Computer's turn
228.             if computerValidMoves != []:
229.                 #drawBoard(board)
230.                 #printScore(board, playerTile, computerTile)
231.
232.                 #input('Press Enter to see the computer\'s move.')
233.                 move = getComputerMove(board, computerTile)
234.                 makeMove(board, computerTile, move[0], move[1])
235.             turn = 'player'
236.
237.
238.
239. print('Welcome to Reversegam!')
240.
241. playerTile, computerTile = ['X', 'O'] #enterPlayerTile()
```

Removing the Player Prompts and Adding a Computer Player

As you can seen, the *AISim1.py* program is mostly the same as the original Reversegam program, except we've replaced the call to `getPlayerMove()` with a call to `getComputerMove()`. We've also made some changes to the text that is printed to the screen so that the game easier to follow. When you run the program, the entire game is played in less than a second!

Again, most of the changes are simply commenting out code. Since the computer is playing against itself, the program no longer needs to run code to get moves from the player or display the state of the board. All of this is skipped so that the board is displayed only at the very end of the game. We comment out code instead of deleting it because it's easier to restore the code by uncommenting it if we need to reuse the code later.

We commented out lines 209 to 214 because we don't need to draw a game board for the player since they won't be playing the game. We also commented out lines 217 to 223 because we don't need to check whether the player enters `quit` or toggles the hints mode. But we need to de-indent line 224 by four spaces since it was in the `else` block that we just commented out. Lines 229 to 232 also draw the game board for the player, so we comment out those lines, too.

The only new code is on lines 216 and 241. In line 216, we just substitute the call to `getPlayerMove()` with `getComputerMove()`, as discussed earlier. On line 241, instead of asking the player whether they want to be *X* or *O*, we simply always assign `'X'` to `playerTile` and `'O'` to `computerTile`. (Both of these players will be played by the computer, though, so you can rename `playerTile` to `computerTile2` or `secondComputerTile` if you want.) Now that we have the computer playing against itself, we can keep modifying our program to make it do more interesting things.

Making the Computer Play Itself Several Times

If we created a new algorithm, we could set it against the AI implemented in `getComputerMove()` and see which one is better. Before we do so, however, we need a way to evaluate the players. We can't evaluate which AI is better based on only one game, so we should have the AIs play against each other more than once. To do that, we'll make some changes to the source code. Follow these steps to make *AISim2.py*:

1. Select **File ▸ Save As**.
2. Save this file as *AISim2.py* so that you can make changes without affecting *AISim1.py*. (At this point, *AISim1.py* and *AISim2.py* still have the same code.)

Sample Run of Simulation 2

Here's what the user sees when they run the *AISim2.py* program.

```
Welcome to Reversegam!
#1: X scored 45 points. O scored 19 points.
#2: X scored 38 points. O scored 26 points.
#3: X scored 20 points. O scored 44 points.
#4: X scored 24 points. O scored 40 points.
#5: X scored 8 points. O scored 56 points.
--snip--
#249: X scored 24 points. O scored 40 points.
#250: X scored 43 points. O scored 21 points.
```

```
X wins: 119 (47.6%)
O wins: 127 (50.8%)
Ties:   4 (1.6%)
```

Because the algorithms include randomness, your run won't have exactly the same numbers.

Source Code for Simulation 2

Change the code in *AISim2.py* to match the following. Make sure that you change the code line by line in number order. If you get errors after typing in this code, compare the code you typed to the book's code with the online diff tool at *https://www.nostarch.com/inventwithpython#diff.*

AISim2.py

```
            turn = 'player'

NUM_GAMES = 250
xWins = oWins = ties = 0
print('Welcome to Reversegam!')

playerTile, computerTile = ['X', 'O'] #enterPlayerTile()

for i in range(NUM_GAMES): #while True:
    finalBoard = playGame(playerTile, computerTile)

    # Display the final score.
    #drawBoard(finalBoard)
    scores = getScoreOfBoard(finalBoard)
    print('#%s: X scored %s points. O scored %s points.' % (i + 1,
      scores['X'], scores['O']))
    if scores[playerTile] > scores[computerTile]:
        xWins += 1 #print('You beat the computer by %s points!
          Congratulations!' % (scores[playerTile] -
          scores[computerTile]))
    elif scores[playerTile] < scores[computerTile]:
        oWins += 1 #print('You lost. The computer beat you by %s points.'
          % (scores[computerTile] - scores[playerTile]))
    else:
        ties += 1 #print('The game was a tie!')

    #print('Do you want to play again? (yes or no)')
    #if not input().lower().startswith('y'):
    #    break

print('X wins: %s (%s%%)' % (xWins, round(xWins / NUM_GAMES * 100, 1)))
print('O wins: %s (%s%%)' % (oWins, round(oWins / NUM_GAMES * 100, 1)))
print('Ties:   %s (%s%%)' % (ties, round(ties / NUM_GAMES * 100, 1)))
```

If this is confusing, you can always download the *AISim2.py* source code from the book's website at *https://www.nostarch.com/inventwithpython/.*

Keeping Track of Multiple Games

The main information we want from the simulation is how many wins for *X*, wins for *O*, and ties there are over a certain number of games. These can be tracked in four variables, which are created on lines 237 and 238.

```
237. NUM_GAMES = 250
238. xWins = oWins = ties = 0
```

The constant `NUM_GAMES` determines how many games the computer will play. You've added the variables `xWins`, `oWins`, and `ties` to keep track of when *X* wins, when *O* wins, and when they tie. You can chain the assignment statement together to set `ties` equal to `0` and `oWins` equal to `ties`, then `xWins` equal to `oWins`. This sets all three variables to `0`.

`NUM_GAMES` is used in a `for` loop that replaces the game loop on line 243:

```
243. for i in range(NUM_GAMES): #while True:
```

The `for` loop runs the game the number of times in `NUM_GAMES`. This replaces the `while` loop that used to loop until the player said they didn't want to play another game.

At line 250, an `if` statement compares the score of the two players, and lines 251 to 255 in the `if-elif-else` blocks increment the `xWins`, `oWins`, and `ties` variables at the end of each game before looping back to start a new game:

```
250.     if scores[playerTile] > scores[computerTile]:
251.         xWins += 1 #print('You beat the computer by %s points!
               Congratulations!' % (scores[playerTile] -
               scores[computerTile]))
252.     elif scores[playerTile] < scores[computerTile]:
253.         oWins += 1 #print('You lost. The computer beat you by %s points.'
               % (scores[computerTile] - scores[playerTile]))
254.     else:
255.         ties += 1 #print('The game was a tie!')
```

We comment out the messages originally printed in the block so now only a one-line summary of the scores prints for each game. We'll use the `xWins`, `oWins`, and `ties` variables later in the code to analyze how the computer performed against itself.

Commenting Out print() Function Calls

You also commented out lines 247 and 257 to 259. By doing that, you took out most of the `print()` function calls from the program, as well as the calls to `drawBoard()`. We don't need to see each of the games since there are so many being played. The program still runs every game in its entirety using the AI we coded, but only the resulting scores are shown. After running all the games, the program shows how many games each side won, and lines 251 to 253 print some information about the game runs.

Printing things to the screen slows the computer down, but now that you've removed that code, the computer can run an entire game of Reversegam in about a second or two. Each time the program printed out one of those lines with the final score, it ran through an entire game (checking about 50 or 60 moves individually to choose the one that gets the most points). Now that the computer doesn't have to do as much work, it can run much faster.

The numbers that the program prints at the end are *statistics*—numbers that are used to summarize how the games were played. In this case, we showed the resulting scores of each game played and the percentages of wins and ties for the tiles.

Using Percentages to Grade the AIs

Percentages are a portion of a total amount. The percentages of a whole can range from 0 percent to 100 percent. If you had 100 percent of a pie, you would have the entire pie; if you had 0 percent of a pie, you wouldn't have any pie at all; and if you had 50 percent of the pie, you would have half of it.

We can calculate percentages with division. To get a percentage, divide the part you have by the total and then multiply that by 100. For example, if *X* won 50 out of 100 games, you would calculate the expression `50 / 100`, which evaluates to `0.5`. Multiply this by `100` to get the percentage (in this case, 50 percent).

If *X* won 100 out of 200 games, you would calculate the percentage with `100 / 200`, which also evaluates to `0.5`. When you multiply `0.5` by `100` to get the percentage, you get 50 percent. Winning 100 out of 200 games is the same percentage (that is, the same portion) as winning 50 out of 100 games.

In lines 261 to 263, we use percentages to print information about the outcomes of the games:

```
261. print('X wins: %s (%s%%)' % (xWins, round(xWins / NUM_GAMES * 100, 1)))
262. print('O wins: %s (%s%%)' % (oWins, round(oWins / NUM_GAMES * 100, 1)))
263. print('Ties:   %s (%s%%)' % (ties, round(ties / NUM_GAMES * 100, 1)))
```

Each `print()` statement has a label that tells the user whether the data being printed is for *X* wins, *O* wins, or ties. We use string interpolation to insert the number of games won or tied and then insert the calculated percentage the wins or ties make up of the total games, but you can see that we're not simply dividing the `xWins`, `oWins`, or `ties` by the total games and multiplying by `100`. This is because we want to print only one decimal place for each percentage, which we can't do with normal division.

Division Evaluates to a Floating-Point Number

When you use the division operator (`/`), the expression will always evaluate to a floating-point number. For example, the expression `10 / 2` evaluates to the floating-point value `5.0`, not to the integer value `5`.

This is important to remember, because adding an integer to a floating-point value with the `+` addition operator will also always evaluate to a floating-point value. For example, `3 + 4.0` evaluates to the floating-point value `7.0`, not to the integer `7`.

Enter the following code into the interactive shell:

```
>>> spam = 100 / 4
>>> spam
25.0
>>> spam = spam + 20
>>> spam
45.0
```

In the example, the data type of the value stored in `spam` is always a floating-point value. You can pass the floating-point value to the `int()` function, which returns an integer form of the floating-point value. But this will always round the floating-point value down. For example, the expressions `int(4.0)`, `int(4.2)`, and `int(4.9)` all evaluate to `4`, not `5`. But in *AISim2.py*, we need to round each percentage to the tenths place. Since we can't just divide to do this, we need to use the `round()` function.

The round() Function

The `round()` function rounds a floating-point number to the nearest integer number. Enter the following into the interactive shell:

```
>>> round(10.0)
10
>>> round(10.2)
10
>>> round(8.7)
9
>>> round(3.4999)
3
>>> round(2.5422, 2)
2.54
```

The `round()` function also has an optional second parameter, where you can specify what place you want to round the number to. This will make the rounded number a floating-point number rather than an integer. For example, the expression `round(2.5422, 2)` evaluates to `2.54` and `round(2.5422, 3)` evaluates to `2.542`. In lines 261 to 263 of *AISim2.py*, we use this `round()` with a parameter of `1` to find the fraction of games won or tied by *X* and *O* up to one decimal place, which gives us accurate percentages.

Comparing Different AI Algorithms

With just a few changes, we can make the computer play hundreds of games against itself. Right now, each player wins about half of the games, since both run exactly the same algorithm for moves. But if we add different algorithms, we can see whether a different AI will win more games.

Let's add some new functions with new algorithms. But first, in *AISim2.py* select **File ▸ Save As** to save this new file as *AISim3.py*.

We'll rename the `getComputerMove()` function to `getCornerBestMove()`, since this algorithm tries to move on corners first and then chooses the move that flips the most tiles. We'll call this strategy the *corner-best algorithm*. We'll also add several other functions that implement different strategies, including a *worst-move algorithm* that gets the worst-scoring move; a *random-move algorithm* that gets any valid move; and a *corner-side-best algorithm*, which works the same as the corner-best AI except that it looks for a side move after a corner move and before taking the highest-scoring move.

In *AISim3.py*, the call to `getComputerMove()` on line 257 will be changed to `getCornerBestMove()`, and line 274's `getComputerMove()` will become `getWorstMove()`, which is the function we'll write for the worst-move algorithm. This way, we'll have the regular corner-best algorithm go against an algorithm that purposefully picks the move that will flip the *fewest* tiles.

Source Code for Simulation 3

As you enter the source code of *AISim3.py* into your renamed copy of *AISim2.py*, make sure to write your code line by line in number order so that the line numbers match. If you get errors after typing in this code, compare the code you typed to the book's code with the online diff tool at *https://www.nostarch.com/inventwithpython#diff*.

AISim3.py

```
162. def getCornerBestMove(board, computerTile):
--snip--
184. def getWorstMove(board, tile):
185.     # Return the move that flips the least number of tiles.
186.     possibleMoves = getValidMoves(board, tile)
187.     random.shuffle(possibleMoves) # Randomize the order of the moves.
188.
189.     # Find the lowest-scoring move possible.
190.     worstScore = 64
191.     for x, y in possibleMoves:
192.         boardCopy = getBoardCopy(board)
193.         makeMove(boardCopy, tile, x, y)
194.         score = getScoreOfBoard(boardCopy)[tile]
195.         if score < worstScore:
196.             worstMove = [x, y]
197.             worstScore = score
198.
199.     return worstMove
200.
201. def getRandomMove(board, tile):
202.     possibleMoves = getValidMoves(board, tile)
203.     return random.choice(possibleMoves)
204.
205. def isOnSide(x, y):
206.     return x == 0 or x == WIDTH - 1 or y == 0 or y == HEIGHT - 1
```

```
207.
208. def getCornerSideBestMove(board, tile):
209.     # Return a corner move, a side move, or the best move.
210.     possibleMoves = getValidMoves(board, tile)
211.     random.shuffle(possibleMoves) # Randomize the order of the moves.
212.
213.     # Always go for a corner if available.
214.     for x, y in possibleMoves:
215.         if isOnCorner(x, y):
216.             return [x, y]
217.
218.     # If there is no corner move to make, return a side move.
219.     for x, y in possibleMoves:
220.         if isOnSide(x, y):
221.             return [x, y]
222.
223.     return getCornerBestMove(board, tile) # Do what the normal AI
           would do.
224.
225. def printScore(board, playerTile, computerTile):
--snip--
257.                 move = getCornerBestMove(board, playerTile)
--snip--
274.                 move = getWorstMove(board, computerTile)
```

Running *AISim3.py* results in the same kind of output as *AISim2.py*, except different algorithms will be playing the games.

How the AIs Work in Simulation 3

The functions getCornerBestMove(), getWorstMove(), getRandomMove(), and getCornerSideBestMove() are similar to one another but use slightly different strategies to play games. One of them uses the new isOnSide() function. This is similar to our isOnCorner() function, but it checks for the spaces along the side of the board before selecting the highest-scoring move.

The Corner-Best AI

We already have the code for an AI that chooses to move on a corner and then chooses the best move possible, since that's what getComputerMove() does. We can just change the name of getComputerMove() to something more descriptive, so change line 162 to rename our function to getCornerBestMove():

```
162. def getCornerBestMove(board, computerTile):
```

Since getComputerMove() no longer exists, we need to update the code on line 257 to getCornerBestMove():

```
257.                 move = getCornerBestMove(board, playerTile)
```

That's all the work we need to do for this AI, so let's move on.

The Worst-Move AI

The worst-move AI just finds the move with the fewest-scoring points and returns that. Its code is a lot like the code we used to find the highest-scoring move in our original `getComputerMove()` algorithm:

```
184. def getWorstMove(board, tile):
185.     # Return the move that flips the least number of tiles.
186.     possibleMoves = getValidMoves(board, tile)
187.     random.shuffle(possibleMoves) # Randomize the order of the moves.
188.
189.     # Find the lowest-scoring move possible.
190.     worstScore = 64
191.     for x, y in possibleMoves:
192.         boardCopy = getBoardCopy(board)
193.         makeMove(boardCopy, tile, x, y)
194.         score = getScoreOfBoard(boardCopy)[tile]
195.         if score < worstScore:
196.             worstMove = [x, y]
197.             worstScore = score
198.
199.     return worstMove
```

The algorithm for `getWorstMove()` starts out the same for lines 186 and 187, but then it makes a departure at line 190. We set up a variable to hold the `worstScore` instead of `bestScore` and set it to `64`, because that is the total number of positions on the board and the most points that could be scored if the entire board were filled. Lines 191 to 194 are the same as the original algorithm, but then line 195 checks whether the `score` is less than `worstScore` instead of whether the `score` is higher. If `score` is less, then `worstMove` is replaced with the move on the board the algorithm is currently testing, and `worstScore` is updated, too. Then the function returns `worstMove`.

Finally, line 274's `getComputerMove()` needs to be changed to `getWorstMove()`:

```
274.                 move = getWorstMove(board, computerTile)
```

When this is done and you run the program, `getCornerBestMove()` and `getWorstMove()` will play against each other.

The Random-Move AI

The random-move AI just finds all the valid possible moves and then chooses a random one.

```
def getRandomMove(board, tile):
    possibleMoves = getValidMoves(board, tile)
    return random.choice(possibleMoves)
```

It uses `getValidMoves()`, just as all the other AIs do, and then uses `choice()` to return one of the possible moves in the returned list.

Checking for Side Moves

Before we get into the algorithms, let's look at one new helper function we've added. The `isOnSide()` helper function is like the `isOnCorner()` function, except that it checks whether a move is on the sides of a board:

```
def isOnSide(x, y):
    return x == 0 or x == WIDTH - 1 or y == 0 or y == HEIGHT - 1
```

It has one Boolean expression that checks whether the `x` value or `y` value of the coordinate arguments passed to it is equal to `0` or `7`. Any coordinate with a 0 or a 7 in it is at the edge of the board.

We'll use this function next in the corner-side-best AI.

The Corner-Side-Best AI

The corner-side-best AI works a lot like the corner-best AI, so we can reuse some of the code we've already entered. We define this AI in the function `getCornerSideBestMove()`:

```
208. def getCornerSideBestMove(board, tile):
209.     # Return a corner move, a side move, or the best move.
210.     possibleMoves = getValidMoves(board, tile)
211.     random.shuffle(possibleMoves) # Randomize the order of the moves.
212.
213.     # Always go for a corner if available.
214.     for x, y in possibleMoves:
215.         if isOnCorner(x, y):
216.             return [x, y]
217.
218.     # If there is no corner move to make, return a side move.
219.     for x, y in possibleMoves:
220.         if isOnSide(x, y):
221.             return [x, y]
222.
223.     return getCornerBestMove(board, tile) # Do what the normal AI
           would do.
```

Lines 210 and 211 are the same as in our corner-best AI, and lines 214 to 216 are identical to our algorithm to check for a corner move in our original `getComputerMove()` AI. If there's no corner move, then lines 219 to 221 check for a side move by using the `isOnSide()` helper function. Once all corner and side moves have been checked for availability, if there's still no move, then we reuse our `getCornerBestMove()` function. Since there were no corner moves earlier and there still won't be any when the code reaches the `getCornerBestMove()` function, this function will just look for the highest-scoring move to make and return that.

Table 16-1 reviews the new algorithms we've made.

Table 16-1: Functions Used for the Reversegam AIs

Function	Description
`getCornerBestMove()`	Take a corner move if available. If there's no corner, find the highest-scoring move.
`getCornerSideBestMove()`	Take a corner move if available. If there's no corner, take a space on the side. If no sides are available, use the regular `getCornerBestMove()` algorithm.
`getRandomMove()`	Randomly choose a valid move to make.
`getWorstMove()`	Take the position that will result in the fewest tiles being flipped.

Now that we have our algorithms, we can pit them against each other.

Comparing the AIs

We've written our program so that the corner-best AI plays against the worst-move AI. We can run the program to simulate how well the AIs do against each other and analyze the results with the printed statistics.

In addition to these two AIs, we've made some others that we don't call on. These AIs exist in the code but aren't being used, so if we want to see how they fare in a match, we'll need to edit the code to call on them. Since we already have one comparison set up, let's see how the worst-move AI does against the corner-best AI.

Worst-Move AI vs. Corner-Best AI

Run the program to pit the `getCornerBestMove()` function against the `getWorstMove()` function. Unsurprisingly, the strategy of flipping the fewest tiles each turn will lose most games:

```
X wins: 206 (82.4%)
O wins: 41 (16.4%)
Ties:   3 (1.2%)
```

What *is* surprising is that sometimes the worst-move strategy does work! Rather than winning 100 percent of the time, the algorithm in the `getCornerBestMove()` function wins only about 80 percent of the time. About 1 in 5 times, it loses!

This is the power of running simulation programs: you can find novel insights that would take much longer for you to realize if you were just playing games on your own. The computer is much faster!

Random-Move AI vs. Corner-Best AI

Let's try a different strategy. Change the `getWorstMove()` call on line 274 to `getRandomMove()`:

```
274.             move = getRandomMove(board, computerTile)
```

When you run the program now, it will look something like this:

```
Welcome to Reversegam!
#1: X scored 32 points. O scored 32 points.
#2: X scored 44 points. O scored 20 points.
#3: X scored 31 points. O scored 33 points.
#4: X scored 45 points. O scored 19 points.
#5: X scored 49 points. O scored 15 points.
--snip--
#249: X scored 20 points. O scored 44 points.
#250: X scored 38 points. O scored 26 points.
X wins: 195 (78.0%)
O wins: 48 (19.2%)
Ties:   7 (2.8%)
```

The random-move algorithm `getRandomMove()` did slightly better against the corner-best algorithm than did the worst-move algorithm. This makes sense because making intelligent choices is usually better than just choosing moves at random, but making random choices is slightly better than purposefully choosing the worst move.

Corner-Side-Best AI vs. Corner-Best AI

Picking a corner space if it's available is a good idea, because a tile on the corner can never be flipped. Putting a tile on the side spaces seems like it might also be a good idea, since there are fewer ways it can be surrounded and flipped. But does this benefit outweigh passing up moves that would flip more tiles? Let's find out by pitting the corner-best algorithm against the corner-side-best algorithm.

Change the algorithm on line 274 to use `getCornerSideBestMove()`:

```
274.                 move = getCornerSideBestMove(board, computerTile)
```

Then run the program again:

```
Welcome to Reversegam!
#1: X scored 27 points. O scored 37 points.
#2: X scored 39 points. O scored 25 points.
#3: X scored 41 points. O scored 23 points.
--snip--
#249: X scored 48 points. O scored 16 points.
#250: X scored 38 points. O scored 26 points.
X wins: 152 (60.8%)
O wins: 89 (35.6%)
Ties:   9 (3.6%)
```

Wow! That's unexpected. It seems that choosing the side spaces over a space that flips more tiles is a bad strategy. The benefit of the side space doesn't outweigh the cost of flipping fewer of the opponent's tiles. Can we be sure of these results? Let's run the program again, but this time play

1,000 games by changing line 278 to `NUM_GAMES = 1000` in *AISim3.py*. The program may now take a few minutes for your computer to run—but it would take *weeks* for you to do this by hand!

You'll see that the more accurate statistics from the 1,000-games run are about the same as the statistics from the 250-games run. It seems that choosing the move that flips the most tiles is a better idea than choosing a side to move on.

We've just used programming to find out which game strategy works the best. When you hear about scientists using computer models, this is what they're doing. They use a simulation to re-create some real-world process, and then do tests in the simulation to find out more about the real world.

Summary

This chapter didn't cover a new game, but it modeled various strategies for Reversegam. If we thought that taking side moves in Reversegam was a good idea, we would have to spend weeks, even months, carefully playing games of Reversegam by hand and writing down the results to test this idea. But if we know how to program a computer to play Reversegam, then we can have it try different strategies for us. If you think about it, the computer is executing millions of lines of our Python program in seconds! Your experiments with the simulations of Reversegam can help you learn more about playing it in real life.

In fact, this chapter would make a good science fair project. You could research which set of moves leads to the most wins against other sets of moves, and you could make a hypothesis about which is the best strategy. After running several simulations, you could determine which strategy works best. With programming, you can make a science fair project out of a simulation of any board game! And it's all because you know how to instruct the computer to do it, step by step, line by line. You can speak the computer's language and get it to do large amounts of data processing and number crunching for you.

That's all for the text-based games in this book. Games that use only text can be fun, even though they're simple. But most modern games use graphics, sound, and animation to make them more exciting. In the rest of the chapters in this book, you'll learn how to create games with graphics by using a Python module called `pygame`.

17

CREATING GRAPHICS

So far, all of our games have used only text. Text is displayed on the screen as output, and the player enters text as input. Just using text makes programming easy to learn. But in this chapter, we'll make some more exciting programs with advanced graphics using the pygame module.

Chapters 17, 18, 19, and 20 will teach you how to use pygame to make games with graphics, animations, mouse input, and sound. In these chapters, we'll write source code for simple programs that demonstrate pygame concepts. Then in Chapter 21, we'll put together all the concepts we learned to create a game.

TOPICS COVERED IN THIS CHAPTER

- Installing pygame
- Colors and fonts in pygame
- Aliased and anti-aliased graphics
- Attributes
- The `pygame.font.Font`, `pygame.Surface`, `pygame.Rect`, and `pygame.PixelArray` data types
- Constructor functions
- pygame's drawing functions
- The `blit()` method for surface objects
- Events

Installing pygame

The pygame module helps developers create games by making it easier to draw graphics on your computer screen or add music to programs. The module doesn't come with Python, but like Python, it's free to download. Download pygame at *https://www.nostarch.com/inventwithpython/*, and follow the instructions for your operating system.

After the installer file finishes downloading, open it and follow the instructions until pygame has finished installing. To check that it installed correctly, enter the following into the interactive shell:

```
>>> import pygame
```

If nothing appears after you press ENTER, then you know pygame was successfully installed. If the error `ImportError: No module named pygame` appears, try to install pygame again (and make sure you typed `import pygame` correctly).

NOTE *When writing your Python programs, don't save your file as* pygame.py. *If you do, the* `import pygame` *line will import your file instead of the real* `pygame` *module, and none of your code will work.*

Hello World in pygame

First, we'll make a new pygame Hello World program like the one you created at the beginning of the book. This time, you'll use pygame to make "Hello world!" appear in a graphical window instead of as text. We'll just use pygame to draw some shapes and lines on the window in this chapter, but you'll use these skills to make your first animated game soon.

The pygame module doesn't work well with the interactive shell, so you can only write programs using pygame in a file editor; you can't send instructions one at a time through the interactive shell.

Also, pygame programs don't use the print() or input() functions. There is no text input or output. Instead, pygame displays output by drawing graphics and text in a separate window. Input to pygame comes from the keyboard and the mouse through *events*, which are covered in "Events and the Game Loop" on page 270.

Sample Run of pygame Hello World

When you run the graphical Hello World program, you should see a new window that looks like Figure 17-1.

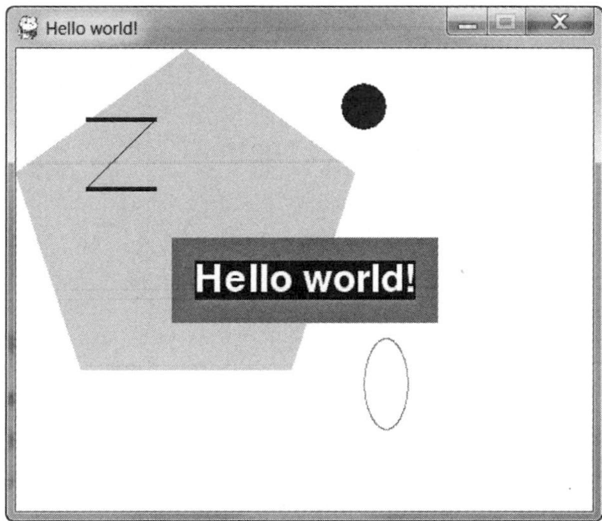
Hello world!
Hello world!

Figure 17-1: The pygame Hello World program

The nice thing about using a window instead of a console is that text can appear anywhere in the window, not just after the previous text you have printed. The text can also be any color and size. The window is like a canvas, and you can draw whatever you like on it.

Source Code for pygame Hello World

Enter the following code into the file editor and save it as *pygameHelloWorld.py*. If you get errors after typing in this code, compare the code you typed to the book's code with the online diff tool at *https://www.nostarch.com/inventwithpython#diff*.

MAKE SURE YOU'RE USING PYTHON 3, NOT PYTHON 2!

pygame HelloWorld.py

```
import pygame, sys
from pygame.locals import *

# Set up pygame.
pygame.init()

# Set up the window.
windowSurface = pygame.display.set_mode((500, 400), 0, 32)
pygame.display.set_caption('Hello world!')

# Set up the colors.
BLACK = (0, 0, 0)
WHITE = (255, 255, 255)
RED = (255, 0, 0)
GREEN = (0, 255, 0)
BLUE = (0, 0, 255)

# Set up the fonts.
basicFont = pygame.font.SysFont(None, 48)

# Set up the text.
text = basicFont.render('Hello world!', True, WHITE, BLUE)
textRect = text.get_rect()
textRect.centerx = windowSurface.get_rect().centerx
textRect.centery = windowSurface.get_rect().centery

# Draw the white background onto the surface.
windowSurface.fill(WHITE)

# Draw a green polygon onto the surface.
pygame.draw.polygon(windowSurface, GREEN, ((146, 0), (291, 106),
  (236, 277), (56, 277), (0, 106)))

# Draw some blue lines onto the surface.
pygame.draw.line(windowSurface, BLUE, (60, 60), (120, 60), 4)
pygame.draw.line(windowSurface, BLUE, (120, 60), (60, 120))
pygame.draw.line(windowSurface, BLUE, (60, 120), (120, 120), 4)

# Draw a blue circle onto the surface.
pygame.draw.circle(windowSurface, BLUE, (300, 50), 20, 0)

# Draw a red ellipse onto the surface.
pygame.draw.ellipse(windowSurface, RED, (300, 250, 40, 80), 1)

# Draw the text's background rectangle onto the surface.
pygame.draw.rect(windowSurface, RED, (textRect.left - 20,
  textRect.top - 20, textRect.width + 40, textRect.height + 40))

# Get a pixel array of the surface.
pixArray = pygame.PixelArray(windowSurface)
pixArray[480][380] = BLACK
del pixArray
```

```

# Draw the text onto the surface.
windowSurface.blit(text, textRect)

# Draw the window onto the screen.
pygame.display.update()

# Run the game loop.
while True:
    for event in pygame.event.get():
        if event.type == QUIT:
            pygame.quit()
            sys.exit()
```

Importing the pygame Module

Let's go over each of these lines of code and find out what they do.

First, you need to import the pygame module so you can call its functions. You can import several modules on the same line by separating the module names with commas. Line 1 imports both the pygame and sys modules:

```
1. import pygame, sys
2. from pygame.locals import *
```

The second line imports the pygame.locals module. This module contains many constant variables that you'll use with pygame, such as QUIT, which helps you quit the program, and K_ESCAPE, which represents the ESC key.

Line 2 also lets you use the pygames.locals module without having to type pygames.locals. in front of every method, constant, or anything else you call from the module.

If you have from sys import * instead of import sys in your program, you could call exit() instead of sys.exit() in your code. But most of the time it's better to use the full function name so you know which module the function is in.

Initializing pygame

All pygame programs must call pygame.init() after importing the pygame module but before calling any other pygame functions:

```
# Set up pygame.
pygame.init()
```

This initializes pygame so it's ready to use. You don't need to know what init() does; you just need to remember to call it before using any other pygame functions.

Setting Up the pygame Window

Line 8 creates a *graphical user interface (GUI)* window by calling the set_mode() method in the pygame.display module. (The display module is a module inside the pygame module. Even the pygame module has its own modules!)

```
7. # Set up the window.
8. windowSurface = pygame.display.set_mode((500, 400), 0, 32)
9. pygame.display.set_caption('Hello world!')
```

These methods help set up a window for pygame to run in. As in the Sonar Treasure Hunt game, windows use a coordinate system, but the window's coordinate system is organized in pixels.

A *pixel* is the tiniest dot on your computer screen. A single pixel on your screen can light up in any color. All the pixels on your screen work together to display the pictures you see. We'll create a window 500 pixels wide and 400 pixels tall by using a *tuple*.

Tuples

Tuple values are similar to lists, except they use parentheses instead of square brackets. Also, like strings, tuples can't be modified. For example, enter the following into the interactive shell:

```
  >>> spam = ('Life', 'Universe', 'Everything', 42)
❶ >>> spam[0]
  'Life'
  >>> spam[3]
  42
❷ >>> spam[1:3]
  ('Universe', 'Everything')
❸ >>> spam[3] = 'Hello'
❹ Traceback (most recent call last):
    File "<stdin>", line 1, in <module>
  TypeError: 'tuple' object does not support item assignment
```

As you can see from the example, if you want to get just one item of a tuple ❶ or a range of items ❷, you still use square brackets as you would with a list. However, if you try to change the item at index 3 to the string 'Hello' ❸, Python will raise an error ❹.

We'll use tuples to set up pygame windows. There are three parameters to the pygame.display.set_mode() method. The first is a tuple of two integers for the width and height of the window, in pixels. To set up a 500- by 400-pixel window, you use the tuple (500, 400) for the first argument to set_mode(). The second and third parameters are advanced options that are beyond the scope of this book. Just pass 0 and 32 for them, respectively.

Surface Objects

The `set_mode()` function returns a `pygame.Surface` object (which we'll call `Surface` objects for short). *Object* is just another name for a value of a data type that has methods. For example, strings are objects in Python because they have data (the string itself) and methods (such as `lower()` and `split()`). The `Surface` object represents the window.

Variables store references to objects just as they store references for lists and dictionaries (see "List References" on page 132).

The `set_caption()` method on line 9 just sets the window's caption to read `'Hello World!'`. The caption is in the top left of the window.

Setting Up Color Variables

There are three primary colors of light for pixels: red, green, and blue. By combining different amounts of these three colors (which is what your computer screen does), you can form any other color. In `pygame`, colors are represented by tuples of three integers. These are called *RGB color* values, and we'll use them in our program to assign colors to pixels. Since we don't want to rewrite a three-number tuple every time we want to use a specific color in our program, we'll make constants to hold tuples that are named after the color the tuple represents:

```
11. # Set up the colors.
12. BLACK = (0, 0, 0)
13. WHITE = (255, 255, 255)
14. RED = (255, 0, 0)
15. GREEN = (0, 255, 0)
16. BLUE = (0, 0, 255)
```

The first value in the tuple determines how much red is in the color. A value of `0` means there's no red in the color, and a value of `255` means there's a maximum amount of red in the color. The second value is for green, and the third value is for blue. These three integers form an RGB tuple.

For example, the tuple `(0, 0, 0)` has no red, green, or blue. The resulting color is completely black, as in line 12. The tuple `(255, 255, 255)` has a maximum amount of red, green, and blue, resulting in white, as in line 13.

We'll also use red, green, and blue, which are assigned in lines 14 to 16. The tuple `(255, 0, 0)` represents the maximum amount of red but no green or blue, so the resulting color is red. Similarly, `(0, 255, 0)` is green and `(0, 0, 255)` is blue.

You can mix the amount of red, green, and blue to get any shade of any color. Table 17-1 has some common colors and their RGB values. The web page *https://www.nostarch.com/inventwithpython/* lists several more tuple values for different colors.

Table 17-1: Colors and Their RGB Values

Color	RGB value
Black	(0, 0, 0)
Blue	(0, 0, 255)
Gray	(128, 128, 128)
Green	(0, 128, 0)
Lime	(0, 255, 0)
Purple	(128, 0, 128)
Red	(255, 0, 0)
Teal	(0, 128, 128)
White	(255, 255, 255)
Yellow	(255, 255, 0)

We'll just use the five colors we've already defined, but in your programs, you can use any of these colors or even make up different colors.

Writing Text on the pygame Window

Writing text on a window is a little different from just using `print()`, as we've done in our text-based games. In order to write text on a window, we need to do some setup first.

Using Fonts to Style Text

A font is a complete set of letters, numbers, symbols, and characters drawn in a single style. We'll use fonts anytime we need to print text on a `pygame` window. Figure 17-2 shows the same sentence printed in different fonts.

Programming is fun!
Programming is fun!
PROGRAMMING IS FUN!
Programming is fun!
Programming is fun!
Programming is fun!

Figure 17-2: Examples of different fonts

In our earlier games, we only told Python to print text. The color, size, and font that were used to display this text were completely determined by your operating system. The Python program couldn't change the font. However, pygame can draw text in any font on your computer.

Line 19 creates a pygame.font.Font object (called a Font object for short) by calling the pygame.font.SysFont() function with two parameters:

```
18. # Set up the fonts.
19. basicFont = pygame.font.SysFont(None, 48)
```

The first parameter is the name of the font, but we'll pass the None value to use the default system font. The second parameter is the size of the font (which is measured in units called *points*). We'll draw 'Hello world!' on the window in the default font at 48 points. Generating an image of letters for text like "Hello world!" is called *rendering*.

Rendering a Font Object

The Font object that you've stored in the basicFont variable has a method called render(). This method will return a Surface object with the text drawn on it. The first parameter to render() is the string of the text to draw. The second parameter is a Boolean for whether or not to *anti-alias* the font. Anti-aliasing blurs your text slightly to make it look smoother. Figure 17-3 shows what a line looks like with and without anti-aliasing.

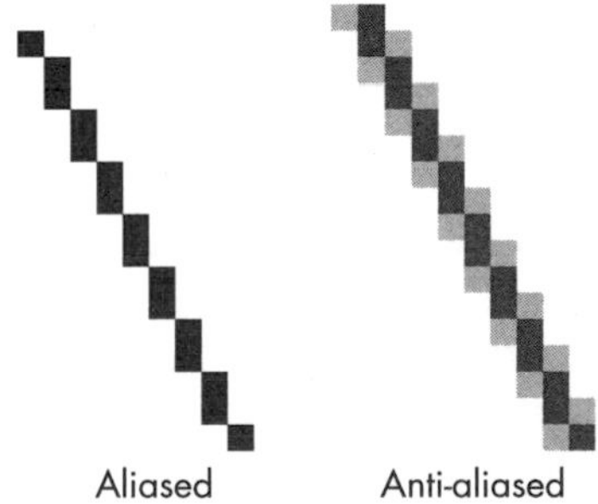

Figure 17-3: An enlarged view of an aliased line and an anti-aliased line

On line 22, we pass True to use anti-aliasing:

```
21. # Set up the text.
22. text = basicFont.render('Hello world!', True, WHITE, BLUE)
```

The third and fourth parameters in line 22 are both RGB tuples. The third parameter is the color the text will be rendered in (white, in this case), and the fourth is the background color behind the text (blue). We assign the Surface object to the variable text.

Once we've set up the Font object, we need to place it in a location on the window.

Setting the Text Location with Rect Attributes

The pygame.Rect data type (called Rect for short) represents rectangular areas of a certain size and location. This is what we use to set the location of objects on a window.

To create a new Rect object, you call the function pygame.Rect(). Notice that the pygame.Rect() function has the same name as the pygame.Rect data type. Functions that have the same name as their data type and create objects or values of their data type are called *constructor functions*. The parameters for the pygame.Rect() function are integers for the x- and y-coordinates of the top-left corner, followed by the width and height, all in pixels. The function name with the parameters looks like this: pygame.Rect(*left, top, width, height*).

When we created the Font object, a Rect object was already made for it, so all we need to do now is retrieve it. To do that, we use the get_rect() method on text and assign the Rect to textRect:

```
23. textRect = text.get_rect()
24. textRect.centerx = windowSurface.get_rect().centerx
25. textRect.centery = windowSurface.get_rect().centery
```

Just as methods are functions that are associated with an object, *attributes* are variables that are associated with an object. The Rect data type has many attributes that describe the rectangle they represent. In order to set the location of textRect on the window, we need to assign its center x and y values to pixel coordinates on the window. Since each Rect object already has attributes that store the x- and y-coordinates of the Rect's center, called centerx and centery, respectively, all we need to do is assign those coordinates values.

We want to put textRect in the center of the window, so we need to get the windowSurface Rect, get its centerx and centery attributes, and then assign those to the centerx and centery attributes of textRect. We do that in lines 24 and 25.

There are many other Rect attributes that we can use. Table 17-2 is a list of attributes of a Rect object named myRect.

Table 17-2: Rect Attributes

pygame.Rect **attribute**	**Description**
myRect.left	Integer value of the x-coordinate of the left side of the rectangle
myRect.right	Integer value of the x-coordinate of the right side of the rectangle
myRect.top	Integer value of the y-coordinate of the top side of the rectangle
myRect.bottom	Integer value of the y-coordinate of the bottom side of the rectangle

Table 17-2 (continued)

pygame.Rect **attribute**	**Description**
myRect.centerx	Integer value of the x-coordinate of the center of the rectangle
myRect.centery	Integer value of the y-coordinate of the center of the rectangle
myRect.width	Integer value of the width of the rectangle
myRect.height	Integer value of the height of the rectangle
myRect.size	A tuple of two integers: (width, height)
myRect.topleft	A tuple of two integers: (left, top)
myRect.topright	A tuple of two integers: (right, top)
myRect.bottomleft	A tuple of two integers: (left, bottom)
myRect.bottomright	A tuple of two integers: (right, bottom)
myRect.midleft	A tuple of two integers: (left, centery)
myRect.midright	A tuple of two integers: (right, centery)
myRect.midtop	A tuple of two integers: (centerx, top)
myRect.midbottom	A tuple of two integers: (centerx, bottom)

The great thing about Rect objects is that if you modify any of these attributes, all the other attributes will automatically modify themselves, too. For example, if you create a Rect object that is 20 pixels wide and 20 pixels tall and has the top-left corner at the coordinates (30, 40), then the x-coordinate of the right side will automatically be set to 50 (because 20 + 30 = 50).

Or if you instead change the left attribute with the line myRect.left = 100, then pygame will automatically change the right attribute to 120 (because 20 + 100 = 120). Every other attribute for that Rect object is also updated.

MORE ABOUT METHODS, MODULES, AND DATA TYPES

Inside the pygame module are the font and surface modules, and inside *those* modules are the Font and Surface data types. The pygame programmers began the modules with a lowercase letter and the data types with an uppercase letter to make it easier to distinguish the data types and the modules.

Notice that both the Font object (stored in the text variable on line 23) and the Surface object (stored in the windowSurface variable on line 24) have a method called get_rect(). Technically, these are two different methods, but the programmers of pygame gave them the same name because they both do the same thing: return Rect objects that represent the size and position of the Font or Surface object.

Filling a Surface Object with a Color

For our program, we want to fill the entire surface stored in `windowSurface` with the color white. The `fill()` function will completely cover the surface with the color you pass as the parameter. (Remember, the `WHITE` variable was set to the value `(255, 255, 255)` on line 13.)

```
27. # Draw the white background onto the surface.
28. windowSurface.fill(WHITE)
```

Note that in `pygame`, the window on the screen won't change when you call the `fill()` method or any of the other drawing functions. Rather, these will change the `Surface` object, and you have to render the new `Surface` object to the screen with the `pygame.display.update()` function to see changes.

This is because modifying the `Surface` object in the computer's memory is much faster than modifying the image on the screen. It is much more efficient to draw onto the screen once after all of the drawing functions have been drawn to the `Surface` object.

pygame's Drawing Functions

So far, we've learned how to fill a `pygame` window with a color and add text, but `pygame` also has functions that let you draw shapes and lines. Each shape has its own function, and you can combine these shapes into different pictures for your graphical game.

Drawing a Polygon

The `pygame.draw.polygon()` function can draw any polygon shape you give it. A *polygon* is a multisided shape with sides that are straight lines. Circles and ellipses are not polygons, so we need to use different functions for those shapes.

The function's arguments, in order, are as follows:

1. The `Surface` object to draw the polygon on.
2. The color of the polygon.
3. A tuple of tuples that represents the x- and y-coordinates of the points to draw in order. The last tuple will automatically connect to the first tuple to complete the shape.
4. Optionally, an integer for the width of the polygon lines. Without this, the polygon will be filled in.

On line 31, we draw a green polygon onto our white `Surface` object.

```
# Draw a green polygon onto the surface.
pygame.draw.polygon(windowSurface, GREEN, ((146, 0), (291, 106),
    (236, 277), (56, 277), (0, 106)))
```

We want our polygon to be filled, so we don't give the last optional integer for line widths. Figure 17-4 shows some examples of polygons.

Figure 17-4: Examples of polygons

Drawing a Line

The `pygame.draw.line()` function just draws a line from one point on the screen to another point. The parameters for `pygame.draw.line()`, in order, are as follows:

1. The `Surface` object to draw the line on.
2. The color of the line.
3. A tuple of two integers for the x- and y-coordinates of one end of the line.
4. A tuple of two integers for the x- and y-coordinates of the other end of the line.
5. Optionally, an integer for the width of the line in pixels.

In lines 34 to 36, we call `pygame.draw.line()` three times:

```
33. # Draw some blue lines onto the surface.
34. pygame.draw.line(windowSurface, BLUE, (60, 60), (120, 60), 4)
35. pygame.draw.line(windowSurface, BLUE, (120, 60), (60, 120))
36. pygame.draw.line(windowSurface, BLUE, (60, 120), (120, 120), 4)
```

If you don't specify the `width` parameter, it will take on the default value of `1`. In lines 34 and 36, we pass `4` for the width, so the lines will be 4 pixels thick. The three `pygame.draw.line()` calls on lines 34, 35, and 36 draw the blue Z on the `Surface` object.

Drawing a Circle

The `pygame.draw.circle()` function draws circles on `Surface` objects. Its parameters, in order, are as follows:

1. The `Surface` object to draw the circle on.
2. The color of the circle.
3. A tuple of two integers for the x- and y-coordinates of the center of the circle.
4. An integer for the radius (that is, the size) of the circle.
5. Optionally, an integer for the width of the line. A width of `0` means that the circle will be filled in.

Line 39 draws a blue circle on the `Surface` object:

```
38. # Draw a blue circle onto the surface.
39. pygame.draw.circle(windowSurface, BLUE, (300, 50), 20, 0)
```

This circle's center is at an x-coordinate of 300 and y-coordinate of 50. The radius of the circle is 20 pixels, and it is filled in with blue.

Drawing an Ellipse

The `pygame.draw.ellipse()` function is similar to the `pygame.draw.circle()` function, but instead it draws an ellipse, which is like a squished circle. The `pygame.draw.ellipse()` function's parameters, in order, are as follows:

1. The `Surface` object to draw the ellipse on.
2. The color of the ellipse.
3. A tuple of four integers for the left and top corner of the ellipse's `Rect` object and the width and height of the ellipse.
4. Optionally, an integer for the width of the line. A width of `0` means that the ellipse will be filled in.

Line 42 draws a red ellipse on the `Surface` object:

```
41. # Draw a red ellipse onto the surface.
42. pygame.draw.ellipse(windowSurface, RED, (300, 250, 40, 80), 1)
```

The ellipse's top-left corner is at an x-coordinate of 300 and y-coordinate of 250. The shape is 40 pixels wide and 80 pixels tall. The ellipse's outline is 1 pixel wide.

Drawing a Rectangle

The `pygame.draw.rect()` function will draw a rectangle. The `pygame.draw.rect()` function's parameters, in order, are as follows:

1. The `Surface` object to draw the rectangle on.

2. The color of the rectangle.
3. A tuple of four integers for the x- and y-coordinates of the top-left corner and the width and height of the rectangle. Instead of a tuple of four integers for the third parameter, you can also pass a `Rect` object.

In the Hello World program, we want the rectangle we draw to be visible 20 pixels around all the sides of text. Remember, in line 23 we created a `textRect` to contain our text. On line 45 we set the left and top points of the rectangle as the left and top of `textRect` minus 20 (we subtract because coordinates decrease as you go left and up):

```
44. # Draw the text's background rectangle onto the surface.
45. pygame.draw.rect(windowSurface, RED, (textRect.left - 20,
      textRect.top - 20, textRect.width + 40, textRect.height + 40))
```

The width and height of the rectangle are equal to the width and height of the `textRect` plus 40. We use 40 and not 20 because the left and top were moved back 20 pixels, so you need to make up for that space.

Coloring Pixels

Line 48 creates a `pygame.PixelArray` object (called a `PixelArray` object for short). The `PixelArray` object is a list of lists of color tuples that represents the `Surface` object you passed it.

The `PixelArray` object gives you a high per-pixel level of control, so it's a good choice if you need to draw very detailed or customized images to the screen instead of just large shapes.

We'll use a `PixelArray` to color one pixel on `windowSurface` black. You can see this pixel on the bottom right of the window when you run `pygame` Hello World.

Line 48 passes `windowSurface` to the `pygame.PixelArray()` call, so assigning `BLACK` to `pixArray[480][380]` on line 49 will make the pixel at the coordinates `(480, 380)` black:

```
47. # Get a pixel array of the surface.
48. pixArray = pygame.PixelArray(windowSurface)
49. pixArray[480][380] = BLACK
```

The `pygame` module will automatically modify the `windowSurface` object with this change.

The first index in the `PixelArray` object is for the x-coordinate. The second index is for the y-coordinate. `PixelArray` objects make it easy to set individual pixels on a `Surface` object to a specific color.

Every time you create a `PixelArray` object from a `Surface` object, that `Surface` object is locked. That means no `blit()` method calls (described next) can be made on that `Surface` object. To unlock the `Surface` object, you must delete the `PixelArray` object with the `del` operator:

```
50. del pixArray
```

If you forget to do so, you'll get an error message that says `pygame.error: Surfaces must not be locked during blit.`

The blit() Method for Surface Objects

The `blit()` method will draw the contents of one `Surface` object onto another `Surface` object. All text objects created by the `render()` method exist on their own `Surface` object. The `pygame` drawing methods can all specify the `Surface` object to draw a shape or a line on, but our text was stored into the `text` variable rather than drawn onto `windowSurface`. In order to draw `text` on the `Surface` we want it to appear on, we must use the `blit()` method:

```
52. # Draw the text onto the surface.
53. windowSurface.blit(text, textRect)
```

Line 53 draws the `'Hello world!'` `Surface` object in the `text` variable (defined on line 22) onto the `Surface` object stored in the `windowSurface` variable.

The second parameter to `blit()` specifies where on `windowSurface` the `text` surface should be drawn. The `Rect` object you got from calling `text.get_rect()` on line 23 is passed for this parameter.

Drawing the Surface Object to the Screen

Since in `pygame` nothing is actually drawn to the screen until the function `pygame.display.update()` is called, we call it on line 56 to display our updated `Surface` object:

```
55. # Draw the window onto the screen.
56. pygame.display.update()
```

To save memory, you don't want to update to the screen after every single drawing function; instead, you want to update the screen only once, after all the drawing functions have been called.

Events and the Game Loop

In our previous games, all of the programs would print everything immediately until they reached an `input()` function call. At that point, the program would stop and wait for the user to type something in and press ENTER. But `pygame` programs are constantly running through a *game loop*, which executes every line of code in the loop about 100 times a second.

The game loop constantly checks for new events, updates the state of the window, and draws the window on the screen. *Events* are generated by `pygame` whenever the user presses a key, clicks or moves the mouse, or performs some other action recognized by the program that should make something happen in the game. An Event is an object of the pygame.event.Event data type.

Line 59 is the start of the game loop:

```
58. # Run the game loop.
59. while True:
```

The condition for the while statement is set to True so that it loops forever. The only time the loop will exit is if an event causes the program to terminate.

Getting Event Objects

The function pygame.event.get() checks for any new pygame.event.Event objects (called Event objects for short) that have been generated since the last call to pygame.event.get(). These events are returned as a list of Event objects, which the program will then execute to perform some action in response to the event. All Event objects have an attribute called type, which tell us the type of the event. In this chapter, we only need to use the QUIT event type, which tells us when the user quits the program:

```
60.     for event in pygame.event.get():
61.         if event.type == QUIT:
```

In line 60, we use a for loop to iterate over each Event object in the list returned by pygame.event.get(). If the type attribute of the event is equal to the constant variable QUIT—which was in the pygame.locals module we imported at the start of the program—then you know the QUIT event has been generated.

The pygame module generates the QUIT event when the user closes the program's window or when the computer shuts down and tries to terminate all the running programs. Next, we'll tell the program what to do when it detects the QUIT event.

Exiting the Program

If the QUIT event has been generated, the program will call both pygame.quit() and sys.exit():

```
62.             pygame.quit()
63.             sys.exit()
```

The pygame.quit() function is sort of the opposite of init(). You need to call it before exiting your program. If you forget, you may cause IDLE to hang after your program has ended. Lines 62 and 63 quit pygame and end the program.

Summary

In this chapter, we've covered many new topics that will let us do a lot more than we could with our previous games. Instead of just working with text by calling `print()` and `input()`, a `pygame` program has a blank window—created by `pygame.display.set_mode()`—that we can draw on. `pygame`'s drawing functions let you draw shapes in many colors in this window. You can create text of various sizes as well. These drawings can be at any x- and y-coordinate inside the window, unlike the text created by `print()`.

Even though the code is more complicated, `pygame` programs can be much more fun than text games. Next, let's learn how to create games with animated graphics.

18

ANIMATING GRAPHICS

Now that you've learned some `pygame` skills, we'll write a program to animate boxes that bounce around a window. The boxes are different colors and sizes and move only in diagonal directions. To animate the boxes, we'll move them a few pixels on each iteration through the game loop. This will make it look like the boxes are moving around the screen.

TOPICS COVERED IN THIS CHAPTER

- Animating objects with the game loop
- Changing the direction of an object

Sample Run of the Animation Program

When you run the Animation program, it will look something like Figure 18-1. The blocks will be bouncing off the edges of the window.

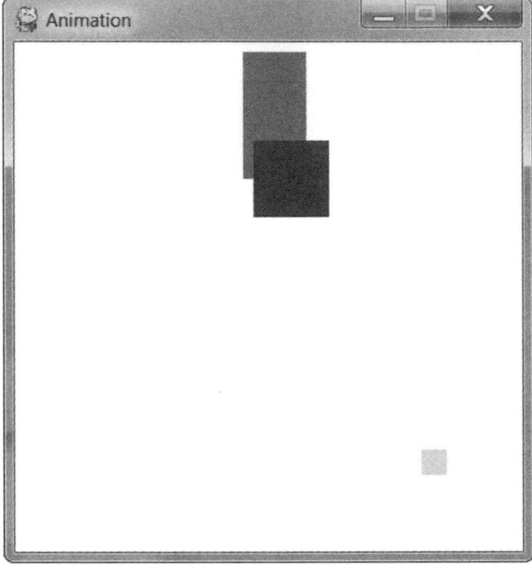
Animation

Figure 18-1: A screenshot of the Animation program

Source Code for the Animation Program

MAKE SURE YOU'RE USING PYTHON 3, NOT PYTHON 2!

Enter the following program into the file editor and save it as *animation.py*. If you get errors after typing in this code, compare the code you typed to the book's code with the online diff tool at *https://www.nostarch.com/inventwithpython#diff*.

animation.py

```
import pygame, sys, time
from pygame.locals import *

# Set up pygame.
pygame.init()

# Set up the window.
WINDOWWIDTH = 400
WINDOWHEIGHT = 400
windowSurface = pygame.display.set_mode((WINDOWWIDTH, WINDOWHEIGHT),
    0, 32)
pygame.display.set_caption('Animation')

```

```
# Set up direction variables.
DOWNLEFT = 'downleft'
DOWNRIGHT = 'downright'
UPLEFT = 'upleft'
UPRIGHT = 'upright'

MOVESPEED = 4

# Set up the colors.
WHITE = (255, 255, 255)
RED = (255, 0, 0)
GREEN = (0, 255, 0)
BLUE = (0, 0, 255)

# Set up the box data structure.
b1 = {'rect':pygame.Rect(300, 80, 50, 100), 'color':RED, 'dir':UPRIGHT}
b2 = {'rect':pygame.Rect(200, 200, 20, 20), 'color':GREEN, 'dir':UPLEFT}
b3 = {'rect':pygame.Rect(100, 150, 60, 60), 'color':BLUE, 'dir':DOWNLEFT}
boxes = [b1, b2, b3]

# Run the game loop.
while True:
    # Check for the QUIT event.
    for event in pygame.event.get():
        if event.type == QUIT:
            pygame.quit()
            sys.exit()

    # Draw the white background onto the surface.
    windowSurface.fill(WHITE)

    for b in boxes:
        # Move the box data structure.
        if b['dir'] == DOWNLEFT:
            b['rect'].left -= MOVESPEED
            b['rect'].top += MOVESPEED
        if b['dir'] == DOWNRIGHT:
            b['rect'].left += MOVESPEED
            b['rect'].top += MOVESPEED
        if b['dir'] == UPLEFT:
            b['rect'].left -= MOVESPEED
            b['rect'].top -= MOVESPEED
        if b['dir'] == UPRIGHT:
            b['rect'].left += MOVESPEED
            b['rect'].top -= MOVESPEED

        # Check whether the box has moved out of the window.
        if b['rect'].top < 0:
            # The box has moved past the top.
            if b['dir'] == UPLEFT:
                b['dir'] = DOWNLEFT
            if b['dir'] == UPRIGHT:
                b['dir'] = DOWNRIGHT
```

```
        if b['rect'].bottom > WINDOWHEIGHT:
            # The box has moved past the bottom.
            if b['dir'] == DOWNLEFT:
                b['dir'] = UPLEFT
            if b['dir'] == DOWNRIGHT:
                b['dir'] = UPRIGHT
        if b['rect'].left < 0:
            # The box has moved past the left side.
            if b['dir'] == DOWNLEFT:
                b['dir'] = DOWNRIGHT
            if b['dir'] == UPLEFT:
                b['dir'] = UPRIGHT
        if b['rect'].right > WINDOWWIDTH:
            # The box has moved past the right side.
            if b['dir'] == DOWNRIGHT:
                b['dir'] = DOWNLEFT
            if b['dir'] == UPRIGHT:
                b['dir'] = UPLEFT

        # Draw the box onto the surface.
        pygame.draw.rect(windowSurface, b['color'], b['rect'])

    # Draw the window onto the screen.
    pygame.display.update()
    time.sleep(0.02)
```

Moving and Bouncing the Boxes

In this program, we'll have three boxes of different colors moving around and bouncing off the walls of a window. In the next chapters, we'll use this program as a base to make a game in which we control one of the boxes. To do this, first we need to consider how we want the boxes to move.

Each box will move in one of four diagonal directions. When a box hits the side of the window, it should bounce off and move in a new diagonal direction. The boxes will bounce as shown in Figure 18-2.

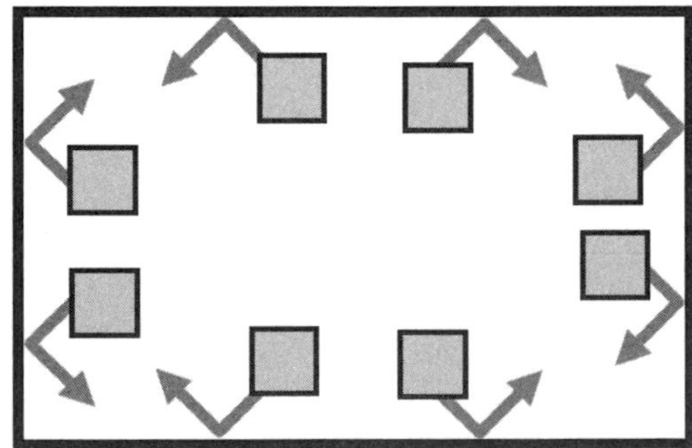

Figure 18-2: How boxes will bounce

The new direction that a box moves after it bounces depends on two things: which direction it was moving before the bounce and which wall it bounced off. There are eight possible ways a box can bounce: two different ways for each of the four walls. For example, if a box is moving down and right and then bounces off the bottom edge of the window, we want the box's new direction to be up and right.

We can use a `Rect` object to represent the position and size of the box, a tuple of three integers to represent the color of the box, and an integer to represent which of the four diagonal directions the box is currently moving in.

The game loop will adjust the x- and y-position of the box in the `Rect` object and draw all the boxes on the screen at their current position on each iteration. As the program execution iterates over the loop, the boxes will gradually move across the screen so that it looks like they're smoothly moving and bouncing around.

Setting Up the Constant Variables

Lines 1 to 5 are just setting up our modules and initializing `pygame` as we did in Chapter 17:

```
 1. import pygame, sys, time
 2. from pygame.locals import *
 3.
 4. # Set up pygame.
 5. pygame.init()
 6.
 7. # Set up the window.
 8. WINDOWWIDTH = 400
 9. WINDOWHEIGHT = 400
10. windowSurface = pygame.display.set_mode((WINDOWWIDTH, WINDOWHEIGHT),
      0, 32)
11. pygame.display.set_caption('Animation')
```

At lines 8 and 9, we define the two constants for the window width and height, and then in line 10, we use those constants to set up `windowSurface`, which will represent our `pygame` window. Line 11 uses `set_caption()` to set the window's caption to `'Animation'`.

In this program, you'll see that the size of the window's width and height is used for more than just the call to `set_mode()`. We'll use constant variables so that if you ever want to change the size of the window, you only have to change lines 8 and 9. Since the window width and height never change during the program's execution, constant variables are a good idea.

Constant Variables for Direction

We'll use constant variables for each of the four directions the boxes can move in:

```
# Set up direction variables.
DOWNLEFT = 'downleft'
```

```
15. DOWNRIGHT = 'downright'
16. UPLEFT = 'upleft'
17. UPRIGHT = 'upright'
```

You could have used any value you wanted for these directions instead of using a constant variable. For example, you could use the string `'downleft'` directly to represent the down and left diagonal direction and retype the string every time you need to specify that direction. However, if you ever mistyped the `'downleft'` string, you'd end up with a bug that would cause your program to behave strangely, even though the program wouldn't crash.

If you use constant variables instead and accidentally mistype the variable name, Python will notice that there's no variable with that name and crash the program with an error. This would still be a pretty bad bug, but at least you would know about it immediately and could fix it.

We also create a constant variable to determine how fast the boxes should move:

```
19. MOVESPEED = 4
```

The value `4` in the constant variable `MOVESPEED` tells the program how many pixels each box should move on each iteration through the game loop.

Constant Variables for Color

Lines 22 to 25 set up constant variables for the colors. Remember, `pygame` uses a tuple of three integer values for the amounts of red, green, and blue, called an RGB value. The integers range from `0` to `255`.

```
21. # Set up the colors.
22. WHITE = (255, 255, 255)
23. RED = (255, 0, 0)
24. GREEN = (0, 255, 0)
25. BLUE = (0, 0, 255)
```

Constant variables are used for readability, just as in the `pygame` Hello World program.

Setting Up the Box Data Structures

Next we'll define the boxes. To make things simple, we'll set up a dictionary as a data structure (see "The Dictionary Data Type" on page 112) to represent each moving box. The dictionary will have the keys `'rect'` (with a `Rect` object for a value), `'color'` (with a tuple of three integers for a value), and `'dir'` (with one of the direction constant variables for a value). We'll set up just three boxes for now, but you can set up more boxes by defining more data structures. The animation code we'll use later can be used to animate as many boxes as you define when you set up your data structures.

The variable b1 will store one of these box data structures:

```
27. # Set up the box data structure.
28. b1 = {'rect':pygame.Rect(300, 80, 50, 100), 'color':RED, 'dir':UPRIGHT}
```

This box's top-left corner is located at an x-coordinate of 300 and a y-coordinate of 80. It has a width of 50 pixels and a height of 100 pixels. Its color is RED, and its initial direction is UPRIGHT.

Lines 29 and 30 create two more similar data structures for boxes that are different sizes, positions, colors, and directions:

```
29. b2 = {'rect':pygame.Rect(200, 200, 20, 20), 'color':GREEN, 'dir':UPLEFT}
30. b3 = {'rect':pygame.Rect(100, 150, 60, 60), 'color':BLUE, 'dir':DOWNLEFT}
31. boxes = [b1, b2, b3]
```

If you needed to retrieve a box or value from the list, you could do so using indexes and keys. Entering boxes[0] would access the dictionary data structure in b1. If we entered boxes[0]['color'], that would access the 'color' key in b1, so the expression boxes[0]['color'] would evaluate to (255, 0, 0). You can refer to any of the values in any of the box data structures by starting with boxes. The three dictionaries, b1, b2, and b3, are then stored in a list in the boxes variable.

The Game Loop

The game loop handles animating the moving boxes. Animations work by drawing a series of pictures with slight differences that are shown one right after another. In our animation, the pictures will be of the moving boxes and the slight differences will be in each box's position. Each box will move by 4 pixels in each picture. The pictures are shown so fast that the boxes will look like they are moving smoothly across the screen. If a box hits the side of the window, then the game loop will make the box bounce by changing its direction.

Now that we know a little bit about how the game loop will work, let's code it!

Handling When the Player Quits

When the player quits by closing the window, we need to stop the program in the same way we did the pygame Hello World program. We need to do this in the game loop so that our program is constantly checking whether there has been a QUIT event. Line 34 starts the loop, and lines 36 to 39 handle quitting:

```
33. # Run the game loop.
34. while True:
35.     # Check for the QUIT event.
36.     for event in pygame.event.get():
37.         if event.type == QUIT:
```

```
38.             pygame.quit()
39.             sys.exit()
```

After that, we want to make sure that windowSurface is ready to be drawn on. Later, we'll draw each box on windowSurface with the rect() method. On each iteration through the game loop, the code redraws the entire window with new boxes that are located a few pixels over each time. When we do that, we're not redrawing the whole Surface object; instead, we're just adding a drawing of the Rect object to windowSurface. But when the game loop iterates to draw all the Rect objects again, it redraws every Rect and doesn't erase the old Rect drawing. If we just let the game loop keep drawing Rect objects on the screen, we'll end up with a trail of Rect objects instead of a smooth animation. To avoid that, we need to clear the window for every iteration of the game loop.

In order to do that, line 42 fills the entire Surface with white so that anything previously drawn on it is erased:

```
41.     # Draw the white background onto the surface.
42.     windowSurface.fill(WHITE)
```

Without calling windowSurface.fill(WHITE) to white out the entire window before drawing the rectangles in their new position, you would have a trail of Rect objects. If you want to try it out and see what happens, you can comment out line 42 by putting a # at the beginning of the line.

Once windowSurface is filled, we can start drawing all of our Rect objects.

Moving Each Box

In order to update the position of each box, we need to iterate over the boxes list inside the game loop:

```
44.     for b in boxes:
```

Inside the for loop, you'll refer to the current box as b to make the code easier to type. We need to change each box depending on the direction it is already moving, so we'll use if statements to figure out the box's direction by checking the dir key inside the box data structure. Then we'll change the box's position depending on the direction the box is moving.

```
45.         # Move the box data structure.
46.         if b['dir'] == DOWNLEFT:
47.             b['rect'].left -= MOVESPEED
48.             b['rect'].top += MOVESPEED
49.         if b['dir'] == DOWNRIGHT:
50.             b['rect'].left += MOVESPEED
51.             b['rect'].top += MOVESPEED
52.         if b['dir'] == UPLEFT:
53.             b['rect'].left -= MOVESPEED
54.             b['rect'].top -= MOVESPEED
```

```
55.         if b['dir'] == UPRIGHT:
56.             b['rect'].left += MOVESPEED
57.             b['rect'].top -= MOVESPEED
```

The new value to set the left and top attributes of each box to depends on the box's direction. If the direction is either DOWNLEFT or DOWNRIGHT, you want to *increase* the top attribute. If the direction is UPLEFT or UPRIGHT, you want to *decrease* the top attribute.

If the box's direction is DOWNRIGHT or UPRIGHT, you want to *increase* the left attribute. If the direction is DOWNLEFT or UPLEFT, you want to *decrease* the left attribute.

The value of these attributes will increase or decrease by the amount of the integer stored in MOVESPEED, which stores how many pixels the boxes move on each iteration through the game loop. We set MOVESPEED on line 19.

For example, if b['dir'] is set to 'downleft', b['rect'].left to 40, and b['rect'].top to 100, then the condition on line 46 will be True. If MOVESPEED is set to 4, then lines 47 and 48 will change the Rect object so that b['rect'].left is 36 and b['rect'].top is 104. Changing the Rect value then causes the drawing code on line 86 to draw the rectangle slightly down and to the left of its previous position.

Bouncing a Box

After lines 44 to 57 have moved the box, we need to check whether the box has gone past the edge of the window. If it has, you want to bounce the box. In the code, this means the for loop will set a new value for the box's 'dir' key. The box will move in the new direction on the next iteration of the game loop. This makes it look like the box has bounced off the side of the window.

In the if statement on line 60, we determine that the box has moved past the top edge of the window if the top attribute of the box's Rect object is less than 0:

```
59.         # Check whether the box has moved out of the window.
60.         if b['rect'].top < 0:
61.             # The box has moved past the top.
62.             if b['dir'] == UPLEFT:
63.                 b['dir'] = DOWNLEFT
64.             if b['dir'] == UPRIGHT:
65.                 b['dir'] = DOWNRIGHT
```

In that case, the direction will be changed based on which direction the box was moving. If the box was moving UPLEFT, then it will now move DOWNLEFT; if it was moving UPRIGHT, it will now move DOWNRIGHT.

Lines 66 to 71 handle the situation in which the box has moved past the bottom edge of the window:

```
66.         if b['rect'].bottom > WINDOWHEIGHT:
67.             # The box has moved past the bottom.
```

```
68.            if b['dir'] == DOWNLEFT:
69.                b['dir'] = UPLEFT
70.            if b['dir'] == DOWNRIGHT:
71.                b['dir'] = UPRIGHT
```

These lines check whether the `bottom` attribute (not the `top` attribute) is *greater* than the value in `WINDOWHEIGHT`. Remember that the y-coordinates start at `0` at the top of the window and increase to `WINDOWHEIGHT` at the bottom.

Lines 72 to 83 handle the behavior of the boxes when they bounce off the sides:

```
72.        if b['rect'].left < 0:
73.            # The box has moved past the left side.
74.            if b['dir'] == DOWNLEFT:
75.                b['dir'] = DOWNRIGHT
76.            if b['dir'] == UPLEFT:
77.                b['dir'] = UPRIGHT
78.        if b['rect'].right > WINDOWWIDTH:
79.            # The box has moved past the right side.
80.            if b['dir'] == DOWNRIGHT:
81.                b['dir'] = DOWNLEFT
82.            if b['dir'] == UPRIGHT:
83.                b['dir'] = UPLEFT
```

Lines 78 to 83 are similar to lines 72 to 77 but check whether the right side of the box has moved past the window's right edge. Remember, the x-coordinates start at `0` on the window's left edge and increase to `WINDOWWIDTH` on the window's right edge.

Drawing the Boxes on the Window in Their New Positions

Every time the boxes move, we need to draw them in their new positions on `windowSurface` by calling the `pygame.draw.rect()` function:

```
85.        # Draw the box onto the surface.
86.        pygame.draw.rect(windowSurface, b['color'], b['rect'])
```

You need to pass `windowSurface` to the function because it is the `Surface` object to draw the rectangle on. Pass `b['color']` to the function because it is the rectangle's color. Finally, pass `b['rect']` because it is the `Rect` object with the position and size of the rectangle to draw.

Line 86 is the last line of the `for` loop.

Drawing the Window on the Screen

After the `for` loop, each box in the `boxes` list will be drawn, so you need to call `pygame.display.update()` to draw `windowSurface` on the screen:

```
88.    # Draw the window onto the screen.
89.    pygame.display.update()
90.    time.sleep(0.02)
```

The computer can move, bounce, and draw the boxes so fast that if the program ran at full speed, all the boxes would look like a blur. In order to make the program run slowly enough that we can see the boxes, we need to add `time.sleep(0.02)`. You can try commenting out the `time.sleep(0.02)` line and running the program to see what it looks like. The call to `time.sleep()` will pause the program for 0.02 seconds, or 20 milliseconds, between each movement of the boxes.

After this line, execution returns to the start of the game loop and begins the process all over again. This way, the boxes are constantly moving a little, bouncing off the walls, and being drawn on the screen in their new positions.

Summary

This chapter has presented a whole new way of creating computer programs. The previous chapters' programs would stop and wait for the player to enter text. However, in our Animation program, the program constantly updates the data structures without waiting for input from the player.

Remember that we had data structures that would represent the state of the board in our Hangman and Tic-Tac-Toe games. These data structures were passed to a `drawBoard()` function to be displayed on the screen. Our Animation program is similar. The `boxes` variable holds a list of data structures representing boxes to be drawn to the screen, and these are drawn inside the game loop.

But without calls to `input()`, how do we get input from the player? In Chapter 19, we'll cover how programs know when the player presses keys on the keyboard. We'll also learn about a new concept called collision detection.

19

COLLISION DETECTION

Collision detection involves figuring out when two things on the screen have touched (that is, collided with) each other. Collision detection is really useful for games. For example, if the player touches an enemy, they may lose health. Or if the player touches a coin, they should automatically pick it up. Collision detection can help determine whether the game character is standing on solid ground or there's nothing but empty air beneath them.

In our games, collision detection will determine whether two rectangles are overlapping each other. This chapter's example program will cover this basic technique. We'll also look at how our `pygame` programs can accept input from the player through the keyboard and the mouse. It's a bit more complicated than calling the `input()` function, as we did for our text programs. But using the keyboard is much more interactive in GUI programs, and using the mouse isn't even possible in our text games. These two concepts will make your games more exciting!

> **TOPICS COVERED IN THIS CHAPTER**
>
> - `Clock` objects
> - Keyboard input in `pygame`
> - Mouse input in `pygame`
> - Collision detection
> - Not modifying a list while iterating over it

Sample Run of the Collision Detection Program

In this program, the player uses the keyboard's arrow keys to move a black box around the screen. Smaller green squares, which represent food, appear on the screen, and the box "eats" them as it touches them. The player can click anywhere in the window to create new food squares. In addition, ESC quits the program, and the X key teleports the player to a random place on the screen.

Figure 19-1 shows what the program will look like once finished.

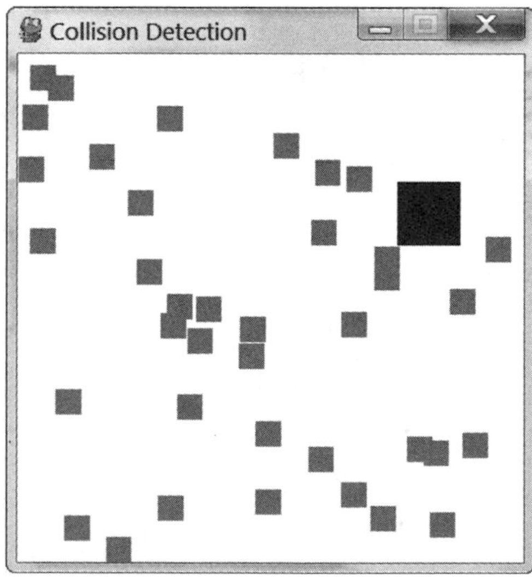

Figure 19-1: A screenshot of the `pygame` Collision Detection program

Source Code for the Collision Detection Program

MAKE SURE YOU'RE
USING PYTHON 3,
NOT PYTHON 2!

Start a new file, enter the following code, and then save it as *collisionDetection.py*. If you get errors after typing in this code, compare the code you typed to the book's code with the online diff tool at *https://www.nostarch.com/inventwithpython#diff*.

collisionDetection.py

```
import pygame, sys, random
from pygame.locals import *

# Set up pygame.
pygame.init()
mainClock = pygame.time.Clock()

# Set up the window.
WINDOWWIDTH = 400
WINDOWHEIGHT = 400
windowSurface = pygame.display.set_mode((WINDOWWIDTH, WINDOWHEIGHT),
  0, 32)
pygame.display.set_caption('Collision Detection')

# Set up the colors.
BLACK = (0, 0, 0)
GREEN = (0, 255, 0)
WHITE = (255, 255, 255)

# Set up the player and food data structures.
foodCounter = 0
NEWFOOD = 40
FOODSIZE = 20
player = pygame.Rect(300, 100, 50, 50)
foods = []
for i in range(20):
    foods.append(pygame.Rect(random.randint(0, WINDOWWIDTH - FOODSIZE),
      random.randint(0, WINDOWHEIGHT - FOODSIZE), FOODSIZE, FOODSIZE))

# Set up movement variables.
moveLeft = False
moveRight = False
moveUp = False
moveDown = False

MOVESPEED = 6

# Run the game loop.
while True:
    # Check for events.
    for event in pygame.event.get():
        if event.type == QUIT:
```

```
                pygame.quit()
                sys.exit()
            if event.type == KEYDOWN:
                # Change the keyboard variables.
                if event.key == K_LEFT or event.key == K_a:
                    moveRight = False
                    moveLeft = True
                if event.key == K_RIGHT or event.key == K_d:
                    moveLeft = False
                    moveRight = True
                if event.key == K_UP or event.key == K_w:
                    moveDown = False
                    moveUp = True
                if event.key == K_DOWN or event.key == K_s:
                    moveUp = False
                    moveDown = True
            if event.type == KEYUP:
                if event.key == K_ESCAPE:
                    pygame.quit()
                    sys.exit()
                if event.key == K_LEFT or event.key == K_a:
                    moveLeft = False
                if event.key == K_RIGHT or event.key == K_d:
                    moveRight = False
                if event.key == K_UP or event.key == K_w:
                    moveUp = False
                if event.key == K_DOWN or event.key == K_s:
                    moveDown = False
                if event.key == K_x:
                    player.top = random.randint(0, WINDOWHEIGHT -
                      player.height)
                    player.left = random.randint(0, WINDOWWIDTH -
                      player.width)

            if event.type == MOUSEBUTTONUP:
                foods.append(pygame.Rect(event.pos[0], event.pos[1],
                  FOODSIZE, FOODSIZE))

        foodCounter += 1
        if foodCounter >= NEWFOOD:
            # Add new food.
            foodCounter = 0
            foods.append(pygame.Rect(random.randint(0, WINDOWWIDTH -
              FOODSIZE), random.randint(0, WINDOWHEIGHT - FOODSIZE),
              FOODSIZE, FOODSIZE))

        # Draw the white background onto the surface.
        windowSurface.fill(WHITE)

        # Move the player.
        if moveDown and player.bottom < WINDOWHEIGHT:
            player.top += MOVESPEED
        if moveUp and player.top > 0:
            player.top -= MOVESPEED
```

```
 91.     if moveLeft and player.left > 0:
 92.         player.left -= MOVESPEED
 93.     if moveRight and player.right < WINDOWWIDTH:
 94.         player.right += MOVESPEED
 95.
 96.     # Draw the player onto the surface.
 97.     pygame.draw.rect(windowSurface, BLACK, player)
 98.
 99.     # Check whether the player has intersected with any food squares.
100.     for food in foods[:]:
101.         if player.colliderect(food):
102.             foods.remove(food)
103.
104.     # Draw the food.
105.     for i in range(len(foods)):
106.         pygame.draw.rect(windowSurface, GREEN, foods[i])
107.
108.     # Draw the window onto the screen.
109.     pygame.display.update()
110.     mainClock.tick(40)
```

Importing the Modules

The pygame Collision Detection program imports the same modules as the Animation program in Chapter 18, plus the random module:

```
import pygame, sys, random
from pygame.locals import *
```

Using a Clock to Pace the Program

Lines 5 to 17 mostly do the same things that the Animation program did: they initialize pygame, set WINDOWHEIGHT and WINDOWWIDTH, and assign the color and direction constants.

However, line 6 is new:

```
6. mainClock = pygame.time.Clock()
```

In the Animation program, a call to time.sleep(0.02) slowed down the program so that it wouldn't run too fast. While this call will always pause for 0.02 seconds on all computers, the speed of the rest of the program depends on how fast the computer is. If we want this program to run at the same speed on any computer, we need a function that pauses longer on fast computers and shorter on slow computers.

A pygame.time.Clock object can pause an appropriate amount of time on any computer. Line 110 calls mainClock.tick(40) inside the game loop. This call to the Clock object's tick() method waits enough time so that it runs at about 40 iterations a second, no matter what the computer's speed is. This ensures that the game never runs faster than you expect. A call to `tick()` should appear only once in the game loop.

Setting Up the Window and Data Structures

Lines 19 to 22 set up a few variables for the food squares that appear on the screen:

```
19. # Set up the player and food data structures.
20. foodCounter = 0
21. NEWFOOD = 40
22. FOODSIZE = 20
```

The `foodCounter` variable will start at the value `0`, `NEWFOOD` at `40`, and `FOODSIZE` at `20`. We'll see how these are used later when we create the food.

Line 23 sets up a `pygame.Rect` object for the player's location:

```
23. player = pygame.Rect(300, 100, 50, 50)
```

The `player` variable has a `pygame.Rect` object that represents the box's size and position. The player's box will move like the boxes did in the Animation program (see "Moving Each Box" on page 280), but in this program, the player can control where the box moves.

Next, we set up some code to keep track of the food squares:

```
24. foods = []
25. for i in range(20):
26.     foods.append(pygame.Rect(random.randint(0, WINDOWWIDTH - FOODSIZE),
          random.randint(0, WINDOWHEIGHT - FOODSIZE), FOODSIZE, FOODSIZE))
```

The program will keep track of every food square with a list of `Rect` objects in `foods`. Lines 25 and 26 create 20 food squares randomly placed around the screen. You can use the `random.randint()` function to come up with random x- and y-coordinates.

On line 26, the program calls the `pygame.Rect()` constructor function to return a new `pygame.Rect` object. It will represent the position and size of a new food square. The first two parameters for `pygame.Rect()` are the x- and y-coordinates of the top-left corner. You want the random coordinate to be between `0` and the size of the window minus the size of the food square. If you set the random coordinate between `0` and the size of the window, then the food square might be pushed outside of the window altogether, as in Figure 19-2.

The third and fourth parameters for `pygame.Rect()` are the width and height of the food square. Both the width and height are the values in the `FOODSIZE` constant.

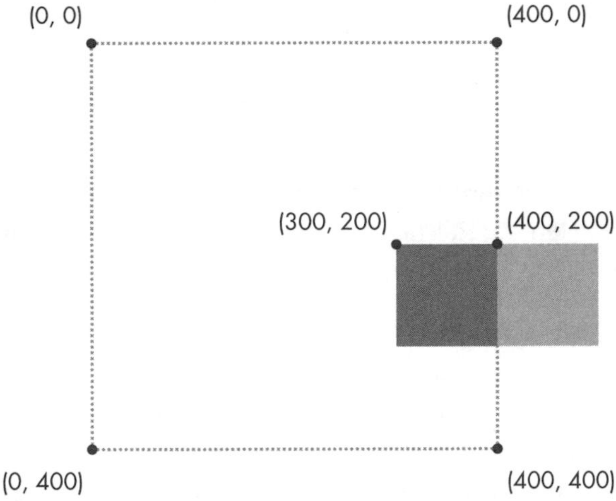

Figure 19-2: For a 100×100 square in a 400×400 window, setting the top-left edge at 400 would place the rectangle outside of the window. To be inside, the left edge should be set at 300 instead.

The third and fourth parameters for `pygame.Rect()` are the width and height of the food square. Both the width and height are the values in the `FOODSIZE` constant.

Setting Up Variables to Track Movement

Starting at line 29, the code sets up some variables that track the movement of the player's box for each direction the box can move:

```
28. # Set up movement variables.
29. moveLeft = False
30. moveRight = False
31. moveUp = False
32. moveDown = False
```

The four variables have Boolean values to keep track of which arrow key is being pressed and are initially set to `False`. For example, when the player presses the left arrow key on their keyboard to move the box, `moveLeft` is set to `True`. When they let go of the key, `moveLeft` is set back to `False`.

Lines 34 to 43 are nearly identical to code in the previous `pygame` programs. These lines handle the start of the game loop and what to do when the player quits the program. We'll skip the explanation for this code since we covered it in the previous chapter.

Handling Events

The pygame module can generate events in response to user input from the mouse or keyboard. The following are the events that can be returned by pygame.event.get():

QUIT Generated when the player closes the window.

KEYDOWN Generated when the player presses a key. Has a key attribute that tells which key was pressed. Also has a mod attribute that tells whether the SHIFT, CTRL, ALT, or other keys were held down when this key was pressed.

KEYUP Generated when the player releases a key. Has key and mod attributes that are similar to those for KEYDOWN.

MOUSEMOTION Generated whenever the mouse moves over the window. Has a pos attribute (short for *position*) that returns a tuple (x, y) for the coordinates of where the mouse is in the window. The rel attribute also returns an (x, y) tuple, but it gives relative coordinates since the last MOUSEMOTION event. For example, if the mouse moves left by 4 pixels from (200, 200) to (196, 200), then rel will be the tuple value (-4, 0). The button attribute returns a tuple of three integers. The first integer in the tuple is for the left mouse button, the second integer is for the middle mouse button (if one exists), and the third integer is for the right mouse button. These integers will be 0 if they are not being pressed when the mouse is moved and 1 if they are pressed.

MOUSEBUTTONDOWN Generated when a mouse button is pressed in the window. This event has a pos attribute, which is an (x, y) tuple for the coordinates of where the mouse was positioned when the button was pressed. There is also a button attribute, which is an integer from 1 to 5 that tells which mouse button was pressed, as explained in Table 19-1.

MOUSEBUTTONUP Generated when the mouse button is released. This has the same attributes as MOUSEBUTTONDOWN.

When the MOUSEBUTTONDOWN event is generated, it has a button attribute. The button attribute is a value that is associated with the different types of buttons a mouse might have. For instance, the left button has the value 1, and the right button has the value 3. Table 19-1 lists all of the button attributes for mouse events, but note that a mouse might not have all the button values listed here.

Table 19-1: The button Attribute Values

Value of button	Mouse button
1	Left button
2	Middle button
3	Right button
4	Scroll wheel moved up
5	Scroll wheel moved down

We'll use these events to let the player control the box with KEYDOWN events and with mouse button clicks.

Handling the KEYDOWN Event

The code to handle the keypress and key release events starts on line 44; it includes the KEYDOWN event type:

```
44.         if event.type == KEYDOWN:
```

If the event type is KEYDOWN, then the Event object has a key attribute that indicates which key was pressed. When the player presses an arrow key or a WASD key (pronounced *wazz-dee,* these keys are in the same layout as the arrow keys but on the left side of the keyboard), then we want the box to move. We'll use if statements to check the pressed key in order to tell which direction the box should move.

Line 46 compares this key attribute to K_LEFT and K_a, which are the pygame.locals constants that represent the left arrow key on the keyboard and the A in WASD, respectively. Lines 46 to 57 check for each of the arrow and WASD keys:

```
45.             # Change the keyboard variables.
46.             if event.key == K_LEFT or event.key == K_a:
47.                 moveRight = False
48.                 moveLeft = True
49.             if event.key == K_RIGHT or event.key == K_d:
50.                 moveLeft = False
51.                 moveRight = True
52.             if event.key == K_UP or event.key == K_w:
53.                 moveDown = False
54.                 moveUp = True
55.             if event.key == K_DOWN or event.key == K_s:
56.                 moveUp = False
57.                 moveDown = True
```

When one of these keys is pressed, the code tells Python to set the corresponding movement variable to True. Python will also set the movement variable of the opposite direction to False.

For example, the program executes lines 47 and 48 when the left arrow key has been pressed. In this case, Python will set moveLeft to True and moveRight to False (even though moveRight might already be False, Python will set it to False again just to be sure).

On line 46, event.key can either be equal to K_LEFT or K_a. The value in event.key is set to the same value as K_LEFT if the left arrow key is pressed or the same value as K_a if the A key is pressed.

By executing the code on lines 47 and 48 if the keystroke is either K_LEFT or K_a, you make the left arrow key and the A key do the same thing. The W, A, S, and D keys are used as alternates for changing the movement variables, letting the player use their left hand instead of their right if they prefer. You can see an illustration of both sets of keys in Figure 19-3.

Figure 19-3: The WASD keys can be programmed to do the same thing as the arrow keys.

The constants for letter and number keys are easy to figure out: the A key's constant is `K_a`, the B key's constant is `K_b`, and so on. The 3 key's constant is `K_3`. Table 19-2 lists commonly used constant variables for the other keyboard keys.

Table 19-2: Constant Variables for Keyboard Keys

pygame constant variable	Keyboard key	pygame constant variable	Keyboard key
K_LEFT	Left arrow	K_HOME	HOME
K_RIGHT	Right arrow	K_END	END
K_UP	Up arrow	K_PAGEUP	PGUP
K_DOWN	Down arrow	K_PAGEDOWN	PGDN
K_ESCAPE	ESC	K_F1	F1
K_BACKSPACE	Backspace	K_F2	F2
K_TAB	TAB	K_F3	F3
K_RETURN	RETURN or ENTER	K_F4	F4
K_SPACE	Spacebar	K_F5	F5
K_DELETE	DEL	K_F6	F6
K_LSHIFT	Left SHIFT	K_F7	F7
K_RSHIFT	Right SHIFT	K_F8	F8
K_LCTRL	Left CTRL	K_F9	F9
K_RCTRL	Right CTRL	K_F10	F10
K_LALT	Left ALT	K_F11	F11
K_RALT	Right ALT	K_F12	F12

Handling the KEYUP Event

When the player releases the key that they were pressing, a `KEYUP` event is generated:

```
58.         if event.type == KEYUP:
```

If the key that the player released was ESC, then Python should terminate the program. Remember, in pygame you must call the pygame.quit() function before calling the sys.exit() function, which we do in lines 59 to 61:

```
59.             if event.key == K_ESCAPE:
60.                 pygame.quit()
61.                 sys.exit()
```

Lines 62 to 69 set a movement variable to False if that direction's key was released:

```
62.             if event.key == K_LEFT or event.key == K_a:
63.                 moveLeft = False
64.             if event.key == K_RIGHT or event.key == K_d:
65.                 moveRight = False
66.             if event.key == K_UP or event.key == K_w:
67.                 moveUp = False
68.             if event.key == K_DOWN or event.key == K_s:
69.                 moveDown = False
```

Setting the movement variable to False through a KEYUP event makes the box stop moving.

Teleporting the Player

You can also add teleportation to the game. If the player presses the X key, lines 71 and 72 set the position of the player's box to a random place on the window:

```
70.             if event.key == K_x:
71.                 player.top = random.randint(0, WINDOWHEIGHT -
                      player.height)
72.                 player.left = random.randint(0, WINDOWWIDTH -
                      player.width)
```

Line 70 checks whether the player pressed the X key. Then, line 71 sets a random x-coordinate to teleport the player to between 0 and the window's height minus the player rectangle's height. Line 72 executes similar code, but for the y-coordinate. This enables the player to teleport around the window by pushing the X key, but they can't control where they will teleport—it's completely random.

Adding New Food Squares

There are two ways the player can add new food squares to the screen. They can click a spot in the window where they want the new food square to appear, or they can wait until the game loop has iterated NEWFOOD number of times, in which case a new food square will be randomly generated on the window.

We'll look at how food is added through the player's mouse input first:

```
74.         if event.type == MOUSEBUTTONUP:
75.             foods.append(pygame.Rect(event.pos[0], event.pos[1],
                  FOODSIZE, FOODSIZE))
```

Mouse input is handled by events just like keyboard input. The MOUSEBUTTONUP event occurs when the player releases the mouse button after clicking it.

On line 75, the x-coordinate is stored in event.pos[0], and the y-coordinate is stored in event.pos[1]. Line 75 creates a new Rect object to represent a new food square and places it where the MOUSEBUTTONUP event occurred. By adding a new Rect object to the foods list, the code displays a new food square on the screen.

In addition to being added manually at the player's discretion, food squares are generated automatically through the code on lines 77 to 81:

```
77.     foodCounter += 1
78.     if foodCounter >= NEWFOOD:
79.         # Add new food.
80.         foodCounter = 0
81.         foods.append(pygame.Rect(random.randint(0, WINDOWWIDTH -
              FOODSIZE), random.randint(0, WINDOWHEIGHT - FOODSIZE),
              FOODSIZE, FOODSIZE))
```

The variable foodCounter keeps track of how often food should be added. Each time the game loop iterates, foodCounter is incremented by 1 on line 77.

Once foodCounter is greater than or equal to the constant NEWFOOD, foodCounter is reset and a new food square is generated by line 81. You can change the rate at which new food squares are added by adjusting NEWFOOD back on line 21.

Line 84 just fills the window surface with white, which we covered in "Handling When the Player Quits" on page 279, so we'll move on to discussing how the player moves around the screen.

Moving the Player Around the Window

We've set the movement variables (moveDown, moveUp, moveLeft, and moveRight) to True or False depending on what keys the player has pressed. Now we need to move the player's box, which is represented by the pygame.Rect object stored in player. We'll do this by adjusting the x- and y-coordinates of player.

```
86.     # Move the player.
87.     if moveDown and player.bottom < WINDOWHEIGHT:
88.         player.top += MOVESPEED
```

```
89.     if moveUp and player.top > 0:
90.         player.top -= MOVESPEED
91.     if moveLeft and player.left > 0:
92.         player.left -= MOVESPEED
93.     if moveRight and player.right < WINDOWWIDTH:
94.         player.right += MOVESPEED
```

If `moveDown` is set to `True` (and the bottom of the player's box isn't below the bottom edge of the window), then line 88 moves the player's box down by adding `MOVESPEED` to the player's current `top` attribute. Lines 89 to 94 do the same thing for the other three directions.

Drawing the Player on the Window

Line 97 draws the player's box on the window:

```
96.     # Draw the player onto the surface.
97.     pygame.draw.rect(windowSurface, BLACK, player)
```

After the box is moved, line 97 draws it in its new position. The `windowSurface` passed for the first parameter tells Python which `Surface` object to draw the rectangle on. The `BLACK` variable, which has `(0, 0, 0)` stored in it, tells Python to draw a black rectangle. The `Rect` object stored in the `player` variable tells Python the position and size of the rectangle to draw.

Checking for Collisions

Before drawing the food squares, the program needs to check whether the player's box has overlapped with any of the squares. If it has, then that square needs to be removed from the `foods` list. This way, Python won't draw any food squares that the box has already eaten.

We'll use the collision detection method that all `Rect` objects have, `colliderect()`, in line 101:

```
 99.     # Check whether the player has intersected with any food squares.
100.     for food in foods[:]:
101.         if player.colliderect(food):
102.             foods.remove(food)
```

On each iteration through the `for` loop, the current food square from the `foods` (plural) list is placed in the variable `food` (singular). The `colliderect()` method for `pygame.Rect` objects is passed the player rectangle's `pygame.Rect` object as an argument and returns `True` if the two rectangles collide and `False` if they do not. If `True`, line 102 removes the overlapping food square from the `foods` list.

DON'T CHANGE A LIST WHILE ITERATING OVER IT

Notice that this `for` loop is slightly different from any other `for` loop we've seen. If you look carefully at line 100, it isn't iterating over `foods` but actually over `foods[:]`.

Remember how slices work. `foods[:2]` evaluates to a copy of the list with the items from the start and up to (but not including) the item at index `2`. `foods[:]` will give you a copy of the list with the items from the start to the end. Basically, `foods[:]` creates a new list with a copy of all the items in `foods`. This is a shorter way to copy a list than, say, what the `getBoardCopy()` function did in Chapter 10's Tic-Tac-Toe game.

You can't add or remove items from a list while you're iterating over it. Python can lose track of what the next value of the `food` variable should be if the size of the `foods` list is always changing. Think of how difficult it would be to count the number of jelly beans in a jar while someone was adding or removing jelly beans.

But if you iterate over a copy of the list (and the copy never changes), adding or removing items from the original list won't be a problem.

Drawing the Food Squares on the Window

The code on lines 105 and 106 is similar to the code we used to draw the black box for the player:

```
104.     # Draw the food.
105.     for i in range(len(foods)):
106.         pygame.draw.rect(windowSurface, GREEN, foods[i])
```

Line 105 loops through each food square in the `foods` list, and line 106 draws the food square onto `windowSurface`.

Now that the player and food squares are on the screen, the window is ready to be updated, so we call the `update()` method on line 109 and finish the program by calling the `tick()` method on the `Clock` object we created earlier:

```
108.     # Draw the window onto the screen.
109.     pygame.display.update()
110.     mainClock.tick(40)
```

The program will continue through the game loop and keep updating until the player quits.

Summary

This chapter introduced the concept of collision detection. Detecting collisions between two rectangles is so common in graphical games that `pygame` provides its own collision detection method named `colliderect()` for `pygame.Rect` objects.

The first several games in this book were text based. The program's output was text printed to the screen, and the input was text typed by the player on the keyboard. But graphical programs can also accept keyboard and mouse inputs.

Furthermore, these programs can respond to single keystrokes when the player presses or releases a single key. The player doesn't have to type in an entire response and press ENTER. This allows for immediate feedback and much more interactive games.

This interactive program is fun, but let's move beyond drawing rectangles. In Chapter 20, you'll learn how to load images and play sound effects with `pygame`.

20

USING SOUNDS AND IMAGES

In Chapters 18 and 19, you learned how to make GUI programs that have graphics and can accept input from the keyboard and mouse. You also learned how to draw different shapes. In this chapter, you'll learn how to add sounds, music, and images to your games.

TOPICS COVERED IN THIS CHAPTER

- Sound and image files
- Drawing and rescaling sprites
- Adding music and sounds
- Toggling sound on and off

Adding Images with Sprites

A *sprite* is a single two-dimensional image that is used as part of the graphics on a screen. Figure 20-1 shows some example sprites.

Figure 20-1: Some examples of sprites

The sprite images are drawn on top of a background. You can flip the sprite image horizontally so that it is facing the other way. You can also draw the same sprite image multiple times on the same window, and you can resize sprites to be larger or smaller than the original sprite image. The background image can be considered one large sprite, too. Figure 20-2 shows sprites being used together.

Figure 20-2: A complete scene, with sprites drawn on top of a background

The next program will demonstrate how to play sounds and draw sprites using `pygame`.

Sound and Image Files

Sprites are stored in image files on your computer. There are several image formats that `pygame` can use. To tell what format an image file uses, look at the end of the filename (after the last period). This is called the *file extension*. For example, the file *player.png* is in the PNG format. The image formats `pygame` supports include BMP, PNG, JPG, and GIF.

You can download images from your web browser. On most web browsers, you do so by right-clicking the image in the web page and selecting Save from the menu that appears. Remember where on the hard drive you saved the image file, because you'll need to copy the downloaded image file into the same folder as your Python program's *.py* file. You can also create your own images with a drawing program like Microsoft Paint or Tux Paint.

The sound file formats that `pygame` supports are MIDI, WAV, and MP3. You can download sound effects from the internet just as you can image files, but the sound files must be in one of these three formats. If your computer has a microphone, you can also record sounds and make your own WAV files to use in your games.

Sample Run of the Sprites and Sounds Program

This chapter's program is the same as the Collision Detection program from Chapter 19. However, in this program we'll use sprites instead of plain-looking squares. We'll use a sprite of a person to represent the player instead of the black box and a sprite of cherries instead of the green food squares. We'll also play background music, and we'll add a sound effect when the player sprite eats one of the cherries.

In this game, the player sprite will eat cherry sprites and, as it eats the cherries, it will grow. When you run the program, the game will look like Figure 20-3.

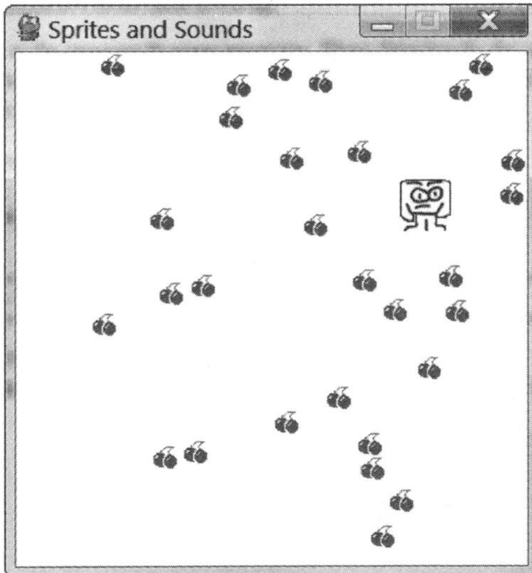

Figure 20-3: A screenshot of the Sprites and Sounds game

Source Code for the Sprites and Sounds Program

Start a new file, enter the following code, and then save it as *spritesAndSounds.py*. You can download the image and sound files we'll use in this program from this book's website at *https://www.nostarch.com/inventwithpython/*. Place these files in the same folder as the *spritesAndSounds.py* program.

If you get errors after entering this code, compare the code you typed to the book's code with the online diff tool at *https://www.nostarch.com/inventwithpython#diff*.

MAKE SURE YOU'RE USING PYTHON 3, NOT PYTHON 2!

spritesAndSounds.py

```
import pygame, sys, time, random
from pygame.locals import *

# Set up pygame.
pygame.init()
mainClock = pygame.time.Clock()

# Set up the window.
WINDOWWIDTH = 400
WINDOWHEIGHT = 400
windowSurface = pygame.display.set_mode((WINDOWWIDTH, WINDOWHEIGHT),
    0, 32)
pygame.display.set_caption('Sprites and Sounds')

# Set up the colors.
WHITE = (255, 255, 255)

# Set up the block data structure.
player = pygame.Rect(300, 100, 40, 40)
playerImage = pygame.image.load('player.png')
playerStretchedImage = pygame.transform.scale(playerImage, (40, 40))
foodImage = pygame.image.load('cherry.png')
foods = []
for i in range(20):
    foods.append(pygame.Rect(random.randint(0, WINDOWWIDTH - 20),
      random.randint(0, WINDOWHEIGHT - 20), 20, 20))

foodCounter = 0
NEWFOOD = 40

# Set up keyboard variables.
moveLeft = False
moveRight = False
moveUp = False
moveDown = False

MOVESPEED = 6

```

```
# Set up the music.
pickUpSound = pygame.mixer.Sound('pickup.wav')
pygame.mixer.music.load('background.mid')
pygame.mixer.music.play(-1, 0.0)
musicPlaying = True

# Run the game loop.
while True:
    # Check for the QUIT event.
    for event in pygame.event.get():
        if event.type == QUIT:
            pygame.quit()
            sys.exit()
        if event.type == KEYDOWN:
            # Change the keyboard variables.
            if event.key == K_LEFT or event.key == K_a:
                moveRight = False
                moveLeft = True
            if event.key == K_RIGHT or event.key == K_d:
                moveLeft = False
                moveRight = True
            if event.key == K_UP or event.key == K_w:
                moveDown = False
                moveUp = True
            if event.key == K_DOWN or event.key == K_s:
                moveUp = False
                moveDown = True
        if event.type == KEYUP:
            if event.key == K_ESCAPE:
                pygame.quit()
                sys.exit()
            if event.key == K_LEFT or event.key == K_a:
                moveLeft = False
            if event.key == K_RIGHT or event.key == K_d:
                moveRight = False
            if event.key == K_UP or event.key == K_w:
                moveUp = False
            if event.key == K_DOWN or event.key == K_s:
                moveDown = False
            if event.key == K_x:
                player.top = random.randint(0, WINDOWHEIGHT -
                  player.height)
                player.left = random.randint(0, WINDOWWIDTH -
                  player.width)
            if event.key == K_m:
                if musicPlaying:
                    pygame.mixer.music.stop()
                else:
                    pygame.mixer.music.play(-1, 0.0)
                musicPlaying = not musicPlaying

        if event.type == MOUSEBUTTONUP:
            foods.append(pygame.Rect(event.pos[0] - 10,
              event.pos[1] - 10, 20, 20))

```

```
 89.     foodCounter += 1
 90.     if foodCounter >= NEWFOOD:
 91.         # Add new food.
 92.         foodCounter = 0
 93.         foods.append(pygame.Rect(random.randint(0, WINDOWWIDTH - 20),
               random.randint(0, WINDOWHEIGHT - 20), 20, 20))
 94.
 95.     # Draw the white background onto the surface.
 96.     windowSurface.fill(WHITE)
 97.
 98.     # Move the player.
 99.     if moveDown and player.bottom < WINDOWHEIGHT:
100.         player.top += MOVESPEED
101.     if moveUp and player.top > 0:
102.         player.top -= MOVESPEED
103.     if moveLeft and player.left > 0:
104.         player.left -= MOVESPEED
105.     if moveRight and player.right < WINDOWWIDTH:
106.         player.right += MOVESPEED
107.
108.
109.     # Draw the block onto the surface.
110.     windowSurface.blit(playerStretchedImage, player)
111.
112.     # Check whether the block has intersected with any food squares.
113.     for food in foods[:]:
114.         if player.colliderect(food):
115.             foods.remove(food)
116.             player = pygame.Rect(player.left, player.top,
                   player.width + 2, player.height + 2)
117.             playerStretchedImage = pygame.transform.scale(playerImage,
                   (player.width, player.height))
118.             if musicPlaying:
119.                 pickUpSound.play()
120.
121.     # Draw the food.
122.     for food in foods:
123.         windowSurface.blit(foodImage, food)
124.
125.     # Draw the window onto the screen.
126.     pygame.display.update()
127.     mainClock.tick(40)
```

Setting Up the Window and the Data Structure

Most of the code in this program is the same as the Collision Detection program in Chapter 19. We'll focus only on the parts that add sprites and sounds. First, on line 12 let's set the caption of the title bar to a string that describes this program:

```
12. pygame.display.set_caption('Sprites and Sounds')
```

In order to set the caption, you need to pass the string `'Sprites and Sounds'` to the `pygame.display.set_caption()` function.

Adding a Sprite

Now that we have the caption set up, we need the actual sprites. We'll use three variables to represent the player, unlike the previous programs that used just one.

```
17. # Set up the block data structure.
18. player = pygame.Rect(300, 100, 40, 40)
19. playerImage = pygame.image.load('player.png')
20. playerStretchedImage = pygame.transform.scale(playerImage, (40, 40))
21. foodImage = pygame.image.load('cherry.png')
```

The `player` variable on line 18 will store a `Rect` object that keeps track of the location and size of the player. The `player` variable doesn't contain the player's image. At the beginning of the program, the top-left corner of the player is located at (300, 100), and the player has an initial height and width of 40 pixels.

The second variable that represents the player is `playerImage` on line 19. The `pygame.image.load()` function is passed a string of the filename of the image to load. The return value is a `Surface` object that has the graphics in the image file drawn on its surface. We store this `Surface` object inside `playerImage`.

Changing the Size of a Sprite

On line 20, we'll use a new function in the `pygame.transform` module. The `pygame.transform.scale()` function can shrink or enlarge a sprite. The first argument is a `Surface` object with the image drawn on it. The second argument is a tuple for the new width and height of the image in the first argument. The `scale()` function returns a `Surface` object with the image drawn at a new size. In this chapter's program, we'll make the player sprite stretch larger as it eats more cherries. We'll store the original image in the `playerImage` variable but the stretched image in the `playerStretchedImage` variable.

On line 21, we call `load()` again to create a `Surface` object with the cherry image drawn on it. Be sure you have the *player.png* and *cherry.png* files in the same folder as the *spritesAndSounds.py* file; otherwise, `pygame` won't be able to find them and will give an error.

Setting Up the Music and Sounds

Next you need to load the sound files. There are two modules for sound in `pygame`. The `pygame.mixer` module can play short sound effects during the game. The `pygame.mixer.music` module can play background music.

Adding Sound Files

Call the pygame.mixer.Sound() constructor function to create a pygame.mixer.Sound object (called a Sound object for short). This object has a play() method that will play the sound effect when called.

```
37. # Set up the music.
38. pickUpSound = pygame.mixer.Sound('pickup.wav')
39. pygame.mixer.music.load('background.mid')
40. pygame.mixer.music.play(-1, 0.0)
41. musicPlaying = True
```

Line 39 calls pygame.mixer.music.load() to load the background music, and line 40 calls pygame.mixer.music.play() to start playing it. The first parameter tells pygame how many times to play the background music after the first time we play it. So passing 5 would cause pygame to play the background music six times. Here we pass the parameter -1, which is a special value that makes the background music repeat forever.

The second parameter to play() is the point in the sound file to start playing. Passing 0.0 will play the background music starting from the beginning. Passing 2.5 would start the background music 2.5 seconds from the beginning.

Finally, the musicPlaying variable has a Boolean value that tells the program whether it should play the background music and sound effects or not. It's nice to give the player the option to run the program without the sound playing.

Toggling the Sound On and Off

The M key will turn the background music on or off. If musicPlaying is set to True, then the background music is currently playing, and we should stop it by calling pygame.mixer.music.stop(). If musicPlaying is set to False, then the background music isn't currently playing, and we should start it by calling play(). Lines 79 to 84 use if statements to do this:

```
79.             if event.key == K_m:
80.                 if musicPlaying:
81.                     pygame.mixer.music.stop()
82.                 else:
83.                     pygame.mixer.music.play(-1, 0.0)
84.                 musicPlaying = not musicPlaying
```

Whether the music is playing or not, we want to toggle the value in musicPlaying. *Toggling* a Boolean value means to set a value to the opposite of its current value. The line musicPlaying = not musicPlaying sets the variable to False if it is currently True or sets it to True if it is currently False. Think of toggling as what happens when you flip a light switch on or off: toggling the light switch sets it to the opposite setting.

Drawing the Player on the Window

Remember that the value stored in playerStretchedImage is a Surface object. Line 110 draws the sprite of the player onto the window's Surface object (which is stored in windowSurface) using blit():

```
109.     # Draw the block onto the surface.
110.     windowSurface.blit(playerStretchedImage, player)
```

The second parameter to the blit() method is a Rect object that specifies where on the Surface object the sprite should be drawn. The program uses the Rect object stored in player, which keeps track of the player's position in the window.

Checking for Collisions

This code is similar to the code in the previous programs, but there are a couple of new lines:

```
114.         if player.colliderect(food):
115.             foods.remove(food)
116.             player = pygame.Rect(player.left, player.top,
                   player.width + 2, player.height + 2)
117.             playerStretchedImage = pygame.transform.scale(playerImage,
                   (player.width, player.height))
118.             if musicPlaying:
119.                 pickUpSound.play()
```

When the player sprite eats one of the cherries, its size increases by two pixels in height and width. On line 116, a new Rect object that is two pixels larger than the old Rect object will be assigned as the new value of player.

While the Rect object represents the position and size of the player, the image of the player is stored in a playerStretchedImage as a Surface object. On line 117, the program creates a new stretched image by calling scale().

Stretching an image often distorts it a little. If you keep restretching an already stretched image, the distortions add up quickly. But by stretching the original image to a new size each time—by passing playerImage, not playerStretchedImage, as the first argument for scale()—you distort the image only once.

Finally, line 119 calls the play() method on the Sound object stored in the pickUpSound variable. But it does this only if musicPlaying is set to True (which means that the sound is turned on).

Drawing the Cherries on the Window

In the previous programs, you called the `pygame.draw.rect()` function to draw a green square for each `Rect` object stored in the `foods` list. In this program, however, you want to draw the cherry sprites instead. Call the `blit()` method and pass the `Surface` object stored in `foodImage`, which has the cherries image drawn on it:

```
        # Draw the food.
        for food in foods:
            windowSurface.blit(foodImage, food)
```

The `food` variable, which contains each of the `Rect` objects in `foods` on each iteration through the `for` loop, tells the `blit()` method where to draw the `foodImage`.

Summary

You've added images and sound to your game. The images, called sprites, look much better than the simple drawn shapes used in the previous programs. Sprites can be scaled (that is, stretched) to a larger or smaller size, so we can display sprites at any size we want. The game presented in this chapter also has a background and plays sound effects.

Now that we know how to create a window, display sprites, draw primitives, collect keyboard and mouse input, play sounds, and implement collision detection, we're ready to create a graphical game in `pygame`. Chapter 21 brings all of these elements together for our most advanced game yet.

21

A DODGER GAME WITH SOUNDS AND IMAGES

The previous four chapters went over the pygame module and demonstrated how to use its many features. In this chapter, we'll use that knowledge to create a graphical game called Dodger.

TOPICS COVERED IN THIS CHAPTER

- The pygame.FULLSCREEN flag
- The move_ip() Rect method
- Implementing cheat codes
- Modifying the Dodger game

In the Dodger game, the player controls a sprite (the player's character) who must dodge a whole bunch of baddies that fall from the top of the screen. The longer the player can keep dodging the baddies, the higher their score will get.

Just for fun, we'll also add some cheat modes to this game. If the player holds down the X key, every baddie's speed is reduced to a super slow rate. If the player holds down the Z key, the baddies will reverse their direction and travel up the screen instead of down.

Review of the Basic pygame Data Types

Before we start making Dodger, let's review some of the basic data types used in `pygame`:

`pygame.Rect`

`Rect` objects represent a rectangular space's location and size. The location is determined by the `Rect` object's `topleft` attribute (or the `topright`, `bottomleft`, and `bottomright` attributes). These corner attributes are a tuple of integers for the x- and y-coordinates. The size is determined by the `width` and `height` attributes, which are integers indicating how many pixels long or high the rectangle is. `Rect` objects have a `colliderect()` method that checks whether they are colliding with another `Rect` object.

`pygame.Surface`

`Surface` objects are areas of colored pixels. A `Surface` object represents a rectangular image, while a `Rect` object represents only a rectangular space and location. `Surface` objects have a `blit()` method that is used to draw the image on one `Surface` object onto another `Surface` object. The `Surface` object returned by the `pygame.display.set_mode()` function is special because anything drawn on that `Surface` object is displayed on the user's screen when `pygame.display.update()` is called.

`pygame.event.Event`

The `pygame.event` module generates `Event` objects whenever the user provides keyboard, mouse, or other input. The `pygame.event.get()` function returns a list of these `Event` objects. You can determine the type of the `Event` object by checking its `type` attribute. `QUIT`, `KEYDOWN`, and `MOUSEBUTTONUP` are examples of some event types. (See "Handling Events" on page 292 for a complete list of all the event types.)

`pygame.font.Font`

The `pygame.font` module uses the `Font` data type, which represents the typeface used for text in `pygame`. The arguments to pass to `pygame.font.SysFont()` are a string of the font name (it's common to pass `None` for the font name to get the default system font) and an integer of the font size.

`pygame.time.Clock`
: The `Clock` object in the `pygame.time` module is helpful for keeping our games from running faster than the player can see. The `Clock` object has a `tick()` method, which can be passed the number of frames per second (FPS) we want the game to run. The higher the FPS, the faster the game runs.

Sample Run of Dodger

When you run this program, the game will look like Figure 21-1.

Figure 21-1: A screenshot of the Dodger game

Source Code for Dodger

Enter the following code in a new file and save it as *dodger.py*. You can download the code, image, and sound files from *https://www.nostarch.com/inventwithpython/*. Place the image and sound files in the same folder as *dodger.py*.

If you get errors after entering this code, compare the code you typed to the book's code with the online diff tool at *https://www.nostarch.com/inventwithpython#diff*.

dodger.py

```
import pygame, random, sys
from pygame.locals import *

WINDOWWIDTH = 600
WINDOWHEIGHT = 600
TEXTCOLOR = (0, 0, 0)
BACKGROUNDCOLOR = (255, 255, 255)
FPS = 60
BADDIEMINSIZE = 10
BADDIEMAXSIZE = 40
BADDIEMINSPEED = 1
BADDIEMAXSPEED = 8
ADDNEWBADDIERATE = 6
PLAYERMOVERATE = 5

def terminate():
    pygame.quit()
    sys.exit()

def waitForPlayerToPressKey():
    while True:
        for event in pygame.event.get():
            if event.type == QUIT:
                terminate()
            if event.type == KEYDOWN:
                if event.key == K_ESCAPE: # Pressing ESC quits.
                    terminate()
                return

def playerHasHitBaddie(playerRect, baddies):
    for b in baddies:
        if playerRect.colliderect(b['rect']):
            return True
    return False

def drawText(text, font, surface, x, y):
    textobj = font.render(text, 1, TEXTCOLOR)
    textrect = textobj.get_rect()
    textrect.topleft = (x, y)
    surface.blit(textobj, textrect)

# Set up pygame, the window, and the mouse cursor.
pygame.init()
mainClock = pygame.time.Clock()
windowSurface = pygame.display.set_mode((WINDOWWIDTH, WINDOWHEIGHT))
pygame.display.set_caption('Dodger')
pygame.mouse.set_visible(False)

# Set up the fonts.
font = pygame.font.SysFont(None, 48)

# Set up sounds.
gameOverSound = pygame.mixer.Sound('gameover.wav')
pygame.mixer.music.load('background.mid')
```

```

# Set up images.
playerImage = pygame.image.load('player.png')
playerRect = playerImage.get_rect()
baddieImage = pygame.image.load('baddie.png')

# Show the "Start" screen.
windowSurface.fill(BACKGROUNDCOLOR)
drawText('Dodger', font, windowSurface, (WINDOWWIDTH / 3),
      (WINDOWHEIGHT / 3))
drawText('Press a key to start.', font, windowSurface,
      (WINDOWWIDTH / 3) - 30, (WINDOWHEIGHT / 3) + 50)
pygame.display.update()
waitForPlayerToPressKey()

topScore = 0
while True:
    # Set up the start of the game.
    baddies = []
    score = 0
    playerRect.topleft = (WINDOWWIDTH / 2, WINDOWHEIGHT - 50)
    moveLeft = moveRight = moveUp = moveDown = False
    reverseCheat = slowCheat = False
    baddieAddCounter = 0
    pygame.mixer.music.play(-1, 0.0)

    while True: # The game loop runs while the game part is playing.
        score += 1 # Increase score.

        for event in pygame.event.get():
            if event.type == QUIT:
                terminate()

            if event.type == KEYDOWN:
                if event.key == K_z:
                    reverseCheat = True
                if event.key == K_x:
                    slowCheat = True
                if event.key == K_LEFT or event.key == K_a:
                    moveRight = False
                    moveLeft = True
                if event.key == K_RIGHT or event.key == K_d:
                    moveLeft = False
                    moveRight = True
                if event.key == K_UP or event.key == K_w:
                    moveDown = False
                    moveUp = True
                if event.key == K_DOWN or event.key == K_s:
                    moveUp = False
                    moveDown = True

            if event.type == KEYUP:
                if event.key == K_z:
                    reverseCheat = False
                    score = 0
```

```
                if event.key == K_x:
                    slowCheat = False
                    score = 0
                if event.key == K_ESCAPE:
                    terminate()

                if event.key == K_LEFT or event.key == K_a:
                    moveLeft = False
                if event.key == K_RIGHT or event.key == K_d:
                    moveRight = False
                if event.key == K_UP or event.key == K_w:
                    moveUp = False
                if event.key == K_DOWN or event.key == K_s:
                    moveDown = False

            if event.type == MOUSEMOTION:
                # If the mouse moves, move the player to the cursor.
                playerRect.centerx = event.pos[0]
                playerRect.centery = event.pos[1]
        # Add new baddies at the top of the screen, if needed.
        if not reverseCheat and not slowCheat:
            baddieAddCounter += 1
        if baddieAddCounter == ADDNEWBADDIERATE:
            baddieAddCounter = 0
            baddieSize = random.randint(BADDIEMINSIZE, BADDIEMAXSIZE)
            newBaddie = {'rect': pygame.Rect(random.randint(0,
                           WINDOWWIDTH - baddieSize), 0 - baddieSize,
                           baddieSize, baddieSize),
                         'speed': random.randint(BADDIEMINSPEED,
                           BADDIEMAXSPEED),
                         'surface':pygame.transform.scale(baddieImage,
                           (baddieSize, baddieSize)),
                         }

            baddies.append(newBaddie)

        # Move the player around.
        if moveLeft and playerRect.left > 0:
            playerRect.move_ip(-1 * PLAYERMOVERATE, 0)
        if moveRight and playerRect.right < WINDOWWIDTH:
            playerRect.move_ip(PLAYERMOVERATE, 0)
        if moveUp and playerRect.top > 0:
            playerRect.move_ip(0, -1 * PLAYERMOVERATE)
        if moveDown and playerRect.bottom < WINDOWHEIGHT:
            playerRect.move_ip(0, PLAYERMOVERATE)

        # Move the baddies down.
        for b in baddies:
            if not reverseCheat and not slowCheat:
                b['rect'].move_ip(0, b['speed'])
            elif reverseCheat:
                b['rect'].move_ip(0, -5)
            elif slowCheat:
                b['rect'].move_ip(0, 1)

```

```
        # Delete baddies that have fallen past the bottom.
        for b in baddies[:]:
            if b['rect'].top > WINDOWHEIGHT:
                baddies.remove(b)

        # Draw the game world on the window.
        windowSurface.fill(BACKGROUNDCOLOR)

        # Draw the score and top score.
        drawText('Score: %s' % (score), font, windowSurface, 10, 0)
        drawText('Top Score: %s' % (topScore), font, windowSurface,
          10, 40)

        # Draw the player's rectangle.
        windowSurface.blit(playerImage, playerRect)

        # Draw each baddie.
        for b in baddies:
            windowSurface.blit(b['surface'], b['rect'])

        pygame.display.update()

        # Check if any of the baddies have hit the player.
        if playerHasHitBaddie(playerRect, baddies):
            if score > topScore:
                topScore = score # Set new top score.
            break

        mainClock.tick(FPS)

    # Stop the game and show the "Game Over" screen.
    pygame.mixer.music.stop()
    gameOverSound.play()

    drawText('GAME OVER', font, windowSurface, (WINDOWWIDTH / 3),
      (WINDOWHEIGHT / 3))
    drawText('Press a key to play again.', font, windowSurface,
      (WINDOWWIDTH / 3) - 80, (WINDOWHEIGHT / 3) + 50)
    pygame.display.update()
    waitForPlayerToPressKey()

    gameOverSound.stop()
```

Importing the Modules

The Dodger game imports the same modules as did the previous pygame programs: pygame, random, sys, and pygame.locals.

```
import pygame, random, sys
from pygame.locals import *
```

The pygame.locals module contains several constant variables that pygame uses, such as the event types (QUIT, KEYDOWN, and so on) and keyboard keys (K_ESCAPE, K_LEFT, and so on). By using the from pygame.locals import * syntax, you can just use QUIT in the source code instead of pygame.locals.QUIT.

Setting Up the Constant Variables

Lines 4 to 7 set up constants for the window dimensions, the text color, and the background color:

```
 4. WINDOWWIDTH = 600
 5. WINDOWHEIGHT = 600
 6. TEXTCOLOR = (0, 0, 0)
 7. BACKGROUNDCOLOR = (255, 255, 255)
```

We use constant variables because they are much more descriptive than if we had typed out the values. For example, the line windowSurface .fill(BACKGROUNDCOLOR) is more understandable than windowSurface.fill((255, 255, 255)).

You can easily change the game by changing the constant variables. By changing WINDOWWIDTH on line 4, you automatically change the code everywhere WINDOWWIDTH is used. If you had used the value 600 instead, you would have to change each occurrence of 600 in the code. It's easier to change the value in the constant once.

On line 8, you set the constant for the FPS, the number of frames per second you want the game to run:

```
 8. FPS = 60
```

A *frame* is a screen that's drawn for a single iteration through the game loop. You pass FPS to the mainClock.tick() method on line 186 so that the function knows how long to pause the program. Here FPS is set to 60, but you can change FPS to a higher value to have the game run faster or to a lower value to slow it down.

Lines 9 to 13 set some more constant variables for the falling baddies:

```
 9. BADDIEMINSIZE = 10
10. BADDIEMAXSIZE = 40
11. BADDIEMINSPEED = 1
12. BADDIEMAXSPEED = 8
13. ADDNEWBADDIERATE = 6
```

The width and height of the baddies will be between BADDIEMINSIZE and BADDIEMAXSIZE. The rate at which the baddies fall down the screen will be between BADDIEMINSPEED and BADDIEMAXSPEED pixels per iteration through the game loop. And a new baddie will be added to the top of the window every ADDNEWBADDIERATE iterations through the game loop.

Finally, the PLAYERMOVERATE stores the number of pixels the player's character moves in the window on each iteration through the game loop (if the character is moving):

```
PLAYERMOVERATE = 5
```

By increasing this number, you can increase the speed at which the character moves.

Defining Functions

There are several functions you'll create for this game. The `terminate()` and `waitForPlayerToPressKey()` functions will end and pause the game, respectively, the `playerHasHitBaddie()` function will track the player's collisions with baddies, and the `drawText()` function will draw the score and other text to the screen.

Ending and Pausing the Game

The `pygame` module requires that you call both `pygame.quit()` and `sys.exit()` to end the game. Lines 16 to 18 put them both into a function called `terminate()`.

```
16. def terminate():
17.     pygame.quit()
18.     sys.exit()
```

Now you only need to call `terminate()` instead of both `pygame.quit()` and `sys.exit()`.

Sometimes you'll want to pause the program until the player presses a key, such as at the very start of the game when the *Dodger* title text appears or at the end when *Game Over* shows. Lines 20 to 24 create a new function called `waitForPlayerToPressKey()`:

```
20. def waitForPlayerToPressKey():
21.     while True:
22.         for event in pygame.event.get():
23.             if event.type == QUIT:
24.                 terminate()
```

Inside this function, there's an infinite loop that breaks only when a `KEYDOWN` or `QUIT` event is received. At the start of the loop, `pygame.event.get()` returns a list of `Event` objects to check out.

If the player has closed the window while the program is waiting for the player to press a key, `pygame` will generate a `QUIT` event, which you check for in line 23 with `event.type`. If the player has quit, Python calls the `terminate()` function on line 24.

If the game receives a KEYDOWN event, it should first check whether ESC was pressed:

```
25.             if event.type == KEYDOWN:
26.                 if event.key == K_ESCAPE: # Pressing ESC quits.
27.                     terminate()
28.                 return
```

If the player pressed ESC, the program should terminate. If that wasn't the case, then execution will skip the if block on line 27 and go straight to the return statement, which exits the waitForPlayerToPressKey() function.

If a QUIT or KEYDOWN event isn't generated, the code keeps looping. Since the loop does nothing, this will make it look like the game has frozen until the player presses a key.

Keeping Track of Baddie Collisions

The playerHasHitBaddie() function will return True if the player's character has collided with one of the baddies:

```
30. def playerHasHitBaddie(playerRect, baddies):
31.     for b in baddies:
32.         if playerRect.colliderect(b['rect']):
33.             return True
34.     return False
```

The baddies parameter is a list of baddie dictionary data structures. Each of these dictionaries has a 'rect' key, and the value for that key is a Rect object that represents the baddie's size and location.

playerRect is also a Rect object. Rect objects have a method named colliderect() that returns True if the Rect object has collided with the Rect object that is passed to it. Otherwise, colliderect() returns False.

The for loop on line 31 iterates through each baddie dictionary in the baddies list. If any of these baddies collides with the player's character, then playerHasHitBaddie() returns True. If the code manages to iterate through all the baddies in the baddies list without detecting a collision, playerHasHitBaddie() returns False.

Drawing Text to the Window

Drawing text on the window involves a few steps, which we accomplish with drawText(). This way, there's only one function to call when we want to display the player's score or the *Game Over* text on the screen.

```
36. def drawText(text, font, surface, x, y):
37.     textobj = font.render(text, 1, TEXTCOLOR)
38.     textrect = textobj.get_rect()
39.     textrect.topleft = (x, y)
40.     surface.blit(textobj, textrect)
```

First, the render() method call on line 37 creates a Surface object that renders the text in a specific font.

Next, you need to know the size and location of the Surface object. You can get a Rect object with this information using the get_rect() Surface method.

The Rect object returned from get_rect() on line 38 has a copy of the width and height information from the Surface object. Line 39 changes the location of the Rect object by setting a new tuple value for its topleft attribute.

Finally, line 40 draws the Surface object of the rendered text onto the Surface object that was passed to the drawText() function. Displaying text in pygame takes a few more steps than simply calling the print() function. But if you put this code into a single function named drawText(), then you only need to call this function to display text on the screen.

Initializing pygame and Setting Up the Window

Now that the constant variables and functions are finished, we'll start calling the pygame functions that set up the window and clock:

```
42. # Set up pygame, the window, and the mouse cursor.
43. pygame.init()
44. mainClock = pygame.time.Clock()
```

Line 43 sets up pygame by calling the pygame.init() function. Line 44 creates a pygame.time.Clock() object and stores it in the mainClock variable. This object will help us keep the program from running too fast.

Line 45 creates a new Surface object that is used for the window display:

```
45. windowSurface = pygame.display.set_mode((WINDOWWIDTH, WINDOWHEIGHT))
```

Notice that there's only one argument passed to pygame.display.set_mode(): a tuple. The arguments for pygame.display.set_mode() are not two integers but one tuple of two integers. You can specify the width and height of this Surface object (and the window) by passing a tuple with the WINDOWWIDTH and WINDOWHEIGHT constant variables.

The pygame.display.set_mode() function has a second, optional parameter. You can pass the pygame.FULLSCREEN constant to make the window fill the entire screen. Look at this modification to line 45:

```
45. windowSurface = pygame.display.set_mode((WINDOWWIDTH, WINDOWHEIGHT),
      pygame.FULLSCREEN)
```

The parameters WINDOWWIDTH and WINDOWHEIGHT are still passed for the window's width and height, but the image will be stretched larger to fit the screen. Try running the program with and without fullscreen mode.

Line 46 sets the caption of the window to the string 'Dodger':

```
46. pygame.display.set_caption('Dodger')
```

This caption will appear in the title bar at the top of the window.

In Dodger, the mouse cursor shouldn't be visible. You want the mouse to be able to move the player's character around the screen, but the mouse cursor would get in the way of the character's image. We can make the mouse invisible with just one line of code:

```
47. pygame.mouse.set_visible(False)
```

Calling `pygame.mouse.set_visible(False)` tells `pygame` to make the cursor invisible.

Setting Up Font, Sound, and Image Objects

Since we are displaying text on the screen in this program, we need to give the `pygame` module a `Font` object to use for the text. Line 50 creates a `Font` object by calling `pygame.font.SysFont()`:

```
49. # Set up the fonts.
50. font = pygame.font.SysFont(None, 48)
```

Passing `None` uses the default font. Passing `48` gives the font a size of 48 points.

Next, we'll create the `Sound` objects and set up the background music:

```
52. # Set up sounds.
53. gameOverSound = pygame.mixer.Sound('gameover.wav')
54. pygame.mixer.music.load('background.mid')
```

The `pygame.mixer.Sound()` constructor function creates a new `Sound` object and stores a reference to this object in the `gameOverSound` variable. In your own games, you can create as many `Sound` objects as you like, each with a different sound file.

The `pygame.mixer.music.load()` function loads a sound file to play for the background music. This function doesn't return any objects, and only one background sound file can be loaded at a time. The background music will play constantly during the game, but `Sound` objects will play only when the player loses the game by running into a baddie.

You can use any WAV or MIDI file for this game. Some sound files are available from this book's website at *https://www.nostarch.com/inventwithpython/*. You can also use your own sound files for this game, as long as you name the files *gameover.wav* and *background.mid* or change the strings used on lines 53 and 54 to match the filename you want.

Next you'll load the image files to be used for the player's character and the baddies:

```
# Set up images.
playerImage = pygame.image.load('player.png')
playerRect = playerImage.get_rect()
baddieImage = pygame.image.load('baddie.png')
```

The image for the character is stored in *player.png*, and the image for the baddies is stored in *baddie.png*. All the baddies look the same, so you need only one image file for them. You can download these images from this book's website at *https://www.nostarch.com/inventwithpython/*.

Displaying the Start Screen

When the game first starts, Python should display the Dodger title on the screen. You also want to tell the player that they can start the game by pushing any key. This screen appears so that the player has time to get ready to start playing after running the program.

On lines 63 and 64, we write code to call the `drawText()` function:

```
61. # Show the "Start" screen.
62. windowSurface.fill(BACKGROUNDCOLOR)
63. drawText('Dodger', font, windowSurface, (WINDOWWIDTH / 3),
      (WINDOWHEIGHT / 3))
64. drawText('Press a key to start.', font, windowSurface,
      (WINDOWWIDTH / 3) - 30, (WINDOWHEIGHT / 3) + 50)
65. pygame.display.update()
66. waitForPlayerToPressKey()
```

We pass this function five arguments:

1. The string of the text you want to appear
2. The font in which you want the string to appear
3. The `Surface` object onto which the text will be rendered
4. The x-coordinate on the `Surface` object at which to draw the text
5. The y-coordinate on the `Surface` object at which to draw the text

This may seem like a lot of arguments to pass for a function call, but keep in mind that this function call replaces five lines of code each time you call it. This shortens the program and makes it easier to find bugs since there's less code to check.

The `waitForPlayerToPressKey()` function pauses the game by looping until a `KEYDOWN` event is generated. Then the execution breaks out of the loop and the program continues to run.

Starting the Game

With all the functions now defined, we can start writing the main game code. Lines 68 and on will call the functions that we defined earlier. The value in the `topScore` variable starts at `0` when the program first runs. Whenever the player loses and has a score larger than the current top score, the top score is replaced with this larger score.

```
68. topScore = 0
69. while True:
```

The infinite loop started on line 69 is technically not the game loop. The game loop handles events and drawing the window while the game is running. Instead, this `while` loop iterates each time the player starts a new game. When the player loses and the game resets, the program's execution loops back to line 69.

At the beginning, you also want to set `baddies` to an empty list:

```
70.     # Set up the start of the game.
71.     baddies = []
72.     score = 0
```

The `baddies` variable is a list of dictionary objects with the following keys:

`'rect'` The `Rect` object that describes where and what size the baddie is.

`'speed'` How fast the baddie falls down the screen. This integer represents pixels per iteration through the game loop.

`'surface'` The `Surface` object that has the scaled baddie image drawn on it. This is the `Surface` that is drawn to the `Surface` object returned by `pygame.display.set_mode()`.

Line 72 resets the player's score to `0`.

The starting location of the player is in the center of the screen and 50 pixels up from the bottom, which is set by line 73:

```
73.     playerRect.topleft = (WINDOWWIDTH / 2, WINDOWHEIGHT - 50)
```

The first item in line 73's tuple is the x-coordinate of the left edge, and the second item is the y-coordinate of the top edge.

Next we set up variables for the player movements and the cheats:

```
74.     moveLeft = moveRight = moveUp = moveDown = False
75.     reverseCheat = slowCheat = False
76.     baddieAddCounter = 0
```

The movement variables `moveLeft`, `moveRight`, `moveUp`, and `moveDown` are set to `False`. The `reverseCheat` and `slowCheat` variables are also set to `False`. They will be set to `True` only when the player enables these cheats by holding down the Z and X keys, respectively.

The baddieAddCounter variable is a counter to tell the program when to add a new baddie at the top of the screen. The value in baddieAddCounter increments by 1 each time the game loop iterates. (This is similar to the code in "Adding New Food Squares" on page 295.)

When baddieAddCounter is equal to ADDNEWBADDIERATE, then baddieAddCounter resets to 0 and a new baddie is added to the top of the screen. (This check is done later on line 130.)

The background music starts playing on line 77 with a call to the pygame.mixer.music.play() function:

```
77.     pygame.mixer.music.play(-1, 0.0)
```

Because the first argument is -1, pygame repeats the music endlessly. The second argument is a float that says how many seconds into the music you want it to start playing. Passing 0.0 means the music starts playing from the beginning.

The Game Loop

The game loop's code constantly updates the state of the game world by changing the position of the player and baddies, handling events generated by pygame, and drawing the game world on the screen. All of this happens several dozen times a second, which makes the game run in real time.

Line 79 is the start of the main game loop:

```
79.     while True: # The game loop runs while the game part is playing.
80.         score += 1 # Increase score.
```

Line 80 increases the player's score on each iteration of the game loop. The longer the player can go without losing, the higher their score. The loop will exit only when the player either loses the game or quits the program.

Handling Keyboard Events

There are four types of events the program will handle: QUIT, KEYDOWN, KEYUP, and MOUSEMOTION.

Line 82 is the start of the event-handling code:

```
82.         for event in pygame.event.get():
83.             if event.type == QUIT:
84.                 terminate()
```

It calls pygame.event.get(), which returns a list of Event objects. Each Event object represents an event that has happened since the last call to pygame.event.get(). The code checks the type attribute of the Event object to see what type of event it is, and then handles it accordingly.

If the type attribute of the Event object is equal to QUIT, then the user has closed the program. The QUIT constant variable was imported from the pygame.locals module.

If the event's type is KEYDOWN, the player has pressed a key:

```
86.            if event.type == KEYDOWN:
87.                if event.key == K_z:
88.                    reverseCheat = True
89.                if event.key == K_x:
90.                    slowCheat = True
```

Line 87 checks whether the event describes the Z key being pressed with event.key == K_z. If this condition is True, Python sets the reverseCheat variable to True to activate the reverse cheat. Similarly, line 89 checks whether the X key has been pressed to activate the slow cheat.

Lines 91 to 102 check whether the event was generated by the player pressing one of the arrow or WASD keys. This code is similar to the keyboard-related code in the previous chapters.

If the event's type is KEYUP, the player has released a key:

```
104.            if event.type == KEYUP:
105.                if event.key == K_z:
106.                    reverseCheat = False
107.                    score = 0
108.                if event.key == K_x:
109.                    slowCheat = False
110.                    score = 0
```

Line 105 checks whether the player has released the Z key, which will deactivate the reverse cheat. In that case, line 106 sets reverseCheat to False, and line 107 resets the score to 0. The score reset is to discourage the player from using the cheats.

Lines 108 to 110 do the same thing for the X key and the slow cheat. When the X key is released, slowCheat is set to False, and the player's score is reset to 0.

At any time during the game, the player can press ESC to quit:

```
111.                if event.key == K_ESCAPE:
112.                    terminate()
```

Line 111 determines whether the key that was released was ESC by checking event.key == K_ESCAPE. If so, line 112 calls the terminate() function to exit the program.

Lines 114 to 121 check whether the player has stopped holding down one of the arrow or WASD keys. In that case, the code sets the corresponding movement variable to False. This is similar to the movement code in Chapter 19's and Chapter 20's programs.

Handling Mouse Movement

Now that you've handled the keyboard events, let's handle any mouse events that may have been generated. The Dodger game doesn't do anything if the player has clicked a mouse button, but it does respond when the player moves the mouse. This gives the player two ways of controlling the character in the game: the keyboard or the mouse.

The `MOUSEMOTION` event is generated whenever the mouse is moved:

```
123.            if event.type == MOUSEMOTION:
124.                # If the mouse moves, move the player to the cursor.
125.                playerRect.centerx = event.pos[0]
126.                playerRect.centery = event.pos[1]
```

`Event` objects with a `type` set to `MOUSEMOTION` also have an attribute named `pos` for the position of the mouse event. The `pos` attribute stores a tuple of the x- and y-coordinates of where the mouse cursor moved in the window. If the event's type is `MOUSEMOTION`, the player's character moves to the position of the mouse cursor.

Lines 125 and 126 set the center x- and y-coordinate of the player's character to the x- and y-coordinates of the mouse cursor.

Adding New Baddies

On each iteration of the game loop, the code increments the `baddieAddCounter` variable by one:

```
        # Add new baddies at the top of the screen, if needed.
        if not reverseCheat and not slowCheat:
            baddieAddCounter += 1
```

This happens only if the cheats are not enabled. Remember that `reverseCheat` and `slowCheat` are set to `True` as long as the Z and X keys are being held down, respectively. While the Z and X keys are being held down, `baddieAddCounter` isn't incremented. Therefore, no new baddies will appear at the top of the screen.

When the `baddieAddCounter` reaches the value in `ADDNEWBADDIERATE`, it's time to add a new baddie to the top of the screen. First, `baddieAddCounter` is reset to `0`:

```
        if baddieAddCounter == ADDNEWBADDIERATE:
            baddieAddCounter = 0
            baddieSize = random.randint(BADDIEMINSIZE, BADDIEMAXSIZE)
            newBaddie = {'rect': pygame.Rect(random.randint(0,
                                WINDOWWIDTH - baddieSize), 0 - baddieSize,
                                baddieSize, baddieSize),
                            'speed': random.randint(BADDIEMINSPEED,
                                BADDIEMAXSPEED),
```

```
135.                               'surface':pygame.transform.scale(baddieImage,
                                      (baddieSize, baddieSize)),
136.                               }
```

Line 132 generates a size for the baddie in pixels. The size will be a random integer between `BADDIEMINSIZE` and `BADDIEMAXSIZE`, which are constants set to `10` and `40` on lines 9 and 10, respectively.

Line 133 is where a new baddie data structure is created. Remember, the data structure for `baddies` is simply a dictionary with keys `'rect'`, `'speed'`, and `'surface'`. The `'rect'` key holds a reference to a `Rect` object that stores the location and size of the baddie. The call to the `pygame.Rect()` constructor function has four parameters: the x-coordinate of the top edge of the area, the y-coordinate of the left edge of the area, the width in pixels, and the height in pixels.

The baddie needs to appear at a random point along the top of the window, so pass `random.randint(0, WINDOWWIDTH - baddieSize)` for the x-coordinate of the left edge of the baddie. The reason you pass `WINDOWWIDTH - baddieSize` instead of `WINDOWWIDTH` is that if the left edge of the baddie is too far to the right, then part of the baddie will be off the edge of the window and not visible onscreen.

The bottom edge of the baddie should be just above the top edge of the window. The y-coordinate of the top edge of the window is `0`. To put the baddie's bottom edge there, set the top edge to `0 - baddieSize`.

The baddie's width and height should be the same (the image is a square), so pass `baddieSize` for the third and fourth arguments.

The speed at which the baddie moves down the screen is set in the `'speed'` key. Set it to a random integer between `BADDIEMINSPEED` and `BADDIEMAXSPEED`.

Line 138 will then add the newly created baddie data structure to the list of baddie data structures:

```
138.             baddies.append(newBaddie)
```

The program uses this list to check whether the player has collided with any of the baddies and to determine where to draw baddies on the window.

Moving the Player's Character and the Baddies

The four movement variables `moveLeft`, `moveRight`, `moveUp`, and `moveDown` are set to `True` and `False` when `pygame` generates the `KEYDOWN` and `KEYUP` events, respectively.

If the player's character is moving left and the left edge of the player's character is greater than `0` (which is the left edge of the window), then `playerRect` should move to the left:

```
140.         # Move the player around.
141.         if moveLeft and playerRect.left > 0:
142.             playerRect.move_ip(-1 * PLAYERMOVERATE, 0)
```

The move_ip() method will move the location of the Rect object horizontally or vertically by a number of pixels. The first argument to move_ip() is how many pixels to move the Rect object to the right (to move it to the left, pass a negative integer). The second argument is how many pixels to move the Rect object down (to move it up, pass a negative integer). For example, playerRect.move_ip(10, 20) would move the Rect object 10 pixels to the right and 20 pixels down and playerRect.move_ip(-5, -15) would move the Rect object 5 pixels to the left and 15 pixels up.

The *ip* at the end of move_ip() stands for "in place." This is because the method changes the Rect object itself, rather than returning a new Rect object with the changes. There is also a move() method, which doesn't change the Rect object but instead creates and returns a new Rect object in the new location.

You'll always move the playerRect object by the number of pixels in PLAYERMOVERATE. To get the negative form of an integer, multiply it by -1. On line 142, since 5 is stored in PLAYERMOVERATE, the expression -1 * PLAYERMOVERATE evaluates to -5. Therefore, calling playerRect.move_ip(-1 * PLAYERMOVERATE, 0) will change the location of playerRect by 5 pixels to the left of its current location.

Lines 143 to 148 do the same thing for the other three directions: right, up, and down.

```
143.         if moveRight and playerRect.right < WINDOWWIDTH:
144.             playerRect.move_ip(PLAYERMOVERATE, 0)
145.         if moveUp and playerRect.top > 0:
146.             playerRect.move_ip(0, -1 * PLAYERMOVERATE)
147.         if moveDown and playerRect.bottom < WINDOWHEIGHT:
148.             playerRect.move_ip(0, PLAYERMOVERATE)
```

Each of the three if statements in lines 143 to 148 checks that its movement variable is set to True and that the edge of the Rect object of the player is inside the window. Then it calls move_ip() to move the Rect object.

Now the code loops through each baddie data structure in the baddies list to move them down a little:

```
150.         # Move the baddies down.
151.         for b in baddies:
152.             if not reverseCheat and not slowCheat:
153.                 b['rect'].move_ip(0, b['speed'])
```

If neither of the cheats has been activated, then the baddie's location moves down a number of pixels equal to its speed (stored in the 'speed' key).

Implementing the Cheat Codes

If the reverse cheat is activated, then the baddie should move up by 5 pixels:

```
154.             elif reverseCheat:
155.                 b['rect'].move_ip(0, -5)
```

Passing -5 for the second argument to move_ip() will move the Rect object upward by 5 pixels.

If the slow cheat has been activated, then the baddie should still move downward, but at the slow speed of 1 pixel per iteration through the game loop:

```
156.             elif slowCheat:
157.                 b['rect'].move_ip(0, 1)
```

The baddie's normal speed (again, this is stored in the 'speed' key of the baddie's data structure) is ignored when the slow cheat is activated.

Removing the Baddies

Any baddies that fall below the bottom edge of the window should be removed from the baddies list. Remember that you shouldn't add or remove list items while also iterating through the list. Instead of iterating through the baddies list with the for loop, iterate through a *copy* of the baddies list. To make this copy, use the blank slicing operator [:]:

```
159.         # Delete baddies that have fallen past the bottom.
160.         for b in baddies[:]:
```

The for loop on line 160 uses the variable b for the current item in the iteration through baddies[:]. If the baddie is below the bottom edge of the window, we should remove it, which we do on line 162:

```
161.             if b['rect'].top > WINDOWHEIGHT:
162.                 baddies.remove(b)
```

The b dictionary is the current baddie data structure from the baddies[:] list. Each baddie data structure in the list is a dictionary with a 'rect' key, which stores a Rect object. So b['rect'] is the Rect object for the baddie. Finally, the top attribute is the y-coordinate of the top edge of the rectangular area. Remember that the y-coordinates increase going down. So b['rect'].top > WINDOWHEIGHT will check whether the top edge of the baddie is below the bottom of the window. If this condition is True, then line 162 removes the baddie data structure from the baddies list.

Drawing the Window

After all the data structures have been updated, the game world should be drawn using pygame's image functions. Because the game loop is executed several times a second, when the baddies and player are drawn in new positions, they look like they're moving smoothly.

Before anything else is drawn, line 165 fills the entire screen to erase anything drawn on it previously:

```
164.        # Draw the game world on the window.
165.        windowSurface.fill(BACKGROUNDCOLOR)
```

Remember that the `Surface` object in `windowSurface` is special because it is the one returned by `pygame.display.set_mode()`. Therefore, anything drawn on that `Surface` object will appear on the screen after `pygame.display.update()` is called.

Drawing the Player's Score

Lines 168 and 169 render the text for the current score and top score to the top-left corner of the window.

```
167.        # Draw the score and top score.
168.        drawText('Score: %s' % (score), font, windowSurface, 10, 0)
169.        drawText('Top Score: %s' % (topScore), font, windowSurface,
              10, 40)
```

The `'Score: %s' % (score)` expression uses string interpolation to insert the value in the `score` variable into the string. This string, the `Font` object stored in the `font` variable, the `Surface` object to draw the text on, and the x- and y-coordinates of where the text should be placed are passed to the `drawText()` method, which will handle the call to the `render()` and `blit()` methods.

For the top score, do the same thing. Pass `40` for the y-coordinate instead of `0` so that the top score's text appears beneath the current score's text.

Drawing the Player's Character and Baddies

Information about the player is kept in two different variables. `playerImage` is a `Surface` object that contains all the colored pixels that make up the player character's image. `playerRect` is a `Rect` object that stores the size and location of the player's character.

The `blit()` method draws the player character's image (in `playerImage`) on `windowSurface` at the location in `playerRect`:

```
171.        # Draw the player's rectangle.
172.        windowSurface.blit(playerImage, playerRect)
```

Line 175's `for` loop draws every baddie on the `windowSurface` object:

```
174.        # Draw each baddie.
175.        for b in baddies:
176.            windowSurface.blit(b['surface'], b['rect'])
```

Each item in the baddies list is a dictionary. The dictionaries' 'surface' and 'rect' keys contain the Surface object with the baddie image and the Rect object with the position and size information, respectively.

Now that everything has been drawn to windowSurface, we need to update the screen so the player can see what's there:

```
        pygame.display.update()
```

Draw this Surface object to the screen by calling update().

Checking for Collisions

Line 181 checks whether the player has collided with any baddies by calling playerHasHitBaddie(). This function will return True if the player's character has collided with any of the baddies in the baddies list. Otherwise, the function returns False.

```
180.         # Check if any of the baddies have hit the player.
181.         if playerHasHitBaddie(playerRect, baddies):
182.             if score > topScore:
183.                 topScore = score # Set new top score.
184.             break
```

If the player's character has hit a baddie and if the current score is higher than the top score, then lines 182 and 183 update the top score. The program's execution breaks out of the game loop at line 184 and moves to line 189, ending the game.

To keep the computer from running through the game loop as fast as possible (which would be much too fast for the player to keep up with), call mainClock.tick() to pause the game very briefly:

```
        mainClock.tick(FPS)
```

This pause will be long enough to ensure that about 60 (the value stored inside the FPS variable) iterations through the game loop occur each second.

The Game Over Screen

When the player loses, the game stops playing the background music and plays the "game over" sound effect:

```
188.     # Stop the game and show the "Game Over" screen.
189.     pygame.mixer.music.stop()
190.     gameOverSound.play()
```

Line 189 calls the stop() function in the pygame.mixer.music module to stop the background music. Line 190 calls the play() method on the Sound object stored in gameOverSound.

Then lines 192 and 193 call the `drawText()` function to draw the "game over" text to the `windowSurface` object:

```
192.        drawText('GAME OVER', font, windowSurface, (WINDOWWIDTH / 3),
              (WINDOWHEIGHT / 3))
193.        drawText('Press a key to play again.', font, windowSurface,
              (WINDOWWIDTH / 3) - 80, (WINDOWHEIGHT / 3) + 50)
194.        pygame.display.update()
195.        waitForPlayerToPressKey()
```

Line 194 calls `update()` to draw this `Surface` object to the screen. After displaying this text, the game stops until the player presses a key by calling the `waitForPlayerToPressKey()` function.

After the player presses a key, the program execution returns from the `waitForPlayerToPressKey()` call on line 195. Depending on how long the player takes to press a key, the "game over" sound effect may or may not still be playing. To stop this sound effect before a new game starts, line 197 calls `gameOverSound.stop()`:

```
197.        gameOverSound.stop()
```

That's it for our graphical game!

Modifying the Dodger Game

You may find that the game is too easy or too hard. Fortunately, the game is easy to modify because we took the time to use constant variables instead of entering the values directly. Now all we need to do to change the game is modify the values set in the constant variables.

For example, if you want the game to run slower in general, change the `FPS` variable on line 8 to a smaller value, such as `20`. This will make both the baddies and the player's character move slower, since the game loop will be executed only `20` times a second instead of `40`.

If you just want to slow down the baddies and not the player, then change `BADDIEMAXSPEED` to a smaller value, such as `4`. This will make all the baddies move between 1 (the value in `BADDIEMINSPEED`) and 4 pixels per iteration through the game loop, instead of between 1 and 8.

If you want the game to have fewer but larger baddies instead of many smaller baddies, then increase `ADDNEWBADDIERATE` to `12`, `BADDIEMINSIZE` to `40`, and `BADDIEMAXSIZE` to `80`. Now baddies are being added every 12 iterations through the game loop instead of every 6 iterations, so there will be half as many baddies as before. But to keep the game interesting, the baddies are much larger.

Keeping the basic game the same, you can modify any of the constant variables to dramatically affect how the game plays. Keep trying out new values for the constant variables until you find the set of values you like best.

Summary

Unlike our text-based games, Dodger really looks like a modern computer game. It has graphics and music and uses the mouse. While `pygame` provides functions and data types as building blocks, it's you the programmer who puts them together to create fun, interactive games.

And you can do all of this because you know how to instruct the computer to do it, step by step, line by line. By speaking the computer's language, you can get it to do the number crunching and drawing for you. This is a useful skill, and I hope you'll continue to learn more about Python programming. (And there's still much more to learn!)

Now get going and invent your own games. Good luck!

INDEX

Symbols

+ (addition), 2, 13
    augmented assignment, 155
    commutative property of, 169
\ (backslash), for escape characters, 41–42
: (colon), in `for` statements, 28–29
{} (curly brackets), for dictionaries, 113
/ (division), 2, 4, 246–247
    augmented assignment, 156
" (double quotes), 42–43
= (equal sign), as assignment operator, 5, 34
== (equal to) operator, 32, 34
> (greater than) operator, 30, 32
>= (greater than or equal to) operator, 32
(hash mark), for comments, 18, 23
< (less than) operator, 30, 32
<= (less than or equal to) operator, 32
* (multiplication), 2
    augmented assignment, 156
!= (not equal to) operator, 32, 36
() (parentheses), and order of operation, 4
>>> prompt, 5, 14
' (single quotes), 42–43
[] (square brackets), for indexes, 92
- (subtraction), 2
    augmented assignment, 155

A

`abs()` function, 170
absolute value of number, 170
addition(+), 2, 13
    augmented assignment, 155
    commutative property of, 169
AI. *See* artificial intelligence (AI)
AISim1.py program
    adding computer player, 242–243
    comparing algorithms, 247–254
    computer playing against itself, 240–247
    sample run, 240–241
    source code, 241–242
AISim2.py program
    keeping track of multiple games, 245
    sample run, 243–244
    source code, 244
AISim3.py program
    how AI works in, 249–252
    source code, 248–249
algorithms, 128
alphabetic order, `sort()` method for, 157–158
`and` operator, 52–53
    short-circuiting evaluation, 140
Animation program
    box data structure setup, 278–279
    constant variables, 277–278
    moving and bouncing boxes, 276–277, 280–282
    running game loop, 279–283
    sample run, 274
    source code, 274–276
anti-aliasing, 263
`append()` method, 95
arguments, 18
arrow keys on keyboard, 293, 294
artificial intelligence (AI), 121, 209
    for Reversegam, 232–233
        comparing algorithms, 247–254
        computer playing against itself, 240–247
    for Tic-Tac-Toe
        creating, 142–145
        strategizing, 128–129
ASCII art, 79, 108
assignment (=) operator, 5, 34
attributes, 264
augmented assignment operators, 155–156

B

background color, for text, 263
background music, 322, 325
  repeating forever, 308
backslash (\), for escape characters, 41–42
Bagels Deduction game
  checking for win or loss, 161–162
  checking string for only numbers, 158–159
  clues, 149
    calculating, 156–157
    getting, 161
  flowchart for, 152–153
  getting player's guess, 161
  `join()` method, 158
  playing again, 162
  sample run, 150–151
  secret number, creating, 160–161
  shuffling unique set of digits, 154–155
  source code, 151–152
  starting game, 159
blank line, printing, 41
`blit()` method, 269–270, 331
blocks of code, grouping with, 27
BMP file format, 302
`bool()` function, 227
Boolean data type, 31
  comparison operators and, 33–34
  conditions for checking, 32
  in Tic-Tac-Toe evaluation, 136–137
Boolean operators, 52–55
`break` statement, 35, 37, 109, 161
breakpoints in debugger, 73–75
brute-force technique, for ciphers, 206–208
bugs, 63
  finding, 70–72
  types, 64–65
`button` attribute, for `MOUSEBUTTONDOWN` event, 292

C

Caesar Cipher program
  brute-force technique, 206–208
  encryption or decryption, 202–205
  getting key from player, 203
  getting message from player, 203
  how it works, 199–200
  sample run, 200–201
  setting maximum key length, 202
  source code, 201–202
  starting program, 206
calling
  functions, 49–50, 60–61
  methods, 94–96
camel case, 20
captions, for windows, 261
Cartesian coordinate system, 163, 209
  grids and, 164–165
  math tricks, 168–169
  negative numbers in, 166–167
case sensitivity, 61
  of variable names, 20
`centerx` attribute, of `Rect` object, 264
`centery` attribute, of `Rect` object, 264
cheat modes, 312
chessboard, coordinates, 164–165
`choice()` function, `random` module, 115–117
cipher, 198
`circle()` function, `pygame.draw` module, 268
clearing window, for animation iteration, 280
`Clock()` function, 289–290
`Clock` object, 313
code. *See* source code
coin flips, program simulating, 73–75
`colliderect()` function, 297, 320
Collision Detection program
  adding food squares, 295–296
  checking for collisions, 297
  clock to pace program, 289–290
  drawing food squares, 298
  drawing player on screen, 297
  event handling, 292–295
  moving player around screen, 296–297
  sample run, 286
  source code, 287–289
  teleporting player, 295
  variables for tracking movement, 291
  window and data structures setup, 290–291
colon (:), in `for` statements, 28–29
color
  filling surface object with, 266
  of pixels, 269–270

RGB values, in `pygame`, 261–262
of text, 263
commenting out code, 242
comments, 17–18
commutative property of addition, 169
comparison operators, 32, 33–34
computer
vs. computer AI simulation, 240
screen coordinate system, 167–168
concatenation
of lists, 94
of strings, 13, 26, 159
conditions, 33–34
constant variables, 91
for keyboard keys, 294
constructor functions, 264
`continue` statement, 161
conversion specifiers, 159–160
coordinate system
Cartesian. *See* Cartesian coordinate system
of computer screen, 167–168
coordinates, 163
corner-best algorithm, 248, 249
vs. corner-side-best algorithm, 253–254
vs. random-move algorithm, 252–253
vs. worst-move algorithm, 252
corner-side-best algorithm, 248, 251–252
vs. corner-best algorithm, 253–254
crashing programs, 64
cryptanalysis, 206
cryptography, 198
cursor, in file editor, 14

D

data structures, 180
for boxes in Animation program, 278–279
for collision detection, 290–291
copying in Reversegam, 229–230
for ocean waves in Sonar Treasure Hunt, 184
for Sprites and Sounds program, 306–307
for Tic-Tac-Toe board, 127–128
data types, 13
Boolean, 31–34
dictionary, 112–115
integers, 2–3, 30–31
lists, 92–94
`pygame.Rect`, 264–265
strings. *See* strings
debugger
breakpoints, 73–75
finding bugs, 70–72
running game under, 66
starting, 65
stepping through program with, 67–70
decryption, 198
in Caesar Cipher, 202–205
`def` block, 49, 50
return statement inside, 55
`def` statement, 49, 50
deleting items in list, 117–118
`del` statement, 117
dictionary data type, 112–113
evaluating with `choice()` function, 115–117
`keys()` and `values()` methods, 114–115
vs. lists, 113–114
variables storing references to, 134
diff tool, 16–17
division (`/`), 2, 4, 246–247
augmented assignment, 156
Dodger game
baddies
adding, 327–328
drawing, 331–332
moving, 328–329
removing, 330
tracking collisions, 320
cheat modes, implementing, 329–330
collision detection, 332
constant variables, 318–319
drawing character, 331–332
drawing text to window, 320–321
drawing window, 330–332
ending and pausing, 319–320
functions, 319–321
game loop, 324, 325–327
game over screen, 332–333
importing modules, 317–318
modifying, 333
moving character, 328–329
rendering text for score, 331
sample run, 313
source code, 313–317
starting game, 324–325

double quotes ("), 42–43
Dragon Realm
  asking to play again, 61
  Boolean operators evaluation, 54
  checking caves, 59
  displaying results, 58–59
  flowchart for, 46–47
  functions, 49–50
  getting player's input, 54–55
  how to play, 45
  importing random and time modules, 48
  return statement, 55–56
  running under debugger, 66
  sample run, 46
  source code, 47–48
  start of program, 60

E

elif statements, 103
ellipse() function, pygame.draw module, 268
else statement, 59, 103
encryption, 198
  in Caesar Cipher, 202–205
end keyword parameter, for print() function, 43–44
end of programs, 19
end='' statements, 97
endswith() method, 105
equal sign (=), as assignment operator, 5, 34
equal to (==) operator, 32, 34
error messages, 64
  ImportError, 256
  IndexError, 93
  NameError, 6, 16
  syntax errors, 4–5
  ValueError, 139
errors. *See* bugs
ESC key, for terminating program, 295, 326
escape characters, 41–42
evaluation, short-circuit, 139–141
event handling, 292–295, 325–326
Event object, 271, 312
events, 270–271
execution of program, 17
exit() function, sys module, 180
exiting program, 19, 271
expressions, 3, 36
  evaluating, 3–4
  in function calls, 19
  function calls in, 18

F

False Boolean value, 31
  for data types, 227
  while keyword and, 51
file editor, 13–16
file extensions, for images, 302
fill() function, 266
find() method, 204–205
float() function, 29–31
floating-point numbers, 2–3, 4
  from division (/), 246–247
  rounding, 247
flow control statements, 26
  elif statements, 103
  if statement, 34, 37
    break statement and, 35
    else statement after, 59
  for statement, 26, 28–29, 37
  while statement, 51–52, 60
flowcharts
  for Bagels Deduction game, 152–153
  benefits, 86
  for Hangman design, 80–85
  for Tic-Tac-Toe design, 127
Font object, 312, 322
  rendering, 263
fonts, 262–263
for statement, 26, 28–29, 37
frame, 318
functions, 18–19, 24. *See also names of individual functions*
  calling, 18, 49–50
  def statements, 49, 50
  parameters, 57–58

G

game loop, 270–271
  for Dodger game, 325–327
  for Reversegam game, 237–238
  for Animation program, 279–283
games. *See names of individual games*
get_rect() method, 264, 321
GIF file format, 302

global scope, 56–57
global variables, 67
graphical user interface (GUI) window, 260
graphics. *See also* pygame module
  ASCII art for Hangman, 79
  downloading from web browsers, 303
  sprites for adding, 302
Guess the Number game, 21
  checking for loss, 35–36
  checking for win, 35
  converting values, 29–31
  flow control statements, 26–29
  generating random numbers, 24–26
  getting player's guess, 29
  importing random module, 23–24
  sample run, 22
  source code, 22–23
  for statement, 28–29
  welcoming player, 26

H

Hacking Secret Ciphers with Python, 198
Hangman game
  ASCII art, 79
  asking to play again, 104–105
  checking for loss, 108
  checking for win, 107
  confirming entry of valid guess, 104
  dictionaries of words in, 115
  displaying board to player, 97–101, 106
  displaying secret word with blanks, 99–101
  elif statements, 103
  ending or restarting, 83, 108–109
  extending
    adding more guesses, 112
    dictionary data type, 112–115
    evaluating dictionary of lists, 115–117
    printing word category, 119
  feedback to player, 85
  flowcharts for design, 80–85
  getting player's guess, 101–103
  getting secret word from list, 96
  how to play, 78
  incorrect guesses, 107–108
  main program, 105–109
  printing word category for player, 119
  review of functions, 105
  sample run, 78–79
  source code, 88–91
hash mark (#), for comments, 18, 23
Hello World program
  creating, 14–15
  how it works, 17–19
  in pygame, 256–259. *See also* pygame module
hypotenuse, 187

I

IDLE
  file editor, 13–14
  interactive shell, 1–9, 13
  starting, xxvi
if statement, 34, 37
  break statement and, 35
  else statement after, 59
image files, 302–303
images. *See* graphics
import statement, 24
ImportError, 256
importing modules, 24
in operator, 94
indentation of code, 27
IndexError, 93
indexes
  for accessing list items, 92–93
  value after deleting item in list, 117
infinite loop, 64, 160–161
input, 37, 39
  validation, 52
input() function, 18–19
installing
  pygame, 256
  Python, xxv–xxvi
int() function, 29–31, 139
integers, 2–3
  converting strings to, 30–31
interactive shell, 1–9, 13
items in lists
  accessing with indexes, 92–93
  changing with index assignment, 93
  deleting, 117–118
iteration, 29

J

join() method, 158
Jokes program
  end keyword, 43–44
  escape characters, 41–42
  how it works, 41
  sample run, 40
  source code, 40
JPG file format, 302

K

key-value pairs, in dictionaries, 113
keyboard
  event handling, 325–326
  user input with, 292–295
KEYDOWN event, 292, 293–294
keys
  for ciphers, 198
  for dictionaries, 113
keys() method, 114–115
KEYUP event, 292, 294–295

L

len() function, 57, 113
line breaks, in printed string, 51
line() function, pygame.draw module, 267
line numbers, xxiv
list() function, 98
lists
  accessing items with indexes, 92–93
  changing item order, 154
  concatenation, 94
  vs. dictionaries, 113–114
  and in operator, 94
  iterating and changes, 298
  methods, 95
  references, 132–135
  slicing, 98–99
  sort() method for, 157–158
load() function, 307
loading previously saved program, 15
local scope, 56–57
loops, 26
  break statement to leave, 35
  nested, 161
  with while statements, 51–52
lower() method, 101–102
lowercase, displaying characters as, 101–102

M

mainClock.tick() function, 289–290, 332
math
  expressions, 3–4
  integers and floats, 2–3
  operators, 2
  syntax errors, 4–5
  tricks, 168–169
math module, 180
methods, calling, 94–96
MIDI file format, 303, 322
modules, importing, 24
mouse
  handling events, 292–293, 327
  making invisible, 322
MOUSEBUTTONDOWN event, 292
MOUSEBUTTONUP event, 292, 296
MOUSEMOTION event, 292, 325, 327
move() method, 329
move_ip() method, 329
MP3 file format, 303
multiline strings, 50–51
multiple assignment, 118–119
multiplication (*), 2
  augmented assignment, 156
music
  background, 322, 325
    repeating forever, 308
  setup, 307–308

N

NameError, 6, 16
names, for variables, 20
nested loops, 161, 226
newline (\n), 42, 43
None value, 142
not equal to (!=) operator, 32, 36
not operator, 53–54
numbers. *See also* math
  absolute value of, 170
  negative, in Cartesian coordinate system, 166–167
  sort() method for ordering, 157–158

O

objects, 261
operators
  Boolean, 52–55
  comparison, 32, 33–34
  math, 2

or operator, 53
order of operations, 3–4
origin, in Cartesian coordinate
system, 167
Othello. *See* Reversegam game
output, 37, 39

P

parameters, for functions, 57–58
parentheses [()], and order of
operation, 4
pausing program, 283, 319–320
percentages, 246–247
PixelArray object, 269
pixels, 167, 260
coloring, 269–270
plaintext, 198
play() method, pygame.mixer.music
module, 309
PNG file format, 302
points, fonts, 263
polygon() function, pygame.draw module,
266–267
print() function, 18, 37
end keyword parameter, 43–44
programs. *See also names of individual
programs and games*
end of, 19
running, 16
saving, 15
writing, 13–15
pygame module
drawing functions
circle, 268
ellipse, 268
line, 267
polygon, 266–267
rectangle, 268–269
events and game loop, 270–271
exiting programs, 271
filling surface object with
color, 266
Hello World program, 256–257
sample run, 257
source code, 257–259
importing module, 259
initializing, 259, 321–322
installing, 256
RGB color values, 261–262
window setup, 260–261
pygame.display module
set_caption() function, 261, 277
set_mode() function, 260, 261, 321
update() function, 266, 270, 282
pygame.draw module
circle() function, 268
ellipse() function, 268
line() function, 267
polygon() function, 266–267
rect() function, 268–269
pygame.event module
Event object, 271, 312
get() function, 271, 292, 312
pygame.font module
Font object, 312, 263
SysFont() function, 263, 322
pygame.image.load() function, 307
pygame.init() function, 259, 321
pygame.locals module, 318
pygame.mixer module, 307
Sound() function, 308
pygame.mixer.music module, 307, 332
load() function, 308, 322
play() function, 308, 325
stop() function, 308
pygame.quit() function, 271, 295
pygame.Rect data type, 264–265
pygame.Rect() function, 264, 290, 328
pygame.Surface object, 261, 312. *See also*
Surface object
pygame.time module
Clock() function, 289–290
Clock object, 298, 313, 321
pygame.transform module, 307
scale() function, 309
Pythagorean theorem, 187–188
Python, installing, xxv–xxvi

Q

QUIT event, 271, 292
quotation marks, for strings, 12, 42–43

R

random module
choice() function, 115–117
importing, 23–24
randint() function, 24–26
shuffle() function, 154–155, 232
random-move algorithm, 248, 250
vs. corner-best algorithm, 252–253
range() function, 26, 98

rect() function, 268–269
Rect object, 309, 312
    colliderect() function, 320
references, to lists, 132–135
remove() method, 189–190
render() method, Font object, 263, 321
rendering fonts, 263
return statement, 55–56
return value, 18
reverse() method, 95
Reversegam game
    AI simulation
        comparing AI algorithms, 247–254
        computer playing against itself, 240–247
    checking for valid coordinates, 225–227
    checking for valid move
        checking eight directions, 223–224
        determining tiles to flip, 224–225
    constants, 220
    corner moves strategy, 232
    data structures
        copying, 229–230
        creating fresh board, 222
        drawing on screen, 221–222
    determining if space is corner, 230
    determining who goes first, 228–229
    game loop, 237–238
    getting computer's move, 232–233
    getting list with all valid moves, 226
    getting player's move, 230–232
    getting player's tile choice, 228
    getting score, 227–228
    hints, 214, 226
    how to play, 210–213
    importing modules, 220
    listing highest-scoring moves, 233
    placing tile, 229
    playing again, 238
    printing scores to screen, 234
    running computer's turn, 236–237
    sample run, 213–215
    source code, 215–220
    starting game, 234–237
Reversi. *See* Reversegam game
RGB color values, 261
right triangle, Pythagorean theorem and, 187–188
round() function, 247
running programs, 16
runtime errors, 64

S

saving programs, 15
scale() function, pygame.transform module, 307, 309
scope, global and local, 56–57
semantic errors, 64
set_caption() function, pygame.display module, 261, 277
set_mode() function, pygame.display module, 260, 261, 321
short-circuit evaluation, 139–141
shuffle() function, random module, 154–155, 232
shuffling unique set of digits, 154–155
simulation
    AI. *See* Reversegam, AI similation
    of coin flips, 73–75
single quotes ('), 42–43
sleep() function, time module, 58, 283
slicing
    lists, 98–99
    operator for, 330
sonar, 171
Sonar Treasure Hunt game
    checking for player loss, 195
    checking for player win, 194
    creating game board, 180–181
    creating random treasure chests, 184–185
    design, 180
    determining if move is valid, 185
    displaying game status for player, 193
    drawing game board, 181–184
    drawing ocean, 183–184
    finding closest treasure chest, 186–189
    finding sunken treasure chest, 194
    getting player's move, 190–191, 193–194
    guessing location, 189
    placing move on board, 185–191
    printing game instructions, 191–192
    quitting, 190

removing values from lists, 189–190
sample run, 173–175
source code, 175–178
starting game, 192–195
termination of program, 195
variables, 193
sort() method, for lists, 157–158
sound file formats, 303
Sound() function, pygame.mixer module, 308
Sound object, 322
sounds
adding, 308
for game over, 332
setup, 307–308
toggling on and off, 308
source code, 14
AISim1.py program, 241–242
AISim2.py program, 244
AISim3.py program, 248–249
Animation program, 274–276
Bagels Deduction game, 151–152
Caesar Cipher program, 201–202
Collision Detection program, 287–289
Dodger game, 313–317
Dragon Realm game, 47–48
Guess the Number game, 22–23
Hangman game, 88–91
Jokes program, 40
reusing, 24
Reversegam game, 215–220
Sonar Treasure Hunt game, 175–178
spaces in, xxiv–xxv, 23
Sprites and Sounds game, 304–306
Tic-Tac-Toe game, 123–126
spaces
in source code, xxiv–xxv, 23
between values and operators, 3
special characters, printing, 42
split() method, 95–96, 190–191
sprites, 302
adding, 307
size changes, 307, 309
Sprites and Sounds game
checking for collision with cherries, 309
drawing player on window, 309
sample run, 303
source code, 304–306
window and data structures setup, 306–307
sqrt() function, math module, 180, 188
square brackets ([]), for indexes, 92
square root, 187
startswith() method, 105
statements, 5. *See also* flow control statements
continue, 161
def, 49, 50
del, 117
end='', 97
for, 26, 28–29, 37
import, 24
statistics, 246
stepping through program with debugger, 65, 67–70
into code, 68
out, 69
stop() function, pygame.mixer.music module, 332
str() function, 31, 35
strings, 12
checking for only numbers, 158–159
comparison operators and, 33–34
concatenation, 13, 26
converting to integer, 30–31
finding, 204–205
interpolation, 159–160
line breaks in, 51
multiline, 50–51
quotes for, 42–43
split() method, 95–96
subtraction (-), 2
augmented assignment, 155
Surface object, 261, 312
creating, 307
drawing on screen, 270
filling with color, 266
syntax errors, 64
in math expressions, 4–5
sys module, 180

T

TAB key (\t), 42
terminating program, 19
ESC key for, 295, 326
text. *See also* strings
drawing to window, 320–321
entry by user, 18
fonts for, 262–263
setting location, 264–265

Tic-Tac-Toe game
- arguments, 143
- artificial intelligence for, 128–129
- checking for full board, 145
- checking corner, center, and side spaces, 144–145
- checking for computer move to win, 143–144
- checking for free space on board, 138
- checking for win, 135–137
  - in one move, 144
- choosing move from list, 141–142
- choosing player's mark, 146
- deciding who goes first, 131
- design with flowcharts, 127–129
- duplicating board data, 137–138
- letting player choose *X* or *O*, 130–131
- placing mark on board, 131–135
- player move, 138–139
- playing again, 148
- printing board on screen, 129–130
- running computer's turn, 147–148
- running player's turn, 146–147
- sample run, 122–123
- source code, 123–126
- starting game, 145–146

`tick()` method, of `Clock` object, 289–290, 298, 313, 332

`time` module
- importing, 48
- `sleep()` function, 58, 283

traceback, 64

`True` Boolean value, 31
- for data types, 227
- `while` keyword and, 51

truth table
- for `not` operator, 54
- for `and` operator, 52–53
- for `or` operator, 53

tuples, 260
- for RGB colors, 261

typing errors, 6

U

`update()` method, `pygame.display` module, 266, 270, 282

`upper()` method, 101–102

uppercase, displaying characters as, 101–102

users
- `input()` function, 18–19
- input with mouse and keyboard, 292–295

V

`ValueError`, 139

values, 3
- assigning new to variable, 7
- converting data type, 29–31
- storing in variables, 5–8

`values()` method, 114–115

variables
- assigning multiple, 118–119
- constant, 91
- names for, 20
- overwriting, 7
- for references to dictionaries, 134
- scope, 56–57, 67, 68
- storing list in, 98
- storing strings in, 102
- storing values in, 5–8

W

WASD keys, 293, 294

WAV file format, 303, 322

`while` statement, 51–52, 60
- infinite loop, 160–161
- leaving block, 103

`windowSurface` object
- `blit()` method, 269–270, 331
- `centerx` and `centery` attributes, 264

worst-move algorithm, 248, 250
- vs. corner-best algorithm, 252

writing programs, 13–15

X

x-axis, 165, 167

x-coordinates, 165
- for `PixelArray` object, 269

Y

y-axis, 165, 167

y-coordinates, 165
- for `PixelArray` object, 269

Z

zero-based indexes, 92, 96

RESOURCES

Visit *https://www.nostarch.com/inventwithpython/* for resources, errata, and more information.

More no-nonsense books from  **NO STARCH PRESS**

SCRATCH PROGRAMMING PLAYGROUND
Learn to Program by Making Cool Games
by AL SWEIGART
SEPTEMBER 2016, 288 PP., $24.95
ISBN 978-1-59327-762-8
full color

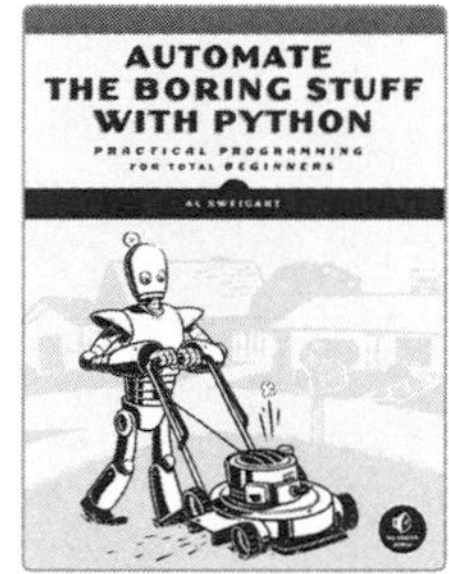

AUTOMATE THE BORING STUFF WITH PYTHON
Practical Programming for Total Beginners
by AL SWEIGART
APRIL 2015, 504 PP., $29.95
ISBN 978-1-59327-599-0

THE LINUX COMMAND LINE, 2ND EDITION
A Complete Introduction
by WILLIAM SHOTTS
MARCH 2019, 504 PP., $39.95
ISBN 978-1-59327-952-3

LEARN TO PROGRAM WITH MINECRAFT
Transform Your World with the Power of Python
by CRAIG RICHARDSON
DECEMBER 2015, 320 PP., $29.95
ISBN 978-1-59327-670-6
full color

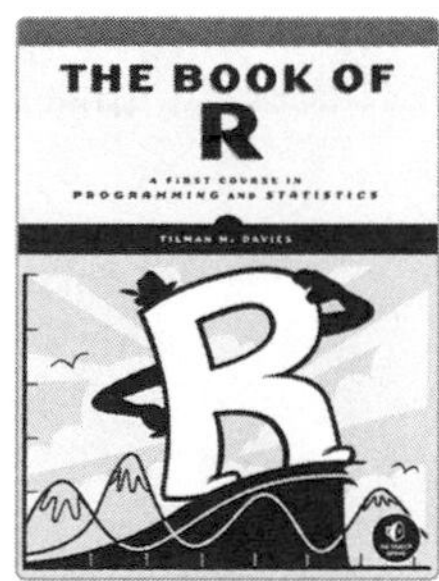

THE BOOK OF R
A First Course in Programming and Statistics
by TILMAN M. DAVIES
JULY 2016, 832 PP., $49.95
ISBN 978-1-59327-651-5

PYTHON PLAYGROUND
Geeky Projects for the Curious Programmer
by MAHESH VENKITACHALAM
OCTOBER 2015, 352 PP., $29.95
ISBN 978-1-59327-604-1

1.800.420.7240 OR 1.415.863.9900 | SALES@NOSTARCH.COM | WWW.NOSTARCH.COM